England's
Post-War Listed Buildings

Including scheduled monuments and registered landscapes

England's
Post-War Listed Buildings

Including scheduled monuments and registered landscapes

Elain Harwood and James O. Davies

BATSFORD

First published in the United Kingdom in 2015 by
Batsford
an imprint of Pavilion Books Company Limited
1 Gower Street
London WC1E 6HD
www.pavilionbooks.com

ISBN 97818499 41464

A CIP catalogue record for this book is available from the
British Library

20 19 18 17 16 15
10 9 8 7 6 5 4 3 2 1

Reproduction by Mission Productions Ltd, Hong Kong
Printed and bound by 1010 Printing International Ltd, China

This book can be ordered direct from the publisher at the
website www.pavilionbooks.com, or try your local bookshop.

Distributed in the United States and Canada by
Sterling Publishing Co. Inc., 1166 Avenue of the Americas,
17th Floor, New York, NY 10036

Previous page: Trellick Tower,
Cheltenham Estate,
Golbourne Road, Kensington,
1968–73, Ernö Goldfinger.

Opposite: Metropolitan
Cathedral of Christ the King,
Mount Pleasant, Liverpool,
1962–7, Frederick Gibberd.

CONTENTS

Identifying the best of the recent past is one of the most important challenges for English Heritage. A tiny percentage of listed buildings – a mere 0.01 per cent – date from after 1945, but what they lack in numbers they assuredly make up in variety, innovation and creativity.

Britain's reputation in modern architecture is second to none. Our leading designers are renowned across the globe. My duty is to ensure that the very best of recent buildings are given the recognition they deserve and added to the National Heritage List for England. Yesterday's cutting-edge buildings can become tomorrow's heritage treasures.

Listing isn't an end in itself, and we go on encouraging creative solutions which ensure that these buildings go on leading useful lives. We are in the vanguard, internationally, in protecting our modern heritage. From bus stations to cathedrals, office blocks to exquisite private houses, there is something here for all tastes to appreciate for a long time to come.

Ed Vaizey, Minister of State for Culture and Digital Industries

FOREWORD

The thirty years after 1945 marked an era of greater prosperity and opportunity for most people, and particularly those born in the 'baby boom' as the era began. Better health provision, better housing, brighter schools and free higher education were visible signs of the new Britain promised during the Second World War and determinedly delivered by both Labour and Conservative governments from the late 1940s to the early 1970s. A part of this welfare state has survived political changes since 1979. The late 1970s, however, also saw fashion move away from the modern architecture that had prevailed over the previous 30 years towards post-modernism and – more potently – conservation. The movement that culminated in 1984 in the creation of English Heritage (since April 2015, Historic England) has since embraced modern architecture, however, and younger architects and historians find the period intellectually challenging and full of buildings that can be beautiful as well as radical.

This is a book about all the sites where there are listed buildings, scheduled monuments and/or registered landscapes, whether one structure or a large group. By 31 December 2013, there were 566 such locations, with many comprising several buildings or a variety of designations. There were also 9 listed K8 telephone kiosks, 8 AA boxes and 72 listed memorials and sculptures. This edition is the first to cover all categories of heritage assets, not just listed ones.

What Is Listing?

Most designated post-war structures are listed. Listing began in the Second World War, when members of the Royal Institute of British Architects raised a concern that major medieval and Georgian buildings that suffered superficial damage were being needlessly destroyed on the grounds of public safety. 'Salvage' lists were hastily drawn up in 1943. The Town and Country Planning Acts of 1944 and 1947 required the government to maintain a list of buildings of 'special architectural or historic interest', and a nationwide survey was begun. The power to make additions to that list now rests with the Minister for Culture and Creative Industries at the Department for Culture, Media and Sport. Historic England is the government's statutory adviser and recommends which buildings should, or should not, be listed.

What makes a building listable? The Secretary of State and his/her ministers can consider only a building's special architectural or historic interest, including any technical innovation. Guidelines are available on the Historic England website. There are three grades of listing and landscape registration. Grade I is reserved for buildings and landscapes of the highest stature, and, in all, only 2.5 per cent are so designated. Those graded II* are outstanding and comprise 5.5 per cent of present listings. Most listed buildings are grade II for their 'special' interest and national significance. Scotland, Wales and Northern Ireland have their own listing systems, with broadly similar criteria for the selection of post-war buildings.

In 2014, England has over 376,000 list entries, which can range from several addresses – such as in a terrace – to a single gravestone. There are additionally over 19,800 scheduled ancient monuments and 1,643 registered parks and gardens. Only 0.2 per cent of these designations are

INTRODUCTION

of structures and sites created after 1945, but they demonstrate a fascinating diversity. Most have been the outcome of thematic surveys, but individual assessments or 'spot listings' are possible when a structure or landscape is under serious threat.

In 1994 the post-war thematic programme and spot listings pioneered a process of consultation with the public, primarily the owners, occupants and local authorities. While the final decision remains that of the government, this process encourages debate and helps to highlight areas of greater or lesser interest within a building. Following this model, consultation now forms part of the assessment process for buildings and sites of all ages and types.

The History of Preservation

The first listings, published in 1948–54 after whistle-stop surveys by historians and architects armed with petrol coupons, concentrated on the most obvious medieval, post-Reformation and Georgian buildings. The Victorian Society was founded in 1958 and a second survey, begun in the mid-1960s, identified more nineteenth- and early twentieth-century buildings for listing. This was encouraged further when in 1970 Nikolaus Pevsner recommended 50 buildings from the inter-war years that he considered the best examples of the Modern Movement in England. The 1980s saw interest in this era extend to more traditional styles and to Art Deco, encouraged by the 'Thirties' exhibition at London's Hayward Gallery in 1979 and the demolition the following summer of Wallis, Gilbert and Partners' Firestone Factory on the Great West Road in outer London. Historic England's forebears at the Department of the Environment rapidly identified 150 examples for listing from the inter-war period, of all styles. Meanwhile, an exhibition on Sir Edwin Lutyens (also at the Hayward Gallery) awakened interest in traditional architecture across the twentieth century. The 1930s found it acceptable to use different styles for different jobs, and studies by building type proved the most successful way of assessing a diverse output, as they focused attention on a candidate's integrity of design and commitment to its original purpose rather than just its good looks.

But why should listing stop at the 1930s? Not every architect's career ended with the war. Giles Gilbert Scott, creator of Liverpool Anglican Cathedral and the red telephone box, in 1947–8 designed Bankside Power Station, now Tate Modern, which throughout the 1980s and early 1990s was seriously threatened with demolition. Bankside, the National Union of Miners' building on Euston Road, the *Financial Times*' offices (Bracken House) opposite St Paul's Cathedral: the post-war buildings threatened with demolition in the mid-1980s were not aggressive, brutal or even made of exposed concrete. These refined, rationalized classical buildings, with subtle brick decoration and works of art, had been overlooked by contemporary critics but could now be appreciated as defining the era as clearly as did the Festival of Britain or the first brightly clad blocks of flats. Bracken House, built in 1955–9 to designs by Sir Albert Richardson, was the first completely post-war building to be listed, in August 1987. Instead of creating replacement offices, for which they had already been commissioned, Michael Hopkins and Partners remodelled Bracken House. Their new centrepiece, replacing the printing works, shows how a listed building can be treated radically yet retain its integrity. At Bracken House the old and new gain so much from their relationship with each other that Hopkins's work was itself recognized in 2013 as contributing to the building's special interest.

A Statutory Instrument in 1987 established the principal of listing buildings more than 30 years old in England, as counted from the date when the first foundations were laid. Buildings less than 30 years old but more than ten years old can very occasionally be listed if they are under severe threat and of outstanding interest, taken by Historic England to mean that they are worthy of the highest grades, I or II*.

After the positive outcome for Bracken House, the next stage of post-war listing, in 1988, came as a set-back. After soliciting suggestions from amenity societies and readers of the *Sunday Times*, English Heritage proposed 70 buildings from the early 1950s. The Government had – as it still has – the final say in listing, and it accepted only 18 of these recommendations. Out of this failure, however, came a high-profile research programme by building type, adjudicated by a steering group that operated for the decade 1992–2002 under the skilful leadership of Bridget Cherry, editor of the Pevsner architectural guides. Its membership across many ages and expertise included Peter Aldington, John Allan, Peter Beacham, Ronald Brunskill, Louise Campbell, Martin Cherry, Catherine Croft, Trevor Dannatt, Jeremy Gould, Diane Green, Neil Jackson, John Partridge, Alan Powers, Martin Robertson, Andrew Saint, Pete Smith, Gavin Stamp and James Sutherland. A series of exhibitions in 1996 held in London and Sheffield, under the general title 'Something Worth Keeping?', described the eventual recommendations in context.

The programme gained clarity and public support in being able to first concentrate on the early 1950s, so it could look anew at the architecture of the welfare state, much of it based on the gentle styles adopted by Scandinavia's social democratic programme in the late 1930s. Building type studies again demonstrated an architectural diversity, however, ranging from the traditionalism of Donald McMorran or Raymond Erith and the mix of Continental and vernacular sources found in Tayler and Green's housing, to the marriage of art and engineering that characterizes offices, education buildings and housing of the time and the drama of Stockwell Bus Garage.

Buildings from the years of Harold Macmillan's premiership of 1956–63, when in his words England 'never had it so good', form the centrepiece of Britain's post-war achievement. The period also saw the beginning of the most radical transformation of Britain's towns and cities seen for nearly a century. Yet media coverage concentrates on shopping centres, houses, flats and car parks, so it is easy to forget that more churches were built then than at any time since the 1860s, public theatres were built for the first time and modern sports facilities first appeared. Private houses became more organic in form as central heating, larger areas of glazing and the end for most families of live-in staff encouraged more open planning. These buildings had not been studied since their completion and they had never previously been explained in terms of their social and functional context. The success of these thematic studies was recognized by the high number of post-war listings in the 1990s, and the first edition of this book in 2000 at the request of the current minister, Alan Howarth. An updated version appeared in 2003. The thematic programme, largely of buildings from 1945 to 1965, gave England a higher tally of listed post-war buildings than anywhere in the world, and has led to widespread interest in our approach from other countries.

The 2015 Edition

This book has 537 individual entries, while the smaller Cold War survivals, sculpture and monuments have separate lists at the end.

New listings in the 2000s recognized thematic studies of buildings for telecommunications and transport, but most were the result of 'spot listings', where an individual building or site has been recommended because it is under threat or new research has highlighted its undoubted interest. Since 2010, however, more thematic work has been undertaken. This includes a study of private houses, while surveys of Roman Catholic churches under the 'Taking Stock' programme jointly funded by English Heritage and many dioceses have transformed the initial Anglican bias of post-war church listings. The brighter colours and semi-abstract works, many by European architects and artists, single out most Roman Catholic churches from their Anglican counterparts. The new edition also includes listings from an on-going survey of monuments from the Cold War, a reminder of Britain's massive commitment in money and materials to defence and the social fears of nuclear war that underlay the entire period. It is significant, too, how many commemorative monuments have been designated since 2002, as the more social and historical aspects of our heritage have gained wider recognition. Historic England is engaged in a four-year programme evaluating war memorials. More buildings associated with popular culture have been designated, notably the Rivoli Ballroom in south London and Liverpool's Casbah Club, the latter for its association with the Beatles. A number of new listings – including High Tech buildings from the 1970s – accompanied the exhibition 'Brutal and Beautiful' held at London's Wellington Arch in 2013, which featured images by James O. Davies that appear in this book.

The National Heritage Protection Plan, inaugurated by English Heritage in 2011 and continued by Historic England to co-ordinate its research and protection strategies, provides a framework for studies devoted to groups of buildings facing particular pressures. The first was of schools – the oldest of the original surveys (1992) and the subject of a major rebuilding programme in the 2000s; the listing of Bromley Hall School in London's East End was the first fruit of this work. A study of libraries prompted the listing of Wallsend Library outside Newcastle, with further examples waiting to be assessed, and more recent surveys have included commercial offices and civic centres. Studies of public art and post-modernism are in the pipeline. A longstanding review of university buildings has already informed several spot listings, which arose out of proposals for alterations.

The Impact of Post-war Listing

Listing does not require a building to open to the public, and most buildings in this guide are strictly private. Further information, for example for church services, is available on the internet.

Interest in the music, fashion and collectables of the 1950s and 1960s has moved beyond a cult zone for retro fans and into serious academia, and is now extending to the 1970s and 1980s. Listing has given confidence to buyers in popular housing developments such as the Golden Lane Estate and Trellick Tower, and has encouraged new housing in a thoroughly modern style. Ernö Goldfinger's Balfron Tower is being restored in 2015–16 for sale on the open market, very different to the uncertain attitude that accompanied the listing of Keeling House in 1992. The youngest listed building in 2014 is Elisabeth Frink's group of sculptures in Worthing, *Desert Quartet*, of 1989–90. Experience has shown that listing has to be one step ahead of fashion if the catastrophe of Firestone is not to be repeated. The listing of Preston Bus Station in September 2013, to general acclaim, was an important step in the appreciation of the most difficult style of the 1960s, monumental brutalism. There is now a general acceptance of the need to identify the best buildings of all periods for the future, and the ultimate success of post-war listing has been to move it from a vanguard into the mainstream of heritage protection.

What does listing achieve? It does not mean that a building has to remain unchanged, but it does require that alterations and additions are thoughtfully designed. Such work requires listed building consent from the local planning authority for grade II buildings, with permission additionally sought from Historic England for buildings graded II* or I, or in local authority ownership. Designation has not prevented the demolition, after listed building consent, of Rhodesway School in Bradford, the Silhouette Corset Factory in Market Drayton, the Harlow Water Gardens and Royal Oak Motel in Newingreen, Kent. These buildings have had regretfully to be removed from the revised edition. Other listings have had more positive outcomes. The Roman Catholic Thanksgiving church of Our Lady of Lourdes by F. X. Velarde in Blackpool was saved from demolition in 1999, after a request for listing by local residents was determined within 48 hours, and has been vested in the Historic Chapels Trust. Listing has prevented the probable demolition of buildings as varied as Manchester's Oxford Road station, the Wills Factory in Newcastle and Northampton's lift-testing tower. The sale of Keeling House for £1.3 million to a private developer showed how listing can 'buy time' while a new owner or use is found for a building, and how public housing can be revitalized. Many post-war buildings have found new uses, as the book reveals.

Post-war listing has led the way in the proactive management of buildings after listing. In 1991, the listing of Foster Associates' Willis Building in Ipswich, offices designed around the ethos of flexibility, prompted the production of management guidelines that closely define the areas of special interest within a building and those that can be changed without controversy. The management of listed buildings at the universities of Sussex and East Anglia have since taken this process further. In April 2014, such heritage partnership agreements assumed statutory force, and more post-war buildings are likely to adopt this dynamic approach.

Elain Harwood

Byker, Newcastle
1970–82, Ralph Erskine.

W. D. and H. O. Wills tobacco factory

Coast Road, Newcastle upon Tyne

1946–50, Cecil Hockin

Listed grade II, 17 November 1986

This factory's sturdy classicism is reminiscent of American factory design of the 1930s, an appropriate image for a firm that was resisting American competition while introducing many of its ideas of branding, advertising and better working conditions. Hockin was architect to the Imperial Tobacco Company, of which Wills formed a part.

Imperial had resolved to decentralize their manufacture and distribution network before the war, and in the late 1940s secured grants encouraging new industry to Tyneside, which is how they could realize so monumental a design. The fast Coast Road was built only in the 1930s and this was architecture designed to be seen at speed, like the inter-war factories of west London.

The factory ranges at the rear were demolished despite their listing, and the surviving office range lay derelict for many years before being converted to flats.

Tyne Pedestrian and Cycle Tunnels

Between Bewicke Street, Howdon, and Tyne Street, Jarrow, Tyne and Wear

1947–51, Mott, Hay and Anderson

Listed grade II, 13 April 2000

A road tunnel under the Tyne was approved by Northumberland and Durham county councils in 1937 and authorized by Parliament in 1946. The road tunnel was delayed until 1961, but in 1947 work started on pedestrian and cycle tunnels to serve the thousands then working in the shipyards on both sides of the Tyne.

Both tunnels are 274.3m (900ft) long, but the cycle tunnel at 3.7m (12ft) is imperceptibly wider than that for pedestrians at 3.2m (10½ft). The escalators, at 25.9m (85ft), were the longest in Britain and perhaps the world when installed. A speed ray regulator, an original feature, ensures that they move more slowly when nobody is using them. The circular entrance pavilions are modest, but the green and cream tiling of the tunnels is impressive, as is their lettering – especially that marking the former county boundary at mid-point.

39-73 (odd) Graham Park Road

Gosforth, Newcastle upon Tyne

1951–2, Clifford Wyld, Gosforth borough architect

Listed grade II, 11 July 2001

Gosforth Urban District Council in 1948 voted to build flats 'of a superior type . . . for better-class people' on a bomb site south of the town centre, inspired by examples in the south-east. Wyld prepared his designs the following year.

The 18 flats have a strong Festival of Britain quality, with circular windows and tiled dados to the staircases, and balconies. At one end is a shelter for prams. Inside, the flats have glazed screens between the living and dining areas, with a hatch to the kitchen, and many retain original fitted cupboards. High skirting boards were designed for ease of cleaning. Letterboxes and rubbish chutes were carefully built in. The flats had garages from the first, and the high standard of finish testifies to the care with which this scheme was designed for its selective market.

The concept of building public housing to be let at commercial rents was popular in the immediate post-war years, but relatively few were built, especially outside London. This is an unusually complete example.

Newcastle Civic Centre

Barras Bridge, Newcastle upon Tyne

Designed from 1950, built 1956–68, George W. Kenyon, city architect

Listed grade II*, 16 November 1995

A new city hall was designed in 1939 but abandoned in the war. New plans were prepared in 1950 but renewing the city's housing stock took priority.

The Civic Centre is part office building, part function suite. First came the Rates Hall range at the rear, with murals by Victor Pasmore, then teaching at Newcastle University. Next followed the 12-storey office range and finally the council chamber and public halls, where the decoration was still more lavish. The centre is approached via the Ceremonial Way, with nine flambeaux by Charles Sansbury, who also designed metal screens to the internal courtyard and, inside, the lift doors. The entrance is dominated by *River God Tyne* by David Wynne, with next to it a carillon tower, culminating in copper fins sporting seahorses and crowns from the city's coat of arms.

Considered old-fashioned when it was completed, the Civic Centre is now appreciated as an exceptional civic ensemble of art and architecture.

Rosehill Theatre

Moresby, near Whitehaven, Cumbria

1959, Oliver Messel with
Gavin Paterson and Son

Listed grade II, 12 June 1998

Sir Nicholas 'Miki' Sekers was a Hungarian émigré who opened silk mills near Whitehaven in 1937 as part of an initiative to reduce unemployment. He also had a passion for the arts, which led him to found the Friends of Glyndebourne, where the architect and designer Oliver Messel had made his reputation. When Sekers decided to build a 'Glyndebourne of the North', Messel was the natural choice of architect. Rosehill is his only building in Britain.

The auditorium was a nineteenth-century barn, which Messel extended with a stage and large foyer lined in silk. It was intended to incorporate parts of a local music hall, the Royal Standard, then being demolished, but part of the barn collapsed on the salvaged timber and only some painted panels survived. The final building was thus more completely Messel's, featuring a classical portico as the proscenium arch and delicate lighting sconces. Sekers attracted a galaxy of stars to Rosehill, and a mix of professional and amateur productions continues today.

Jesmond Branch Library

St George's Terrace,
Newcastle upon Tyne

1962–3, Harry F. Faulkner Brown
of Williamson, Faulkner Brown
and Partners

Listed grade II, 24 April 1998

Faulkner Brown secured the commission when lecturing at the nearby university. Responding to the corner site, the plan is the wheel of a circular saw, serrated so there are places for a ring of bookcases, with full-height windows bringing daylight across the book spines so their titles can be easily read. The circular plan aided security, while the big windows drew people in.

Red marble aggregate and contrasting dark granite setts were substituted for marble because of cost, but by producing a much smaller building than the council had intended there was money for good bronze and stainless-steel fittings, rubber floors and a high-quality control desk. Faulkner Brown designed or sourced all the fittings, including the bookshelves, which were made by a Newcastle firm. Its success led to further branch libraries in Heaton and Wallsend from Williamson, Faulkner Brown and Partners, who later specialized in large university libraries.

In June 2013 the City Council closed the library, and it is now run by a voluntary group.

Kingsgate
Footbridge

New Elvet, Durham

1962–3, Ove Arup and Partners

Listed grade I, 24 April 1998

Kingsgate Bridge was commissioned by Durham University to link the historic city peninsula to new departments across the River Wear. It is an exceptional response to an outstanding setting.

    The bridge was conceived as a thin band stretched taut above the gorge on slender, V-tapered stilts. Each half of the main span was built at right angles to its final position, one on each bank. The two arms were then turned and fixed with neat bronze locks, which serve as expansion joints. For Arup they symbolized the bond between the city and its university. Made of concrete with Shap gravel aggregate, the balustrade with its chamfered top is pleasing both visually and to touch. It forms a symbiotic group with the Architects' Co-Partnership's solid, stepped Dunelm House alongside, complementing each other to the enhancement of both.

    Sir Ove Arup (1895–1988) had a considerable personal input into the bridge's design and it remained a favourite work. His ashes were scattered here.

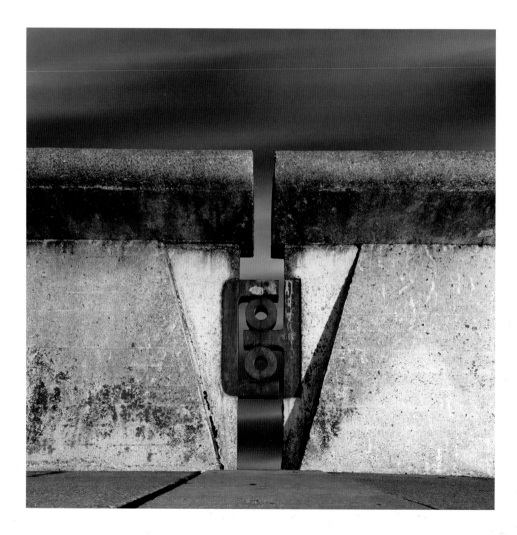

Cummins Engine Factory

Yarm Road, Darlington

1964–6, Kevin Roche and John Dinkeloo

Listed grade II*, 23 September 1992

The American Cummins Engine Company and its independent associate Chrysler Cummins were attracted to Darlington by government grants, and built separate factories on adjoining sites. The factory for Chrysler Cummins (1963–4), by James Cubitt and Partners, is a good British design of the period, but it is totally upstaged by its American-designed neighbour.

The Cummins engine factory was the first work by Roche and Dinkeloo, former associates of the late Eero Saarinen. They created an exceptional design, in which there is no external differentiation between the offices and the factory floor. Delicate glazing is contrasted with a heavyweight Saarinen material for the welded frame: CorTen steel, which oxidizes within three years to a tactile, rust-brown finish that is maintenance free.

Roche and Dinkeloo also continued Saarinen's experiments with neoprene gaskets, a means of fixing glazing derived from the car industry, here used for internal partitions as well as outside.

Wallsend Library

Ferndale Avenue, Wallsend,
North Tyneside

1965–6, Harry F. Faulkner Brown
of Williamson, Faulkner Brown
and Partners

Listed grade II, 20 December 2013

Following the success of Jesmond Library, Faulkner Brown was commissioned to build a larger library as the first stage in rebuilding Victorian Wallsend. The distinctive saw-tooth façades are repeated: part glass, part blind panels with bookshelves behind them. Here, however, the building is square rather than round, its concrete podium floating in a sea of cobbles, and the quality and rigour of the delicate steel and glass façade extends right through the interior. Natural light streams from an internal courtyard and is reflected in the steel ceiling, a grid of little pyramids that indicates the constraints of the grid. The courtyard features a sculpture of a Roman head by Murray McCheyne, master of sculpture at Newcastle University.

Faulkner Brown later expanded the flexible design of Wallsend as a series of principles for planning university libraries, notably at Nottingham. It closed in December 2013, when listing stalled its demolition as part of a new regeneration scheme.

Billingham Forum Theatre

Queensway, Billingham,
Stockton-on-Tees

1965–8, Elder and Lester
Job architect, A. J. Ward

Listed grade II, 1 October 2004

Billingham Forum combines a theatre, skating rink, swimming pool and sports halls in one building, the centrepiece of a new town centre by the same architects. It is an exceptional piece of patronage, built when wealthy Billingham Council blew its financial reserves before it was absorbed into the Borough of Teesside.

Only the theatre is listed. It was designed with 647 seats, for a mixture of touring plays and productions by a resident company, with a well-equipped backstage area and a lavish front of house. The auditorium is remarkable for its horseshoe plan, based on a traditional Italian auditorium and closely resembling an opera house with the audience populating its walls in three tiers of balconies and boxes, reflecting the growing understanding of theatre history emerging in the mid-1960s. The result is a refined enclosed space that combines intimacy with good sight lines, with no seat more than 18.2m (60ft) from the large, traditional stage.

British Gas Research Engineering Station

Station Road, Killingworth,
North Tyneside

1966–7, Ryder and Yates

Listed grade II*, 27 January 1997

In 1963 Ryder and Yates had built Northern Gas's offices in Killingworth, then worked with the regional board to win a national competition for a research station. The discovery of North Sea gas in 1965 meant that the laboratories and workshops had to be designed with maximum flexibility, as their requirements were unknown. They are housed in a steel-framed shell at the rear, for which the architects developed a system of demountable partitions and services.

The frontage range of offices, canteen, kitchen and library is most remarkable. The cool, Corbusian building of white concrete appears to float behind landscaped mounds, which are sliced vertically to reveal the basement car park. Entry is over a drawbridge and through a square arch, whose acute taper contrasts with six rooftop funnels that mask the services.

Ryder and Yates had worked under Berthold Lubetkin at Peterlee, and understood the artistic nature of modernism as well as its solid, clear proportions. They then formed one of Britain's first multidisciplinary practices, integrating architecture, servicing and engineering.

Trees

Middle Drive, Woolsington,
Newcastle upon Tyne

1967–8, Gordon Ryder
of Ryder and Yates

Listed grade II, 27 October 2010

Ryder and Yates met while working for Berthold Lubetkin at Peterlee and formed a practice in 1953. Private houses formed the backbone of their early practice, in which Ryder provided the planning and Yates the panache. This is the sole example from the mid- to late 1960s, after larger commissions like the Research Station (see opposite) had come their way.

Trees is largely symmetrical, save for the protruding triangular entrance halfway down one side of its box-like exterior. Thence Ryder devised a progression through a double-height living room modelled on Le Corbusier's for his Unités d'Habitation, with a gallery leading to the master bedroom. The ground-floor children's area has a separate circulation.

Designed to minimize noise from the nearby airport, large windows are limited to the entrance, the master bedroom giving on to an enclosed roof garden and the living room, whose arched window reflects the vault of the roof. Concave and convex parabolic vaults were frequently used by the firm, derived from that by Lubetkin over his penthouse at Highpoint II of 1938.

Radio mast for the Durham County Police

Aykley Heads, Durham

Designed 1965, built 1968,
Ove Arup and Partners, engineers

Listed grade II, 26 March 2003

The radio mast was the work of Britain's foremost firm of engineers of the time, a modest but considered response to a sensitive site overlooking Durham Cathedral.

Concrete enabled a mast to be built within the required wind tolerances, avoiding bending, which would distort the narrow radio frequencies. The key was the tripod base that enabled the mast to be very slender; a white concrete with a fair face finish also gave greater elegance. The structure was cast in five sections, a triumph for Britain's advanced precast concrete industry, and cost £10,000. It won a special mention in the Concrete Society Awards for 1969.

The mast at Aykley Heads has a significance disproportionate to its size because it shows what can be done to make an interesting structure out of a functional brief. It was saved from demolition in 2012, but may be moved to the new police headquarters nearby.

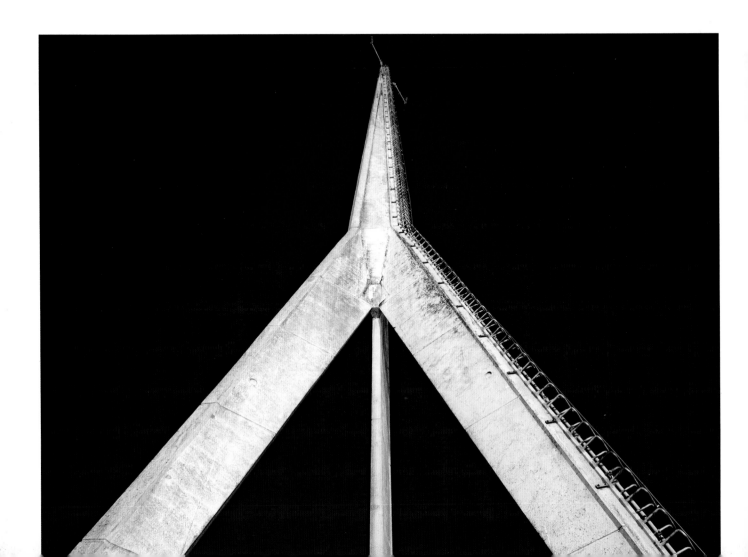

Apollo Pavilion

Oakerside Drive, Peterlee,
Co. Durham

Designed 1967, built 1969–70,
artist Victor Pasmore

Listed grade II*, 14 December 2011
Landscape registered 29 April 2002

The artist Victor Pasmore was invited in 1955 to reinvigorate the layout of Peterlee, a new town for the mining industry. He developed distinctive drifts of close-packed housing amid open landscaping, layouts that survive despite alterations to the houses themselves. His involvement with Peterlee lasted until 1977.

Pasmore was to see in architecture and landscape a way of reaching dimensions in space and time that his art could not realize. South of Peterlee the land falls sharply and a small lake was created at the plateau's edge. There Pasmore designed 'an architectonic feature large enough to dominate the scene', as a church might have in more religious times. It is a sculptural, two-storey bridge through which one can walk, its complex form enhanced with abstract patterning. Its construction coincided with the launch of Apollo XI: hence Pasmore's choice of name.

The structure was saved by a brilliant local pressure group formed in 2002 and was restored by Burns Architects in 2009, having secured Heritage Lottery Funding ahead of its listing.

Byker, Newcastle

1970–82, Ralph Erskine
Partner in charge, Vernon Gracie
Landscape architects,
Pär Gustafsson and Gerry Kemp

Listed grade II*, 22 January 2007

Partial clearance for a motorway blighted Byker's southern terraces after 1960. System-built slabs to shield a proposed motorway were superseded by Erskine's more imaginative scheme, based on his experience of Arctic Sweden.

Erskine leased an undertaker's shop as his British office and a drop-in centre for residents, meeting the 1969 Skeffington Report's recommendations on public consultation. Residents' comments informed the bright colours, courtyards and play areas, but they had no say in internal planning, nor in the perimeter wall of flats that contains half the housing units and shields the low-rise elements from the road and metro, and from north winds.

Erskine's 'Plan of Intent', retaining schools, churches, pubs and the Shipley Street Baths in the new development, was approved in 1970. To preserve the community, the fringes were developed first, to which residents from the central core were decanted. Neighbourhoods of 250 units had variations in house types and decoration, and included a shop and community facilities.

Most distinctive is the Byker Wall, with its snaking blue roofs. Patterned brick, cheery ventilators and tiny windows face north, while to the south a riot of balconies and walkways exploit the benign microclimate and extensive views. The early low-rise housing has similar roofs and timberwork, and over-scaled downpipes topped with bird boxes derived from Erskine's Arctic work. Later areas use concrete blocks, over-sized 'metric' bricks and earthier colours. Salvaged Victorian architectural features contribute to the careful landscaping.

Listing was prompted by threats to demolish Bolam Coyne, an isolated block that has since been restored. Although Erskine built very extensively in Sweden, Byker is his finest work.

THE NORTH WEST

Radar Training
Station, Fleetwood
1961–2, Lancashire
County Council

Adam Bridge

Wallgate, Wigan

1946, London, Midland and Scottish
Railway, W. K. Wallace, chief engineer

Listed grade II, 23 March 2001

This is the earliest prestressed railway viaduct in England – worldwide, only examples in Switzerland are certainly earlier. The London, Midland and Scottish Railway had commenced experimenting with precast concrete at its Derby research institute in the 1930s. Precast units were strong, long-lasting, cheap and quick to install, but the great depth of the beams required for large spans had made them of limited use for underbridges and viaducts where traffic had to pass underneath. The prestressed beams could be more slender. They were used for emergency repairs in the war, but this was their first use in a new structure.

The Adam Bridge spans a river and new road near the Wigan Pier canal basin. It has four spans, and high-tensile rods tie the beams so they act together under live loads. A precast concrete parapet and handrail survive on the eastern elevation.

Lewis's department store

Ranelagh and Renshaw Streets, Liverpool

Designed 1947, built 1951–3, 1954–7, Gerald de Courcy Fraser, succeeded by Fraser, Sons and Geary

Listed grade II, 4 June 2007

Lewis's, founded in 1856 and rebuilt by Fraser in c.1910–23 as Liverpool's leading store, was reconstructed after war damage in two main phases. The entrance was completed in 1956 with Jacob Epstein's male nude, *Liverpool Resurgent*, and relief panels depicting children.

The interior featured marble entrances and Art Deco staircases, including fluted columns derived from Selfridge's, then under Lewis's ownership. As trade diminished in 1987, some upper floors (including the restaurants, hair salon and function room) were closed off to the public, to linger in decrepit splendour. The cafeteria was tiled by Carter's of Poole (1953), for whom Alfred Burgess Read specialized in depictions of food and crockery. Other walls have a knife and fork or wave motifs, while hanging lights and metal screens enforced the Festival of Britain idiom.

In 2012–13, Lewis's was subdivided by the developers Merepark, when the cafeteria tiles and screens were incorporated into the breakfast room of a hotel. Incised panels by Susan Einzig from the more select Mersey Room restaurant survive in an adjoining corridor.

20 Forthlin Road

Liverpool

1949, Liverpool City Architect's Department

Listed grade II, 28 February 2012

The inclusion of this modest terraced council house is a reminder that buildings can be listed for their special historic interest, as this was the adolescent home of Paul McCartney.

McCartney (b.1942) moved here from Speke with his family in 1955, and met John Lennon at the Woolton church fête nearby two years later. McCartney's mother had died in the interim, and his musician father encouraged his guitar playing, with the bathroom favoured because of its acoustics. McCartney and Lennon wrote many songs here.

Few original fittings survive at Forthlin Road, save perhaps the bedroom linoleum, but since acquiring the house in 1996 the National Trust has restored the house to its post-war appearance, reusing windows from across the street. Part of the Beatles' songwriting skill was in celebrating the ordinary, so it is fitting that McCartney and Lennon's teenage homes should be preserved. Lennon's house, Mendips (1933), is also listed.

English Martyrs RC Church

St George's Road, Wallasey

1952–3, Francis Xavier Velarde

Listed grade II, 30 July 2003
Upgraded to II*, 18 September 2013

Velarde's earlier churches, mainly Roman Catholic, are well known, but his later work was little published. Most architects were compromised by limited budgets in the 1950s, but Velarde's work blossomed, despite limited mobility after a car accident. He had a Spanish father and studied that country's early churches, an influence that came to the fore in his adoption of a brick Romanesque style, enlivened with brilliant colour and silver leaf.

This is Velarde's first major post-war church, defining his later style with its large offset tower, pyramidal baptistery and sumptuous interior. Within the massive bulk of brickwork, his windows are deliberately small and round-arched to heighten the sense of massiveness. The nave arcade has giant round piers banded in black and silver, with jagged bands of brilliant orange and white in the ceilings, and diamonds and circles of blue or opaque white glass in the windows. Silver angels float across the altar and font. Another surprise is a further chapel in the first floor of the tower, set behind a metal screen.

Lovell Telescope

Jodrell Bank Centre for Astrophysics, Goostrey, near Macclesfield, Cheshire

1952–7, (Sir) Bernard Lovell, astronomer
Charles Husband, engineer

Listed grade I, 13 June 1988

In 1945 Bernard Lovell installed a radar transmitter at the University of Manchester's botanical station, Jodrell Bank, to prove that meteors were part of the solar system. He then constructed a paraboloidal reflector, whose success in detecting radio waves from the Andromeda Galaxy prompted him to propose a giant telescope that could be pointed at any part of the sky. Charles Husband designed a 76m (249ft) dish that could be tilted from supports on either side and moved on a circular track. As construction commenced, discoveries elsewhere demanded a more precise steel bowl to detect wavelengths of a few centimetres. It was welded from 7,100 panels, each 2.1mm thick.

The telescope achieved immediate fame when, in 1957, it tracked the first satellite, Sputnik 1, though astronomical study – particularly of pulsars – remains its principal function. In 1970–1, two circular girders were placed under the bowl as additional supports. It is now the third-largest fully steerable radio telescope in the world, and is linked to seven dishes around England.

St Joseph's RC Church

Moreton Road, Upton

1953–4, Adrian Gilbert Scott

Listed grade II, 15 November 2011

Although not as well known as his brother Giles or grandfather Sir George, Adrian Gilbert Scott was a notable mid-twentieth century architect who worked extensively for the Roman Catholic Church. St Joseph's was his smallest church, yet its bold composition, with a dominant south-west tower, makes an imposing presence. The stripped Perpendicular Gothic styling and clean lines, enhanced by well-placed and subtle ornamentation, create an elegant building that blends modern and traditional detailing and influences to successful effect.

The interior is dominated by the Scott's characteristic parabolic arches, an efficient form adopted by Antoni Gaudí, which was first used by Sir Giles in his unrealized design for Coventry Cathedral. At Upton they are complemented by a tall dado of blue Hornton stone from Oxfordshire, as at his slightly earlier church in Lansbury (see p.428), set below pale plastered walls to produce a dignified space that is enhanced by tall, elegant windows.

Heaton Park Pumping Station

Heywood Road, Prestwich, Salford

1954–5, Alan Atkinson, Manchester City Engineer's Department
Mitzi Cunliffe, sculptor

Listed grade II, 15 April 1998

An Act to bring water to Manchester from the Lake District was secured in 1919, and the Haweswater Reservoir was completed in 1934. It was only in 1947–55, however, that an aqueduct and pipeline was constructed to Manchester, a distance of 82 miles and costing £14 million. The feat and those who had realized it were recorded by Cunliffe in four panels on the walls of the pumping station at the end of the pipeline at Heaton Park Reservoir; above it is a large relief showing the route from the Lake District. The building itself is clad in Westmorland greenstone and Yorkshire sandstone.

The interior, lined in marble, features relief diagrams in sycamore wood tracing the route of the pipe. It is extraordinary to find so much artwork on an industrial building in an unfrequented suburban location, and shows the preoccupation with public art in the early 1950s. Cunliffe, an American artist living locally, is best known as the designer of the BAFTA award.

Former Sugar Silo

173 Regent Road, Liverpool

1955–7, Tate and Lyle
Engineer's Department

Listed grade II*, 23 September 1992

The storage of granular substances such as grain posed particular problems (due to their fluidity) before the development of heavily reinforced concrete silos in the USA c.1900. At Billingham, Imperial Chemicals built several tunnel silos to store fertilizers in the 1920s using a parabolic arched construction inspired by Eugene Freyssinet's hangars at Orly, which followed the natural shape of a mound of phosphate or grain.

David Bailey of Tate and Lyle Engineer's Department adopted the same principle to store sugar in Liverpool. At 161m (528ft) long and 26.5m (87ft) high, in 12 ribbed sections, this is the largest parabolic silo in England. The interior is smooth. Raw sugar was loaded via conveyor belts from the dockside and reclaimed by gravity through a band of hoppers set down the centre of the floor into another conveyor below. Although the parabolic arches were not innovatory, the silo's prestressed floor was an advance over the Billingham models and its size and shape are phenomenally impressive. It has since been used to store grain.

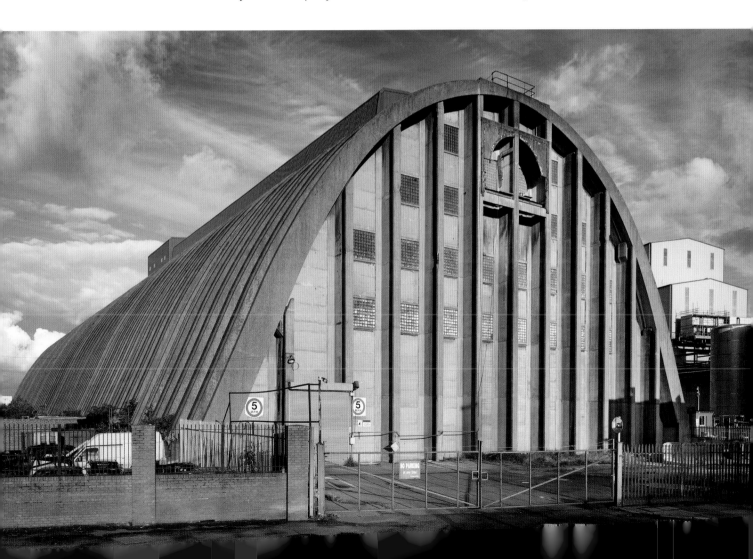

St Theresa's RC Church

Upholland, Lancashire

1955–7, Francis Xavier Velarde

Listed grade II, 25 November 1999

St Theresa's is a prominent church on a hillside outside the new town of Skelmersdale, close to St Joseph's College and a convent, its tall campanile with round-arched openings typical of Velarde's work. It also has a remarkable quantity of external carving, including reliefs between the paired windows, a pietà, and a line of angels topping the buttresses – all by Velarde's favourite sculptor, Herbert Tyson Smith, who designed Velarde's memorial following his death in 1960.

However, it is the interior that is most impressive: long and low, dark yet rich, with an exceptional use of gilding and touches of brilliant colour. The long, low hall is reminiscent of the earliest Christian churches, albeit in brick. This is achieved by the massive construction and small windows, mostly paired, and by an aisle of round gold columns. Their blue capitals complement the painted ceiling, while the sanctuary has predominantly orange panels to its ceiling and reredos.

Thanksgiving Shrine of Our Lady of Lourdes

Whinney Heys Road,
Blackpool, Lancashire

1955–7, Francis Xavier Velarde

Listed grade II*, 30 June 1999

This shrine to the patron saint of the Lancaster diocese was conceived by Bishop Thomas Flynn as a thanksgiving for its survival through the Second World War. All its parishes subscribed to the cost of £50,000. Blackpool was chosen for its central location and convenience for visitors.

Velarde's work has a jewel-box quality. The exterior is dominated by the carved relief and figurative corner pinnacles by local sculptor David John. Inside are columns of gold mosaic, blue and pink glass and a trompe l'oeil ceiling divided into facets by gold bands, painted blue in the nave and red in the sanctuary – the ingredients of Velarde's later parish churches on a tiny scale. John designed the reredos and altar, set behind bronze railings.

Spot listing – in just two days – pre-empted the shrine's demolition by the diocese, which had already stripped the interior of movable fittings. The building has since been vested in the Historic Chapels Trust, which is raising £500,000 for its repair.

Runcorn–Widnes Bridge

Queensway, A533 at Runcorn Gap

1956–61, Mott, Hay and Anderson, engineers

Listed grade II, 29 March 1988

This bridge replaced a transporter bridge of 1901 that linked Runcorn and Widnes across the Mersey. Its graceful arches share the powerful aesthetic found in interwar bridges, such as the same firm's Sydney Harbour Bridge of 1929–32. Here, however, there are no stone terminal towers, so that the engineering stands for itself, elegant and expressive of the new England encapsulated in the road's name of Queensway.

The bridge was designed as a two-pinned arch that includes the side spans. When built, its main span of 330m (1,082ft) made it the largest steel arch in Europe and third largest in the world. The side spans are of 76m (249ft), and with end cantilevers the total length is 496m (1,627ft). To meet the movements that arise in large-span bridges, a joint was designed consisting of 42 steel plates laid on edge across the carriageway, inlaid with rubber cushions and prestressed. The bridge remains the principal road link between Liverpool and the south.

Holy Cross
RC Church

Hoylake Road, Bidston

1957–9, Francis Xavier Velarde

Listed grade II, 30 July 2003

Holy Cross's entrance façade has three components: a low tower, a narthex with corner pinnacles of almost mosque-like acuteness, and a square baptistery on the street corner with a central cupola. Its tower is stubbier than those of Velarde's earlier churches, but also more geometric.

This was Velarde's favourite church, the last completed before his death. It enjoys a richly decorated interior; the entrance is tiled in large black and white squares with gold crosses, and the baptistery has red and white diagonal tiles incorporating gold fish. The arcade is lined in marble, with white mosaic for the low piers and blue mosaic crossed with gold in the apse. Windows line the aisles, leaving the body of the church glowing under a painted ceiling. A Lady chapel has more blue and gold mosaic, with a mural depicting the Virgin and Child surrounded by angels. Velarde's square and diamond patterns of blue and white glass in a square lattice has Italian forebears but remains distinctive.

Domus

542 Colne Road, Reedley, Burnley

1958, Alan Chambers

Listed grade II, 12 June 2012

Domus was designed for Eric Cookson, a major local developer, and demonstrates the glitz as well as luxury of post-war living. The living spaces are on the upper storey, whose white concrete frame with its shallow arched roof vaults stands out against subsidiary areas clad in brick, including a lower floor set into the hillside for hobbies and entertaining. Windows have been renewed but retain red glazing in the hallway, below which a pool is fed by a cascade running over local stone.

The principal floor is entered through a marble-lined porch into a hall floored in terrazzo marble tiles. The open-plan living and dining room is partly screened by a free-standing wall lined with rosewood veneer panels; more timber lowers the ceiling height over the dining area. The lower floor, reached by a broad open-tread stair, includes a party room with its own rosewood-lined bar and glass dance floor. The Cooksons occupied Domus until the twenty-first century, when it was sensitively modernized by new owners.

Entwood

Westwood Road, Birkenhead

1958, Dewi-Prys Thomas

Listed grade II, 15 July 1998

Dewi-Prys Thomas was one of a distinctive group of architects working in the Liverpool area who experimented with unorthodox plans and novel roof structures in private houses. He was also a charismatic and inspirational lecturer at the School of Architecture.

This house is formed from three linked pavilions on a pinwheel plan, which gives the house an interesting shape from every angle, and quarter-pyramid roofs to each room. The entrance is in an angle between the house and garage, with the main living room in the pavilion to the right, its high timber roof dropping down into a snug bay window area. The white-painted Tyrolean rendered brick walls also suggest vernacular influences, which distinguish Thomas's work from that of his contemporaries.

Upholland High School

Sandbrook Road,
Upholland, Lancashire

1958–60, Lyons, Israel and Ellis

Listed grade II, 30 March 1993

Under partner Tom Ellis, this practice was among the first to adopt a heavy concrete aesthetic for secondary school buildings, beginning with one at Falmouth won in competition in 1953 that fitted its long mass to the rugged landscape and used local granite aggregates. Further schools followed, of which this is one of the most mature and least altered.

The site was a tight one, and the brief imposed a limit of two storeys. Ellis's team designed a series of pale-brick cross-walls to define the width of the classrooms, science laboratories and handicraft rooms that protrude like a series of half-open drawers and give the school its distinctive profile. Each is fully glazed above a thick timber dado, while the entrance is a square glass box.

The school has been extended using the same brick and concrete idiom.

Hollings Building (the Toast Rack)

Manchester Metropolitan University
Wilmslow Road, Manchester

1958–60, Leonard C. Howitt,
Manchester City Architect's
Department
Job architect, Derek Hill

Listed grade II, 24 April 1998

Manchester's Domestic and Trades College was designed in three linked sections around courses in catering and fashion design. It is dominated by the six-storey classroom block, whose tapered form was inspired by the need for rooms of different sizes. Its concrete parabolic arched construction is testimony to Howitt's fascination with creating picturesque forms from concrete technology, seen also at Manchester Crown Courts and Blackley Crematorium. The name Toast Rack describes its proto-pop sensibilities perfectly.

The college's tailoring workshops were placed in a separate steel-framed, top-lit building at the rear to minimize disturbance from their noisy machinery. The low range in front was built as a circular hall for catwalk shows with a silver-service restaurant wrapped around it, to which the public were invited as guinea pigs for the cookery course. There was also a hair salon. This hub was raised a storey by Mills, Beaumont, Leavey, Channon in 1995–6 to create a library and information technology centre. The university closed the Toast Rack in 2013.

Casbah Club

8 Hayman's Green, Liverpool

1959 conversions

Listed grade II, 15 September 2006

The basement of an unassuming 1860s villa in a suburb of Liverpool is a remarkable survivor from the early days of Liverpool's epoch-making beat culture.

In 1959 Mona Best opened a coffee bar club in the basement of her home, after her two sons took to hanging out there with their mates. She took the name Casbah Club from the 1938 film *Algiers*. A local musician, Ken Browne, brought in fellow guitarists George Harrison, John Lennon and Paul McCartney to play on the opening night, and they helped with the last-minute decorations. They played there regularly until a row over their £3 fee. Mona's eldest son, Pete Best, later joined them on drums to form the Silver Beetles, and the Casbah remained their base camp until his sacking in 1962. It closed soon after, reopening for tours only in 1999.

The club is a maze of tiny interconnecting rooms. In addition to ceilings painted with Aztec runes and silver stars, there are murals by Cynthia Powell (Cynthia Lennon) and Mona Best.

Cedarwood

50 Beaconsfield Road, Liverpool

1959–60, Gerald Beech and
Dewi-Prys Thomas

Listed grade II*, 25 April 2007

Cedarwood, by lecturers from the Liverpool University School of Architecture, was designed as the *Women's Journal* House of the Year and visited by 50,000 people in March 1960 before it was occupied. It encapsulated the best in contemporary design, with an emphasis on modular planning and flexible living spaces.

As the name suggests, Canadian cedar figures extensively outside and in, defining the first floor set above clerestory glazing. Modern materials abound inside, among them a concertina vinyl Lionide screen to the dining area, 'Citron' Formica surfaces in the kitchen and bathroom, and exposed Glulam beams of Douglas fir in the living room.

One of the most distinctive features is the egg-shaped cloakroom capsule in the hall, clad and lined in cedar, with original sanitary fittings and coat hooks in the shape of stiletto heels. Outside, the driveway was once heated to prevent icing. Beech and Thomas's work extended to the landscaping of the garden, including a patio, reflecting pool, artificial mounds and trees.

Oxford Road Station

Manchester

1959–60, British Railways
London Midland Region

Listed grade II, 24 November 1995

London, Midland and Scottish Railways was dubbed a 'cradle of prefabrication' for prototype stations devised under Leslie Martin's supervision in 1945. After nationalization, his successors adopted lightweight steel for rebuilding stations in the region's electrification programme.

Manchester Oxford Road was the only large station rebuilt by prefabricated methods, made necessary by the weakness of the viaduct on which it sits. The architect Max Clendinning turned to Hugh Tottenham, then engineering shell roofs for the Timber Development Association, and they produced three conoid shells, ranging 13–29m (42–95ft) in span, made of three layers of laminated timber and supported on a cruck-like frame. Timber was also used for the shopfronts, café and bench seating, giving the station its rich, cohesive appearance. Smaller crucks support curved canopies over the platforms. Timber-shell roofs were a peculiarly English achievement, and Oxford Road's is the finest. Clendinning later became well known for designing interiors.

St Ambrose RC Church

Heathgate Avenue, Speke, Liverpool

1959–61, Weightman and Bullen
Job architects, Alfred Bullen and
Jerzy Faczynski

Listed grade II, 16 November 2007

Liverpool Corporation began building at Speke in 1936, but the model suburb dates mainly from the 1950s. As in the new towns, the Catholic church is outside the centre, where there was more land, but its tall campanile makes it unmissable. The church behind is equally striking, a square box with an exposed concrete frame and clerestory glazing.

St Ambrose was Liverpool's first liturgically planned church, designed when the Metropolitan Cathedral was still being debated. Under the broad, trabeated ceiling the sanctuary and altar are free-standing, with a processional aisle beyond the slender concrete columns on all four sides. The Lady chapel has glass by Patrick Reyntiens from 1976, while Gounil and Philip Brown designed that in the entrance hall and former baptistery.

Faczynski, who trained at Liverpool's Polish School of Architecture opened in 1944, painted Our Lady and carved the triptych, while his countryman Adam Kossowski produced Stations of the Cross. The grandest feature, however, is perhaps the organ set over the entrance.

Co-operative Insurance Society offices and New Century House

Miller and Dantzic Streets, Manchester

1959–62, Sir John Burnet, Tait and Partners (Gordon Tait) with George S. Hay

Listed grade II, 24 November 1995

The Co-operative group's buildings round Miller Street demonstrate the development of office building in the twentieth century, the most impressive built following a tour of Chicago in 1954 by incoming Co-operative Insurance Society (CIS) manager Robert Dinage. They are a 25-storey office tower for the CIS and a 14-storey building for the Co-operative Wholesale Society (CWS) that includes a conference hall for shareholders' meetings. CIS's tall service tower and elevated site mean that it dominates the city.

Dinage called for modern offices for 2,500 staff, partly open-plan. The Design Research Unit designed the executive interiors to make a prestigious headquarters comparable with those in the corporate world, including in London. Massing, materials and detailing were disciplined to the highest standards, with Italian mosaic and glass curtain walling selected as the cladding materials to withstand the grimy air for which Manchester was still notorious.

The simpler interiors of the CWS building are today better preserved. They were designed by Hay's in-house team, with decorative panels in the conference hall by Stephen Sykes.

Former Pilkington Brothers' head offices

Borough Road, St Helens

1959–64, Fry, Drew and Partners
(E. Maxwell Fry and Peter Bond)

Listed grade II, 24 November 1995
Landscape registered 25 April 2013

Pilkington's had glass works and offices across St Helens, until it resolved to build a single prestigious headquarters in its suburbs. An open valley was selected in 1953 and Maxwell Fry appointed through the auspices of Robert Gardner-Medwin of Liverpool University. He immediately proposed a lake. His office tower and canteen are set within a landscape of water and greenery developed with Peter Youngman, which together comprise his finest post-war work.

The 48.46m (159ft) office tower was always a scintillating advertisement for Pilkington's products. An aluminium glazing system was specially devised, notable for its elegant profile and simple fixing, while the spandrel panels are an opaque blue glass contrasted with green slate end walls. A white Vitrolite canteen block closed the northern end of the lake, where first-floor restaurants enjoyed spectacular views.

The quality of the environment was originally matched by fine art within it. The canteen had two abstract reliefs in wood by Victor Pasmore, while the main building features a glass panel in the main entrance hall by Avinash Chandra.

The Solar Campus

Leasowe Road, Wallasey, Wirral

Emslie A. Morgan, 1960–1

Listed grade II, 22 January 1996

This school is one of the earliest, largest and most successful passive solar energy buildings in the world, and was designed by a junior borough architect.

St George's was planned for boys, but merged with the adjoining girls' school before it opened. Morgan designed a long, cranked block facing almost south and with a double-glazed solar wall 70m (229ft) long in total. It has two skins of glass, 610mm (24in) apart, the inner one translucent and with some reversible aluminium panels, which are painted black on one side to absorb heat in winter. Roofs are heavily insulated, while the massive construction ensures equable temperatures as well as giving the school its distinctive appearance. A window in each room opens for ventilation.

Morgan died suddenly in 1964 while he was applying for patents and the mathematics behind the design were never revealed. The school remained a one-off. It closed in 1994 and the building now houses the borough's youth and community services.

Meols Hall

Botanic Road, Churchtown, Southport

1960–4, Roger Fleetwood Hesketh

Listed grade II*, 15 November 1972

Shippon

1952, Roger Fleetwood Hesketh

Listed grade II, 15 July 1998

An early seventeenth-century fragment with a wing of 1695, Meols Hall was inherited in 1938 by Hesketh. The war and a political career delayed his remodelling of it.

Hesketh was an enthusiast for Palladian architecture, as adapted to the English country house. He rescued stone quoins and a doorcase from a demolished wing at Lathom Hall, near Ormskirk, by the first English translator of Palladio's *Il Quattro Libri dell'Architettura*, Giacomo Leoni, and bricks from Tulketh Hall, Preston. The chief addition is a flat-roofed library with a semi-circular bow, which houses the largest pictures and a fireplace from Bold Hall, also by Leoni. Other details copy Alberti or local eighteenth-century motifs. This mix of textbook models and Lancastrian variations gives Meols an unusually convincing illusion of natural growth.

Hesketh also erected two gazebos modelled on an eighteenth-century original at the family's former home at Rossall and – best of all – a tripartite Palladian shippon with concrete quoins for his prizewinning cows.

Radar Training Station

Fleetwood Nautical College, Esplanade, Fleetwood

1961–2, Lancashire County Council Job architects, Eric Morris Hart and John Hatton

Listed grade II, 26 March 2003

A concrete caravan on legs, this jovial folly serves a serious function. It was designed as a radar station for training the masters and crews of coastal craft in navigation as part of Fleetwood's historic nautical college. The delicacy of the design, from its oval shape on little pilotis to the framing of the fenestration, was created with great care and earned a Civic Trust Award in 1965. The site was chosen for the proximity of the fishing fleet but is also particularly picturesque; on one side it faces the wilds of the sand dunes in which it sits, on the other Decimus Burton's Lower Lighthouse of 1839–40, a judicious juxtaposition of new and old navigational technology.

The building is now part of Blackpool and The Fylde College, and still provides training in the use of radar for navigation at sea.

St Raphael the Archangel RC Church

Huddersfield Road,
Millbrook, Stalybridge

1961–3, Edward J. Massey

Listed grade II, 13 December 2011

St Raphael's is striking for its central dome and modern materials, particularly its bold concrete arcade facing Huddersfield Road. It was also liturgically novel in 1960, when Massey explained 'the new manner' of his design that enabled mass to be said from both sides of the altar and the congregation to sit on three sides. The sanctuary is set under the dome, whose clerestory fills the church with light, flanked by small galleries and seating areas. The Blessed Sacrament chapel at the (liturgical) east end is visible through a screen.

Massey was discerning in his choice of artworks. A tile mural of St Raphael on the outside wall was replaced by abstract concrete panels after weather damage, but inside St Raphael still dominates the *dalle de verre* infilling the arcade by Pierre Fourmaintraux.

Faced with falling rolls and rising maintenance bills, St Raphael's closed in 2011 and its future is uncertain. Ceramic stations of the cross and water stoops by Alan Boyson have been removed.

University Sports Pavilion

Geoffrey Hughes Athletics Ground, Wyncote, Allerton, Liverpool

1961–63, Gerald Beech

Listed grade II, 2 December 1997

This is an elegant little bar and café with views of surrounding rugby and football pitches. It is linked to changing rooms and stores on one side, and to concrete terracing on the other that serves as a grandstand.

Wyncote House was given to Liverpool University as a sports ground in 1922, and was developed with new pitches and a running track in 1957. Gerald Beech taught at the School of Architecture, and his work is notable for its thoughtfulness and imagination.

A pond and trees mask the bulk of the changing rooms, linked by a bridge to the elegant bar and café, set one above the other. They dominate their surroundings despite their tiny scale, striking for their sleek, continuous glazing, renewed since listing. The *Architects' Journal* questioned 'whether the best place to hold a post-rugger bottle party is a glass box', but the building has survived well.

Adell Diner
(Tower Garage)

Wilmslow Road, Alderley Edge

1962, Berkeley Moir
of Moir and Bateman

Listed grade II, 6 June 2012

This is a remarkable survival of a 1960s garage. Berkeley Moir was a Rochdale architect who designed petrol stations for Shell (often with his wife Winifred Bateman) as well as this garage and showroom for the Total Oil Company.

The eye-catching image of a circular garage, and its convenience for displaying cars as well as for circumnavigation by drivers, had been recognized since the 1930s. What makes this example striking is the combination of narrow window frames and canted glazing, reducing reflections, with a soaring, cantilevered canopy supported on internal columns. The result hovers like a lunar landing pod at a time when high canopies were beginning to be superseded by flatter models.

Declining sales saw the petrol pumps removed c.1978, but the showroom and offices remained until 2011 when they were converted into a diner.

40 Kingston Road

Didsbury, Manchester

1962–3, John Parkinson Whittle

Listed grade II, 19 March 2010

John Whittle and his wife Petronella met when studying architecture at Manchester University. They chose this site, formerly allotments, in 1960 as it was convenient for the office of Halliday and Meecham where Mr Whittle worked. Designing his own home enabled him to indulge his taste for simple Scandinavian design, finessed with details inspired by Mies van der Rohe.

The single-storey house crosses the width of its narrow, sloping site. The main spaces are set around an internal courtyard, with a children's wing (including an au pair's room) extending into the rear garden where there are views across the adjoining park and flood plain. The living spaces flow into each other and into the courtyard, with natural light flooding the south-facing lounge.

The dark grey facing bricks provide a tougher interpretation of Scandinavian architecture than was found in the 1950s, when pale bricks predominated. The interior continues this strong palette of natural finishes, where brick is contrasted with timber ceilings and built-in fittings, the latter with touches of bright colour.

St Mark's Church

Milne Street, Chadderton, Oldham

1962–3, George Gaze Pace

Listed grade II, 25 September 1998

Posted to work in Yorkshire in the war, Pace became a prolific designer of churches and fittings across northern England. His work is imbued with a simple faith and the Arts and Crafts tradition, developed with a longstanding team of Yorkshire craftsmen, but became increasingly radical.

As non-orthogonal plans from Europe became better known in the late 1950s, so Pace's spaces became more organic and his use of rough stone, concrete and brick more expressive. His characteristically small rectangular openings evolved from a Romanesque symmetry to a loose patterning reminiscent of Le Corbusier's Notre Dame du Haut, Ronchamp.

This process reached its maturity at St Mark's, which apes the local industrial aesthetic in its glossy, unadorned engineering brick, and includes a sharp saddleback tower at right angles to the church that recurred in Pace's later work. The interior's barn-like quality is enforced with giant forked posts of laminated timber, while the great east window interweaves ribbons of grey and multicoloured panes, the latter made from fragments of Victorian glass.

Metropolitan Cathedral of Christ the King

Mount Pleasant, Liverpool

1962–7, Frederick Gibberd

Listed grade II*, 25 September 1998

The English city with the highest proportion of Roman Catholics gained a cathedral only after an ambitious design by Sir Edwin Lutyens was abandoned in 1959 with just the crypt completed. A competition was held for an alternative, when Archbishop Heenan requested that the congregation be set close to the celebration of the mass.

Gibberd's design beat 289 other entries, the assessors concluding that it 'powerfully expresses the kingship of Christ, because the whole building is conceived as a crown'. He roofed over Lutyens's crypt as a space for outdoor services, and designed a new church to the south. An axis through the entrance, denoted by a free-standing belfry resembling that by Marcel Breuer at St John, Collegeville, Minnesota, and the large Blessed Sacrament chapel, was intended to be a link. Gibberd's 16-sided church has a perfectly central altar under a glazed corona. While most cathedrals reveal themselves slowly as you explore them, entering Liverpool is to be struck by a single, arresting image of a vast auditorium bathed in red and blue light.

John Piper and Patrick Reyntiens designed the main glass, and Margaret Trahearne that in the Lady chapel. The stone belfry and bronze outer doors feature relief panels by William Mitchell, and the Chapel of the Blessed Sacrament has a mural by Ceri Richards. Many of these artists had worked at Coventry, yet in the very different context their work is entirely subliminated to the overall effect, strong and sublime.

The structure of 16 concrete buttresses tied by ring beams was innovative, but following water ingress the original mosaic tiling has been overclad.

St Mary's Priory Church

Broadfield Drive, Leyland, Lancashire

1962–4, Jerzy Faczynski
of Weightman and Bullen

Listed grade II, 29 September 1998

Leyland grew rapidly in the 1950s as an overspill town for the Manchester conurbation, but gained few new amenities save this lavish Catholic church planned in 1959.

Father Edmund FitzSimons was inspired by Swiss and French churches to request a centrally planned church. The result is a drum with a low ambulatory, zigzag concrete roof, and a central corona over the altar supported on V-shaped columns. Its Continental flavour is due also to the involvement of Polish architects and artists. The latter's work is largely figurative, yet modern: a tapestry of the Trinity by Faczynski and a hanging cross by Adam Kossowski, together with inscriptions by George Thomas and bronze Stations of the Cross by Arthur Dooley sitting in the 'V' of the columns. More dramatic are 36 abstract panels of *dalle de verre* glass around the ambulatory, based by Patrick Reyntiens on the Creation. Reyntiens was indebted to Fernand Léger's glass at Sacré Coeur, Audincourt, France, but St Mary's is the more powerful composition.

Pennine Tower Restaurant

Forton (now Lancaster) motorway service area, M6 motorway

1964–5, T. P. Bennett & Sons
Architect in charge, Bill Galloway
Job architect, Ray Sanderson

Listed grade II, 15 October 2012

The development of Great Britain's motorway network commenced in the 1950s with bypasses for Preston and Lancaster, integrated into the M6 in 1962–5. Forton, built for Top Rank Motor Inns and among the first service stations, has a striking 22m (72ft) tower with a cantilevered restaurant and sun deck on the northbound side.

Originally intended to be even taller, the tower's character and structural integrity survives largely as built. It was designed as a beacon to attract motorists, while the waitress-service restaurant offered spectacular prospects over the motorway and surrounding countryside towards the Lake District and Morecambe Bay. The hexagonal form resembled that of airport control towers, evoking the glamour of 1960s air travel; it also drew on the briefly popular fascination for city towers housing restaurants and observation platforms.

The restaurant closed in 1989. The lower buildings have been altered and extended and they, with the footbridge, are excluded from the listing.

Former chapel at Hopwood Hall College

Rochdale Road, Middleton

1963–5, Frederick Gibberd, in association with Reynolds and Scott

Listed grade II, 22 January 1996

Gibberd refined many of his ideas for Liverpool Cathedral at this small chapel for the De La Salle College founded here in 1946 and whose principal, Brother Augustine, had admired Cambridge's round Holy Sepulchre Church as a student. The small scale enabled Gibberd to set the altar under a funnel-like corona and give three of the eight sides to subsidiary spaces rather than place seating behind it, including the organ and a small weekday chapel.

The structure comprises eight concrete trusses linked by ring beams and cross-bracing in the roof, with concrete block infill. Colour and interest are provided by its copper roof and the glazing of the central corona with simple rectangles in red, yellow and green hues by David Atkins. This conical tower is visible across the semi-open countryside from a considerable distance.

Although the chapel was deconsecrated after the college passed to local authority use in 1992 and became used as a hall for examinations and sports, the space remains impressive.

William Temple Memorial Church

Simonsway, Wythenshawe, Manchester

1964–5, George Gaze Pace

Listed grade II, 25 September 1998

That this is the most challenging of Pace's church interiors is not immediately evident externally, for like his best works it resembles a broad barn with high dormers and has only a stubby tower, derived from Le Corbusier's La Tourette. Pace's characteristic oblong windows fill the gable end.

Inside, the difference is the use of steel. Rolled I-beams and exposed girders define the building's functions within a single rectangular space and impart an industrial aesthetic that led the church to be called 'a workshop for worship' by the critic Dennis Sharp. The large, railed sanctuary, with a curved clerical bench behind, is set diagonally, with blocks of pews to either side. An enclosed chapel occupies the fourth corner, with the choir set in front. In the middle the font is encased in a steel framework that also supports the roof. Pace also introduced a contrast between his own oak fittings and some Victorian pews brought, like many of the congregation, from the heart of old Manchester.

St Jude RC Church

Poolstock Lane, Worsley Mesnes,
Wigan

1964–5, Lionel A. G. Prichard and Son

Listed grade II, 26 April 2003

St Jude's is a triangular church in a busy housing area. Built using a hefty concrete frame to withstand mining subsidence, this expensive (£90,000) building was funded by football pools and bingo sessions run by the priest, Fr Tobin. The seating forms a fan around an apron-shaped sanctuary placed against the rear wall, its altar lit by a concealed rooflight. The other sides each have six full-height windows filled with semi-abstract *dalle de verre* designed by Robin Riley, loosely based on Christ's crucifixion and resurrection and glistening with a sense of movement.

Above the altar is a large mosaic depicting the crucifixion by Hans Unger and Eberhard Schulze, perhaps their largest collaboration. Ungers is known elsewhere for his stained glass and posters for London Transport and the Post Office. The baptistery, a circular building on the street corner, was converted to a shrine to St Jude in 1993.

Pall Mall Court

55 King Street, Manchester

1966–8, Brett and Pollen
Partner in charge, Harry Teggin

Listed grade II, 4 December 2000

Pall Mall Court was commissioned as a prestige headquarters for the London Assurance Group, for whom Teggin had designed offices in Sloane Street. The insurers were taken over by the Sun Alliance Group as work began, and the building has always been occupied by a variety of tenants.

In shape, the building is an inverted 'Z', a five-storey range to King Street sheltering a 12-storey block and a public piazza. Teggin wanted the building 'to have the impact of a jet stone' by using bronze glass, sharp angles and opaque facets to glisten in the soot-blackened Manchester atmosphere. The cleaning of the surrounding buildings tempered this effect, but it attests to the sumptuousness and mystery that a black building can bring to the streetscape. Its beautiful detailing was achieved by using only the best foremen to lay the dark bricks facing the piazza.

Liverpool Playhouse Theatre

Williamson Square, Liverpool

Extensions 1966–8,
Hall, O'Donahue and Wilson

Listed grade II*, 26 March 1999

The Liverpool Playhouse opened in 1911 as one of England's first repertory theatres, in a building remodelled by Sir Charles Reilly and Stanley Adshead from the 1865 Star music hall. By the 1960s its minimal foyer and backstage facilities were proving debilitating and the redevelopment of the adjoining markets enabled land to be secured for an extension.

A workshop was built behind the stage, with five storeys of dressing rooms. In front, foyers, bars and a restaurant were cantilevered over Williamson Square in two glazed circular structures, reached via a circular staircase from the entrance and box office. They make a fascinating sequence because of their changing levels and cross-vistas between the two circles, and look exciting without compromising Reilly and Adshead's stuccoed block, sparkling enticingly when lit at night. The precise finishes are typical of this elegant but little-known local firm.

Since the building was listed the workshops have been remodelled as retail spaces.

St Augustine's RC Church

Grosvenor Square, Manchester

1966–8, Desmond Williams
and Associates

Listed grade II, 16 November 2007

A chapel of the Holy Family on this site was rebuilt using War Damage Commission funding from the bombed St Augustine's in York Street. It was Salford diocese's first church built in full accordance with the principles of Vatican II: a simple plan with a sloping floor devised to give as many worshippers as possible a clear view of the altar.

The church is top-lit between its Vierendeel trusses as it is hemmed in to either side, where tall, recessed windows are filled with colourful French 'chipped' glass by Whitefriars Studio. Brick and timber finishes are left exposed and enriched by a dominating, crustily ceramic mural depicting Christ in Majesty by Robert Brumby. He also designed the holy water stoups, wall lights, the centrally placed font, the altar table with its bronze inset, and an extraordinarily three-dimensional memorial from the mangled plate of the earlier church.

Such richness is in contrast to the stark brick exterior, relieved only by a ceramic plaque and a figure of the Madonna, again by Brumby.

Central Bus Station and Car Park

Tithebarn Street, Preston

1968–9, Building Design Partnership
Job architects, Keith Ingham and
Charles Wilson

Listed grade II, 23 September 2013

Preston was the centre of an extensive bus and coach network that created so much congestion the council commissioned a bus station in 1960. There was a hiatus while the site was assembled, and a design combining Europe's largest bus station with car parking followed a survey in 1965.

The concrete's smooth finish derives from moulds of glass reinforced polyester (GRP), with upswept balcony fronts devised by engineers Ove Arup and Partners for economy and elegance. Signage and fittings are also of GRP. The tall ground floor provides height for double-deckers, and each stand has sliding doors to shelter passengers in bad weather. Ingham sought to provide the luxury of air travel. The car park has nine stepped parking levels and pre-cast ends clad in white tiles, a rigidity broken by swirling ramps at either end, one enclosing the taxi rank. A 48.77m (160ft) pylon was dubbed 'Britain's tallest lamp post'.

The building was long threatened with demolition and its eventual listing belatedly indicates a growing appreciation of brutalism.

Addleshaw Tower

Bell Tower Walk, Chester

1973–5, George Gaze Pace

Listed grade II, 9 July 2012

When in 1963 Chester Cathedral's medieval tower was found to be suffering cracking from bell-ringing, it was decided to construct a new, free-standing tower or 'bell house'. Named after its commissioner, Dean Addleshaw, the result is the first free-standing bell-tower to be built by a cathedral since the fifteenth century, and Pace's last major work.

Addleshaw Tower embodies Pace's philosophy that church architecture should progress beyond strict historicism, though its sloping sides and pyramidal top contain local vernacular references. It was likened by its detractors to a silo and also dubbed the 'Chester Rocket'. It uses both modern and traditional materials in its construction, including Bethesda slate, reinforced concrete and *dalle de verre* glass. It is a highly functional solution that suits its sensitive site.

Farnley Hey, Farnley Tyas
1953–4, 1956,
Peter Womersley

9 and 11 Ellers Lane

Auckley, Doncaster

1948

Listed grade II, 19 September 2007

These are rare surviving examples of timber houses commissioned from Sweden by the government to ease Britain's housing shortage at the end of the war. Prefabricated timber housing proved popular in Sweden from the 1920s as it was quick to build, well insulated and used cheap offcuts. Following an exhibition in 1944, 10,000 units were ordered to two British designs – one with a full second storey; one with dormers in the roof as here – based on earlier Ministry of Health prototypes for farmworkers' cottages. They have distinctive outshuts for the coal shed and wash house. Sweden encouraged the scheme to ease unemployment problems, but it was curtailed by Britain's dollar crisis of 1947 and only 2,444 were exported.

The Swedish houses are distinctive because of their timber boarding. No. 11 Ellers Lane retains built-in cupboards and wardrobes, a response to post-war shortages of furniture.

Fearing fire, the Swedish houses were erected only in the countryside. Scottish conditions proved too wet, but they have fared better in eastern England, especially around Doncaster.

Friarwood Valley Gardens

Pontefract, West Yorkshire

1950–4, R. W. Grubb, borough parks and cemeteries superintendent

Registered grade II, 2 April 2001

Pontefract's Dominican Friary once stood somewhere in this steep valley, which, following the dissolution, became a cemetery and later orchards. The land was acquired when the arterial Southgate was widened in the 1930s, but in 1947 the council recommended that the remainder become public gardens. Grubb reported that the sheltered location and rich soil could support every sort of tree and shrub, and proposed a variety of gardens, with terraces, rockeries, a stream and lily pools.

The mayor planted a cherry tree to mark the start of work, and flowering trees became a feature of the gardens, slowly replacing the fruit trees. An open-air theatre, bowling green, rose garden and an aviary were added, and the gardens' informal layout was developed around a stream, later culverted because of pollution. Today the dominant feature is the sheltering retaining wall to the road, with steps and gate pillars brought from the demolished Byram Park at Knottingley. The theatre has gone, but otherwise Grubb's concept survives remarkably well.

West Block, Christopher Pickering Homes

Hessle Road, Hull

1952, J. H. Hirst

Listed grade II, 21 January 1994

Christopher Pickering (1842–1920) was a Hull fish merchant and by 1881 a ship owner, who quickly made his fortune. He invested in land, where in 1914 he commissioned a model village that included a church, park, children's home and almshouses, to which this terrace of eight dwellings is an addition. The symmetrical composition, with a central bay incorporating a commemorative plaque and stone mullioned windows, reflects the style of the earlier work, with which this forms a listed group.

Almshouses have a long tradition, but the need for more old people's sheltered accommodation was identified with the wartime dispersal of many extended families. Thereafter public housing schemes began to include small bungalows for the elderly and the first communal old people's homes. Most other charitable foundations built new almshouses after 1945 only when their original foundations were commandeered for road widening.

Farnley Hey

Farnley Tyas, near Huddersfield

1953–4, 1956 and later,
Peter Womersley

Listed grade II, 15 July 1998

Farnley Hey exemplifies the 'contemporary' style, which mixed traditional materials and modern planning in a new departure for executive living. A plinth of rough local stone provides a platform on the steep hillside, and the timber frame is infilled with glass and weatherboarding. The main spaces flow into each other and extend on to outdoor terraces, with the dining area separated from the double-height living room by a planting trough. Stairs ascend to a gallery serving bedrooms (minimizing corridors) and a cantilevered balcony, now glazed and infilled below.

Womersley was inspired by visiting Le Corbusier's Pavillon Suisse, and also Italy, where Gio Ponti and Piero Fornassetti were experimenting with new plastics. Completed as licences were lifted, with only 153sq. m (1,650sq. ft) of accommodation, a framed roof terrace over the carport was infilled as an additional bedroom and nursery in 1956, when a Formica balustrade was added to the open-tread stair. Farnley Hey was the first of three houses designed by Womersley for his brother, John (see Vista Point, p.409), and remains magnificent.

Bathhouse at Thomas Broadbent & Sons Ltd

Queen Street South, Huddersfield

1955, Andrew Buck and Geoffrey Rowe of Abbey Hanson Architects

Listed grade II, 18 November 2009

This ablutions block was designed for workers at a foundry company. Highly unusual outside the coal industry, the facility has survived virtually unchanged.

The exterior, built in coursed and finely cut stone and arranged as a series of rectangles, shows the influence of Frank Lloyd Wright and Willem Dudok in its balance of vertical and horizontal elements, with a curtain-walled centrepiece. It is grander than contemporary brick-built pithead baths. Internally the layout is unchanged, with a central main washroom flanked by showers, a 'dirty' locker room, a 'clean' locker room (with original lockers) and toilets. A remarkable number of original fixtures survive, ranging from light fittings, flooring, doors and wall tiles to footbaths, a drinking fountain, showers, washbasins and urinals.

The local newspaper, the *Huddersfield Examiner*, reported on the building's opening, with a headline 'So Optimistic – They've Even Built a Sun Lounge!' This room, situated on the flat roof and accessed externally, survives alongside a canopy supported on steel columns.

University Library and Arts Tower

Western Bank, Sheffield

1956–9, 1961–5,
Gollins, Melvin, Ward and Partners

Listed grade II*, 30 March 1993

Sheffield was unique among universities in the early 1950s in holding a public competition for new buildings, remembered today for the unplaced schemes by the Smithsons and James Stirling that heralded the New Brutalism. The winners, in 1953, were inspired by the American office architecture of Mies van der Rohe and Gordon Bunshaft, and no other British firm achieved the simplicity of American curtain walling with such confidence.

Gollins, Melvin and Ward completely redesigned their buildings after the competition. The library was built first, of Portland stone and tinted glass. Stairs lead through a foyer and a former catalogue hall, spaces that increase in size and opulence and climax in the mighty main reading room, restored in 2009–10 by Avanti Architects.

The library's low bulk acts as a foil to the 19-storey Arts Tower, which fulfilled the university's aim of creating a prominent landmark. There are lecture theatres in the basement, departmental and tutorial rooms in the tower, refurbished in 2009–11, and the School of Architecture at the top.

Park Hill

Sheffield

1957–61, Jack Lynn and
Ivor Smith, Sheffield City
Architect's Department

Listed grade II*, 22 December 1998

No other provincial authority produced a greater range of post-war housing than did Sheffield under Lewis Womersley, city architect. His reputation attracted the young Jack Lynn and Ivor Smith, whose student project for 'streets in the sky' envisaged a total community of housing, shops and pubs linked by long, raised decks, following an unsuccessful entry by Lynn for the Golden Lane competition. Park Hill also owes something to the Quarry Hill flats built by rival Leeds City Council in 1935–9 (demolished).

Park Hill's flats were assembled from a three-bay, three-storey module, with an access deck every third floor and containing a mix of flats and maisonettes. There were also four pubs, shops and a community centre. The architects boasted that no complete elevations were drawn out, though an artist, John Forrester, determined the graded brick cladding. Street decks suited the sheer slopes of 'Little Chicago', a slum cleared before the war, because all save the topmost of the three give on to actual ground level at some point. The development ranges from four to 13 storeys with the fall of the land, so as to maintain a constant roofline.

What was remarkable was not that Park Hill had problems, but that it worked. By the mid-2000s, however, it was run down and the city brought in the developers Urban Splash to revamp the largest ranges for sale. Their controversial scheme demolished the shops, reduced the width of the walkways and replaced the brick infill with bright panels. After long delays, the first flats were completed and sold in 2012.

St Paul's Church

Wordsworth Avenue, Sheffield

1958–9, Basil Spence and Partners

Listed grade II*, 25 September 1998

This is the most refined of Spence's parish churches, clean and chaste like a lemon sorbet. It had its genesis in three small commissions for new Coventry suburbs from 1955, using War Damage Commission compensation for a single bombed church. Spence and Gorton were developing ideas for a completely glazed west end at Coventry Cathedral and Spence experimented with the idea elsewhere. Glazed ends were further made fashionable by the Sirens' Otaniemi Chapel of 1957 in Finland.

St Paul's presence is denoted by an open bell-tower, linked by a covered way to the simple church. The roof appears to float on glass, rather than the brick side walls, which are slightly cranked to provide support. The church is glazed at both ends, though the western window is bisected by the gallery carrying the choir and organ, while to the east a screen was inserted during construction to conceal nearby shops. Spence designed and donated the altar fittings.

Church of St Catherine of Siena

Richmond Road, Sheffield

1958–60, Basil Spence and Partners

Listed grade II, 13 June 1997

This is the second and larger of Spence's parish churches in Sheffield, designed in 1957 after he had visited Le Corbusier's chapel at Ronchamp. It replaced the city's bombed St Philip's, and the War Damage Commission insisted on a 'plain church' for 500 worshippers.

The tall bell-tower is formed of two brick curves that resemble an eye on plan. An incised inscription by the slate-hung entrance is by Ralph Beyer, then carving the hallowing places at Coventry Cathedral, and a large bronze crucifixion was later added to the side.

Lines of benches lead the eye to the sanctuary, a carefully managed stage. The ceiling slopes gently upwards to the east end where a hidden window shines light directly on to the altar in an apse resembling a theatrical cyclorama. Altar, pulpit and font have equal prominence, set in a line, the rich fittings indicating the church's relatively generous funding.

Since the building was listed the porch has been extended, to provide coffee facilities.

St Joseph's RC Church

Green Lane, Newby, Scarborough

1958–60, Francis Johnson

Listed grade II, 16 November 2007

Johnson is known mainly for his country houses, for which he adopted a late eighteenth-century classical idiom. His church work reflects an earlier interest in Italian and Scandinavian design of the 1920s, however, and he considered this the best example.

Johnson, who lived in Bridlington, was commissioned by the local priests Monsignor Lynn and Father Loveday to build a Catholic church for Scarborough's expanding northern suburbs. The most dramatic element is the brick west elevation, a stripped-down reinterpretation of a Romanesque European westwerk and particularly indebted to P. V. Jensen Klint's Grundtvigs Church in Copenhagen, which he visited in 1934. The calm, delicate interior was entirely furnished by Johnson, with altar rails and light fittings by the local designer William Dowson.

Johnson resented the success found by Croydon-born George Pace in Yorkshire. His own churches are more traditional, particularly in their correct Georgian fittings, but with twists and quirks in the elevations, especially of his towers.

Scargill Chapel

near Kettlewell, North Yorkshire

1958–61, George Gaze Pace

Listed grade II*, 25 September 1998

Scargill House in the Yorkshire Dales was bought by a group of Manchester Anglicans as a holiday and conference centre. Pace was commissioned to design a chapel for the founders to erect themselves, although it was eventually entrusted to a local builder for speed.

Pace conceived a chapel that would 'appear to grow out of the dale'. It is built of local limestone, like the drystone walls of the valley below. It combines simplicity with great power, especially in the relationship between the square hall and its curved entrance passage and staircase, emphasized by a sweeping roof of cedar shingles. The interior is large and austere, Pace's feeling for the local vernacular continuing in the timber crucks supporting the roof.

The building is an early demonstration of the Liturgical Movement, with the altar set forward of the long side wall, and marked a turning point in Pace's career. Here he developed the personal language of rough stonework, unadorned timber stanchions and liturgical planning that made his subsequent churches so extraordinary.

St Mark's Church

Broomfield Road, Broomhill, Sheffield

1958–63, George Gaze Pace

Listed grade II, 9 December 1999

Pace was appointed surveyor to the Diocese of Sheffield in 1949, and although his schemes to extend the cathedral were frustrated, he secured some commissions for new churches. Most ambitious was the replacement of W. H. Crossland's church of 1868–71, bombed in 1940 leaving only its tower – a rare opportunity to build on a large, inner-city scale. A first design dates from 1950–1. It was followed by a more experimental cantilevered concrete construction, a reduced version of which was eventually realized.

The exterior is faced in local stone, and has the thick, rectangular piercings that are typical Arts and Crafts features of Pace's work. The plan is a broad hexagon that accommodates a large chapel to the side of the sanctuary.

The unexpectedly modern interior is impressive in its scale and lightness. It is a synthesis of expressionist concrete trusses and limed oak furniture also by Pace, and is dominated by the organ case and brilliantly coloured windows by Harry Stammers and John Piper.

1 Park Lane

Sheffield

1959–60, Patric Guest

Listed grade II, 20 December 2000

Between 1960 and 1972 the metal designer David Mellor made all his limited editions and prototypes in this house and studio. He was then a bachelor and the kitchen was a corner of the lounge, where a wardrobe incorporated a pull-out bed. The tiny entrance hall doubled as the receptionist's office. The workshop is set down five steps on the sloping site, and as there is a constant roofline, extra height is achieved. The ceilings are of cedar, with full-height teak doors. On his marriage to Fiona MacCarthy in 1966, Mellor added a bedroom and study; a later children's annexe is now a separate house.

The combination of living and working functions in one narrow rectangle has proved surprisingly flexible. Later owners have adapted the drawing office to a kitchen, though it retains its glazed screen to the corridor. More recently the photographic studio has become an office and the workshop a spacious living room.

Patric Guest was working for Gollins, Melvin, Ward and Partners in Sheffield at the time.

Wentbridge Viaduct

A1 near Darrington, Wakefield

1959–61, F. A. (Joe) Sims of
West Riding County Council with
Maynard Lovell, consultant engineers

Listed grade II, 29 May 1998

'At last Britain has a bridge to show which by virtue of its sheer size, its taut, pared-down elegance, its dramatic impact, can hold its own with any of the great bridges of the continent.' So claimed New York's Museum of Modern Art in 1964, likening the Wentbridge Viaduct to the exciting bridges of Italy's Autostrada del Sole.

This prestressed concrete viaduct carries the A1 over the River Went and was once the largest in Europe. Unusually, the three-span structure acts as a continuous beam, supported at abutments and by sloping legs pinned by precast concrete hinges at the top and bottom. There are two side spans of 43m (141ft) and a centre 58m (190ft) wide, with a span at the leg supports of 94m (308ft). The deck is of concrete cellular construction with cantilevered footpaths and is fixed only at the south abutment, where the risk of horizontal thrust is combated by hemispherical bearings.

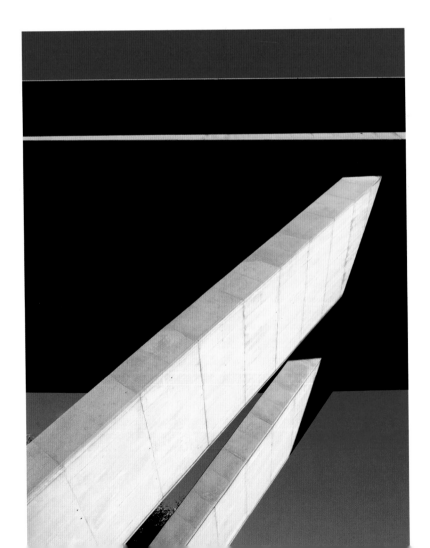

Royal Observer Corps Group Headquarters (Cold War Bunker)

Monument Close, York

1961, Ministry of Works

Scheduled 21 June 2000

The Royal Observer Corps was a mainly volunteer force, which in 1955 was tasked to report explosions and track radioactive fallout in the event of nuclear war. It established a network of 1,561 underground monitoring posts (each for three men) and 25 group headquarters, of which York is the outstanding survivor. It follows a standard 1958 Air Ministry specification to house 60 staff. Steps added in the 1980s serve a concrete entrance block, with the rest of the building sunk into the surrounding embankment. Its centrepiece is the operations room, where explosions and fallout could be recorded and passed to the Ministry of Defence to inform its response. Male and female dormitories were provided, together with an officer's room.

How effective this building would have been in a nuclear attack is questionable, despite a complex air relay system. It was abandoned in March 1992 with most of its equipment intact, and in 2006 was opened to the public by English Heritage.

Several of the monitoring posts are also scheduled or listed.

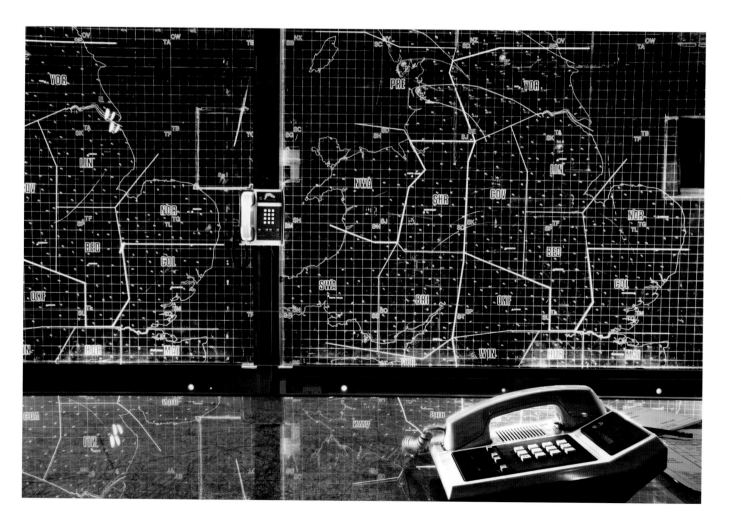

Castle House (Co-op store)

Angel Street, Sheffield

1961–4, G. S. Hay, Co-operative Wholesale Society (CWS) architect

Listed grade II, 31 March 2009

The Brightside and Carbrook Co-operative Society rebuilt their war-damaged central stores after passing their original site to the city for its Castle Market.

Hay's near-blind, granite-faced exterior, encouraging a standardized interior based around the display of goods in artificial light, followed a visit by the Society's secretary, Mr L. Hartle, to Dirk Brouwer's stark additions of 1935–7 at Amsterdam's De Bijenkorf store. At its opening in 1964, the store was described as 'luxurious', with its marble fascias, mosaics, fitted carpets and air conditioning offering a fashionable yet cultured image consciously different from the Society's humble roots.

Stanley Layland of the CWS designed the interior, including the metal relief of a cockerel and fish at the top of a domed staircase hall lined in Carter's tiles, which announced the adjoining restaurant. The boardroom, with a horseshoe-shaped table under a matching lighting canopy, has suffered water damage. The store later incorporated the adjoining (unlisted) Hornes Brothers store of 1962 but closed in 2009. The ground floor remains in use, but its future is uncertain.

Sunderlandwick Hall

near Great Driffield, East Yorkshire

1962–3, Francis Johnson

Listed grade II, 15 July 1998

Sunderlandwick Hall was Johnson's favourite commission, built to replace a heavily altered eighteenth-century mansion that burned down during VJ Day celebrations in 1945.

The clients were Johnson's cousin and her husband, Sir Thomas Ferens, who wanted a house capable of holding its own against the surviving 1840s stables. Johnson produced an L-shaped plan, with the drawing room, dining room and study facing the park, where an elliptical bow in the centre flanked by tripartite windows under blind arches repeats one of his most distinctive motifs. There exudes a comfortable largesse under the hipped roof with no unnecessary gimmicks or details, nor is there the pinched quality found in many post-war classical houses. This confidence continues inside, where fireplaces, pedimented doorcases and a curved staircase strengthen the semblance of a villa in the tradition of Carr of York. On one side is a pedimented garden pavilion, on the other a staff house in a more contemporary idiom.

Francis Johnson achieved national renown in the 1980s for his Yorkshire country houses.

Church of the Holy Redeemer

Boroughbridge Road, Acomb, York

1962–4, George Gaze Pace

Listed grade II, 25 September 1998

Many cities with a surfeit of old churches have demolished selectively to endow new suburban parishes, but the procedure has become increasingly controversial. Pace prepared 22 schemes in 1959 for incorporating elements of St Mary Bishophill Senior, York, into his church at Acomb.

The south entrance front tells the story. There are Pace's characteristic oblong windows and a saddleback tower, but also two lancets and a small doorway of c.1200 in a wall built largely of medieval masonry. In the porch is another late twelfth-century doorway. Enter, and you are in a wide nave with two aisles, the left with an arcade of modern brick piers and concrete beams, the other defined by circular piers from c.1200. The west window is Victorian. An iron cross incorporates a carved Saxon stone and another is built into the pulpit.

The grouping together of a forward altar, font, pulpit and lectern demonstrates, Pace believed, that the 'ministry of both the word and the sacraments are of equal importance'.

The Lawns

Northgate, Cottingham, Hull

1963–7, Gillespie Kidd and Coia

Listed grade II*, 30 March 1993

In Scotland the designers Isi Metzstein and Andy MacMillan are noted for their radical new churches, but in England they worked in the university sector, mainly through the auspices of Sir Leslie Martin, who was master planner for Hull University's expansion.

Financial cutbacks ensured that only half the scheme was built and an intended lake was aborted, while the adjoining social centre was pared down. However, the six linked halls enjoy an open parkland setting, and maturity has imbued a feeling of conclusiveness. This is due to the clever plan of each hall: a self-contained quadrangle of three-storey student bedsitters with a lower range behind housing for the warden and tutorial staff. The medium is brick, with staggered cross-walls forming a series of parallelograms defining groups of five single study bedrooms and two double rooms per floor, each of which shares a kitchen and 'parlour'. Each room has its own balcony, concealed from its neighbour by the stepped plan that belies the limited funding.

Leeds University additions

1963–78, Chamberlin, Powell and Bon

Roger Stevens Building
Listed grade II*, 10 June 2010

Senior Common Room, teaching buildings, the Edward Boyle Library and Henry Price Residences
Listed grade II, 10 June 2010

Leeds University, on a steep hillside site, was Britain's fastest-growing university in the post-war years. Appointed master planners in 1958, Chamberlin, Powell and Bon's exceptionally detailed report in 1960 proposed the building of flexible departmental buildings around a block of shared lecture theatres. Only one quadrangle was fully realized, Chancellor's Court, with the senior common room to its west and the lecture theatres and physics building to the east. An undergraduates' library was added northwards in 1973–5 and a social sciences building in 1978, adjoining Alfred Waterhouse's original college. These long slabs of glass and concrete were delineated only by pairs of beams, on a strict grid with service ducts between them. Codes following the colours of the rainbow denote the floors and level pedestrian routes through the buildings to the lecture theatres, from the Red Route starting at the top of the hill and becoming a high-level walkway, to the Purple Route linking the lower southern buildings.

The lecture theatre block (Roger Stevens Building) is the one distinctive building, redesigned in 1964 to fulfil a new brief that Leeds take 10,000 students by 1970. Lecture theatres with stepped seating are entered through narrow doors at the end of each row from ramps rising through the building, a structure reflected in the steps of the external ducting.

Chamberlin also recommended building student flats to enliven the campus, including the Henry Price Residences – realized by Bon in 1963–4 – using traditional red brick to contrast with the teaching buildings. There has been some rebuilding and expansion, but Leeds's ambitious programme of the 1960s has served it well.

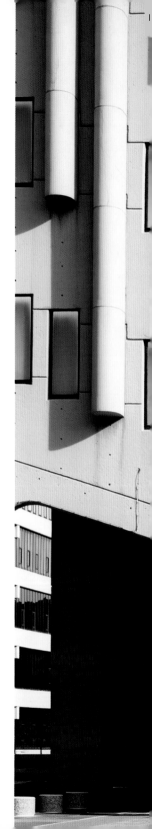

RC Church of the Holy Family

Chequerfield Road, Pontefract

1964, Derek Walker

Listed grade II, 27 August 2008

This is the first of three churches built by Walker near Leeds before he became the chief architect of Milton Keynes. One has been demolished and one is now a mosque; Holy Family closed in 2008, the diocese citing a dwindling congregation and a shortage of priests.

Walker admired his client, Fr John Hudson, for his 'uncluttered' attitudes and a radical brief that in 1961 alarmed the local hierarchy but anticipated later Vatican reforms. The sanctuary is the width of the nave, but short transepts enabled worshippers to sit on three sides, with the choir in a gallery over the south transept. A colonnade separates the Lady chapel from the nave.

The materials are simple and strong: load-bearing ivory brick and concrete. Behind the altar is a large ceramic depicting Christ in Majesty by Robert Brumby, and Roy Lewis designed the stained glass. The central tower was removed in the late 1990s following vandalism and leakage, but the interior, with its fine fittings, survived almost intact before its closure.

St Peter's Church

Reney Avenue, Greenhill, Sheffield

1964–5, Oxley and Bussey
Architect in charge, Peter Sargent

Listed grade II, 18 February 1999

Housing estates were built from the 1920s in Greenhill, where St Peter's pyramidal spire is a prominent hilltop landmark. Although the site was acquired in 1930, the church was planned only in 1963, when Father Andrews asked local architects Oxley and Bussey to seat 450 people 'as near the sanctuary as possible'.

The timber footings to the spire form an archway within the church. Otherwise the building is a series of brick segments that together form a broad, staggered semi-circle. At the centre of the outer arc lies the sanctuary, whose rear wall shields the vestry and makes a cool, cream contrast to vibrant glass and dark brick walling elsewhere. The largest segment houses the weekday chapel, which has a wall of abstract stained glass. The rich collection of fittings fulfils the early 1960s aesthetic of clean lines, solid craftsmanship and good materials, with the steel cross suspended over the altar a fitting tribute to Sheffield's most famous industry.

St Saviour's Church

Ings Way, Fairweather Green,
Bradford

1964–5, 1971, George Gaze Pace

Listed grade II, 6 January 2007

The parish of St Saviour's was created in 1883. Land was given for a larger church in 1924, but Pace was appointed only in 1961.

Pace's maturity as a designer coincided with rising inflation, and from the mid-1960s his new churches grew smaller. This is a very complete example, a rectangular building with steep-pitched roofs that rise to a monopitch tower – effectively a high dormer lighting the altar. The interior resembles a barn, concrete beams contrasted with timber posts and trusses, the roof rafters forming patterns of oblongs repeated in the window openings and pew fronts. The sanctuary is set on a diagonal with ranks of pews on its two main sides; the choir sits in the opposite corner. Pace's limed oak furnishings and black metal light fittings are combined with pews from St John's Church, Little Horton, whence also came a mosaic in the side chapel; the bell came from St James's Church, Manchester Road, Bradford. Pace added a church hall in 1969–71.

Assembly hall

Bootham School, Bootham, York

1965–6, Trevor Dannatt

Listed grade II, 31 March 2007

Bootham School, founded for boys by the Society of Friends in 1823, occupies a tight site in central York. Dannatt was commissioned to add an assembly hall that was entirely modern yet fitted comfortably amidst the surrounding buildings and views of York Minster. It had to be suitable as a meeting room for worship and also as a concert hall or theatre.

The hall, for 440 people, forms a sculptural centrepiece to the school, distinguished by its board-marked concrete, with stairs to the balcony expressed between setback glazing and with a copper mansard roof. There are foyers on two sides, also finished in concrete and with paved floors, and the balcony is set over these. The auditorium is lit by a high clerestory and features a stage at one end that is concealed by an elm screen when not needed, a material also used on the balcony fronts. The strong, pure qualities, the honestly expressed natural materials, and a rare humane sensibility that infuses Dannatt's best works are well seen here.

Electricity Substation

Moore Street, Sheffield

1965–7, Bryan Jefferson
of Jefferson, Sheard and Partners

Listed grade II, 18 September 2013

Electricity distribution in Sheffield called for a 275 kilovolt cable ring around the city centre with transformer and switching substations to supply the local 33 kilovolt system. Land shortages saw the building of one of these as a prominent three-storey building adjoining the new ring road.

The electricity board demanded an uninterrupted interior for the two transformers and switchgear, with minimum heights and exceptional floor loadings, so Jefferson chose a reinforced concrete structure with deep portal frames. The equipment required no windows, so he designed a building that expressed its structure, restricting ornament to the spiral escape stairs. The *in situ* concrete's strength is emphasized by a board-marked finish that retains the bolt marks of the formwork and daywork joints. Dark engineering brick forms a ground-floor plinth, with concrete plank cladding above, set outside the frame on the first floor, and a tough canopy set between the projecting beam ends of the frame. It powerfully expresses the hidden force of energy.

New Chapel

University of York St John,
Lord Mayor's Walk, York

1966–7, George Gaze Pace

Listed grade II, 30 September 2003

York St John University has its origins in two Anglican teacher training colleges built in the nineteenth century, based in York and Ripon, which merged in 1975. As student numbers grew, so in 1962 the York college commissioned a new chapel from Pace, who had already refurbished its existing one. In 1965 he determined a Y-shaped plan, with wings on either side of a forward altar that could be used as transepts for major services or as side chapels. The building tapers towards the rear, where there is a narrow gallery housing the organ and choir.

Pace designed the original fittings, and pews by him for the old chapel were also redeployed. However, the building has gained additional interest as the repository of artworks by the students, including fine stained glass.

The college closed its Ripon campus in 2001 and sought English Heritage's advice on the listing of the chapel before producing a master plan for expansion on its York site.

3A Ellers Road

Doncaster

1967–8, Peter Aldington
of Aldington and Craig

Listed grade II, 28 January 2009

In 1967 Peter Aldington was invited by a childhood friend Brian Wilkinson to design a house in the garden of an existing property for himself, his wife and three daughters. Trees were retained and the new property made subordinate to its neighbour. The resulting flat roof differentiates it from Aldington's earlier work, but the plan resembles that of his own house, Turn End. A discreet entry adjoining a carport leads to the kitchen, set in the central section of a three-sided courtyard plan and with built-in counters and fittings. Concrete block walls and full-height sliding aluminium windows are topped by a boarded ceiling. The central courtyard (later enclosed by Aldington) is the dominant feature, with a smaller one lighting the larger bedrooms; these indoor and outdoor spaces are linked by similar tiled floors.

The *Architectural Review*'s Lance Wright felt, in 1972, that the single-storey courtyard house was 'perhaps Modern Movement's greatest contribution to domestic architecture' for its adaptability to awkward infill sites. This is a rare example from outside London.

Theatre Royal additions

St Leonard's Place, York

1967, Patrick Gwynne
R. A. Sefton Jenkins, engineer

Additions listed grade II*,
14 March 1997

The Theatre Royal dates largely from 1879–80, its baronial Gothic exterior more typical of a chapel than a theatre, and with the remains of a twelfth-century undercroft below. It had little foyer or workshop space, no common entrance and tiny bars. The director, Donald Bodley, decided to build on an adjoining garden that housed the scenery hut.

Bodley came to London for advice and ate at Gwynne's Serpentine Restaurant in Hyde Park. Immediately he determined on his architect. Gwynne had been inspired by umbrellas to create a structure of mushroom columns at the Serpentine, and repeated them here supporting linked hexagons. Two double-height columns, unglazed, advertise the building to the street, with seven set in two tiers within. Spherical rooflights backlight the interior by day; at night the building shines like a lantern. Best of all is the sweeping staircase, cantilevered from a single free-standing post, engineered by Jenkins without calculations. The Theatre Royal is Gwynne's most accessible design since the Serpentine Restaurant was demolished in 1990–1.

Queensgate Market

Huddersfield

1968–70, Gwyn Roberts of
J. Seymour Harris Partnership

Listed grade II, 4 August 2005

The 1960s saw local authorities exploiting the consumer boom by redeveloping their town centres. Huddersfield sold a large freehold plot that included its Victorian market to the developer Murrayfield, whose architects were used by the borough for a new market alongside.

The loss of the landmark Victorian market seems to have inspired its successor to be technologically interesting – a Gothic building in modern form inspired by the Spanish architect/engineer Felix Candela. The roof comprises 21 free-standing columns, functioning independently and ranging from 3.3m (11ft) to 7.5m (24½ft) tall, each supporting an asymmetrical hyperbolic paraboloid concrete shell umbrella 3m (10ft) deep. Thus the shells cantilever further to one side than the other, creating a striking repeated pattern while the alternating tall and short rows permit clerestory glazing between them. Roberts was a friend of the German sculptor Fritz Steller, who decorated the ring road elevation with nine semi-abstract ceramic panels, *Articulation in Motion*. He also produced a steel mural, *Commerce*.

Arqiva Tower

Jagger Lane, Emley Moor,
near Huddersfield

1969–71, Sir Ove Arup and Partners

Listed grade II, 26 March 2003

This television tower was built for the Independent Television Association to replace a steel guyed mast erected in 1966, which collapsed in 1969 thanks to high winds and heavy icing. Concrete was chosen for the replacement as it offered the only means of withstanding winds up to 241km/h (150mph), and it was relatively cheap. Good looks were also important in this environmentally sensitive moorland setting, where there was vehement local opposition.

At 330m (1,082ft), the concrete shell was the third-highest tower in Europe on completion, and it takes seven minutes by lift to reach the top. The wall thickness reduces from 533 to 343mm (21 to 13½in) over this height, giving an elegant profile that is also compatible with the distribution of vertical bending movement. It is a building that combines perfect technical performance with architectural elegance.

Crucible Theatre

Norfolk Street, Sheffield

1969–71, Renton Howard Wood Associates, job architects Nicholas Thompson and Robin Benyon

Listed grade II, 1 November 2007

A new repertory theatre was built as part of an expansion of Sheffield's civic centre. It was planned in consultation with Tanya Moiseiwitsch, former assistant to Tyrone Guthrie, who in the 1940s developed the thrust stage, a tongue-like structure around which the audience sat on three sides. The pretence at creating an outdoor courtyard indoors, with spotlights for stars, reflects the form's derivation in antique theatre and its initial revival for festivals. The intimacy created between actors and audience – despite holding over 1,000 people – is reflected in the success of the Crucible in hosting the World Snooker Championship since 1977.

The foyers originally had vividly coloured carpet and banners, and bold signage designed by Clare Ferraby in deliberate contrast to the shabby chic courted by many 1970s theatres; externally, bronzed fascias were contrasted with shiny red panels. That look was denuded over the years, but informed Burrell Foley Fischer's striking refurbishment of 2007–10.

Halifax Building

Trinity Road, Halifax

1970–4, Building Design Partnership
Partner in charge, H. W. (Bill) Pearson

Listed grade II, 23 January 2013

The Halifax Building Society, so named from 1928 when it was already the largest in Britain, commissioned a new headquarters in 1968 to increase its efficiency and security, and to give staff a better working environment.

BDP, Britain's largest multidisciplinary practice, faced an awkward, wedge-shaped site near the town centre. They covered the entire plot, bridging it with a massive construction that proclaimed the institution's strength and stability, with diamond-shaped concrete piers and planters that defined public pedestrian routes beneath overhanging floors of bronzed curtain walling. Open-plan offices are laid out on the third floor across the whole site, with an executive suite on top. The ground and mezzanine floors have recreational facilities and a basement was originally dedicated to an innovatory computerized file retrieval system. Although a huge building that dominates Halifax from a distance, it is only partially seen close to because it sits so tightly within the street plan, while expensive finishes exemplified pride in the Society.

St Margaret Clitherow RC Church

Threshfield, North Yorkshire

1972–3, Peter Langtry-Langton

Listed grade II, 5 April 2012

The first designs in 1966 for a church at Threshfield were by Jack Langtry-Langton, architect of Bradford's circular English Martyrs church in 1935. When he and the diocese could not agree a solution, his son Peter designed a simpler building in 1968 for a different site, inspired by a drawing of an African church made of palm leaves and branches.

St Margaret's comprises two intersecting squares, whose corners of limestone rubble project as triangles from a pyramidal roof formed around four concrete beams clad in zinc. A giant skylight is adorned with a lead Celtic cross by John Ashworth and John Loker of LA Studios, responsible also for a bas-relief of Christ over the altar. Two large *dalle de verre* windows are by Jane Duff for John Hardman Studios, in swirling semi-abstract shapes and primary colours. Peter Langtry-Langton designed the curved pews and fittings.

Despite the church's striking form, the colours and textures of the materials ensure it blends comfortably into its rural setting between Threshfield and Grassington.

WEST MIDLANDS

Cathedral Church of
St Michael and All
Angels, 1956–62,
Sir Basil Spence.

397-427 (odd) Wake Green Road

Birmingham

1945, Phoenix (John Laing, McAlpine and Henry Boot contractors)

Listed grade II, 15 July 1998

These prefabs are among the rare survivors of 156,623 bungalows erected in 1945–8 under the temporary housing programme initiated by Winston Churchill in March 1944. It was a response to an acute housing shortage exacerbated by the war.

'Temporary prefabs' were built by a number of commercial firms to a standard size and two-bedroom plan determined by the Ministry of Works. Most had built-in kitchens and bathrooms based on a prototype by the Ministry, and at a time when fittings and furniture were in short supply they were thought luxurious. Examples were erected by local authorities across Britain, sometimes on sites prepared by prisoners of war, and including some (as here) on the edge of a public park. Leftover Anderson shelters were erected as garden sheds.

The Phoenix was one of the rarest and least known types, but its solid covering of asbestos cement sheeting made it among the most durable. It was intended to last 15 years, but these surviving examples are still popular with residents today.

Broadgate House

Broadgate, Coventry

1948–53, Coventry City
Architect's Department

Listed grade II, 24 January 2013

This was the first building erected in central Coventry after its wartime destruction. It was the only six-storey block of offices and shops realized according to the 1941 master plan by Donald Gibson, city architect, with lower units preferred elsewhere.

Gibson's rationalized neoclassical style, indebted to Lewis Mumford's *The Culture of Cities* and with carvings by John Skelton, gave way to a Festival of Britain idiom for the clock tower. This celebrates Coventry's history and incorporates the salvaged market hall bell. On the hour appears a curvaceous Lady Godiva riding her white horse, while from a window leers Peeping Tom; their artist, Trevor Tennant, carved more figures facing Hertford Street. A mosaic in the office entrance by Hugh Hosking and Rene Anoniette depicting the Coventry Martyrs confirms how Coventry was seeking to reaffirm its history by pictorial means.

Although Gibson's plan introduced novel pedestrian precincts elsewhere, Broadgate House was built as a bridge over traffic entering Broadgate from Hertford Street, blocked in 1968.

War memorial bus shelter

Barnard's Green, Malvern,
Worcestershire

1949

Listed grade II, 18 May 2011

This tiny building, opened in October 1949, performs its function of sheltering passengers from inclement weather with unusual panache. This is because it is also a memorial to local men lost in the Second World War, part of a brief movement for bus shelters as practical monuments.

A late exercise in 1930s-style commercial modernism with an oversailing canopy, the three-bay shelter is curved at one end. At the other is a clock tower, stubby yet charmingly enlivened with the motif of projecting fins first conceived by Walter Gropius, in his entry to the Chicago Tribune competition of 1922, and popularized by Willem Dudok's Hilversum Town Hall and T. S. Tait's clock tower for Glasgow's 'Empire Exhibition' in 1938. The designer is unknown, leaving unexplained such curious incongruities as recessed panels adorned with poppies, a traditional motif creating a link with the First World War enhanced by a more recent plaque reminding us that: 'The war to end all wars didn't'.

Memorial Gardens

Church Hill, Walsall

1951–2, Geoffrey Jellicoe

Registered grade II, 20 April 1999

Medieval Walsall was swept away in a 1930s slum clearance scheme, yet its neglected hilltop is quietly beautiful thanks to Jellicoe's war memorial gardens, commissioned in 1947. Their high walls have classical aedicules framing views of St Matthew's church, while a slightly later chapel – resembling a gazebo from the garden – has concrete mullions and pilotis under its traditional pyramidal copper roofs. A Greek key pattern of paths defines beds of shrubs and trees. To the south a terrace offers views across the town, truncated since the gardener's cottage was sold in 1998.

The mix of architecture and landscape, and of modernism with classical Italian motifs, is indicative of Jellicoe's career at a time when he was regarded as a specialist in housing as much as in landscape. A gateway in the garden wall forms an axis to the Brotherhood (parish) Hall added by Jellicoe in 1955–6 at the end of a delightfully decorative terrace of old people's flats built by him in 1951–4.

Limbrick Wood School

Jobs Lane, Tile Hill, Coventry

1951–2, Ministry of Education/
Coventry City Architect's Department

Listed grade II, 30 March 1993

Stirrat Johnson-Marshall left Hertfordshire County Council in 1948 to found a development group at the Ministry of Education dedicated to researching new building methods. Though preoccupied with secondary schools, he was also inspired to modify the Bristol Aeroplane Company's prefabricated primary school, a system of aluminium panels and trusses developed when peace threatened the aircraft industry.

Donald Gibson, chief architect at Coventry, had been Johnson-Marshall's boss in the 1930s, and offered a site in the new suburb of Tile Hill. The infants' department was built first, followed by a separate junior school. Both elements set pairs of classrooms and cloakrooms around a central assembly hall, a cheaper and more informal solution than BAC's long lines of classrooms thanks to its three-dimensional grid. Limbrick Wood is contemporary with Greenfields School (see p.186), designed by Hertfordshire to a similar plan, and did much to promote a tighter approach to primary school planning.

Woodlands Academy

Broad Lane, Tile Hill, Coventry

1952–4, extended 1955–6,
Michael Smith, Ministry of Education

Listed grade II, 30 March 1993

Because four direct-grant grammar schools creamed off Coventry's best students, the city embarked on a pioneering comprehensive system, generously funded by rates from the car industry. Only a large school could provide a viable sixth form, and the Ministry of Education insisted on a ten-form entry.

Woodlands Academy was built for 1,500 boys. Such a massive school could have become impersonal, but Smith devised a system of houses with their own meeting rooms and dining areas so that the boys could identify with a smaller group. Single-storey blocks serving pairs of houses surround the taller teaching buildings. All used a version of the prefabricated system developed for Hertfordshire schools (see pp.186–7) pushed by the Ministry for multistorey use. The informal planning and 21 hectare (52 acre) site give the school its character. The hall is decorated with Greek figures, and the library, now a sixth-form centre, has murals by Norman Adams depicting scenes from Homer's *Odyssey*. One building was rebuilt in 1992 following a fire.

Church of St Michael and All Angels

Church Road, Tettenhall, Wolverhampton

Largely rebuilt 1952–5, Bernard Miller

Listed grade II, 29 July 1950 (for the medieval tower)

The medieval church of Tettenhall Regis was consumed by a fire in 1950, which spared only the fourteenth-century tower and the 1882 south porch.

Bernard Miller, student and lecturer at the Liverpool School of Architecture, built several churches in the 1930s with Art Deco flourishes. Tettenhall, by contrast, is strongly influenced by the Arts and Crafts Movement, with low, broad arcades supported on foliage capitals, and boldly reticulated windows that cast pools of light into the church. The wide nave is spanned by a timber roof that harmonizes with Miller's intricate furnishings. His symbol of a bee can be found on one of the painted altar rails. Only the massive font, clad in swirling blue mosaics by G. Mayer Marten, retains Art Deco elements.

The altar has always been in the church's crossing. It was, however, originally set against a low wall that divided the main space from a Lady chapel, a device popular in the 1930s. An open timber screen was installed in 1985. The east window is by G. Cooper-Abbs.

Grosvenor House

Bennetts Hill, Birmingham

1953–4, Cotton, Ballard and Blow

Listed grade II, 18 February 1999

This is a rare example of an office building erected before restrictive building licences were revoked in November 1954. It enhances its corner site by adopting a wavy nautical motif reminiscent of the Festival of Britain, with jaunty projecting sills, cornices and balconies. These form an unusually cohesive ripple of contrasting planes, which culminate in a distinctive prow to the corner with New Street. Most prominent of all is an oversailing glass cornice that projects over its uppermost storey.

Cotton, Ballard and Blow was the architectural practice behind Jack Cotton, the Birmingham-born entrepreneur responsible for much of its earlier city centre rebuilding and one of England's leading land speculators by the 1960s. His most ambitious scheme was for Monico at Piccadilly Circus, an unsuccessful London development fronted for a time by Walter Gropius. This is one of the few listed speculative office buildings, and an example of rare wit and integrity.

Christ Church

Frankpledge Road,
Cheylesmore, Coventry

1954–8, Alfred H. Gardner

Listed grade II, 10 August 1998

Christ Church was derided as 'Pleasure Gardens pastiche' in 1958, but it is this charming style that makes it so enjoyable. The architect was imposed on this traditionally evangelical parish by Coventry's Anglo-Catholic Bishop Gorton. It replaced a city-centre church bombed in 1941.

The church hall, tower, vestibule, vicarage and caretaker's house are separately expressed in different materials. The belfry's chequerboard motif is repeated throughout the interior, which has a nave and aisles of similar width, and only a shallow sanctuary. The plaster vault is decorated with wheels and ribbons representing Coventry industries. Square patterns dominate the side walls and particularly the east end, in timber and purple acoustic tiles edged in gold. Gold, too, are the light fittings, inspired by the hanging birdcage in the Lion and Unicorn Pavilion at the Festival of Britain. The sculpture of Christ the Sower, woodcarving and clock are by John Skelton, the Coventry-born nephew of Eric Gill. The thick stained glass depicting the life of Christ is by Pierre Fourmaintraux.

Goldfinger House

off Cranmore Boulevard,
Shirley, Solihull

1955–6, Ernö Goldfinger

Listed grade II, 25 November 1995

This diminutive but distinctive office building was designed as the headquarters of a paper manufacturer, Carr and Co. It was Goldfinger's first truly mature work, and early designs show him systematically abandoning the brick cladding still found in his Regent's Park flats, London (see p.438) in favour of an unadorned concrete frame distinguished by a high parapet and contrasting planes of glazing.

The water tanks and lift motor room are housed in a perfect concrete cube raised high above the roof, intended to allow access beneath to a roof garden. Below, another cube, entirely glazed, forms an entrance hall between ground-floor pilotis. These volumes, and the concrete spiral escape stairs to the side, contrast with the strict rhythm of the overall 84cm grid (2ft 9in) of concrete and glass that makes up the rest of the building.

The ground floor was partly infilled with listed building consent in a refurbishment by AJA Architects completed in September 2010.

Stonecrop

Campden Hill, Illmington,
Warwickshire

1955 onwards, Robert Harvey
of Yorke, Harper and Harvey

Listed grade II*, 27 March 2007

Robert Harvey was one of the first generation of architects to be inspired by Frank Lloyd Wright, whose work came to British attention in the late 1930s. He relished private house commissions, which he ran from a Stratford-upon-Avon office inherited from F. W. B. Yorke while his partner Ross Harper undertook larger projects from Birmingham.

Harvey believed that planners were the curse of modern housebuilders and acquired this orchard site, with north-facing views, for his own house after frustrations elsewhere. He chose long pieces of Cotswold stone resembling those used by Wright at Taliesin, with English oak and elm, and floor slabs of polished Hornton stone. For economy, many of the materials were second-hand and Harvey, his brother and brother-in-law undertook much of the work themselves.

A large chimney and hearth provide the central accent, around which the L-shaped plan revolves. The flowing space allows views of the landscape from different levels, and the main bedroom has a wide balcony overlooking the living room.

79 Lovelace Avenue

Solihull, West Midlands

1955–9, D. Rosslyn Harper

Listed grade II, 23 May 2003

Birmingham was perhaps the first school of architecture in England to become obsessed by the work of Frank Lloyd Wright, in the 1930s. It inspired Ross Harper as well as his partner Robert Harvey, and the former skilfully adapted Wright's early Prairie style into this house for himself and his family.

The house of oak, cedar and Shropshire brick nestles against woodland and the garden flows easily from its terrace. The sweeping horizontal planes of the Prairie style inspired its massing, emphasized by its carport and verandah roof, the cedar boarding and recessed horizontal joints to the brickwork. The shallow hipped roof appears to hover over the frameless corner first-floor windows. Inside, the open-plan living area evolves around a central hearth with similarly detailed brickwork. There is a substantial staircase with polished vertical panelling, built-in furniture and geometric light fittings.

With its warm materials, broad massing and close relationship with the landscape, this house is a successful translation of the Prairie style to the West Midlands.

Granelli

The Rise, Hopwood, Alvechurch, Worcestershire

1960–1, Remo and Mary Granelli

Listed grade II, 20 August 2007

Remo Granelli and Mary Graham met while working for Birmingham City Council, married, and in 1959 founded their own practice after winning a housing competition. They had bought a site overlooking National Trust land in 1955, and now they designed a house and studio that maximized the extensive views.

The Granellis adopted a T-shaped plan around a wide corridor, with pergolas extending into the garden at both ends. The sloping ground allowed the south-facing sitting room to be set lower to give a greater ceiling height. They used Leicester bricks and vertical cedar boarding externally, and sourced fittings from local Birmingham manufacturers, including the motor trade for the chromium-plated pipes of the staircase balustrade. Remo Granelli's father, Anthony, manufactured terrazzo, which adds elegance to the hall and cantilevered staircase and suited the underfloor heating. The house exudes an easy spaciousness, yet was achieved for £4,000.

114 Kenilworth Road

Coventry

1956–7, Robert Harvey
of Yorke, Harper and Harvey

Listed grade II, 8 December 2004

This modest house for his brother is the best of a pair by Harvey for his family in Kenilworth Road. Completed before his own house at Ilmington, it was the first to demonstrate his romantic style and the powerful influence of Frank Lloyd Wright, with whom he had corresponded.

The house is concealed from the road, and presents an inscrutable brick façade that cowers under its deep eaves and is pierced only by narrow, high-set windows. To the rear the house flows naturally into the garden from a raised terrace. Timber dominates the interior, particularly the living room and the adjoining linked kitchen. To the right, a wing for the Harveys' three boys has a wagon roof and built-in furniture that captures the spirit of a Wild West bunkhouse. This was the first house where Harvey forsook traditional downpipes as inappropriate to his big roofs, instead copying Wright's preference for metal chains as a conduit for rainwater.

Belgrade Theatre

Belgrade Square, Coventry

1956–8, Coventry City
Architect's Department
Job architect, Kenneth King

Listed grade II, 12 June 1998

The Belgrade was Britain's first repertory theatre built after the war, and the first for a local authority. It had its own workshops and 21 bedsits overlooking Corporation Street for resident actors, who were expected to become part of the Coventry community.

The main elevation, with its double-height glazing, is a modest version of Mannheim's Nationaltheater, designed in 1953. Pendant lights are by Bernard Shottlander, with murals by Martin Froy.

The auditorium has a single gallery over shallow rear stalls, with a conventional proscenium stage and stepped boxes either side reminiscent of those at the Royal Festival Hall. The name comes from the panelling: President Tito, visiting Coventry, made a gift of beech wood. The lengths were too short for the theatre, however, so Yugoslavian timber can be found in local council housing, while the theatre used West African hardwoods moulded into curves by the Building Research Station to give excellent acoustics. A concrete representation of Belgrade, based by Jim Brown on a seventeenth-century print, enlivens the Corporation Street elevation.

Retail Market

Queen Victoria Road, Coventry

1957–8, Coventry City
Architect's Department
Job architects, Douglas Beaton,
Ralph Iredale and Ian Crawford

Listed grade II, 18 June 2009

Many city centres had relied heavily on their markets following bomb damage during the war, and they were consequently a prominent feature of redevelopment plans. Coventry's new market replaced the war-damaged Barracks and Rex markets and occupied a quadrant of its cruciform pedestrian shopping precinct, when planned in 1941 the first in Europe.

The market's round shape offers several entrances of equal importance and encourages shoppers to circulate around all the stalls, many of which retain their vintage lettering. A mural by Dresden students depicting farming and industrial scenes was commissioned through that city's burgomaster. A feature of the Rex Market had been a children's merry-go-round, so David Mason designed a replacement, which stood outside the market until in about the year 2000 it was moved to its centre. A series of ramps links the market into a network of rooftop car parks.

An adjacent engineering works was converted into a fish market, and the mermaids, sailors and Neptunes with which Jim Brown decorated its columns were incorporated into the circular market when it was demolished.

Cathedral Church of St Michael and All Angels

Priory Street, Coventry

1956–62, Sir Basil Spence
Engineers, Ove Arup and Partners

Listed grade I, 29 March 1988

The medieval church, raised to cathedral status in 1918, was devastated in a great air raid on 14 November 1940. No building competes with its rebuilding as a symbol of post-war revival, and it made Spence a household name.

A scheme by Sir Giles Gilbert Scott, incorporating the surviving tower and apse, was abandoned in 1946 and a competition held in 1950. There was no restriction as to style or materials, or compulsion to retain more than the tower and two crypts.

Spence's winning design in August 1951 incorporated the ruins as a forecourt to a new building sited at right angles on a new site orientated north–south. It is a stone-walled structure, but for economy Spence recast the interior in 1955–6 using concrete blocks, with concrete-framed side chapels, after Arup had refined a lighter, faceted concrete vault. He redesigned the porch as a massive *porte cochère* linking the old and new buildings, having already conceived a great, clear-glazed west window etched with angels by John Hutton.

Spence quickly commissioned the principal artworks to ensure their realization, though this inhibited subsequent changes to the east end. They included Graham Sutherland's tapestry of Christ in Majesty and ten windows by Laurence Lee, Keith New and Geoffrey Clarke. John Piper's baptistery window and Jacob Epstein's sculpture of St Michael quashing the devil followed in 1954–5. Subsequent commissions, especially in the side chapels, indicate a greater toughness emerging in Spence's work.

The cathedral, criticized on its opening by modernists and traditionalists alike, is now recognized as one of the great 1950s repositories of art and culture.

Oldbury Wells School

Oldbury Wells, Bridgnorth, Shropshire

1957–8, 1959–60,
Lyons, Israel and Ellis
Job architects, Tom Ellis,
Alan Colquhoun and Paul Yarker

Listed grade II, 30 March 1993

Lyons, Israel and Ellis's (LIE) mature style emerged in this pair of buildings at Bridgnorth, built as separate schools for boys and girls but since 1972 combined as a single comprehensive.

The boys' school, built first, is an urbane, curtain-walled building, the lines of glazing set firmly within an exposed concrete frame. A line of rooflights over the main hall (now used for teaching) is a distinctive feature of the architects' work. It was extended in 1964.

The girls' school is one of the firm's most sophisticated compositions, with a dramatic water tank set high over the set-back entrance. The entrance is a cube of concrete over low doors, almost free-standing within the building's dominating frame, countered by the cubic water tank.

The schools confirmed LIE's place at the cutting edge of the new brutalism in these years. Peter Smithson, who studied under Ellis at Newcastle, remembered him as among the kindest of men and a supreme draughtsman, and many able assistants later achieved independent fame.

The Vale

Egbaston, Birmingham

1959–65, Casson and Conder with
Mary Mitchell, landscape architect

Landscape registered grade II,
6 December 2000

This land formed part of the Calthorpe Estate developed by successive Lords Calthorpe with villas for Birmingham businessmen from the 1830s onwards. By the 1950s most were occupied by institutions, including the university, which in 1955 acquired The Vale, Wyddrington and Maple Bank with 19 hectares (47 acres) of land to provide desperately needed student accommodation.

Casson and Conder were invited to prepare a master plan in 1956. They proposed enhancing the park-like character of this steeply sloping wooded site, grouping residential halls among trees and creating a lake in the low-lying, damp centre. Mitchell extensively recontoured and replanted the land but retained nineteenth-century trees. Conder designed a bridge, though an adjoining coffee bar and library was never built, and guided the design of the central Wyddrington and Lake Halls by H. T. Cadbury-Brown. These were remodelled in 2002–4 as Shackleton Hall and the other halls were rebuilt in 2006–14.

The Rotunda

New Street, Birmingham

1960–5, James A. Roberts

Listed grade II, 9 August 2000

The Rotunda is the principal landmark of central Birmingham's post-war redevelopment, and Roberts was one of Britain's leading commercial architects.

It is rare to find a 1960s office building designed as a cylinder set on a podium, and it reflects the move in art and design at that time towards simpler shapes. 'As it was at the top of the hill and it had no back or front it struck me that the building should be circular . . . like a drum', Roberts explained in 1995. A 12-storey tower was first planned in 1960, when the foundations were poured; it took its 24-storey form only as work progressed. The podium is sympathetically concave on its west elevation.

The building's white mosaic cladding was replaced in 2005, when the Rotunda was converted from offices to flats and serviced apartments. A mural of *ciment fondu* wrapped around the central drum by John Poole, a local artist, was designed for a banking hall but is now mostly concealed.

Coventry Station

Station Square, Coventry

1961–2, British Railways,
London Midland Region
Job architect, Derrick Shorten

Listed grade II, 24 November 1995

Coventry's special position as a symbol of England's post-war regeneration and promises to the bishop, Cuthbert Bardsley, ensured that its station was generously funded and completed as intended. It replaced a station that had only two platforms with the present four.

Shorten studied Pier Luigi Nervi's unrealized design of 1954 for Naples' Central Station, and hit on building the station at right angles to the tracks; the section he produced over a first frantic weekend determined the realized design. Connecting bridges were hung from stainless-steel rods devised by the engineer Peter Dunican of Ove Arup and Partners, with staircases overlooking the double-height booking hall finished in white Swedish tiles; the large areas of glazing were made possible by neoprene gaskets, then novel, and balustrading was formed from heat-toughened Pilkington glass. Finer still are the fascias and signage, the latter in a modified version of the typeface being designed by Jock Kinneir for the motorway system and for which Coventry and Glasgow Queen Street were trial stations.

Ashley and Strathcona Buildings

Birmingham University

1961–2, Howell, Killick, Partridge and Amis

Listed grade II, 30 March 1993

Birmingham was the first of a series of university commissions that resulted from the success of Howell, Killick and Partridge in the Churchill College competition of 1959. Amis joined in 1961.

Birmingham's Faculty of Commerce and Social Science had just been amalgamated from different departments. The taller, snail-shaped Ashley Building was devised as a means of bringing the disparate staff together by setting 69 tutors' rooms around a five-storey atrium off a circular stair. It is built of the storey-high precast panels developed by the firm when assistants at the London County Council, with projecting sills to throw off rainwater. Strathcona is a curving tail housing lecture theatres and seminar rooms, built of concrete blocks but with a similar rhythm of projecting floor beams to its neighbour.

This aesthetic is enhanced internally by the architects' 'Chinese-style' slatted ceilings and staircase joinery. Their subsequent Oxbridge work refined these ideas, but the Birmingham buildings have an earthy panache, and the atrium remains one of their finest spaces.

Roman Catholic Church of Our Lady

Valley Road, Lillington,
Royal Leamington Spa

1962–3, Henry Fedeski
of Fedeski and Rayner

Listed grade II, 19 September 2011

A new parish was created in 1958 to serve the expanding Leamington suburbs. Local architect Henry Fedeski worked closely with the incumbent, Fr C. J. Thornton, to produce a large, cruciform church with equal arms but with a central altar placed under the crossing, denoted externally by a copper flèche.

The result is an impressive internal space. The church's glory, however, is its extensive scheme of vibrant *dalle de verre* glass by Dom Charles Norris of Buckfast Abbey, which fills the walls at clerestory level and is used for all the ground-floor glazing. Figurative panels in the transepts depict the Annunciation and the ground-floor chapels and baptistery are decorated with symbols appropriate to their functions; the clerestory glazing is in abstracted patterns which become more rational towards the east end, representing God bringing order from chaos. The blind east end is occupied by a monumental chi-rho mosaic (a symbol repeated on the altar) by Steven Sykes, who had worked with Basil Spence at Coventry Cathedral.

The Folly

near Leominster, Herefordshire

1962–3, 1973–6, Raymond Erith

Listed grade II, 15 July 1998

The Folly was devised with the aid of the client, Mrs M. A. Willis, as a *jeu d'esprit* following her divorce. It is one of Erith's most distinctive compositions.

The building stands at the head of a wooded valley, which it dominates from a distance. The elevations were developed from the elliptical plan, and Erith also claimed to have been inspired by the lunar cycle. The plan consists of semi-oval rooms set one above the other and connected by a spiral stair. Erith's device of using a Venetian foot of almost 35.5cm (14in) makes details like stairs more generous within the building's limited size. Most domed roofs are taller than they are wide to counter the flattening effect of perspective when viewed from below, but Erith eschewed this conceit, though he gave height by placing a viewing platform on top. A single-storey addition linked by a Regency-inspired verandah was added in 1973–6.

Mrs Willis later wrote that The Folly was 'the best thing I have achieved in my life'.

The Shakespeare Centre

Henley Street, Stratford-upon-Avon

1962–4, Lawrence Williams
of Wood and Kendrick and Williams

Listed grade II, 19 October 2010

Shakespeare's birthplace had been acquired as a national memorial by a trust in 1847, but by the late 1950s it could no longer accommodate its collections. Boldly, the trustees determined on a new building 'of its time' that would be an exposition of modern building materials, though its scale and massing had to respect its neighbour. A detailed brief was prepared by the director, Levi Fox, who also ran the extensive fundraising campaign that saw the building completed for the quatercentenary of Shakespeare's birth.

Williams's solution is a carefully designed and detailed concrete-framed structure, its precast concrete beams giving an arcaded effect. The ground floor has a main reception space, The Room, leading to a lecture hall and the Nuffield Library, with a conference room above. Among the many artworks and commemorative features are glazed panels engraved with Shakespearean characters by John Hutton, sculpture by Douglas Wain-Hobson and carved panels by Nicolete Gray and John Skelton. Much of the bespoke and built-in furniture is by Gordon Russell.

St Matthew's Church

Birdbrook Road, Perry Beeches, Birmingham

1962–4, Maguire and Murray

Listed grade II, 16 June 1997

Maguire and Murray secured this commission through the New Churches Research Group, a multi-denominational group of architects and clergy founded in 1957.

St Matthew's features their most complicated geometry. Maguire divorced the altar from a place under a central lantern by creating seven stepped clerestories, which rise in a circle from the low baptistery around the rear of the congregation to the sanctuary set forward of the longest wall. This means that the sanctuary and font are physically close, as liturgists were beginning to demand, yet are separately defined and at opposite ends of the processional route. The original structure was devised as an Archimedes spiral swirling into infinity, but a hexagonal roof structure was eventually built on grounds of cost.

The cool quality of the practice's St Paul's Church, Bow Common (see p.446) is repeated in bands of exposed grey brick and concrete walling, blue paviour flooring and bench seating, but here the client refused a baldacchino. This is perhaps the firm's most beautiful interior.

Central Baths

Fairfax Street, Coventry

1962–6, Michael McLellan
and Paul Beney, Coventry City
Architect's Department

Listed grade II, 2 December 1997

Wartime bombing destroyed four of Coventry's five pools. In a radio broadcast in 1941 the city architect, Donald Gibson, identified a new central pool as one of his priorities, along with a shopping precinct and a ring road. Detailed plans date from 1956.

The 1944 Education Act recommended that children be taught to swim, but it was only from 1960 that baths were built in large numbers. Set in a great glazed hall, Coventry's 50m (164ft) main pool is T-shaped, including a diving area that projects southwards into a garden designed to include sunbathing terraces. A bank of 1,174 seats has changing rooms and slipper baths underneath. A teaching pool nestles underneath a café set on a bridge, and there is a children's pool beyond.

The white mosaic external finish has been overclad and the building extended, but nowhere else produced a swimming hall of such grandeur, and this survives.

German Military Cemetery

Cannock Chase, Staffordshire

1962–67, Diez Brandi
and Harold Doffman

Registered grade I,
17 September 2002
Cemetery building listed grade II,
4 April 2006

In 1959 a treaty was concluded by the British and Federal German governments to build a cemetery for the remains of 4,939 German nationals who died in Britain during the two world wars. Cannock Chase resembles the heathland of northern Germany, and a Commonwealth War Graves Commission cemetery already existed nearby.

Designed by the German church architect Diez Brandi, with buildings by local architect Harold Doffman, the cemetery occupies a shallow valley. The First World War dead are buried on the south-west-facing slope while those from the Second World War are interred opposite and on level ground to the west. The planting of Scots pine and silver birch, with beds of heather for the rows of upright headstones, has a powerful simplicity, resembling the woodland cemeteries of northern Europe admired in the mid-twentieth century and flowing naturally into the surrounding landscape. The dark Hall of Honour, with its bronze sculpture of a fallen warrior, evokes the Valhalla of German mythology and contrasts with more specifically religious chapels in British and American cemeteries.

Keele University Chapel

near Newcastle-under-Lyme, Staffordshire

1964–5, George Gaze Pace

Listed grade II, 25 September 1998

The chapel is the one distinguished building at Britain's first post-war university, opened in 1950. Its size is due to the personal faith of its founders and the sponsorship of the Ecumenical Institute of the World Council of Churches, which resolved to build an experimental chapel shared by all denominations at its Birmingham meeting in 1959. Pace was commissioned because of his ecumenical chapel at Ibadan University, Nigeria (1951–4).

There are two drum-shaped chapels, and the sharing of one of these by Anglicans and non-conformists was exceptional in the mid-1960s. The other serves the Roman Catholic congregation. These chapels form the twin end towers that give the building its impact, and their internal voids are dramatic. The long hall with a gallery on one side can be used for a variety of worship, or for the university's ceremonial events.

Keele is an interesting balance between Pace's masterful use of timber, particularly for the barn-like hall, and a brutalist aesthetic seen in the use of industrial engineering brick.

New Street Signal Box

Navigation Street, Birmingham

1964–6, Bicknell and Hamilton

Listed grade II, 24 November 1995

John Bicknell and Paul Hamilton had designed Harlow Station and many signal boxes for British Railways before setting up their own practice.

The electrification of the Euston line included automatically locking signals, requiring bigger signal boxes. Birmingham controls 350 signals, and was the first multi-storey box on a central city site. Hamilton felt that the prominent location demanded a formal expression of its purpose, while also likening the completed building to a 'log house'. The heavily textured precast panels were chosen because of the tight site and restricted access.

The accommodation is laid out on five levels around a central shaft projecting above the roof. The top-floor control room is surrounded by a deep, cantilevered fascia to shade the console from the sun. The technical brief demanded heavy floor loadings and exceptional sound insulation, while sensitive electronic equipment had to be shielded by blank walls.

Minerals and Physical Metallurgy Building

Birmingham University

1964–6, Philip Dowson and Arup Associates

Listed grade II, 30 March 1993

Arup Associates emerged as a multidisciplinary practice out of the engineers Ove Arup and Partners in 1963, and this was the defining building for its architect partner, Philip Dowson.

Dowson had already designed several laboratory buildings, for private companies as well as universities. Here, four linked laboratories provided a northern terminus to the campus. Like Howell, Killick, Partridge and Amis, Dowson was experimenting with precast units, here with internal gutters to prevent rainwater streaking the façade, and he made every drawing himself. What makes the building special is the use of a 'tartan' grid to incorporate the heavy servicing. It is a collection of square units, each with a column at every corner; where four corners meet there is space for services and ventilation between the four columns, denoted by rooftop ventilators. Tartan grids were used by other architects, but became a feature of Arup Associates' subsequent university and office buildings.

While the building was under construction the Robbins Report was published, recommending more university places, and, Dowson recalled, they simply doubled the size.

South Winds

Cryfield Grange Road, Coventry

1965–6, Robert Harvey of
Yorke, Harper and Harvey

Listed grade II, 24 April 2012

Harvey designed this house for a builder, R. M. Wilson, who wanted 'a house which would be noticed' and who did not stint on the budget or interfere with the design. One of Harvey's last domestic buildings, the references to Frank Lloyd Wright are clear in the contrast of roughly textured stone with sleek wood and glass, and emphatically in the flat roofs and sweeping horizontality that distinguish it from his earlier, more modest designs.

The centrepiece is a large, central carport under the *piano nobile* between a circular indoor swimming pool and the entrance. A glazed screen conceals the rear garden and views, and to the entrance front there is only a narrow strip of upper windows serving the kitchen and a corridor. The main rooms face south, reached via a spiral staircase and with a continuous balcony giving views towards Kenilworth Castle.

The house is so striking that Jaguar used it in publicity shoots for its XJS car.

Debden Hollow

Barford Hill, Barford, Warwickshire

1966–7, Robert Harvey

Listed grade II, 15 April 2010

Debden Hollow has a prime location on rising ground close to the River Avon. Preliminary drawings show that Harvey placed it carefully to ensure the best angles for the sun and drama of the setting, which he enhanced with some recontouring of the ground.

It was Harvey's last major house, and that he remained fiercely loyal to Wright is indicated by the series of oversailing planes. The principal floor is embedded in the earth at its southern end but projects northwards: with its strong horizontal lines set against the slope it appears to be pushing its way out from the ground to take flight. White-painted concrete enhances this effect, with sliding glass doors of full height and balconies to all sides overlooking the river and garden. Tucked below is a carport and a basement floor of dark bricks containing service rooms and a small flat for a maid. It retains original features in the open-plan living area. A white cube addition was added with listed building consent in 2011.

Our Lady Help of Christians RC Church

East Meadway, Tile Cross, Birmingham

1966–7, Richard Gilbert Scott (Sir Giles Gilbert Scott, Son and Partner)

Listed grade II, 18 February 1999

St Thomas More RC Church

Horse Shoes Lane, Sheldon, Birmingham

1968–9, Richard Gilbert Scott

Listed grade II, 12 October 2012

Richard Gilbert Scott joined his father Giles in partnership in 1953, but inherited these two commissions from his uncle, Adrian Gilbert Scott, whose designs had proved too expensive. Both have centralized plans, Our Lady being T-shaped and St Thomas More adopting a broad fan.

Scott sought the Gothic sensibility of his father's works, but using a modern idiom. His choice was a fireworks display of 1960s shapes and materials. Our Lady is dominated by a soaring, ribbed tent of copper-coated concrete, while St Thomas More has dramatically thick concrete buttresses that rise to a cross-shaped steeple. Internally, both are remarkable for their semi-abstract glass by Scott's friend John Chrestien, a painter who died shortly after St Thomas More was completed. His brilliant colours shine like neon against the rippling concrete shapes, Our Lady in strong reds, the more abstract shapes at St Thomas More in cooler yellows and blues.

Scott brought an extreme bravura and joyfulness to church architecture, and the two churches are his most expressive and inventive works. The photograph shows the more complex interior of Our Lady Help of Christians.

St Dunstan's RC Church

Kingsfield Road, Birmingham

1966–8, Jack Edmondson
of Desmond Williams and Associates

Listed grade II, 16 October 2012

The Second Vatican Council's *Sacrosanctum Concilium* in 1963 encouraged far greater lay participation in the church's liturgy, based on a stone altar forward of the east end. As a completely central altar still left the priest's back turned to some of the congregation, Edmondson and his client, Father Eugene O'Sullivan, determined on a semicircular design with a side chapel, vestries and confessionals all tucked to the rear in a smaller segment.

St Dunstan's is tall and its brickwork austere, yet it has great drama. The engineers Sir Ove Arup and Partners were consulted for the roof, a stepped spiral which revolves around a needle-like central tower that acts as a central post. The processional route follows this ascending spiral around the outer wall, its mystery achieved by concealing windows in the 'riser' to each step, with only small clerestories in the wall visible from the entrance. Strategically placed works of art include a large sculpture of the Risen Christ by John Poole and *dalle de verre* glass by John Hardman Studios.

Houses for Visiting Mathematicians

Warwick University,
Gibbet Hill Road, Coventry

1968–70, Howell, Killick,
Partridge and Amis

Listed grade II*, 7 June 2007

Christopher Zeeman, Professor of Mathematics and an algebraic theoretician of topological space, founded a Mathematics Research Centre in 1966, with funding from the Nuffield Foundation for five houses and two flats for visiting foreign mathematicians and their families.

Single-storey wings to the houses contain studies. In pure mathematics, complex speculative equations are still best set out on blackboards and Bill Howell curved the walls to make these continue all around the room. Corners to the other rooms were also made curved, creating a ripple of convex or concave corners like Borromini without ornament – well seen in the entrance porches and enhanced by their yellow brickwork laid with emphatic horizontal joints. The curves were exaggerated further by the houses being set in a reel around a central green. The shape suggests sociability but doors and windows are turned away from each other for maximum privacy. A resemblance to toy forts is enhanced by the massive scale of the rest of the university. The houses are still used by visiting academics.

Sports pavilion at King Edward VI Grammar School

Manor Road, Stratford-upon-Avon

1971, Robert Harvey

Listed grade II, 12 September 2011

King Edward's School wanted a pavilion that could be used for both summer and winter sports. Harvey produced a building at the centre of their extensive playing fields, set above an earth embankment that formed a grandstand. Changing rooms were placed below and a tearoom above.

As often with Harvey, there is a contrast between the bunker-like basement, which has plum-coloured bricks laid with raked horizontal mortar and only a few slit windows, and the airy upper floor made of creosoted railway sleepers with large glass windows and skylights. A scoring box for cricket is jauntily attached. Above, a generous roof with a central valley projects on all sides and forms a canopy over the entrance. Standard components were used throughout to cut costs and these have stood the test of schoolboy handling remarkably well. Harvey later reported that it was the building that gave him the greatest pleasure to design.

Edinburgh Sports Dome

Malvern St James Girls' School, Imperial Road, Malvern

1977–8, Michael Godwin (architect) and John Faber (engineer) with Norwest Holst Construction

Listed grade II, 21 May 2009

This large sports hall was erected using a system devised by the Italian architect and inventor Dante Bini. Bini had erected his first concrete dome in 1964, but this was only the second in England. Godwin knew his work and visited domes with members of the school; he liked the football shape, while the girls asked that the building should be naturally lit and be adaptable for social events.

The dome was created by inflating a nylon-reinforced neoprene membrane, over which a network of reinforcement bars were laid and slathered in wet concrete. A second PVC membrane was put over the dome to permit the concrete to be vibrated – all featured on the BBC's *Tomorrow's World* programme. Godwin's innovation was to cut and glaze arched openings in the bottom of the dome and to set it in a moat, which improved stability and added to its beauty. Inside, squash courts and changing rooms were placed against the north side beneath a balcony.

NO SMOKING

North Lincolnshire
Civic Centre, 1960–2,
Charles B. Pearson,
Son and Partners

Regional Seat of Government

Chalfont Drive, Nottingham

c.1952–3, extended c.1963,
Ministry of Defence

Listed grade II, 18 July 2003

Fearing the breakdown of central government, initially from the threat of revolution or a general strike, in the 1920s the country was divided into 12 home defence regions. Each was provided with a war room in the early 1950s, designed to protect a commissioner and around 50 staff from atomic bombs, with a central operations room surrounded by cabins. All were purpose-built save that at Newcastle, and were among the first buildings planned to survive nuclear attack.

The semi-sunken Nottingham building was absorbed into a larger block when in the late 1950s the regional organization was remodelled to challenge the greater threat posed by the H-bomb. Planned as the Berlin Wall went up and endemic of the escalation of the Cold War with the Cuban Missile Crisis, it attempted to protect some 200 staff from radiation. Its novelty is its naive grandeur amidst other government buildings, where the windowless, partly cantilevered concrete structure appeared impregnable to visiting dignitaries, with a fashionably brutalist result. The interior survives little altered.

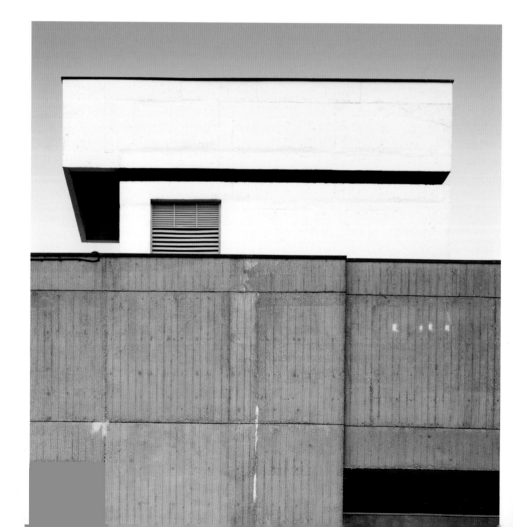

Clipstone Colliery headstocks

Mansfield Road, Clipstone, Nottinghamshire

1953–4, National Coal Board

Listed grade II, 19 April 2000

The nationalization of Britain's mines made capital available for major works, including new deep shafts on the Nottinghamshire coalfields. Of particular interest was the friction winding system for the large loads needed to make these deep seams economic.

The Koepe winding system uses a single loop of rope, or two or more ropes in parallel, and a powered pulley or Koepe wheel rather than the standard drum. It is under balance, needing less power for operation, and was invented in Germany in 1877 by Frederick Koepe. Unusually, at Clipstone the NCB went for ground-based winders, rather than installing winders in towers over the shafts. This required headframes, and the ones at Clipstone used pulley wheels or 'sheaves' located one above the other, rather than the more normal sheaves positioned next to each other. They were the tallest in the UK when built, standing about 65m (213ft) high.

The other buildings at Clipstone have been demolished since the pit closed in 2003, and the headstocks are themselves threatened.

22 Avenue Road

Leicester

1954–5, Fello Atkinson and Brenda Walker of James Cubitt and Partners

Listed grade II, 15 July 1998

When in 1953 Mr and Mrs Goddard commissioned a new house, building restrictions constrained them to a floor area of 457sq. m (1,500sq. ft). They decided not to waste space on stairs, and encouraged the architects to create a free-flowing plan without prescribed circulation areas. The result is a rare early survival of the influence of American open planning.

The house has a timeless quality. It hugs the road, where there is little to see: a neatly lettered gate and a garage. The plan is an L-shape overlooking a generous former orchard to the rear. There is no hall, a lobby leading straight into the living–dining space, with the master bedroom to the right. These two rooms have full-height glazing on to a patio. The fully fitted, tiny kitchen still has its original colourful cupboards, with a hatch to the dining area. The ceiling-high doors and careful detailing are reminders that Atkinson was an experienced exhibition designer, and he brought the same care to this house.

The Pediment

Aynho, Northamptonshire

1956–7, Raymond Erith

Listed grade II, 29 March 1988

Croquet shed
at The Pediment

1964, Raymond Erith

Listed grade II, 14 August 2012

Erith found an exceptional client in Elizabeth Watt, a lawyer, art collector and horticulturalist, whose interest in classical architecture matched his own. She acquired the rectory paddock, a large site for a village centre, and her new house needed an architectural presence. Erith suggested a pedimented square structure which, he observed, 'would have the charm that one occasionally sees in eighteenth-century buildings when they are at once very small and very architectural'. The large stone blocks give scale, and flanking walls tether it to the ground. The south-facing garden elevation is lighter, with a trellis to the ground floor. In the equally formal interior a neo-Gothic niche in the study contrasts with a heavy Palladian stone fireplace in the drawing room.

Erith also designed several garden buildings, and was still working here at his death in 1973. The croquet shed was inspired by Kent's pyramidal pavilions at Badminton, eventually realized around a carved pillar conceived as a giant gate pier with a flaming urn on top.

Intake Farm School

Bancroft Lane, Mansfield, Nottinghamshire

1956–7, Nottinghamshire County Council Architect's Department Job architects, Bevis Fuller and Henry Swain

Listed grade II, 30 March 1993

The price of prosperity in Nottinghamshire's post-war coalfields was subsidence, and schools were fracturing as coal was extracted below them. This problem faced Donald Gibson on his arrival as county architect from Coventry in 1955. He and a team of fervent assistants adapted the Brockhouse cold-rolled frame, already used in Coventry and by the Ministry of Education, with pin joints and rocker bases to ride subsidence, and claddings of timber and overlapping tiles.

Little Intake Farm pioneered the system. Its nickname of the 'rock and roll school', was topical. With its prefabrication, an assembly hall from which classrooms are offset in pairs, and a mural by Fred Millett (long overpainted) it established Nottinghamshire as the successor authority to Hertfordshire. That the system not only solved the subsidence problem but lasted into the twenty-first century was due to Gibson bringing in other authorities to expand its development. Hence its name: the Consortium of Local Authorities' Special Programme, or CLASP.

Newton Building

Nottingham Trent University,
Burton Street, Nottingham

1956–8, T. Cecil Howitt and Partners

Listed grade II*, 24 April 1998

In 1948 Nottingham University College was split between a 1920s suburban campus that became Nottingham University, and a central nineteenth-century site, which was developed as a technical college. Howitt designed for both institutions, but the outstanding building was for the college. It is only half of a larger scheme from 1952, which was truncated when the college decided to retain the adjoining Arkwright Building of 1877.

The Newton Building is a local landmark, its giant façades of Portland stone dominated by a great glazed staircase and lift tower. Its brooding, American-style classicism also owes a little to Howitt's tour of French technical colleges in 1937, though the final design was by his assistant Charles Hyde. The tower contains classrooms; to either side, low stone walls screen an early form of podium, where lecture theatres by Hopkins Architects have replaced the original workshops (with listed building consent). Hopkins has also created a glazed link with the Arkwright Building that includes a new entrance to the university, completed in 2011.

Cripps Hall

Beeston Lane, University
of Nottingham

1957–9, McMorran and Whitby

Listed grade II, 29 March 1988

Despite a fine suburban site given by Sir Jesse Boot in 1921, Nottingham's university status was long obstructed by an over-paternalistic city council. Its award in 1948 prompted a building boom, but while modern styles were adopted in its science area, halls of residence were built in a classical idiom until the 1970s. Donald McMorran was among the most imaginative of traditional architects, sparing in his detail and using fine materials and proportions to create simple quadrangles.

Cripps Hall was the most ambitious of the halls for men, where donations from the Cripps family from Northamptonshire (motor components manufacturers, who also endowed St John's College, Cambridge, see p.249) allowed some embellishments. A clock tower denotes the dining hall while lean pairs of giant, baseless Ionic columns frame the entrance, both features indebted to Swedish classicism of the 1920s. This is the finest of a group of buildings by McMorran.

Thor missile sites, RAF Harrington and RAF North Luffenham

Daventry and Rutland respectively

1958–9, US Air Force and Royal Air Force

Listed grades II and II* respectively, 17 June 2011

Named after the Norse god of thunder, Thor was an operational ballistic missile developed by the US Air Force but operated by the RAF. It was a 19.8m (65ft) rocket with a range of 2,414km (1,500 miles), sufficient to reach Moscow. Under 'Project Emily', Thor missiles were installed in England on 20 sites manned by the RAF, though the nuclear warheads remained under American control. During the Cuban Missile Crisis of October 1962, they were made ready for launching.

Thor missiles were withdrawn in 1963, superseded by longer-range missiles, but at Harrington and Luffenham (a group headquarters site that controlled four other bases) the structures associated with them remain. Each base had three cross-shaped launch pads where the missiles were stored, reinforced concrete blast walls, fuel bays, theodolite sheds and ancillary buildings. They had a short operational life, but these surviving structures are gaunt reminders of 13 days when the world held its breath.

RAF North Luffenham is now St George's Barracks, while RAF Harrington is farmland.

College Court

formerly College Hall,
Knighton Road, Leicester

1958–60, Sir Leslie Martin
and Trevor Dannatt

Listed grade II, 30 March 1993

Leslie Martin was appointed consultant in June 1956, and his master plan was published the day Leicester was granted university status in March 1957. Accommodation for women students was urgently needed, for which land was granted at nearby Knighton.

This was Martin's first post-war work in independent practice, where he sought to establish a 'tradition' of modern architecture working with younger men. Dannatt had assisted on the Royal Festival Hall and was emerging as a designer of undemonstrative buildings using honest materials. College Hall was one of England's first halls of residence in a modern style, realized on a limited budget. Its clean lines are enhanced by concrete projections and a sculptural spiral staircase. It was planned for 170 students, around a dining hall and a small senior common room, set behind the high table, both with low ceilings of natural timber.

The college closed in 2005 and was threatened with demolition, but in 2012–13 it was converted by Associated Architects into a residential conference centre, College Court.

Former Lincolnshire Motors

Brayford Wharf, Lincoln

1959, Hugh Segar (Sam) Scorer of Denis Clarke Hall, Scorer and Bright

Listed grade II, 9 August 2000

The 1950s saw the building of many sleek showrooms that proclaimed the luxurious image of the limousine. Few survive. Lincolnshire Motors is a feat of technical construction that has withstood many changes of use, having been converted into a public library before it was listed and now divided into restaurants. Scorer took on the commission in return for a fast car, one of his great enthusiasms.

The circular corner projection was the manager's office, and petrol pumps originally faced Brayford Pool. Behind, the former showroom has a reinforced concrete hyperbolic paraboloid shell roof to give a clear, unobstructed area. There are four shells, each 15m (49ft) square and 7cm (3in) thick, with more enforcement around the edges. Sam Scorer became interested in shell constructions as a student in c.1950, and considered them 'a fascinating game of geometry' all his life. This was one of many collaborations with the Hungarian engineer Dr K. Hajnal-Kónyi, who pioneered shell construction in Britain following his arrival here in 1936.

Canopy to former petrol station

A1, Markham Moor, Nottinghamshire

1960–1, Hugh Segar (Sam) Scorer

Listed grade II, 27 March 2012

This is Scorer's most dramatic and best-known work, a garage built with K. Hajnal-Kónyi for A. H. Turner and seen by millions of motorists on the A1 each year.

Thin concrete shells were developed in Germany around 1920 as a means of achieving large spans with limited materials at little cost. Their strength is in their shape, for they carry loads by forces in the plane of the shell rather than by the weight of their materials. The anticlastic shell, with a double curvature, was developed c.1950 in Mexico by Félix Candela, whose favourite shape was the hyperbolic paraboloid for its strength and ease of shuttering. This was also Scorer's preferred form.

The Markham Moor garage comprises a single shell over 18m (59ft) square: two corners rise to apexes of 11.4m (37½ft), while those opposite are only 1.5m (5ft) above ground. In c.1980 a restaurant was inserted underneath (later a Little Chef), but the structure was not compromised. The Highways Agency spared it from demolition in 2004.

North Lincolnshire Civic Centre

Ashby Road, Scunthorpe

1960–2, Charles B. Pearson,
Son and Partners
Job architect, Dennis T. Burnside

Listed grade II, 24 April 1998

Charles B. Pearson and his son Charles Edward practised extensively around their native Lancaster, but this is probably their finest building. Scunthorpe developed as a steel town in the 1930s, when a town hall was first proposed and Charles E. Pearson won a competition for its design. Several schemes followed before it was eventually built on a new site further south.

The building makes expressive use of local steel, as panels are combined with slate and hardwoods, jauntily contrasted with end walls of brick. The oval council chamber resembles the 'egg in a box' of the Royal Festival Hall and is clad in Portland stone. Its form, however, is fully visible through a tall, open screen of square columns.

The interior is particularly distinguished, with a double-height entrance hall finished in marble and copper, which houses a Roman mosaic excavated at nearby Winterton. The council chamber is lined with slatted timber to give excellent acoustics, with fine original furnishings and inset lighting.

Engineering Building, Leicester University

Major's Walk, Leicester

1960–3, James Stirling
and James Gowan
Engineer, Frank Newby of
Felix Samuely and Partners

Listed grade II*, 30 March 1993

This is a building of international significance, which defined modernism's late-1950s shift towards a greater individualism and gave it a truly British character. Leicester eschewed Scandinavian influences for liver red Accrington brick and Dutch tiles, with aluminium-framed patent glazing, an updating of the industrial architecture of England's nineteenth-century cities. Such a use of Victorian elements combined with constructivist forms and a twelve-storey tower is dramatic.

Leicester has the tightest site of the post-war universities, and the architects had to squeeze in workshops for heavy machinery, laboratories, lecture theatres, and a 30.5m (100ft) water tank to serve hydraulic experiments. The workshops, covering two-thirds of the area, had to have north-light glazing, but the plot does not run north–south. So while the building uses its site efficiently, the glazing runs at a diagonal, developed as a low-cost solution by Newby but denoted by wilful, lozenge-shaped terminals devised by Gowan. The interior is overwhelming because of the glowing, translucent light that results.

Comparisons can be made with Frank Lloyd Wright's Johnson Wax complex at Racine, Wisconsin, the saturated light of the large, single-storey interiors similarly contrasted with their banded towers. The shapely forms of Leicester's tower, thrust out on the stepping of two projecting lecture theatres, are credited to Stirling, again as refined by Newby.

The synthesis between Stirling and Gowan's contrasting approaches gives the surprisingly skinny building its tautness. The partnership collapsed soon afterwards and, despite their subsequent individual achievements, for most critics this remains the sublime monument of the new brutalism. Perhaps the true partnership was between the architects and their engineer.

Vaughan College

St Nicholas Circle, Leicester

1960–2, Trevor Dannatt
Engineers, Ove Arup and Partners

Listed grade II, 30 March 1993

Vaughan College is a more refined working of ideas explored by Dannatt with Leslie Martin in their earlier College Hall.

The Reverend Vaughan founded a Working Men's College in 1862, which became the University's Department of Adult Education. However, his buildings were cleared for a ring road, and their replacement buildings are set on a three-lane intersection. Adjoining them is a substantial chunk of Roman wall and the excavated site of Leicester's Roman baths. Dannatt's scheme had to incorporate a museum at this low level.

The college itself is set on a terrace, a few steps above the road, cantilevered on double beams over the clear-glazed museum and its coffered terrace overlooking the dig. It is a deliberately low-key foil to the ancient structures and has a calm sense of rightful purpose in the simple interiors. The main building has a hall, library, and a common room overlooking the excavations, all with beautiful timber floors. The college closed suddenly in 2013 but the museum is still there.

Nottingham Playhouse

Wellington Circus, Nottingham

1961–3, Peter Moro

Listed grade II*, 14 July 1994

Moro's finest work, the playhouse was made possible with compensation for the privatization of Nottingham's gas company. He had worked on the Royal Festival Hall, and Nottingham repeats the idea of a square foyer wrapped around a separately expressed auditorium. Behind, the fly tower is set over a large stage and basement workshops where the land falls away to the rear.

The circular auditorium gives the playhouse its intimacy, with its large balcony bringing actors and audience close together, and flexibility. The stage, developed with the specialist designer Richard Southern, is conventional but a large apron can be raised from the orchestra pit and seats rearranged to create a large thrust stage. A lighting rig suspended over this apron is a major architectural feature.

The decorative treatment of narrow verticals in the façade reappears in the auditorium as timber slats and lighting troughs, with a metal mural by Geoffrey Clarke in the double-height foyer. The restaurant wing was remodelled and raised a storey in 1993–5 by Marsh Grochowski.

RC Church of the Good Shepherd

Thackeray's Lane, Woodthorpe,
Nottinghamshire

1961–3, Gerard Goalen

Listed grade II*, 25 September 1998

Gerard Goalen's church at Harlow (see p.216) was hugely admired by Father Mooney, who asked for a new church for his expanding congregation at Woodthorpe. By then Goalen was working for Frederick Gibberd and both had entered the Liverpool Metropolitan Cathedral competition. Disappointed when Gibberd's design was preferred, the Nottingham commission enabled Goalen to set up his own practice.

The Good Shepherd's plan is a foreshortened hexagon, its roof of four hexagonal shell vaults supported on four slender columns, like inward-blown umbrellas. It creates a broad worship space that slopes steeply to the sanctuary, one of the first to adopt the preferred liturgical solution of a fan shape that pulls congregation and celebrant close together. Limited funds were directed to glass at the east end, where Patrick Reyntiens produced three large windows of *dalle de verre* in rich blues, greens and reds on abstracted tree themes. These strengthen the numinous, organic experience of the church, their pattern of heavy mullions repeated in the organ case.

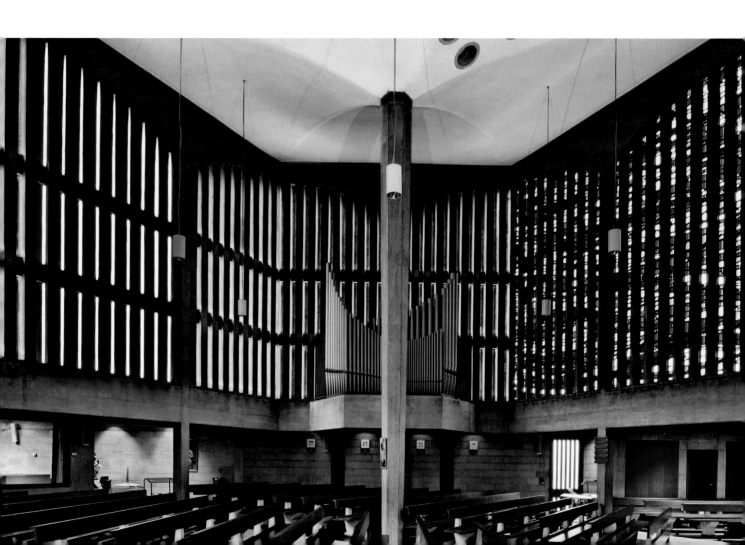

Church of St John the Baptist

Sudbrooke Drive,
Ermine East, Lincoln

1962–3, Hugh Segar (Sam) Scorer
of Clarke Hall, Scorer and Bright

Listed grade II*, 19 January 1995

St John's resembles a dark whale beached in a suburban housing estate. The hexagonal solution to the question of the new liturgy adopted here, with the congregation set in an arc around the sanctuary, was also chosen at the contemporary Good Shepherd in Nottinghamshire. But here the plan is dwarfed by Scorer's hyperbolic paraboloid concrete roof just 8cm (3½in) thick. The two lower ends reach the ground, where pools catch cascading rainwater. The high prows are lopped off, because there was to have been a bell tower – never erected because of lack of money, but shown in a model in the church.

The altar and pulpit were made of primitive cast concrete by local sculptor Charles Edward Sansbury. The east window is by Keith New, who had worked at Coventry Cathedral. This is his first work in brilliant colours, and economies made by painting rather than firing the glass reinforce the composition's abstract quality. The combination of technical ingenuity and liturgical planning are homogeneous with each other.

Winthorpe Road Bridge

Newark bypass, Newark

1964, Alfred Goldstein of
R. Travers Morgan and Partners

Listed grade II*, 29 May 1998

The Winthorpe Bridge carries the Newark bypass over the River Trent. It is a three-span, continuous, prestressed concrete bridge 158m (518½ft) long, with a central span of 79m (260ft) over the river formed of nine small box girders cast *in situ* on falsework. The abutment wing walls are cantilevered and are based on a concave cylindrical section, giving them a rare architectural elegance.

The fluted faces of the bridge and the horizontal fascia along the top edge are carefully detailed, the latter formed by precast concrete units with a blue Shap granite aggregate finish.

The character of this bridge appears to be transitional between the 1950s and 1960s in its construction, having modern continuous box girders, with no edge cantilever. It was listed for its exceptional elegance and quality of finish.

Former magistrates' court

West Bars, Chesterfield, Derbyshire

1963–5, J. S. Allen and
Roy Keenleyside

Listed grade II, 10 August 1998

Few courts were built in the post-war years, save at Chesterfield. Joe Allen, invited in 1961 to replan Chesterfield's town centre, was an 'enabler', and the building's detailed design was made by his former student, Roy Keenleyside, who was killed in a car crash shortly afterwards.

The building sits in a park and was designed to be seen from all sides. It has a double fan-shaped plan, with three courtrooms in the larger eastern fan, and offices in the smaller western one. White marble mullions and gables for the curved sides are contrasted with grey Welsh and green Westmorland slate. Inside, the courtrooms are panelled in rosewood and Norwegian quartz, with a grand imperial staircase in the full-height central entrance hall. This had an electrically operated glass screen, which could separate adults from juveniles if their courts were sitting at the same time.

Listing was prompted by the construction of new courts, and the building is now used by the local authority as its Connexions information centre.

Horton Rounds

The Drive, Horton, Northamptonshire

1966, Arthur A. J. Marshman
of Marshman, Warren and Taylor

Listed grade II, 12 September 2012

Architects who make their living producing large commercial developments sometimes build strikingly original one-off houses for themselves. Such is this house by a major designer of offices in provincial cities. It is set on former tennis courts to the demolished Horton Hall, overlooking open countryside, its curious plan enlivened by natural stone, weatherboarding and shingles.

The plan resembles a snail, centred on a near-circular first-floor living room reached by an open-tread circular staircase or a short lift, set around a central stone fireplace and inglenook. Further stairs ascend to a rooftop eyrie. Bedrooms are in the tail over a carport, or in a separate circular pod reached by a short bridge that led Sir Nikolaus Pevsner to describe the house as a comma and full stop.

Horton Rounds works because it combines 1960s showmanship with genuine architectural skill, for the sweeping horizontal weatherboarding is reminiscent of Frank Lloyd Wright, while the stonework makes an ingenious interplay of convex and concave forms.

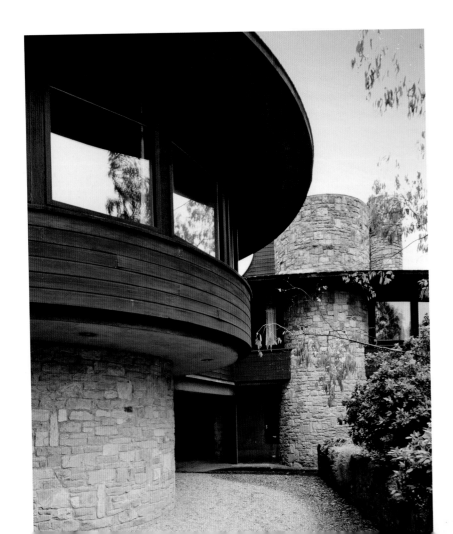

D90 building, Boots

Thane Road, Nottingham

1967–8, Skidmore, Owings and
Merrill with Yorke, Rosenberg
and Mardall

Listed grade II*, 28 August 1996

The Chicago office of Skidmore, Owings and Merrill's (SOM), under Bruce Graham, was selected to give Boots a sophisticated transatlantic image. Graham's office developed independently from SOM in New York, and a greater influence was Mies van der Rohe, who in 1957 had designed offices for Bacardi Rum in Cuba. This unbuilt scheme was designed as a doughnut of offices that appears to be single-storey, but is set over a sunken service floor lit from an internal courtyard. Building D90 repeats this plan, but with an elegant steel frame rather than concrete.

Yorke, Rosenberg and Mardall provided much of the internal detailing. On one side, a sleek executive suite of offices survives with storey-high doors; elsewhere, open-plan spaces were originally defined by lines of timber carrels or low cubicles, now gone. 'Would you let your daughter work in an open-plan office?' queried the *Observer Magazine*, a reminder of their rarity in 1968. D90 was the outstanding transatlantic collaboration of the late 1960s. The listing ensured that an addition, D90A, was sensitively designed by Frank Duffy of DEGW.

Mobil canopies at Esso filling station

Loughborough Road,
Red Hill, Leicester

1978–9, John Ward and Associates
to a design by Eliot Noyes

Listed grade II, 27 March 2012

In 1964 the architect and industrial designer Eliot Noyes was commissioned by the Mobil oil company to give an instantly recognizable image to its 19,000 petrol stations around the world. The first of his 'Pegasus' stations, named after the company's logo (which he simplified), opened in Connecticut, USA, in 1966 with stainless-steel pumps and parasol canopies. Ivan Chermayeff and Thomas Geismar designed the graphics. The circular design recalled the oil drum, used symbolically in American petrol stations since their earliest days, but it also contrasted with the square and V-shaped canopies adopted by other companies at the time. Similarities with Arne Jacobsen's circular concrete canopy at Strandvejen, Copenhagen, were probably coincidental.

The Red Hill canopies were not erected until 1978–9, after an earlier scheme had been thwarted by local allotment holders. What makes them so distinctive is the way they overlap each other – and their rarity, for few examples survive anywhere in the world. They have been repainted and rebranded, but remain a remarkable piece of international design history.

Express Lift Tower

St James's Road, Northampton

1980–2, Stimpson and Walton

Listed grade II, 30 October 1997

This 127m (417ft) landmark was built for testing lifts and their components, training staff in installation and maintenance, and simulating faults in lifts around the world. Its pure form is thus a skyscraper core without offices, but with three lift shafts. The high-speed shaft was for testing lifts at speeds of up to 7.5m (25ft) per second. The tallest shaft contains a service lift and gives access to a laboratory above the fast lift. The third and lowest one contains four lifts for testing and training.

The tower was designed to produce the least wind resistance. It tapers parabolically from bottom to top, where its pierced shape provides added bracing. The lower parts were slip-formed in three weeks by continuous pouring. Between it and the lift shafts lies a clear internal space housing the staircase.

This was the only testing tower in Britain, and Europe's only other is in Romania. Listing saved the tower from demolition, but it is now surrounded by housing and has no obvious use.

29A Loom Lane,
Radlett, Hertfordshire
1962–5, George Marsh

American Military Cemetery

Madingley, Cambridge

1944–56, Perry Stuart and Hepburn, Kehoe and Dean

Listed grade II*, 25 September 1998
Registered grade I, 3 January 2002

This is the only American Second World War cemetery in Britain, built on land given by the University of Cambridge in recognition of the area's concentration of airbases. A total of 3,811 servicemen and women are buried in long, curved rows, each with a marble cross or Star of David in the smooth lawn. The landscaping is by the Olmsted Brothers.

More formal still is the monument to the 5,126 airmen and sailors with no known grave, by American architects with Peter Bicknell as their British consultant. Their names are recorded on a long wall beside a canal, interrupted by giant military figures from English sculptors. This axis leads to the memorial: part chapel, part museum to American endeavour. An incised map shows the larger stations where Americans were based, while inside a relief explains the principal American operations across Europe and the Atlantic. A mosaic depicting the Resurrection and Last Judgement dominates the sanctuary and continues across the ceiling, where ghostly aircraft are escorted by angels on their final flight.

Rushmere Hall School

Lanark Road, Ipswich

1947–9 by Birkin Haward
of Johns, Slater and Haward

Listed grade II, 25 July 2013

Haward specialized in schools, especially primary schools, and his work for Ipswich Education Department chronicles their evolution from the 1940s into the 1970s. This, his first post-war building, combines a light steel frame and concrete cladding in the manner of Hertfordshire schools (where he also worked) but with brick end walls; Haward's schools had to be economical but working for a small authority gave him freedom from repetition. The plan, on a large site in a new housing estate, is a winding zigzag with a central office range, kitchen and canteen, and separate assembly halls for infants and juniors. From these extend two lines of classrooms along extended corridors, each with an external patio space. At one end are classrooms for nursery children; at the other are those for the oldest boys and girls. The relative generosity of school budgets in the late 1940s is evident in this spacious school, which even had cinema projection facilities. The school won a Festival of Britain Merit Award in 1951.

**Burleigh School
(juniors' building),
Blindman's Lane, Cheshunt**
1946-8
Listed grade II, 29 March 1988

**Essendon School,
School Lane, Essendon**
1947-8
Listed grade II, 30 March 1993

**Morgans School
(Juniors' building),
Morgans Road, Hertford**
1948-9
Listed grade II*, 6 May 1998

**Aboyne Lodge School,
Etna Road, St Albans**
1949-50
Listed grade II, 24 March 2010

**Templewood School,
Pentley Park Road,
Welwyn Garden City**
1949-50
Listed grade II*, 30 March 1993

**Danegrove Infants' School,
Ridgeway Avenue,
London Borough of Barnet**
1950-1
Listed grade II, 30 March 1993

**Greenfields School,
Ellesborough Close,
South Oxhey**
1951-2,
Listed grade II, 30 March 1993

Schools by Hertfordshire County Council

In 1944 the Ministry of Education recommended standardization to meet a backlog in school building exacerbated by the war. Hertfordshire received many evacuees from London, especially in the new towns, and needed to build ten primary schools a year to meet rapidly rising birth rates. Private builders were using prefabricated techniques developed for wartime huts to produce temporary classrooms, and Hertfordshire's architects refined a light, steel-framed system by Hills of West Bromwich. The mastermind was Stirrat Johnson-Marshall, appointed deputy architect in 1945, who recruited a team of idealistic young assistants with wartime experience of designing from first principles to adapt Hills's 2.51m (8ft 3in) frame to a more flexible three-dimensional grid. Every element was considered from a child's perspective, including low windows and tiny sinks.

Burleigh School in Cheshunt was the first school. In the former infants' section, by Mary Crowley, the grid is seen in the projecting classrooms and linked cloakrooms, while the juniors' part, by David Medd and Bruce Martin, has pitched roofs and the blond concrete panels have a Scandinavian quality. These ingredients were repeated at Essendon, a tiny village school, where a sculpture by Georg Ehrlich launched a county art programme. A range of bright colours was chosen to stimulate the children – strong in the corridors, with more muted shades for classrooms.

Morgans School (originally Morgan's Walk), a year later, saw Bruce Martin exploiting the grid to group the classrooms off the corners of a central hall. Roofs were now flat. The former infants' rooms have projecting bays, creating a separate space for messy play and a stepped profile. At Aboyne Lodge, Templewood and Danegrove, a staggered plan of classrooms permitted more full-height glazing at a time of concern for children's eyesight, with vertical concrete cladding panels to allow more variety in window sizes. Despite sharing these ingredients, Templewood (by Cleeve Barr) has a greater panache, thanks to its careful massing and three striking murals by Pat Tew in the entrance area and dining hall (shown in the photograph). Barnet was in Hertfordshire before 1965, so a few schools are now in Greater London, including Danegrove. Danegrove was also unusual in being designed by the Architects' Co-Partnership, whose Anthony Cox had worked for Hertfordshire and whose other partners equally shared the county team's vision.

By 1950 the Hertfordshire programme was proven, and Johnson-Marshall, Crowley and David Medd had moved on to the Ministry of Education. Government budgets were cut that year and more oppressively from 1951 onwards, leading to the elimination of corridors and separate dining halls. At Greenfields School, South Oxhey, corridors were absorbed into the room space; large classrooms could be divided organically into messy areas and quiet corners where children could work in small groups. The recompense came in the large assembly hall, whose high arched roof and exposed trusses impart a surprising grandeur.

The Hertfordshire schools programme was one instance of prefabrication proving successful on every social and architectural level. It was imitated elsewhere in Britain and around the world, for example by Ezra Ehrenkrantz in California, who in turn inspired the young Norman Foster.

**Windmill Green
Ditchingham, Norfolk**

1947-9
Listed grade II,
19 November 1998

**Agnes Hood Terrace,
Scudamore Place
and Thwaite Road,
Ditchingham, Norfolk**

1950-1, 1958-9, 1964
Listed grade II,
19 November 1998

**Church Road, Bergh
Apton, Norfolk**

1951, 1956-7
Listed grade II,
19 November 1998

**Forge Grove and
Kenyon Row,
Gillingham, Norfolk**

1955, 1957
Listed grade II,
19 November 1998

**Davy Place,
Loddon, Norfolk**

1963
Listed grade II,
19 November 1998

Housing by Tayler and Green for Loddon Rural District Council

Piped water, mains electricity and sewers were still rarities in rural England in 1945, and better housing was needed to keep farmworkers on the land. In Norfolk, the problem was grasped by Loddon Rural District Council and their consultants Tayler and Green.

David Green had returned to his native Lowestoft to run his father's practice, having met Herbert Tayler while studying at London's Architectural Association. Tayler was the designer, Green the committee man and service engineer. Ernst May's Frankfurt housing inspired the long terraces of Windmill Green, preferred to the ubiquitous 'semi' because they respected the long lines of the open landscape. But these are unusual terraces: each house is very broad, and incorporates a walk-through passage-cum-store leading to the back garden. As only poor Fletton bricks were available, the houses were colour-washed in a range of pinks, blues and creams, a local tradition like the pantiled roofs.

Council bungalows for pensioners were a post-war innovation, and Loddon commissioned their first in 1948. The single-storey Agnes Hood Terrace is unusual for Tayler and Green in its curved plan. It faces a larger scheme of sheltered housing, Scudamore Place, where the corner warden's house and community hall is an eye-catching juxtaposition of contrasting volumes. Rows of terraced bungalows are linked by crinkle-crankle walls (traditional double-curved walls for protecting fruit trees), used by Tayler to conceal scruffy back gardens.

Although Tayler and Green designed the entire scheme at Bergh Apton in 1949, its short terraces were built in phases only as government loans permitted. A recurring pattern of one taller gable in each terrace, denoting a larger house, was derived from an eighteenth-century silk mill and adjoining cottages at Ditchingham. After 1951 Tayler abandoned colour washing in favour of contrasting colours and patterns of brickwork, to save on maintenance costs and because better bricks were available. Sometimes one house in a row would be colour-washed.

A quintessential scheme was at Gillingham, where two contrasting terraces are linked by a crinkle-crankle wall. The incorporation of dates into the gable brickwork is another local feature that became a Tayler and Green trademark, along with diaper patterns and alternating projecting headers, arched window openings, bargeboards, trellises and landscaping. Tayler justified his brick patterns as 'cheap, and the men noticeably sing while building them'; fortunately, traditional local builders could meet his exacting standards.

Davy Place is the most distinctive of Tayler and Green's later works for Loddon, a scheme for pensioners on a sloping site left by gravel working. The gable ends are particularly elaborate, one contrasting alternating bricks with the bottoms of wine bottles set in cement. In 1962 Nikolaus Pevsner called Tayler and Green's incorporation of traditional details 'post-modern', before that epithet achieved popular currency.

Tayler and Green designed 709 housing units for Loddon Rural District Council between 1945 and 1973. Their retirement coincided with the absorption of the authority into the larger South Norfolk District Council, which has developed an enlightened policy for the conservation of Tayler's most imaginative elevations through design guidelines.

Barclay School

Walkern Road, Stevenage,
Hertfordshire

1947–9, 1951, F. R. S. Yorke,
Eugene Rosenberg and Cyril Mardall

Listed grade II, 30 March 1993

This was the first important secondary school built after the war. Although it was built using the Hills system of light-weight steel refined by Hertfordshire County Council, Rosenberg gave it an individual architectural character by using brick and stone as well as concrete cladding. His proposed curved layout was modified by Yorke, however, to form an H-shaped, two-storey set of classrooms, with an assembly hall adjoining the entrance. A spacious vestibule is floored in Hornton stone and punctuated by open-tread staircases, with a mural by Kenneth Rowntree.

Along the main classroom spine, the upper floor rooms are separated from the corridor and cloakrooms by short spurs, so rooflights in the intervening wells can light the corridor on the floor below, a split section repeated at subsequent Yorke, Rosenberg and Mardall schools.

Hertfordshire's chief education officer, John Newsom, secured Henry Moore's *The Family of Man* when Henry Morris, his pioneering Cambridgeshire counterpart, could not raise sufficient money for it. Originally by the front door, it is now in the entrance hall.

The Lawn

Mark Hall Moors, Harlow

1950–1, Frederick Gibberd

Listed grade II, 22 December 1998

Orchard Croft terraces

3–13 and 161–5 (consecutive) Mardyke Road, Harlow

1952–4, Frederick Gibberd

Listed grade II, 22 December 1998

Harlow was the fourth new town to be designated after Stevenage, in 1947, but was developed quickly. Unlike at other new towns, its master planner Frederick Gibberd was retained as its consultant architect for 35 years and stamped his personality on the town.

Gibberd believed in 'mixed development', designing a variety of flats and houses to serve all ages and family sizes. The ten-storey Lawn was Britain's first point block, its expense justified by the desire to preserve seven oak trees, but really a visual contrast to the surrounding two-storey houses. Gibberd likened its unique trapezoidal plan, giving all four flats on each floor south-facing living rooms and balconies, to a butterfly, while its elevations are Scandinavian in style, with patterned brick cladding and render. Lack of demand for flats in new towns ensured that it was not repeated for many years.

Gibberd developed Mardyke Road with three-storey terraces incorporating garages, after seeing Fortfield Terrace at Sidmouth. Its curve is well seen from the cricket field opposite.

Anti-aircraft operations rooms

1951, Ministry of Works

Shrubland Road, Mistley, Essex
Listed grade II, 22 May 2007

Beacon Hill, Frodsham, Cheshire
Listed grade II, 18 March 2013

A total of 32 anti-aircraft operations rooms were built in the UK to chart the approach of hostile aircraft and allocate targets to gun batteries in their area. The system, devised in the late 1940s, grew out of wartime air defences and was designed to counter the threat of Soviet planes carrying atomic bombs.

Most operations rooms were built to a standard design. They are square, reinforced concrete structures of two storeys, many like Mistley sunk into the ground with a distinctive square air shaft surmounting the roof. Frodsham is more unusual in being set wholly above ground against a hillside. Inside, both have a double-height plotting and operations room overlooked by a gallery on two sides, in which the functions of receiving, analysing and communicating information can still be discerned. These examples survive because they were adopted by their respective county councils for civil defence in the early 1960s, and they serve as reminders of the global tension that surrounded the Korean War. The photograph is of Mistley, now a museum.

RAF Wittering, near Peterborough

Nuclear fissile core stores and nuclear bomb store buildings

1952-3

Listed grade ll*, 11 July 2011

Gaydon hangar, electrical testing building, and nuclear bomb loading crane

1952

Listed grade ll, 11 July 2011

Blue Steel servicing facility

c.1963

Listed grade ll, 9 January 2012

RAF Wittering has played an important role in military history since its establishment in 1916 to counter Zeppelin attacks. Its runway was extended in 1952–4 for Britain's V-bombers, when a hangar was built to house the Vickers Valiant (with a wingspan of 34.8m/ 114ft) using innovative tubular steel trusses.

To one side of the airfield there quietly appeared nine small kiosks and six squat concrete bunkers half-hidden under earth embankments. In November 1953 they became the first buildings to house Britain's inaugural atomic weapon, codenamed Blue Danube. Beneath the kiosks, their wavy-edged roofs designed for camouflage, nuclear cores were stored in stainless-steel-lined vessels. Cases containing high explosives were held in the bunkers. Apart, the two components were relatively safe, but together they could create a nuclear explosion. A fixed-gantry crane and maintenance building also survive. A hangar was added for Britain's later, more sophisticated, Blue Steel missile, but the bomber squadrons were disbanded in 1968 as the Victor bombers could no longer evade Soviet radar.

Smithdon High School

Downs Road, Hunstanton

1951–3, Alison and Peter Smithson

Listed grade II*, 30 March 1993

Alison Smithson was 21, and Peter 26, when in 1950 they won a competition to design a secondary modern school in Hunstanton with a building very different to the Ministry of Education's contemporary complex for St Crispin's, Wokingham (see p.322). The symmetrical plan harks back to interwar grammar schools, its central hall set between two courtyards, around which classrooms and laboratories on the upper floors are reached by spindly steel staircases from a ground-floor gyratory of corridors and cloakrooms.

A welded steel frame, designed on the principle of plastic design (that there is no single weak point), was inspired by classical forms and Mies van der Rohe. The early phases of Mies's Illinois Institute of Technology are recognizable, though the Smithsons' corner detailing, an inset post between two I-beams, is weightier. There is a surprising complexity, too, in the projecting and receding rhythm of square glazing panels and slightly proud infill panels of brick in the end walls and free-standing gymnasium. Inside, the unadorned steel ceilings and exposed plumbing are striking. A triumphant use of off-the-peg components culminates in a centrally placed Braithwaite tank.

The term 'New Brutalism', coined by Alison in 1953, originally stood for truth to materials and found objects, as demonstrated here, but was appropriated by later concrete expressionism, a style at odds with Hunstanton's classical neutrality, whose ultimate origins lay in the work of Rudolf Wittkower.

The direct glazing into the steel frame caused shattering as the building alternately overheated or chilled, solved successfully in 1984–91 by introducing wooden subframes and black dado panels save for an inset section retained to show the original fenestration.

Regional Seat of Government

Gilpin Road, Cambridge

c.1952–3, extended 1963

Listed grade II, 18 July 2003

The two-stage evolution from war room to Regional Seat of Government is more apparent at Cambridge than at Nottingham (see p.158). Again there are some careful concrete details and finishes.

The 1950s part is entered first: a two-storey bunker set around a double-height war room now floored over and surrounded by plant rooms and living accommodation. Curved Perspex windows to smaller control rooms still surround the lower part. A corridor leads to the later extension with its own escape doors and a very large plant room, complete with a standby generator and air filtration equipment. There are extensive dormitories, a canteen and kitchen, and a BBC studio. The juxtaposition demonstrates the change in government planning from a small regional centre to counter the devastation caused by an atomic bomb, to a larger structure that would protect some 400 staff from fallout so they could control the region after Britain had been attacked with hydrogen bombs. Other government buildings here have been demolished and the building now adjoins the distinguished Accordia housing estate.

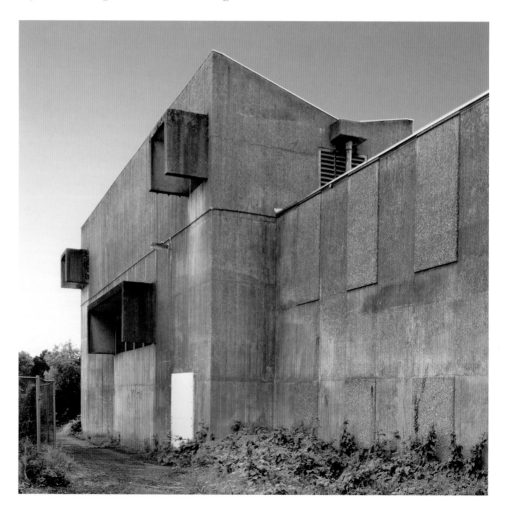

Flight Test Hangar

former De Havilland site, Comet Way, Hatfield, Hertfordshire

1952–4, James M. Monro and Son with SMD Engineers Ltd

Listed grade II*, 21 September 1998

The jet-engined Comet passenger aircraft was the great hope of the British aircraft industry. Commercial services began in May 1952, but then three planes exploded in flight after their thin aluminium shells suffered fatigue.

This story overshadows the use of aluminium for De Havilland's maintenance hangar. It was built of a strain-hardened alloy, HE, less prone to oxidization than its predecessors, and when built was the world's largest permanent aluminium structure at 100.5m (330ft) long and 13.7m (45ft) high, with a span of 61m (200ft). Its structure of portal-framed trusses, with pin joints on welded steel bases and concrete prestressed tie beams, inspired subsequent military hangars.

A steel and brick annexe was added in 1953–4, including a five-storey tower topped by a control room, whose zigzag 'Festival-style' balconies are repeated in the stepped profile of the fire station also integrated into the building. The hangar has been adapted as a hotel and leisure centre, with the folding doors left open and a glazed frontage inserted.

5 Pennyfathers Lane

Harmer Green, Welwyn, Hertfordshire

1953–4, Mary and David Medd

Listed grade II, 18 April 2007

The schools architects Mary Crowley and David Medd married in 1949, after they had left Hertfordshire for the Ministry of Education. Crowley had designed three houses in 1936 at nearby Tewin, but it was only when they stopped off in Copenhagen after a gruelling visit to Poland in 1952 that they resolved to build their own home. Their inspiration was the simple gabled cottage created by artists Carl and Karin Larsson from 1888 onwards at Sundborn, Sweden, and modern Scandinavian design. Much of their furniture was laboriously shipped from Denmark, with David making a built-in settle and other pieces himself.

This tiny house is important, too, as a rare, little-altered example of a private dwelling built while licensing controls were in force. Begun in the war and imposed vigorously (albeit with variations) between July 1947 and November 1954, licences limited a house's size to around 140 sq. m (1,500 sq. ft), and pegged its cost to that of council housing (here £4,000). A loophole, however, allowed David to build a large workshop alongside.

All Saints Church

Bawdeswell, Norfolk

1953–5, James Fletcher Watson

Listed grade II, 25 September 1998

Bawdeswell's modest 1840s church was struck in 1944 by an RAF Mosquito bomber limping back to a nearby base. The replacement, with a three-stage tower and simple pedimented porch, harked back to New England, suggesting a style transported and thence returned. Its simple basilica plan with an apse is a reminder of the harmony between communion and the word in eighteenth-century Anglicanism.

Only the altar rails were salvaged from the old church, though an old organ was brought from nearby Shotesham. The other fittings were by local architect Watson, including a three-decker pulpit, a barrel-vaulted ceiling and chandeliers, a feature of his country house work. The result has the neatness of a doll's house. The external flint walling followed a study of Norfolk examples by Watson and the site foreman, but was combined with projecting headers in pure 1950s style.

Watson's work continued a gentle neo-Georgian tradition based on the local brickmaking and craftsman traditions that also served Tayler and Green so well.

Trinity United Reformed (former Presbyterian) Church

Unthank Road, Norwich

1954–6, Bernard Feilden
with Edward Boardman and Son

Listed grade II, 5 October 2007

Trinity Church was destroyed in 1942 and its site purchased by the council for redevelopment. One of the congregation had acquired the Unthank Road Baptist Chapel as a store, and offered it for the new church. Its foundations determined the building's modest footprint and thence the plan of a first-floor church over an entrance meeting area.

Bernard Feilden joined local architects Edward Boardman and Son in 1950. He was solely responsible for Trinity and when Boardman refused him a partnership, set up his own practice. The tower with its entasis and copper cupola has Scandinavian influences, but Feilden was also inspired by Sant' Apollinare Nuovo in Ravenna, seen in the war. Most striking is the centralized steel roof structure clad in African hardwood, its triangular roof lights symbolizing the Trinity and forming a cross over the main chandelier. Decoration is confined to the natural materials, save for small reliefs in the Westmorland slate panels on the exterior.

Feilden became surveyor to Norwich Cathedral, York Minster and St Paul's Cathedral.

Atomic bomb store RAF Barnham

Gorse Industrial Estate
Thetford, Norfolk

1954–9, Air Ministry

Scheduled 29 May 2003
Five buildings listed at grade II and II*,
24 June 2011

This is the survivor of two central storage and servicing facilities built for the RAF's first operational atomic bomb, Blue Danube, close to the airfields that would use it. Land was purchased in 1953 and the pentagonal compound enclosed by a double fence became operational in 1956. Three buildings for the non-nuclear components of the bombs, so big and heavy that they required cranes, were set in earthen banks around a central yard. Two survive, flanked by lines of kiosks or hutches that housed the fissile cores in the ground. An inspection and repair workshop was added in 1959, although it had been recognized that small stores at airfields like Wittering were more efficient. Probably fewer than ten warheads were ever held here.

Barnham became obsolete with the development of the stand-off missile Blue Steel and closed in 1963. It demonstrates Blue Danube's big, crude character very legibly, and scheduling, with the listing of the main buildings (now industrial units), has prompted a maintenance and repair programme.

82-125 Knightsfield

Welwyn Garden City

1955–6, Louis de Soissons, Peacock, Hodges and Robertson

Listed grade II, 22 December 1998

Louis de Soissons was appointed in 1920 as the first architect and town planner at Welwyn Garden City, which he developed in a largely neo-Georgian style.

Welwyn and Hatfield were jointly designated as a new town in 1947, with de Soissons as Welwyn's planner. He expanded the town to the north and south-east with a mixture of public and private housing. While private housebuilders used a variety of styles, he determined that a prominent group of houses and flats at the main intersection in the northern neighbourhood should continue the Georgian tradition.

Knightsfield has a consistent Regency detailing, with big first-floor balconies under prominent copper canopies. The bold massing hides a complex variety of dwellings, with houses at the ends and flats or maisonettes in central units that resemble three-storey town houses. The individual unit is thus subsumed in favour of four mirrored terraces set around a village green.

Listing was prompted by piecemeal window replacement, which was halted before it could undermine the group's consistent character.

St Luke's Church

High Road, Leagrave, Luton

1955–6, Hon. John Seely
(Lord Mottistone) and Paul Paget

Listed grade II, 25 September 1998

Nikolaus Pevsner dismissed St Luke's as 'startlingly out of touch with its age', but the diversity of functions contained under one roof makes it more suited to contemporary needs than many overtly modern churches. The plan is novel in Seely and Paget's extensive church work.

The rectangular church itself is set to the rear, behind butterfly wings containing ancillary accommodation, which are disturbingly domestic in appearance. Their elevations are in an eighteenth-century Georgian brick style, and the cross on the roof ridge is the chief external evidence of a church.

The church itself is on two levels behind a round-arched arcade. A Lady chapel forms a gallery behind a round-arched arcade to one side, where it can be used as an overflow space. Otherwise the design is quietly neoclassical, dominated by pendant candelabra and an enormous altar painting by Norman Blamey; Seely and Paget enjoyed incorporating murals in their churches and this stylized *Christ in His Glory* was one of Blamey's first major religious works.

2 Farm Field

Watford

1955–6, Alison and Peter Smithson

Listed grade II, 3 July 2012

Derek Sugden, an engineer with Ove Arup and Partners, met Peter Smithson in 1951 through his colleague Ronald Jenkins. He had bought some land but had only £2,500 with which to build a house, and needed an architect. Smithson was already becoming well known and Sugden was surprised when he offered to take the commission.

A covenant on the land required the house to be built of brick with a tiled roof. Sugden wanted 'an ordinary house, a simple house, but that should not stop it from being a radical house', the latter suggested externally only in the irregular pitched roof and L-shaped windows. But already the Smithsons were defining the new brutalism, the honest expression of natural brick, timber and concrete in a marriage of vernacular construction with De Stijl and Le Corbusier that reacted against Scandinavian modernism. Sugden's house reveals these aims internally, with its exposed brickwork and concrete beams, unpainted doors, open-tread stairs and tiled floors. It is little altered, even retaining its built-in kitchen fittings by Alison.

Castle Hill United Reformed Church

Dryden Road, Ipswich

1955–7, Birkin Haward
of Johns, Slater and Haward

Listed grade II, 25 September 1998

Birkin Haward first worked with the engineer Felix Samuely when assisting Erich Mendelsohn on the Bexhill Pavilion in 1934–5. He subsequently became interested in shell roofs for schools around Ipswich, where he based his post-war practice.

The Castle Hill church is an early folded concrete slab developed with Samuely, a high pitched roof engineered as a series of thin, inverted, V-shaped wedges slung between two concrete frames and post-tensioned. Upswept eaves to either side, including the entrance vestibule, reduce the stresses in the main planes and taper to just 12cm (4¾in) thick.

The interior is a high, light hall, with a sanctuary at one end and a stage at the other. The side walls are formed of diamond-shaped blocks, another Haward speciality, and precast in three patterns inset with glass, which are also used to form the cross over the altar. Instead of stained glass, for economy clear glass was sprayed with oil paint and varnished. The Compton organ comes from a demolished cinema in Clacton.

Rushbrooke

near Bury St Edmunds, Suffolk

1956, 1956–9, 1960–63,
Llewelyn Davies and Weeks

Listed grade II, 22 December 1998

Rushbrooke is a minute estate village in hedge-less Suffolk sugar beet country. John Weeks's modernistic rebuilding contrasts with Tayler and Green's farmworkers' housing in Norfolk.

Richard Llewelyn Davies had met Victor Rothschild at Cambridge in the 1930s. He and Weeks went on to specialize in hospital design, but in 1950 Rothschild commissioned them to build estate cottages. A linked pair and a house for the village nurse by Weeks established an idiom of white-painted brick with big mono-pitched roofs and black trimmings, inspired by Italian vernacular buildings seen on holiday, which he repeated in rebuilding the main village street around an old well house. The houses have south-facing living rooms, a large walk-in store, and a first-floor playroom or store. The style is coincidentally reminiscent of Arne Jacobsen's Søholm, outside Copenhagen, and also to designs made in 1954 by the Smithsons, Howells, James Stirling and other friends of Weeks for 'Habitat', a first theoretical project organized by the international group of architects later known as Team 10.

The Gibberd Garden

Marsh Lane, Harlow, Essex

1957–84, Frederick Gibberd

Registered, 9 February 1995

Frederick Gibberd bought a smallholding on the edge of Harlow in 1957. He was refused permission to rebuild the 1907 bungalow, but he remodelled and extended it while creating the surrounding garden. Picture windows offer different views of surrounding garden rooms enclosed by shrubs and hedges. Prospects lead from one to the next, inspired by town planning theorist Camillo Sitte, with greater spontaneity than seen in Gibberd's work elsewhere. Leaf textures dominate over flowers. Away from the house the garden is less formal, and an Edwardian lime walk leads to the dank Pincey Brook and a children's castle. In 1974, Gibberd salvaged two of Macvicar Anderson's columns from Coutts' Bank, Strand, and placed them here.

The garden was transformed following Gibberd's marriage in 1972 to Patricia Fox-Edwards, an authority on sculpture, and Marsh Lane became their permanent home. Their collection now dominates the garden. A trust was founded in 1995 to acquire the garden.

Richardson Candles

St John's Street, Trinity Street,
King's Parade, Trumpington Street,
Benet Street, Wheeler Street and
Silver Street, Cambridge

1957, Sir Albert Richardson

19 street lights
Listed grade II, 6 May 2011
12 street lights
Listed grade II, 4 April 2013

As the economy improved in the 1950s, Cambridge decided to replace its gas street lights, but could find no modern electrical fittings that suited its architecture. So, following Grey Wornum's successful new light for Westminster, the city commissioned Sir Albert Richardson to design one for Cambridge. For Richardson it was a chance of redemption after losing a battle against unsympathetic street lights in his beloved Ampthill.

Birmingham's engineers had produced a post-topped or 'candle' lamp for the Festival of Britain, working with the REVO Electric Company of Tipton. Its fluted and decorated column was classical, yet the fluorescent tube and Perspex diffuser represented the latest technology. The combination appealed to Richardson, who kept the fluting, but removed the fussy capital detail and simplified the scalloped and grooved lantern caps to give the unit a smooth silhouette.

Richardson's Candles give little downward light, but suit Cambridge's narrow central streets. They were set to be replaced before the first listings in 2011; more listings followed in 2013.

St Paul's Church

College Square, Harlow

1957–9, Humphrys and Hurst

Listed grade II, 16 November 2007

St Paul's is arguably the most lavish Anglican church in any new town. Frederick Gibberd suggested that it should be the one town centre building faced in brick rather than concrete, a contrast emphasized by gold touches. Canon Knight, the first incumbent, was a major influence, seeking 'the best of traditional design, but making imaginative use of modern materials'.

The interior is painted in dark red, blue and yellow, with plain and lemon yellow (quasi-grisaille) glass. This contrasts with the black background of John Piper's mural depicting Christ in the house at Emmaus, a theme chosen to suggest that Christ is always present. It was installed days ahead of that at the BBC's Television Centre (see p.440). The fittings were largely designed by Reginald W. Hurst, but completed by Derrick Humphrys after Hurst's death in 1958, and form a glorious ensemble with the mural. The organ was installed in 1967.

The architects had worked for N. F. Cachemaille-Day before forming their own practice and this is their principal work.

Clock Tower

Town Square, Stevenage,
Hertfordshire

1957–9, Leonard Vincent,
Stevenage Development Corporation

Listed grade II, 22 December 1998

Stevenage was Britain's first modern new town, designated in November 1946. The clock includes a memorial to Lewis Silkin, the Minister of Town and Country Planning who secured legislation to ease London's overcrowding by building satellite towns resembling the garden cities pioneered by Ebenezer Howard. Satellite towns were also crucial to Patrick Abercrombie's *Greater London Plan* of 1945. Silkin was unpopular in Stevenage: on the day of designation signs on the railway station appeared renaming the town 'Silkingrad'.

Stevenage had the first pedestrian-only new town centre, based on a design made by Peter Shepheard when working for Abercrombie. The clock tower is its centrepiece, an open concrete frame with black granite cladding. On the east face is a map in painted ceramic tiles showing Stevenage and its principal industries.

The pool has been modified to include an inner pool and fountain. Nearby is Franta Belsky's listed sculpture, *Joy-ride*, a mother and child symbolic of the new town.

Water Gardens

Hemel Hempstead, Hertfordshire

1957–60, Geoffrey Jellicoe

Registered, 1 February 2010

Geoffrey Jellicoe prepared the master plan for Hemel Hempstead new town in 1947. But in 1949 the Hemel Hempstead Development Corporation rejected his proposals for the town centre, including a grid of public buildings and formal gardens defined by a canalized River Gade.

However, in 1957 Jellicoe was invited back to design gardens to hold back storm water once the Gade valley was developed. He united the river's two channels into one, which wriggles through open parkland before sweeping round a gentle mound. Thence the canal is straight, with bridges and projecting balconies giving views over the water and planting by Jellicoe's wife Susan – now badly overgrown. Finally it debouches into a lake, for Jellicoe the head of a serpent with a fountain as its eye.

Inspired by a Paul Klee painting, the water gardens were one of Jellicoe's first exercises in landscape design as a fine art form, in which he explored its subconscious symbolism. Proposals for the restoration of the gardens are being prepared in 2015.

Church of St Andrew and St George

St George's Way, Stevenage

1957–60, Hon. John Seely
(Lord Mottistone) and Paul Paget

Listed grade II, 25 September 1998

This church opened as St George's, the 'mother church' of the new town.

At the architects' first church, St Faith's, Lee-on-the-Solent, Seely argued that the most stable form of structure was the catenary arch – the form that a chain naturally takes when draped over a rail – and developed this in reinforced concrete. At Stevenage similar arches were precast, prestressed and set in pairs, extending outwards to give the effect of flying buttresses and appearing internally as pointed arches at their intersection. Also built of prestressed columns is the adjoining open campanile, with tuned metal rods instead of bells.

Seely and Paget's favourite artist, Brian Thomas, created the gloriously colourful east window in 1966. The undercroft was adapted as the town museum in 1977, when Thomas's murals for the basement Lady chapel were moved to the high altar. The organ, side chapels and vestry are enclosed in afromosia wood, while the nave altar was devised from fittings brought from St Andrew's, Bedwell (closed in 1963).

Corpus Christi, Sidney Sussex, Wolfson and Girton Boathouse

Cutter Ferry Lane, Cambridge

1958, David Roberts

Listed grade II, 2 December 1997

This was Cambridge's first new boathouse since 1930, and the first designed to be shared by two colleges, Corpus Christi and Sidney Sussex. With its blond brick and modest scale, it reacted against the jauntily vulgar Queen Anne style still in vogue between the wars with a pure, functional design. It comprises a ground-floor store and workshop with a small pavilion and changing rooms on top. From a first-floor balcony, two spiral staircases wind down to the water, their duality reflecting the shared occupancy of the premises. Shared boathouses are now more common, and Wolfson's and Girton's later arrival is denoted by additional flagpoles. Extensions have been added to either side without destroying the elegant symmetry of the original composition.

Many boathouses later followed Roberts's winning formula. That shared by Selwyn, King's, Churchill and the Leys School is a bigger variant in Cambridge, as is the one built for Emanuel School at Barnes in 1960 by Laurence King, the first post-war boathouse on the Thames.

3 Clarkson Road

Cambridge

1958, Trevor Dannatt

Listed grade II, 26 April 2004

Trevor Dannatt was introduced to Peter and Janet Laslett by their landlady, Rachel Rostas. They sought a modern interpretation of a Cambridge don's house, and Dannatt devised a prototype for modest professional housing. It was his second house, but the first to be completed, and owes much to his earlier work with Peter Moro and Leslie Martin, and to Erik Sørenson's house at Vedbæk near Copenhagen.

Dannatt took the client's demand for an upper-level living room, and a slope in the land, to produce a sectional arrangement full of surprises. He set the living room on a half level over the low garage, not reflected externally in the line of the cedar cladding to the upper floor and denoted only by a large picture window. The device made the room a high, double cube, lined in cedar above the low windowsills and fireplace. There are diagonal vistas to the ground-floor dining area through the open stairwell, making a more complex plan than Moro's own house in Blackheath Park (see p.562).

School of Architecture extension

1 Scroope Terrace, Cambridge

1958–9, Colin St John Wilson and Alex Hardy

Listed grade II, 16 January 2013

Cambridge University offered a full diploma course in architecture only from 1956, when Leslie Martin became professor and recruited Wilson as his assistant. Hardy taught building services. Third-year students participated in design studies for this extension, and visiting lecturers advised as engineers and quantity surveyors. The materials were brick and concrete, exposed inside and out, with a budget of just £4 per square foot.

The extension followed a rigorous grid of 2.74m (9ft), while the Golden Section determined floor heights and the proportions of the ground-floor tutors' rooms. A central service area with concrete shelves and pigeonholes enforces similarities with Stirling and Gowan's work and adjoins a sunken common room. The first floor houses a lecture theatre, top-lit by timber louvres originally controlled from the concrete stand installed for the projectionist. It is entered through doors on central pivots like those created by Le Corbusier. Though technically listed with the rest of the terrace in 1972, the special interest of the extension was not then recognized.

Our Lady of Fatima RC Church

Howard Way and First/Mandela Avenue, Harlow

1958–60, Gerard Goalen

Listed grade II, 20 December 2000

Gerard Goalen was working for Harlow Development Corporation when he was asked to design the town's principal Roman Catholic church. The incumbent, Father Francis Burgess, asked that 500 parishioners be accommodated close to a large sanctuary and free-standing altar. This was a radical brief for 1953. Had the church been built then, it would have been among the first in Britain inspired by the Liturgical Movement, but no building licence was available.

The church has a T-shaped plan, with the sanctuary at the junction of three equal arms that house the congregation. The church is dominated by brightly coloured fused slab glass windows from Dom Charles Norris's studio at Buckfast Abbey. Goalen was an expert in modern French glass, and found Norris's the closest English approximation available in large quantities. High on the fourth wall is the organ and a figure of Christ by Daphne Hardy Henrion.

St John's Church

Bishop's Rise, Hatfield, Hertfordshire

1958–60, Peter Bosanquet
of Brett, Boyd and Bosanquet

Listed grade II, 25 September 1998

Lionel Brett, Lord Esher, was appointed master planner to Hatfield new town in 1948. This church by his partner was planned for a congregation of 200, plus a choir of up to 50 seated in a rear gallery, but seems larger because of its massive pitched roof and a prominent hilltop site. There is a strong resemblance to Frank Lloyd Wright's Unitarian church at Shorewood Hills, Wisconsin, designed in 1947. The fall of the land makes the sanctuary seem still higher.

Thick timber roof trusses resembling an upturned boat dominate the panelled interior, supported on reinforced concrete columns and on the gable walls, whose curves brace them against the wind after gales had lifted roofs on nearby housing. A window in the form of a cross lights the sanctuary amid small windows of coloured glass, which glow at dusk. A design for a 24.4m (80ft) campanile, compared by *The Builder* to a fire station, was never built.

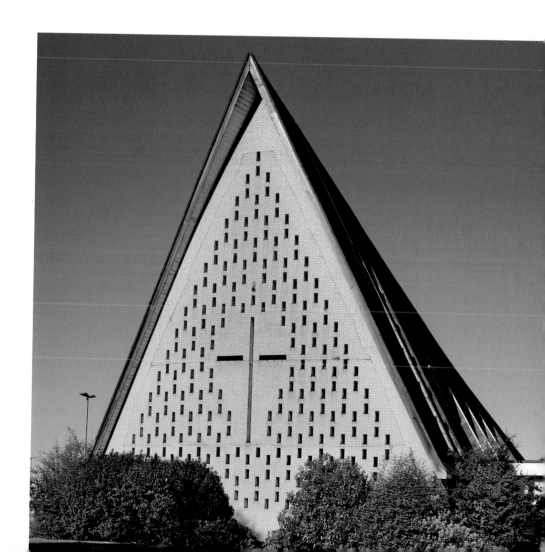

St Alban's College of Further Education, now Oaklands housing

Hatfield Road, St Albans

1958–60, Hertfordshire
County Council
Job architect, John Wakely

Listed grade II, 14 February 2003

Post-war higher education was dominated by the university sector, socially and architecturally. Founded in 1957 to provide O- and A-level courses, vocational and evening classes, St Alban's was a rare example of a local authority college designed with panache.

Hertfordshire architects had continued building for schools using the Hills system, retooled by Jack Platt in 1956 to use common 'Blue Standard' components. Bruce Martin had experimented with metric proportions, but Platt found 0.81m (2ft 8in) neater for sizing doors and lavatories. This module was first tested here, where Wakely designed a series of linked two- and four-storey blocks on the sloping site on a rectangular grid, replacing Victorian villas but retaining the old trees. With aluminium cladding and large areas of glass, the result was neater and more sophisticated than the earlier schools.

When the college sold the site for housing, a survey identified key buildings for listing and the rest were demolished. The listed blocks were remodelled in 2008–11 as flats by John Pardey.

1A-37 Highsett

Hills Road, Cambridge

1958–60, Eric Lyons
for Span Developments Ltd

Listed grade II, 22 December 1998

Highsett I is arguably Lyons's most successful work outside London. The land was owned by Jesus College, where Span partner Leslie Bilsby knew the bursar. Lyons, encouraged by Leslie Martin, proposed a 15-storey tower for part of the site, which was refused permission in 1958.

Also part of the original scheme was a long quadrangle, resembling a college down to its manicured central lawns, entered between pilotis and with glazed staircase halls to front and rear. Three sides of the court have variously sized flats. The fourth has maisonettes over garages, giving a greater variety of elevations than found in earlier Span blocks. Lyons believed that flat-roofed buildings fitted most naturally into his lushly planted landscapes, while his signature tile-hanging offered the comfort of traditional materials. They are contrasted with dark brick, and the structural cross-walls are concealed to give a greater horizontality and fluidity of design than in his earlier work. Like all Span schemes, Highsett is a cunning integration between architecture, landscaping and careful management.

Arts Faculty buildings

Sidgwick Avenue, Cambridge

1958–64, Casson, Conder and Partners

Listed grade II, 30 March 1993

The squalor of the science sites prompted the arts faculties to carefully plan their new precinct, on a site selected in 1950. A competition was held in 1952 between Sir Hugh Casson and Robert Atkinson. Casson's was the first large post-war university plan, and led to his major Birmingham commission. But at Sidgwick Avenue it proved impossible to secure all the land required, and a revised scheme of 1963 was abandoned save for James Stirling's history faculty.

Casson and Conder provided an urbane integrated environment of refined buildings in partly load-bearing brick and stone, walkways and a central lawn that is Cambridge's best teaching campus. The centrepiece is a three-sided cloistral building on a low plinth set on chunky pilotis to allow vistas through. It houses language departments, whose libraries have undergone extensive alterations with listed building consent. The building to the west includes the well-preserved Marshall Library for economics. At the entrance to the site is the Lady Mitchell Hall, completed in 1964 only after many revisions to Conder's designs.

Westcliff Library

London Road, Westcliff-on-Sea, Southend

1959–60, Patrick Burridge, borough architect

Listed grade II, 24 April 1998

Southend was a progressive library authority, and had recognized the need for a branch in the expanding district of Westcliff in the 1930s. There were no suitable buildings for conversion, so a bombsite was selected and in 1956 Burridge prepared designs.

The result is an unusually handsome small library, thanks to the quality of the timber roofs and detailing, and large areas of glass. The lending library was set in the body of the building, lit by a clerestory, with children's and reference areas in the aisles to either side. The children's section was later moved to the far end to allow better supervision, where a low window gives good light for the smallest readers. A curved bench was built to screen the newspaper tables, and books can be taken into the secure rear courtyard.

Staff admire the building for its flexibility and generous rear workroom. Burridge repeated the plan elsewhere in Southend, but never with the same quality of materials.

Harlow Town Station

Station Approach, Harlow

1959–60, British Railways Eastern Region: Paul Hamilton, Ian Fraser and John Bicknell

Listed grade II, 24 November 1995

Harlow, a rebuilding of Burnt Mill Station to serve the new town, fulfilled Hamilton's 'pent-up urge to build' after years just producing standard plans for the London County Council and a timber system for British Railways. The subsoil was poor, so he decided to use as little of it as possible, placing the waiting room on the bridge and making a feature of the lifts, which then principally served parcel traffic. This concept had been pioneered by Western Region in 1956–8 at Banbury.

Hamilton chose chunky detailing and robust finishes capable of withstanding hard knocks and little maintenance. The result is a series of thick, horizontal, concrete and timber slabs, covering the glazed booking hall, adjoining brick offices and the stairs from the platforms, rising to the covered bridge and crowned by the lift towers. Brick, mosaic and thick timber are the main finishes. Hamilton acknowledged references to Frank Lloyd Wright, whom he much admired, and to the Japanese pavilion at the 1958 Brussels World's Fair.

Broxbourne Station

Broxbourne, Hertfordshire

1959–61, British Rail Eastern Region
Job architect, Peter Reyniers

Listed grade II, 2 March 2009

The station was rebuilt and resited as part of the electrification of the Liverpool Street–Bishop's Stortford line, and complements that at nearby Harlow. Its plan is similar, though smaller; three lift towers, of yellow stock and purple brick placed over the irregularly spaced island platforms, support a wholly enclosed bridge that is more normally reached via glazed-in staircases, their thick, oiled wood handrails adding to the sense of solidity and mass. The straightforward use of stock brick and concrete creates rich contrasts with light from the great staircase window.

The simple strength of Broxbourne was much admired by the contemporary critic Ian Nairn, who preferred it to the better-known Harlow; other opinions vary, but nobody can doubt the impact made by the presence of two similar stations of exceptional quality so close together. A signal box (still unlisted) completes the ensemble.

Garret Hostel Bridge

Garret Hostel Lane, Cambridge

1960, Timothy Morgan
of Guy Morgan and Partners

Listed grade II, 29 September 1998

The sixth bridge on the site since records began in 1455, this replaced William Chadwell Mylne's cast-iron bridge of 1837. It had to be higher than its predecessor and to withstand occasional car traffic; the steep camber serves as a brake to speeding cyclists.

The construction was engineered by Guy Morgan and Partners, and designed by Guy's son Timothy, then studying at the Cambridge School of Architecture but who sadly died soon after the bridge was completed.

The bridge is a two-hinged arch of prestressed concrete, 27m (88½ft) in span, with a keel-shaped underside. The concrete portal frame is supported on a concrete hinge at one end and steel rollers at the other to minimize the depth of the deck to just 53cm (1ft 9in) at the crown, although it incorporates two water mains and electric gables. The abutments appear weightier by being concealed in York stone, also used to pave the bridge. The handrails are of bronze.

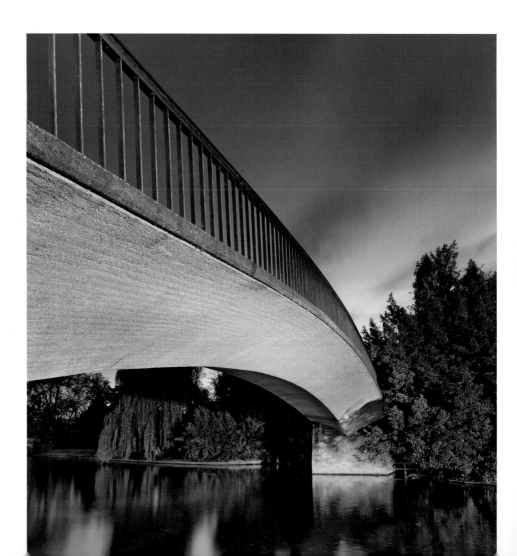

The Spinney

108 Westerfield Road, Ipswich

1960, Birkin Haward
of Johns, Slater and Haward

Listed grade II, 2 December 2009

Birkin Haward acquired a poorly drained site in 1957 shortly after the death of his wife and designed this house for himself, his sister and teenage children. Best known for his schools, he wrote in 1996 that it was 'the only individual dwelling . . . that I felt able to conceive in an entirely uninhibited manner'. The materials are Fletton brick with an upper floor of timber on concrete posts, left largely exposed internally.

The plan is based around a central double-height hall, which contains the open-tread stair, with a living room and studio at the ends and more private rooms to the sides. Haward likened the plan, reflected in the W-shape of the roof, to that of the local timber vernacular tradition. Central halls were also appearing in his schools and the house anticipates the deep, rectangular plans of his later work. Haward lived here until his death in 2002, making small additions to the glazed entrance and garden elevations.

Keelson

Hills Avenue, Cambridge

1960–1, Eric Sørensen

Listed grade II, 15 July 1998

The crystallographer Olga Kennard bought a plot in 1960 and looked for a British architect in vain. So she turned to her professional contacts in Denmark, whence the great physicist Niels Bohr responded, 'Sørensen and no one else!' Although Scandinavian influences were strong in post-war architecture, few foreign architects built in Britain in the 1950s and 1960s. Dr Kennard remains delighted with her decision.

Keelson is a single-storey house the width of the narrow site, and Sørensen made a U-shaped plan around a courtyard overlooked by the bedrooms, with a large living area facing the rear garden. Its understated elegance owes much to its slender timber frame, which is infilled with white-painted brickwork to a carefully irregular pattern to the front and large areas of glass to the rear. Sørensen also suggested some of the Danish furniture. The result is a well-integrated blend of quiet sophistication coupled with practical domesticity.

Dr Kennard was the founder of Cambridge Crystallographic Data Centre, which in 1992–3 also commissioned a major building from Sørensen.

Harvey Court

Gonville and Caius College,
West Road, Cambridge

1960–2, Sir Leslie Martin
and Patrick Hodgkinson

Listed grade II*, 30 March 1993

Harvey Court, developed from a project by Colin St John Wilson for King's College in the city centre, is a hostel separated from its parent college, like James Stirling's similarly controversial Florey Building at Oxford (see p.355).

Martin and Hodgkinson reappraised the traditional Cambridge brick quadrangle for 100 graduate students. The top-lit breakfast room is on the ground floor, with a south-facing lounge overlooking beautiful grounds. Their roof forms a raised courtyard, reached up two sets of stairs and surrounded by three storeys of bedsitters stepped like the flats subsequently developed by Hodgkinson at London's Brunswick Centre. Staircases project between the brick piers that dominate the walls to the street and sides.

Leslie Martin usually worked with younger architects. Many recurrent themes first appeared at Harvey Court: the orthogonal planning, the stepped section and brick, the similarities with Aalto's Säynätsalo town hall and Baker House, Massachusetts. His work has a coolness and logic, but with an underlying romance in its sculptural elevations and quirky plan.

Brooke House

East Square, Basildon

1960–2, Anthony B. Davies of
Basildon Development Corporation

Listed grade II, 22 December 1998

Most of the new towns experimented with tall flats in their central shopping areas to generate a permanent population and some life in the evenings, copying the early 1950s model of Rotterdam's Lijnbaan. Only at Basildon was a block of exceptional quality produced, where Brooke House forms a vertical node at the junction of the two main parades.

Brooke House, built on 14 floors and with six flats to a floor, was aimed at professionals without families. Its structure is based around four concrete boxes of great strength, which contain the kitchen, bathroom and duct units, and these are carried down on to the piled foundations via extremely tall pilotis. The entrance hall could thus be designed as a virtually free-standing glass box between them, and it contains a sculpture by F. E. McWilliam given to Basildon in 1959 by the politician Harold Lever. The elegant glass detailing is continued upwards in the ranks of canted windows that enliven the façade.

Churchill College

Storey's Way, Cambridge

1960–8, Richard Sheppard,
Robson and Partners

Listed grade II, 30 March 1993

A trust was founded in 1958 to establish a Cambridge college in Sir Winston Churchill's honour, largely for science and engineering. With a vast site and sponsorship from industry and trade unions, it was intended for 600 men and to last 500 years. A two-stage competition among 20 firms saw the emergence of young practices such as Howell, Killick and Partridge, and of a more monumental style thereafter popular for large commissions.

The winner, Richard Sheppard, assisted by William Mullins, created a language of exposed concrete floor slabs and brick walling based on Le Corbusier's Maisons Jaoul, conservative yet appropriately majestic. They adopted a traditional plan, placing residential accommodation off staircases in groups of quadrangles. Generous common rooms are gathered behind Cambridge's largest dining hall, vaulted in concrete. A separate block houses libraries, lecture halls and archives. A chapel included in the original brief proved controversial and Mullins added an ecumenical building in concrete and brick at the far end of the site in 1967–8.

Barstable School

Timberlog Lane, Basildon

1961–2, Yorke, Rosenberg
and Mardall
Partners in charge, Cyril Mardall
and David Allford

Listed grade II, 30 March 1993

This is one of Yorke, Rosenberg and Mardall's last schools, built as they turned to larger commercial and civic schemes following their success at Gatwick Airport (1958–63). It demonstrates the tougher aesthetic in their work that followed the recruitment of a younger generation led by Brian Henderson and David Allford.

Barstable was built as a grammar school but is now a bustling comprehensive for 11 to 16-year-olds. The exposed concrete frame of its main three-storey teaching block is contrasted with infill panels of dark, bluish brick. It forms a strong contrast with a long, lower range at right angles that contains a large assembly hall with a folded plate concrete roof, and a swimming pool.

Windows have been replaced and the concrete painted following repair work. The school has also been greatly extended with the building of new blocks for science and technology. The original building retains its vigour, but it is now part of a larger urban complex that has the feel of a small township.

44 West Common Way

Harpenden, Hertfordshire

1961–3, Povl Ahm from a design by Jørn Utzon, extended 1972–4 by Ulrick Plesner

Listed grade II, 15 July 1998

When the engineer Povl Ahm was working for Ove Arup on the Sydney Opera House he persuaded its architect Jørn Utzon to design him a house. The result followed Utzon's drawings, save that Ahm introduced an intermediate truss to reduce the depth of the pre-cast concrete beams that support the gently pitched roof. Exposed along the long, fully glazed frontage, concealed side-on to the road, these contrast with cool brickwork elsewhere.

The house is single-storeyed, but the hall and carport are at a slightly lower level to the living room, and further steps rise to the dining and kitchen area beyond. This progression is an important feature, as is the consistency of finish, with Swedish Hogamass white tiles throughout the house and adjoining terrace. Joinery details follow those of Utzon's houses at Fredensborg.

Plesner worked for Arup Associates, and his wing facing the road provides separate children's accommodation in a sympathetic style. The combined result is a beautifully detailed house in the idiom of an internationally important architect.

2 and 2A Grantchester Road

Cambridge

1961–4, Colin St John Wilson

Listed grade II, 13 April 2000

No. 2A was built for academics Peter and Natasha Squire, while No. 2 was Wilson's house and studio, where he combined teaching with architectural practice. The house plans are similar, save that the Squires had a single-storey living room and extra bedroom, while Wilson had a double-height living space with a gallery supported on columns like a triumphal arch, and an open-well staircase. His house is furthermore set back behind an office wing that forms a continuous street façade with No. 2A, its colonnade described by Colin Rowe as 'the smallest monument in Cambridge'.

These were the first houses in Britain built of ferro-concrete blocks, which impart a rigorous austerity. From them Wilson derived a tartan grid of 1.2m (4ft) that he described as 'railway lines', which let him 'push things up and down'. Even the patio paving follows these proportions. From the office entrance separate stairs and a bridge-like landing lead to a first-floor drawing office. Now a private house, it remains a perfect setting for displaying art and sculpture.

John Lewis's warehouse

Gunnel's Wood Road,
Stevenage, Hertfordshire

1962–3, Yorke, Rosenberg and
Mardall with Félix Candela

Listed grade II, 24 November 1995

John Lewis built its main distribution depot at Stevenage for its proximity to the A1. Eugene Rosenberg invited the Spanish architect-turned-engineer Félix Candela to collaborate on the structural design after they had met in Mexico, although Candela's work was already fashionable here. He had escaped Franco's Spain in 1939 and in Mexico developed concrete folding plates and hyperbolic paraboloid shells as a cheap and architectural means of bridging large spans. This is his only English work.

The 142m (466ft) building is roofed with shells of board-marked reinforced concrete, 127mm (5in) thick, supported on square columns. Each unit resembles an inside-out umbrella, or warped parallelogram, and is tilted to create a string of north-facing roof lights between each of the 11 rows of 15 shells. Candela first used the system for a clothing factory in Mexico City and Tulancingo wool mill in 1955, but the 15 half-shells projecting over the loading bays at Stevenage may be unique. The building is still owned by John Lewis, but is no longer in use.

29A Loom Lane

Radlett, Hertfordshire

1962–5, George Marsh

Listed grade II, 18 February 1999

George Marsh was one of Richard Seifert's first partners, and designed Centre Point. Here he enjoyed an unaccustomed freedom in designing a house for himself.

The Marshes had previously lived in a flat in Kensington with high ceilings, and the decision to make the principal rooms open-plan on a single level reflects its influence. The site slopes steeply so the principal rooms at entrance level give on to a south-facing balcony built over a playroom and sauna. As soon as the house was completed, Marsh added a wing for his in-laws.

Marsh found similarities between concrete and timber construction. The complex room heights are made possible by two hyperbolic paraboloid (or hypar) timber roofs, supported on a light steel frame at three points, with the 'granny flat' under a third. The hypar form was constructed first, allowing the builders to work under cover, and its overhangs prevent solar gain. The flooring, mosaics and glass, by Jupp Dernbach Mayen, are repeated at Centre Point.

Murray Edwards College, formerly New Hall

Huntingdon Road, Cambridge

1962–6, Chamberlin, Powell and Bon

Listed grade II*, 30 March 1993

New Hall was opened in 1954 as Cambridge's third women's college, to improve an 11:1 male to female ratio. However, although Peter Chamberlin was appointed architect in 1958 following an invited competition, fundraising lagged behind that for new male colleges.

At the core of the college are the dining room and library, built of white brick and concrete around a courtyard. The abiding image is of the domed first-floor dining hall set sentinel over a reflective pool, its double skin resembling a half-peeled orange and testimony to fine precision precasting. A dumb waiter rises into the centre of the cruciform space. Still more powerful is the library, with two galleries reached via a soaring central staircase. The residential Orchard Court followed, its variety of room configurations reflected in the busy patterning of its façades.

The college's bold forms were at first deemed inappropriate for cosy Cambridge, but it gave a progressive institution a strong identity. Extensions have been made in a lighter idiom.

Ferrum House

Grange Court Road,
Harpenden, Hertfordshire

1963, John S. Bonnington

Listed grade II, 15 July 1998

John Bonnington was a partner of Basil Spence, with particular responsibility for the firm's growing number of civic commissions, when he designed this neat house for himself. It is one of the very first steel-framed houses in England, inspired by a visit in c.1955 to Mies van der Rohe's Farnsworth House. It is maintained in immaculate condition.

It is the principal first floor which is steel-framed, and its black outline is complemented by yellow brick cross-walls on the ancillary lower floor. Mies's influence is evident in the precision of the planning, using a brick module of 22.9cm (9in) and a grid of 91.4cm (3ft). Storey-high windows in aluminium frames fit naturally into this grid. An addition in similar style was made in the 1970s for the Bonningtons' growing family.

The interior is equally sophisticated, with Swedish white glass mosaic floors and ceilings boarded in sitka spruce. There are large hardwood sliding doors and partitions, and timber is also used for the extensive built-in cupboards and shelving, and for the built-in radiogram.

Long Wall

Newman's Green, Acton, Suffolk

1963, Philip Dowson and
Peter Foggo of Arup Associates

Listed grade II, 28 February 1997

Long Wall was devised as a weekend-cum-retirement home for a doctor and his wife. It takes its name from the brick wall that runs through and beyond the house, separating it from the former garage, giving privacy and sheltering a large rear terrace. It also houses the chimney in what is otherwise a lightweight structure. The other external walls are glazed, creating an open, Miesian pavilion, but realized in timber. Boarded ceilings and exquisite lines of cupboards make timber also the dominant material of the interior. Dowson wrote that: 'We wanted to establish a relationship between the hearth and the horizon and the spaces develop, each with their own function and influence, in graduated steps between these extremes.' But for the strong, sheltering eaves, the house would appear diminutive in the big Suffolk landscape.

Dowson was a co-founder of Arup Associates, a multidisciplinary practice that grew out of the engineers Ove Arup and Partners. The house was restored by Hugh Pilkington in 1995 in consultation with him.

RAF Neatishead
Norfolk

Type 84 radar modulator building
c.1963
Scheduled 27 February 2008

R30 operations room
1942, remodelled 1970s
Listed grade II*, 22 February 2008

R3 operations block and standby generator house
c.1952
Listed grade II, 22 February 2008

R12 equipment building
1967
Listed grade II, 22 February 2008

RAF Neatishead is the largest continuously occupied radar station in Britain, if not the world, and demonstrates the most important changes in Britain's air defences since 1941. Rebuilding to accompany the British Experimental Rotor Programme in the 1950s included a standby generator house in the nearby village disguised as a chapel, and the underground R3 operations block whose entrance guardroom masquerades as a bungalow.

More important structures were associated with Linesman, a 1960s fully computerized air defence system established at just five sites. The Type 84 radar is a local landmark, with its array of parabolic reflector dishes supported on a rotating rooftop steel girder frame. Following a fire in the original R3 bunker in 1966, the flat-roofed R30 operations room was adapted in 1972 from a wartime radar station to house the Improved United Kingdom Ground Defence Environment. It has an extraordinarily intact and evocative 1970s interior, with banks of computers and radar control consoles, and now forms part of the RAF Air Defence Radar Museum.

Former Ampthill Rural District Council offices

Dunstable Street, Ampthill, Bedfordshire

1963–5, Sir Albert Richardson and E. A. S. Houfe

Listed grade II, 27 April 2004

This is one of Richardson's last buildings, designed with his son-in-law in 1961–4 and completed after his death. In 1919 he had acquired Avenue House in Ampthill, whose late Georgian style came to inspire his post-war work, and he campaigned tirelessly to preserve the town's historic character. In his last years, Richardson had become one of the most outspoken critics of the Modern Movement, and encouraged a public image as 'last of the Georgians'. Nevertheless, his best works combine classical with early twentieth-century elements.

Avenue House's details are reflected in these council offices, with their neoclassical proportions and delicate iron balustrades. The copper cupola with its ball finial is a neo-Scandinavian touch. Inside is one of Richardson's most impressive spaces – a tall, octagonal council chamber with a public gallery under a central skylight, since remodelled.

The council vacated the offices in 2006. Richardson's work has been converted to offices, with the rest of the site redeveloped as housing.

George Thompson Building, Leckhampton

Corpus Christi College,
off Grange Road, Cambridge

1963–4, Philip Dowson
of Arup Associates

Listed grade II, 30 March 1993

Two linked blocks were built behind Leckhampton House, a Victorian villa concealed down a long private drive. It was the first accommodation in Cambridge designed solely for research fellows and graduates, who are provided with large study bedrooms and some fellows' 'sets' of rooms over a shared ground-floor common room and library.

Dowson had built two blocks in 1962 at Somerville College, Oxford, for undergraduates and graduates respectively. Leckhampton is a refinement of ideas on precasting first explored there, to a refined plan whose echelon layout gives every room a view of the mature gardens. Dowson was concerned that dirt-laden water from glass surfaces should not discharge over the concrete and cause streaks. His solution was to set the glass behind the frame, which more importantly serves as a screen, giving privacy and a sense of security despite the large windows. The result resembles a lattice kit of parts, set over solid brick piers and walls that link the two blocks.

William Stone Building

Peterhouse, Trumpington Street, Cambridge

1963–4, Leslie Martin and Colin St John Wilson

Listed grade II, 30 March 1993

A massive legacy from an American centenarian enabled the building of Cambridge's first tower of student accommodation. A double cluster of rooms and staircases was originally proposed by Martin and Wilson, a development of their Harvey Court, but an eight-storey tower was chosen to preserve Peterhouse's extensive parkland.

Each floor has three undergraduate bedsitters and a fellow's 'set' of three rooms, which can be divided by sliding partitions into two separate units if required. The staggered profile of south-facing windows is the building's defining image. As in the architects' earlier collaborations, there are affinities with Alvar Aalto's work, here his flats at Bremen, Berlin, and Tapiola (Finland). A basement storage area is shielded by the earth bank in front of the tower.

This was the first Oxbridge college building to have a lift, and the funding ensured high-quality interior fittings. The only economy was the choice of load-bearing brickwork, making it one of the first blocks to show that cellular buildings could be built high without reinforcement.

3 Church Walk

Aldeburgh, Suffolk

1963–4, H. T. and Elizabeth
Cadbury-Brown

Listed grade II, 4 December 2000

In 1957, H. T. (Jim) Cadbury-Brown designed an opera house in Aldeburgh for Benjamin Britten. It was never built, but Cadbury-Brown was given first option on the site. He and his wife Betty designed two houses there, one for Britten's assistant Imogen Holst and the larger one for themselves.

Their house lies concealed in a wild garden, where gaps in the boundary walls and enveloping creeper allowed views of Aldeburgh church. The house, of pinkish brick, is long and low, with an entrance courtyard enclosed by a projecting bedroom. The land falls to the south, so while the roof remains a constant height, the architects gained height for their living room by setting it down steps, creating what Betty termed her 'passion pit'. Betty's detailing also includes full-height doors, a leitmotif of the 1960s, and tall skylights or 'light scoops' that illuminate the central bathroom, the living area, kitchen sink and beds. After lying derelict following Jim's death in 2009, the house was restored in 2013–14.

New North Court

Jesus College, Jesus Lane,
Cambridge

1963–5, David Roberts
and Geoffrey Clarke

Listed grade II, 30 March 1993

David Roberts began working in a pale-brick Scandinavian idiom in Cambridge in the 1950s, beginning at his own Magdalene College. By the early 1960s his designs had become more modern, with aid from Leslie Martin, who as a fellow of Jesus College secured this commission.

New North Court replaced a house by Sir Alfred Waterhouse, also the architect of the adjoining range. Its boomerang plan divides the college's gardens and sports ground. It somewhat resembles Michael Powers's earlier 'Beehives' at St John's College, Oxford (see p.328), but instead of hexagons, New North Court is formed of linked cubes set at right angles to the line of the block. Alternating central cubes contain staircases and service rooms, with four study bedrooms at the corners of each landing. Each has a projecting, fully glazed window at its apex, and the reflection of the clouds sends a translucent shimmer down the façades. New North Court was admired for the quality of its accommodation and for gently updating the college's character.

The Ryde

Hatfield, Hertfordshire

1963–6, Phippen, Randall and Parkes

Listed grade II, 22 December 1998

In 1962 Michael Baily, a *Times* correspondent, advertised for people to join a cooperative housing venture 'to work out afresh the real needs of the family of today and the type of structure which would best answer them'. This became the Cockaigne Housing Group, named from William Morris's *News from Nowhere*, when Hatfield Development Corporation leased them land.

Peter Randall and David Parkes were architects at the Ministry of Housing and Local Government, and Baily admired their model 'adaptable house' at the Ideal Home Exhibition. For Cockaigne they produced staggered terraces of long and narrow single-storey, two-, three- or four-storey dwellings lit by skylights and internal courtyards – high-density 'patio planning' inspired by Hugo Häring and Hannes Meyer's work from 1920s Germany. Exposed timbers span concrete block cross-walls, construction described by Randall as 'earthy, economic and pragmatic', indebted to Le Corbusier and early Habitat shops. There are private and shared gardens, a tennis court, a community centre and lodgings for visitors. Collectively managed, it remains popular, and inspired subsequent Phippen, Randall and Parkes schemes elsewhere.

103 Main Street

Caldecote, Cambridge

1964, John Meunier

Listed grade II, 12 July 2002

John Meunier designed this house while lecturing at Cambridge University. Made possible by a mortgage scheme for faculty members with no savings, it is austere, but makes a feature of its cheap Fletton brickwork inside and out.

Meunier saw architecture in terms of the cube and the square, and the plan comprises two intersecting cubes. The larger one contains the open-plan living, dining and kitchen areas, while the lower cube has an enclosed study and bedrooms. The intersection contains the bathroom and service core. The house is raised on a square brick plinth, which forms two terraces. The façades follow a sequence from a completely blank north face to the totally glazed south face.

Meunier has stated that a house should be noble and elevating rather than comfortable. This he describes as 'an English Brutalist version of a Frank Lloyd Wright Usonian house', which understates the classical proportions that also informed his subsequent work with Barry Gasson. Since the listing he has extended the house.

Water tower

Temple Lane, Tonwell
near Bengeo, Hertfordshire

1964, Edmund C. Percey
of Scherrer and Hicks

Listed grade II, 15 May 2007

Edmund Percey became a specialist in the design of water towers for the Lee Valley Water Company, and later also worked in the Thames Valley. This is an early and elegant example of his work, a relatively small tank holding 227 cu. m (50,000 gallons) supported on eight canted piers around a central access column. The result resembles an ice-cream cone. Percey explained in 1975 that he chose the design to break down the tank's bulky appearance into separate sections, creating a balanced design that he felt was important close to housing, and in so doing he also emphasized its verticality. The Tonwell tank was cast *in situ* using smooth plywood shuttering, but later Percey turned to precast panels to give a more precise and interesting finish, contrasting heavy aggregates with board-marked *in situ* work to conceal staining.

Other examples of Percey's work in the Lee Valley are at Arkley and Cockfosters at the edge of London, and at Springwood and Silver Leys near Bishop's Stortford. Note, too, his later tanks at Baydon, Wiltshire, and Tadley, Hampshire.

Mural at Lee Valley Water Company

Chantry Lane, Hatfield, Hertfordshire

1964–5, William Mitchell

Listed grade II, 23 October 2012

Mural at the Three Tuns

Bull Yard, Coventry

1966, William Mitchell

Listed grade II, 15 September 2009

William George (Bill) Mitchell trained at the Southern College of Art, Portsmouth, and at the Royal College of Art before in 1957 he and Anthony Hollaway were employed by the London County Council as in-house artists. Mitchell established a successful consultancy producing concrete reliefs and sculptures, working with many leading architects.

Mitchell claimed that his mural – 5 x 2.43m (16½ x 8ft) – at Hatfield for a headquarters building, designed in 1961 by Edmund Percey of Scherrer and Hicks, was the largest single cast ever created. He created a negative mould by carving 25.4cm (10in) blocks of polystyrene set on formwork, over which the concrete was poured. It includes floral and Aztec totemic motifs (shown below), over which originally flowed a cascade of water. It was moved in 2014 and now forms part of a block of flats.

More Aztec motifs decorated the façade of a pub for Coventry architects W. S. Hattrell and Partners, a distinctive feature in an extension to the shopping precinct, Bull Yard.

University Centre

Granta Place, Cambridge

1964–7, Howell, Killick, Partridge and Amis

Listed grade II, 18 February 2013

The University Centre was constructed as a response to the 1962 Bridges Committee, which identified a need for a meeting place for non-collegiate graduate students and young lecturers. It was funded by the Wolfson Foundation.

Bill Howell designed a series of precast concrete modules with chamfered corners, faced in Portland Roach stone panels very clearly bolted on as cladding. Howell, Killick, Partridge and Amis was one of the first firms to successfully exploit precasting, which gave a smooth, precise finish to their post-and-lintel construction. The building's highlight is the off-centre former fire escape stair leading from the roof, a turret of contrasting board-marked *in situ* concrete.

Inside, there are lead treads to the stairs (a traditional Victorian feature, reflecting Howell's tastes), which ascend to a series of meeting rooms designed for flexibility and adaptation. These are set on two sides of a double-height dining hall raised over the kitchen, the first in a series by the firm, its timber roof and pyramidal central lantern supported on steel ties.

Cripps Building
St John's College

St John's Street, Cambridge

1964–7, Powell and Moya

Listed grade II*, 31 March 2009

When St John's College appealed for donations towards a new building in 1958, it received support from an alumnus, C. Humphrey Cripps, who with his father funded the entire project. A site was selected by Leslie Martin, west of the River Cam and straddling the Bin Brook.

Powell and Moya's wriggling terrace, doubling back to create three-sided courtyards in confrontations with itself or the older buildings around it, was chosen ahead of pyramids proposed by Denys Lasdun. Its study bedrooms and fellows' flats are reached off eight staircases from an open ground-floor cloister. The generous budget permitted Portland Whitbed and Roach stone for the building's hefty vertical piers, whose rhythm is countered by bands of windows in bronze frames from Cripps's firm, bold concrete floor plates and overhangs to the penthouse roofs. The timber joinery to the stairs and rooms was skilfully detailed by the architects.

Powell and Moya's common room was replaced in 1987 by the bulky Fisher Building, but their residential accommodation was carefully refurbished in 2011–14.

Norfolk Terrace and Suffolk Terrace (the Ziggurats) teaching wall and library

University of East Anglia, Norwich

1964–8, Denys Lasdun and Partners

Listed grade II* (ziggurats) and grade II, 16 October 2003

Lasdun was commissioned in 1962 to produce a master plan and the first buildings for this new university, the third after Sussex had opened the way for new foundations. A large site was chosen alongside the River Yare, from which a lake was formed only in 1975–7. Lasdun was determined to preserve this open landscape, and placed his buildings where the valley starts to rise.

Lasdun's aim, like that of Chamberlin at Leeds, was for a 'five-minute university' with departmental buildings and residential accommodation close together. He thus proposed a long teaching spine flanked by students' flats, with a library in a central green 'dry dock', all linked by high-level walkways. The cranked spine also symbolized the links between subject areas where academic research was concentrating in the 1960s. The concrete construction combined *in situ* work with panels precision-cast on site, *in situ* service towers projecting from Lasdun's distinctive, crisply finished and very long horizontals.

Flats for students were cheaper than traditional halls and recognized as more progressive, with 12 students sharing a kitchen/diner and creating a supportive social grouping equivalent to that of the Oxbridge staircase. Each flat is set back and partially lowered so that its sill level meets the roof of the flat below. This stepped section and continuous profile, with each elevation at 90 degrees to the next, has led to the terraces becoming known as the Ziggurats. Only two lines of ziggurats were completed before Lasdun's contract was terminated in 1968, but they remain the boldest architecture of any new university.

Since the listing the library has been extended, and the university continues to expand.

History Faculty

Sidgwick Avenue, Cambridge

1964–8, James Stirling

Listed grade II, 13 April 2000

In December 1962 Stirling and James Gowan were invited to enter a competition for a history faculty building. The design was substantially Stirling's and the partnership split a year later.

The centrepiece of the building is the great library, its glass roof inspired by nineteenth-century reading rooms. It is bookended by two blocks at right angles housing common rooms, seminar rooms and tutors' rooms. The impact comes from the library's segmental, easily supervised form, clear space and exposed roof structure. The building occupies a pivotal place in Stirling's oeuvre, in which his synthesis of Le Corbusier's Maisons Jaoul with industrial England's red-brick tradition was first tempered by a symmetry inspired by Sant'Elia.

The building remains controversial. Despite an innovative ventilation system and subsequent enhancements it can overheat, a problem not aided by its southern orientation after Stirling adapted the design to a reduced site. In 1980 falling tiles from its façades led the university to consider demolition; instead, most were replaced with brickwork.

39 New Road

Barton, Cambridgeshire

1965, Barry Gasson and
John Meunier

Listed grade II, 3 July 2012

John Wendon had purchased the British licence for a Swedish heating system and wanted a house to publicize it. Leslie Martin introduced him to the architects. Their scheme revolved around a central square light well, defined by giant piers and with a family living area at its base, from which a Corbusian ramp climbed to the other rooms. At the top a kitchen, dining room and parlour, with a roof terrace, fulfilled Wendon's brief for separate parents' spaces. The entrance was originally via external stairs to a midway point, but a later architect owner, Viren Sahai, made a new ground-floor entrance in 1997.

The house has a fortress-like demeanour. Each external wall is punctuated only by two vertical windows, of the same width as the ramp and running the full height of the building. There is an overriding intellectual formality here, in the plan and in the modular concrete block construction. Gasson and Meunier met while teaching at Cambridge, and similar qualities define their better-known Burrell Collection Museum, Glasgow, designed in 1971.

Spring House (Cornford House)

Conduit Head Road, Cambridge

1965–7, Colin St John Wilson and M. J. Long

Listed grade II, 13 April 2000

Christopher Cornford, painter and Dean of the Royal College of Art, wanted a house suitable for displaying works of art and for entertaining, and a secluded studio. Wilson based his design around a double-height living space, with a separate studio wing flanking the entrance forecourt. Their massing and the interplay of mono-pitched roofs are reminiscent of Alvar Aalto's Säynätsalo town hall (1950–2).

Inside is a more rigorous geometry. As at Wilson's Grantchester Road houses, there is a module, this time of 1.85m (6ft). A dominating axis leads from the hearth in one corner to a cutaway glazed section diagonally opposite, where an outdoor patio and stairs to a first-floor verandah link the indoor and outdoor worlds. This cut-out corner is at the apex of an internal timber gallery that overlooks the living room on two sides and gives access to the bedrooms. Under it are set the kitchen and dining areas. The strongly braced gallery, open roof and timber partitions give the house its great character and beauty.

Maltings Chase

Bures Road, Wissington, Suffolk

1967–8, Edward Cullinan

Listed grade II, 4 October 2007

Cullinan designed a series of houses while working part-time for Denys Lasdun. Maltings Chase was the second of two he produced for Gerald and Rosemary Knox, who became close friends.

Maltings Chase, which replaced a tuberculosis sanatorium, comprises two long, narrow wings, each reminiscent of Cullinan's own house in Camden Mews (see p.460). One is for adults and one for children, linked by a dining room-kitchen to form a courtyard plan. Although largely single-storey and with roofs of a constant height, the steep slope permits a double-height, galleried living room to the front and low stabling to the rear, where a grassed ramp leads on to the kitchen roof.

The walls are of Suffolk white brick, salvaged from a demolished chapel and farmhouse. Maltings Chase is thus the coolest of Cullinan's houses but also the most monumental, thanks to its Palladian proportions and deep eaves and exposed concrete beams that hint at Lasdun's contemporary Hill House, Hampshire. Cullinan's long, narrow, single-sloping (and often single-aspect) units also informed his public housing.

The Studio

Ulting, near Maldon, Essex

1967–9, Richard and Su Rogers
with John Young

Listed grade II, 3 July 2012

Richard and Su Rogers's first independent work was a house and studio for the artist and photographer Humphrey Spender, who in 1966 wanted a smaller house. His students at the Royal College of Art recommended that he approach Rogers or Norman Foster.

The site was the orchard of Spender's old house, where the architects set two single-storey rectangular units of identical size, one a house, the other the studio and carport. The roof light from Team 4's Creekvean (see p.301) was repeated at the centre of Spender's enclosed studio, but otherwise the appearance is very different, for here the architects adopted a braced yellow-painted steel external frame clad in lightweight steel sheeting. The house's front and rear elevations are entirely glazed, with sliding doors. Rogers and Foster had discovered steel to be more flexible and aesthetically satisfying than wet construction when working at Reliance Controls, Swindon (demolished), and Ulting repeats its braced structure. Inside are sliding purple doors.

Marychurch

Salisbury Square, Hatfield,
Hertfordshire

1970–1, George Mathers

Listed grade II, 4 April 2013

A Roman Catholic church was built at Hatfield in 1930, but became too small for the post-war new town. Proposals for expansion were delayed while the village centre was redeveloped, until as part of a bypass scheme land was secured in 1966 for a new building south of the old.

Although its faceted walls are actually twelve-sided, the church with its thickly rendered, piecrust walls and conical roof appears circular. The oculus to this cone is the brightest point within the church, for the inset windows round the sanctuary have *dalle de verre* in dusky green and blue by Dom Charles Norris and Dom Paulinus Angold of Buckfast Abbey that is the building's chief glory. The raised sanctuary area lies opposite the broad entrance hall and baptistery, where lighter glass prevails behind the large, abstract-shaped font by Andrea Godfrey, who also designed the welded steel screen that separates the seating and circulation spaces within the church. Paler glass is also found in the Lady chapel to the side.

Studio at Chapel House

Horham, Suffolk

1971

Listed grade II, 16 October 2002

Benjamin Britten was driven out of his home-cum-office in Aldeburgh by the sound of US aircraft, the pressures of public life and nosy tourists. Peter Pears, his partner, found them a retreat in Horham, some 24km (15 miles) away, in 1970. Later that year they commissioned a tiny brick studio, which was built at the furthest corner of the garden.

Britten agreed the design with his builder rather than his architect, Peter Collymore, who was extending the seventeenth-century house (separately listed). The result was no architectural gem – just a brick shed with a simple pantiled roof – but it has a large window giving a view across the Suffolk countryside so important in Britten's work. It was here that he composed his last major works, including the opera *Death in Venice*, the cantata *Phaedra* and his third string quartet.

The modest structure is listed for its historic interest, Britten perhaps consciously following Gustav Mahler in choosing an outdoor 'composing house' or shed for calm and isolation.

72-74 Water Lane

Histon, Cambridgeshire

1972, David Thurlow

Listed grade II, 3 July 2012

These semi-detached houses, their upper floors set within a continuous steep-pitched roof, present similar street frontages yet are very different inside. Thurlow's distinctive style of house, first established while working with Colin St John Wilson, is low-lying and fills the width of a plot. Flexible internal plans respond to the needs of his clients – here fellow architects Gerry Craig and Richard Powell, with their families – according to their different means. The former Craig House is largely open-plan, while the Powells' richer interior is a flowing sequence of living, kitchen and dining areas, with a concealed snug.

The houses' outstanding features are their sections. The cross-wall construction permits extensively glazed façades, while the first floor is suspended in the centre of each house, allowing extra height at each side to the room below. The recessed dormers serving the bedrooms have glazed cheeks that throw light into these living areas.

214 Chesterton Road

Cambridge

1972, Marcial Echenique

Listed grade II, 3 July 2012

Echenique was teaching planning at Cambridge University when he designed this two-storey, three-bedroom house in 1971. He looked to timber construction to realize a larger house than he could otherwise have afforded, designing a bolted frame of chemically impregnated Canadian hemlock built to a strict 3.8m (12½ft) grid around a central post. Walter Segal's contemporary and similar system became well known in the 1970s and 1980s, but Echenique's light yet substantial-looking house remains a one-off. It is clad in enamelled panels, which are left exposed inside and out – Echenique would not even hang paintings.

The house is set on stilts to combat a change in levels and to preclude damp-proofing. The double-height, south-facing living room incorporates a large glazed conservatory and a gallery lined with shelving for Echenique's many books. His office adjoined it at this level to one side, while a dining area adjoins the lower level on the other. Although Echenique lived here only a short time, the house remains remarkably little altered, and still requires little maintenance.

RAF Alconbury

Hardened aircraft shelters (4109 and 4110) and Avionics Building

Huntingdonshire

1983 and 1989, US Air Force

Listed grade II*, 10 September 2007

Established as a RAF base in 1938, Alconbury Airfield was used by the US Air Force during the Second World War and from 1959 for its reconnaissance squadrons. In 1983, U2/TR-1 spy planes were based there, leading to the construction of 13 aircraft shelters to accommodate their 31.39m (103ft) wingspan, which is unique in Europe. The shelters were 'hardened' to withstand the impact of a 227kg (500lb) bomb using reinforced concrete and steel, with round-arched roofs. Two are listed.

Images taken by the planes were processed in the avionics building, usually known as the 'Magic Mountain', the most sophisticated hardened Cold War structure remaining in England. Its prominent flat top was reinforced to resist a direct missile strike, and in addition to film processing, servicing and computer facilities it housed decontamination units and life support systems, including a compressed air repressurizing system in case of attack.

This is an unusual group of Cold War buildings. Operations ceased here in 1995.

Willis, Faber and Dumas, now the Willis Building

16 Friars' Street, Ipswich

1972–5, Foster Associates

Listed grade I, 25 April 1991

Nothing in this building seems dated. Yet its balance of technical innovation and extensive social facilities could only have been created in the early 1970s, when Willis, Faber and Dumas, the insurance broker, relocated its administrative staff to Ipswich and commissioned Foster Associates from a shortlist.

The four-storey, deep-plan building answers the contorted plot with a sinuous glass sheath hugging the road, supported on internal glass fins using patch fixings that have a 50mm (2in) tolerance. Reflective by day, dusk reveals glimpses of the spectacular interior created by Foster after careful studies of Willis's working practices. A concrete frame, its columns a mighty 14m (46ft) apart, and a sprinkler system enable the offices to open directly off paired escalators running up the building. The early service floor makes it easy to absorb changes in computer technology. The highlight is the top-floor restaurant and roof garden, where turf provides insulation and a recreational facility complete with a parapet hedge.

The dark glass, compact shape and services make this a low-energy building, while the yellow and green decoration repeats predominant colours within the lighting system. Willis was the first building of the 1970s to be listed, an indication of its seminal position in the evolution of High Tech from low-cost architecture into a richly detailed executive style, when there were proposals to infill a ground-floor swimming pool for more office space. It is now visible below glass slabs.

Willis pioneered the strategy of management guidelines that identify those elements crucial to the building's architectural integrity and working areas whose inherent flexibility should be acknowledged.

Sainsbury Centre for Visual Arts

University of East Anglia, Norwich

1977–8, Foster Associates

Listed grade II*, 19 December 2012

Sir Robert Sainsbury began an art collection in the 1930s, and with his wife Lisa donated it to UEA in 1973, promising a building where it could be enjoyed by students, staff and the public as part of their daily lives. Few art galleries had been built in Britain since 1945, and Denmark's Louisiana (Humlebaek) and Kunsten (Aalborg) museums of modern art provided models for a naturally lit, informal environment. The brief given Foster in 1974 also demanded teaching facilities and a restaurant.

Foster placed everything in a single, undefined space evoking a giant barn or airship hangar. It adjoins Lasdun's terraces but is separately aligned so the university cannot be seen from inside, and it appears to float in the landscape. Engineered by Anthony Hunt, a largely prefabricated portal frame gives a clear span, while a double skin (a late but crucial revision) conceals mechanical services; ancillary stores are in a semi-basement. Two mezzanines form exhibition floors over teaching rooms. The side walls and roof are clad in aluminium panels, installed in 1988 after previous panels and their insulation reacted chemically, with glazed ends as already used by Foster for the manufacturers Modern Art Glass. Inside the natural light is filtered through rooftop glazing, controlled by bands of aluminium louvres, and through further louvres at the sides. Circular fans are a design feature; the building's great height also aids natural ventilation.

Norman Foster's first public building, the Centre established his popular reputation. His Crescent Wing of 1991 is too young to be considered for listing yet, though the two buildings were linked by a long basement gallery in 2006.

Creekvean,
Feock, Cornwall,
1964–7, Team 4

Dartington Hall

near Totnes, Devon

Gardens redeveloped by Avray Tipping and Beatrix Farrand, and from 1945 by Percy Cane

Landscape registered grade II*, 12 August 1987

Leonard and Dorothy Elmhirst acquired the medieval Dartington Hall in 1925, where they promoted rural industries and a school to revive the extensive estate. They laid out grounds on rising ground south and west of the hall, aided in their private garden by Avray Tipping in 1927 and more extensively by Beatrix Farrand in 1933–9. Her work was continued in 1946–8 by Percy Cane, who made great steps down Heath Bank and opened vistas.

The centrepiece is the so-called tiltyard. This ornamental post-medieval ground, perhaps dating from as late as c.1800, was first adapted in 1954–5 as an open-air theatre, its wedge-shaped lawn surrounded by stepped grass terraces. Cane continued Farrand's emphasis on grass, shrubs and forest trees, with paved paths that acknowledged the stone of the ancient hall, and control of colour by giving camellias and rhododendrons their own walks. The one herbaceous border was revived by Preben Jakobsen in the 1980s. Exceptional sculptures include a donkey by Willi Soukop, and Henry Moore's memorial *Reclining Woman*, itself listed grade II*.

Locomotive turntable

Yeovil Junction Station,
Barwick, Somerset

1947, Cowans, Sheldon & Co.

Listed grade II, 4 September 2005

Yeovil Junction was opened by the London and South Western Railway in 1860. It became a busy junction for freight when, in 1864, the Great Western built a link to its Weymouth line, with a transfer shed (itself listed) and turntable.

A giant 21.33m (70ft) turntable was installed in 1947 for the new Bulleid Pacific locomotives operating passenger services from London, operated by the engine's vacuum brake system. It was used for engineers' track machines after the transfer shed was closed in 1952 and steam engines withdrawn in the 1960s. When, in 1993, British Rail proposed to remove the turntable, the South West Main Line Steam Company was formed, which today runs it as part of the Yeovil Railway Centre.

Large locomotive turntables in working order are rare, and it forms part of a historic group of railway structures.

Queen's Park

Groundwell Road, Swindon

1949–53, 1959–64, J. Loring-Morgan
and Maurice J. Williams,
Swindon Borough Council

Registered grade II, 8 August 2001

Proposals to convert a disused quarry and brickworks into a central park were first made in 1937, and were confirmed in W. R. Davidge's wartime plan for Swindon. Work began with a garden of remembrance, its flower beds aligned on an axis with a nearby church spire, which opened in 1950 on the site's north-west corner. The main park was completed in 1953 for Queen Elizabeth II's coronation, and is dominated by a big lake created from the clay pits. Eastward additions from 1960–4 were centred on an elaborate terrace with a pergola and conservatory, the latter demolished c.1992 save for raised brick display beds in its footings.

Post-war urban parks are rare. Queen's Park's fine ornamental trees and shrubs are displayed more informally than in its Victorian counterparts.

Barbara Hepworth Sculpture Garden

Barnoon Hill, St Ives, Cornwall

1949–61, Barbara Hepworth

Registered grade II, 30 January 2001

Barbara Hepworth (1903–75) moved to St Ives in 1939 with her then husband, Ben Nicholson. She purchased Trewyn Studio in 1949, and made it her home from 1951.

A sculptor who drew heavily on landscape for inspiration, Hepworth soon created a garden on the sloping, embanked site that was also an open-air studio and a setting for her work. She retained many artist's casts and 18 bronzes, including late works of monumental proportions, which with large stone carvings are displayed on three main terraces running north–south and a lower lawn to their east. There are mature Victorian trees and a small pool, between which Hepworth set plants chosen for their textural and sculptural qualities. The result is dense, green and almost sub-tropical. She extended the garden in 1965 when she acquired a greenhouse and adjoining land from a fellow artist.

The Tate Gallery opened the complex to the public after Hepworth's death in a fire there, in accordance with her wishes.

Former bus depot

Mallard Road, Charminster,
Bournemouth

1950–1, Jackson and Greenen

Listed grade II, 17 August 1999

Larger garages were needed for motor buses than for trams and trolleybuses. They also required uninterrupted spans, which strained steel supplies in the early 1950s, but which could be met by concrete shells. Reinforced concrete only 14cm (5½in) thick has massive tensile strength when cast as a cylinder or cone, as used in Germany from the 1920s. The earliest surviving shell roof in England is at the Wythenshawe bus garage, Manchester, of 1939–42.

This is the survivor of two garages in Mallard Road. The engineer Alfred Goldstein created the largest shell roof of its day, 91.4m (300ft) long by 45.7m (150ft) wide, and its nine cylinders were among the first British examples of prestressing to be published. The wavy roof and patterned brickwork walls add charm. The garage was originally built to take trolleybuses as well as motor buses, which determined its great height. Alongside is a wash house.

The depot closed in 2006 and was converted to a Homebase store, but the basic structure, including the main doors, survives.

Barclays Bank building

Armada Way, Plymouth

1950–2, Christopher Green
of Curtis Green, Son and Lloyd

Listed grade II, 22 September 2003

This was the first bank in Plymouth's civic precinct, one of the zones within Sir Patrick Abercrombie's ambitious plan for rebuilding the city centre following crippling war damage.

Barclays became a joint stock bank in 1896 and expanded rapidly across England. The London architect Curtis Green built a string of prestigious buildings for them in the 1920s in a classical style, and his son succeeded him in an extensive post-war programme. Classicism long remained popular for bank design as it suggested the durability of tradition and hence of savings entrusted there. On this prominent site the austere but subtly detailed exterior is enhanced by contrasts of Portland stone and granite, and by William McMillan's sculpted figures from Plymouth's old and recent history: Francis Drake and a Second World War fireman stand guard over the entrances to the banking hall.

Two further storeys were added in 2005–7, based on Green's original intentions, in a scheme by the Architects Design Group that converted the bank to restaurants and flats.

Festival of Britain bus shelter

Farmington, near Northleach, Gloucestershire

1951, Gerald J. Green

Listed grade II, 22 January 2008

The Council for the Preservation of Rural England and the National Association of Parish Councils both suggested that building bus shelters would be an appropriate way for villages to celebrate the Festival of Britain of 1951.

This was the first building by Green, a local surveyor, earning him £100 when it won the competition at Farmington. The site and materials were given by the local landowner, Colonel Raymond Barrow, who suggested a circular building modelled on his dovecote, but Green liked playing with angles and produced an octagonal design inspired by the 1898 pump house on the village green. The National Association recommended local materials 'so that the structures will fit harmoniously into the surrounding landscape'. Four local craftsmen realized the design in rubble and ashlar limestone, with a gable above the open front and a conical roof covered in Cotswold stone slates.

Garden Ground

193 Bulford Road,
Durrington, Wiltshire

1951–2, Robert Townsend

Listed grade II, 3 May 2007

Townsend is today largely remembered for his factory for Wilton Carpets and its innovatory timber shell roof (demolished), but he was personally more interested in designing houses and championing the genius of Frank Lloyd Wright. He wrote of Wright's houses reflecting man's soul, of having 'ying and yang', and they inspired his use of stone or – as here – earthy red brick, which he combined with timber eaves in a translation of the Usonian house to Wessex.

Townsend designed Garden Ground in 1949 for himself and his wife, a doctor whose surgery and dispensary occupied the front portion of the house. The centrepiece is a double-height living area set diagonally to the other rooms, as found in all Townsend's most ambitious houses. The interior is dominated by timber: hardwoods in the living room and kitchen with plywood elsewhere, including boarded roofs and built-in cupboards and shelving.

Townsend's career changed again when in 1965 he became a deacon of the Roman Catholic Church, for whom he produced most of his later work.

Medlycott Building and war memorial

Sherborne School, Abbey Road, Sherborne, Dorset

1954–6, Oswald S. Brakspear

Listed grade II, 4 October 1973

Sherborne School has medieval origins, but was expanded by an energetic Victorian headmaster, the Revd H. B. Harper, whose architects developed the old abbey in Gothic and Tudor styles.

Amazingly, Sherborne suffered bomb damage. By the 1950s, too, it needed more space, to provide improved teaching facilities as well as accommodate increasing rolls. A block of four classrooms was built with a central staircase and with two entrances to ease congestion between lessons. Named after Sir Hubert Medlycott, a long-serving school governor, its style was the seventeenth-century vernacular as popularized around Lacock in Wiltshire by Oswald's father, Harold Brakspear. Medlycott looks diminutive, yet its classrooms are surprisingly light and comfortable for large groups. It was listed, long before a '30-year rule' was formalized, as a prominent element in the school's central quadrangle or Great Court.

Brakspear also restored R. H. Carpenter's 'Big School' or assembly hall of 1879, remodelling the interior with a stage and large gallery, and adding a war memorial as part of a new entrance.

Royal Bank of Scotland

Old Town Street, Plymouth

1955–8, National Provincial Bank
Architect's Department
Chief architect, Brian C. Sherren
Assistant in charge, A. E. Souter

Listed grade II, 20 August 2009

This quirky building perfectly suits one of Plymouth's most important sites, being the visual terminus of the department stores lined along Royal Parade. The National Provincial Bank, established in 1918, quickly showed the greatest architectural ambition among Britain's clearing banks and Sherren's vigorous department continued this tradition in the 1950s.

The granite columns of the square portico stand sharp against a background of turquoise mosaic, particularly striking when backlit at night, while the curved copper roof is crowned by an illuminated clock tower of blue glass. Cladding panels are consciously expressed as a veneer. Other ornamentation celebrates the heritage of Plymouth and the bank itself, with gold emblems in the mosaic and in the glass side doors, while the bronze front doors are studded with roundels depicting ancient coins. Such stripped yet richly decorated neoclassicism, its sources in 1920s Scandinavia and Italy, was regularly depicted in post-war reconstruction plans but rarely realized. St Petersburg's curiously similar Finland Station is slightly later.

AA box 137,
A39 west of
Porlock, Somerset
9 January 1989

AA box 372,
A556, Chester Road,
Mere, Cheshire
31 January 1989

AA box 442,
A684 east of Aysgarth,
North Yorkshire
6 April 1988

AA box 456,
A3052, Half Way
Inn, near Newton
Poppleford, East Devon
9 January 1989

AA box 487,
A591 between
Grasmere and
Thirlmere, Cumbria
27 January 1987

AA box 530,
A149 west of
Brancaster
Staithe, Norfolk
20 November 1987

AA box 573,
Garrowby Lodge,
near Bishop Wilton,
East Yorkshire
11 July 1991

AA box 817,
B1340, Beadnell,
Northumberland
17 November 1987

AA boxes

1956, Enham Industries for the Automobile Association

Listed grade II

The Automobile Association was founded in 1905. Its first sentry box was installed at Newingreen, Kent, in 1911 as a shelter for patrolmen, but later boxes housed telephones so that AA members could contact a breakdown patrol or make emergency calls. By the 1930s they were also a shelter for motorists, and provided maps and a fire extinguisher.

In 1956 a new standard Mark IV design was introduced: square timber boxes painted black and yellow, with a gable on each side containing the AA's winged logo. Other crests and the box number appeared on the sides and there was originally a small window in the door.

There were 787 numbered boxes across Great Britain when they began to be phased out in 1968, of which 21 survive *in situ* with others in museums. The biggest concentration is in the Grampians, but eight in England are listed. Their winged logos were restored in the 1990s, and the box at Mere was largely rebuilt after being hit by a motorist.

The photograph shows the AA box at Porlock.

Church of the Ascension

The Lawns, Crownhill, Plymouth

1956–7, Potter and Hare

Listed grade II, 25 September 1998

Robert Potter trained under W. H. Randoll Blacking, who was a pupil of Sir Ninian Comper, a church architect greatly admired by John Betjeman. The rectangular plan and free-standing baldacchino of Comper's St Philip's Church, Cosham (1937) inspired similar features here.

Potter and Hare's use of local stone enriches the 'contemporary' styling of the angled walls, tapered tower and a concrete butterfly roof painted red. Placing the choir in a rear gallery, rather than in front of the congregation, had been explored in the 1930s, but Potter refined the idea by setting his gallery in front of a full-height baptistery so that sound could filter down from front and back. Jacob Epstein was commissioned to design glass roundels behind the sanctuary but died after making only a few sketches, and Geoffrey Clarke substituted more abstract designs. Robert Medley decorated the baldacchino. This church defined Potter and Hare's distinctive mix of traditional materials with modern construction, bold stylistic form and works of art.

Mary Harris Memorial Chapel of the Holy Trinity

Exeter University

1956–8, E. Vincent Harris

Listed grade II, 29 March 1988

Few modern university campuses have a free-standing chapel, but this was a personal bequest from its architect Vincent Harris in memory of his mother. A perspective was exhibited as early as 1943, which shows a symmetrical composition at the centre of a formal axis down the hillside towards the city. Harris continued the scheme even after he was dismissed in 1953 in favour of William Holford, who abandoned the axis. He softened his original neo-Georgian proposals with two pairs of tall Elizabethan bay windows similar to those on his nearby laboratories of the 1930s. One of his smallest and most perfect buildings, it was delayed until building licences were lifted.

The interior has a tranquil austerity, its oak pews set in collegiate fashion facing whitened walls, gently lit by clear-glazed bay windows. The only colour is in the ceiling, a muted mural of abstract geometry by Thomas Monnington, who had just painted a similarly subtle ceiling for Harris at his Council House in Bristol (1937–56).

Unitarian Church

Notte Street, Plymouth

1957–8, Richard Fraser
of Louis de Soissons Partnership

Listed grade II, 17 September 2008

Baptist Church
and Hilliard Hall

Catherine Street, Plymouth

1957–8, Richard Fraser
of Louis de Soissons Partnership

Listed grade II, 10 December 2008

Plymouth's two oldest dissenting congregations, with seventeenth-century origins, both occupied large chapels that were destroyed in 1941. Under Patrick Abercrombie's plan for Plymouth's rebuilding, they were offered sites behind the restored parish church close to the civic centre.

Louis de Soissons came to prominence as the architect of Welwyn Garden City, but his enlarged post-war practice also opened an office in Plymouth. Comparisons with neo-Georgian-style churches in New England seem particularly pertinent here. These examples are sideways to each other: the Unitarians' square with a central spire; the Baptists' complex, including a hall and schoolroom linked by an arcade to the church, its spire completed only in 1959. Overhanging gables on brackets have their source in Inigo Jones's St Paul's Church, Covent Garden.

Both churches have little-altered interiors that are brightly lit and dominated by murals, that in the Unitarian Church by local artist Jack Pickup, that for the Baptists painted by leading church muralist Hans Feibusch in 1960.

Devon County Hall

Topsham Road, Exeter

1957–64, Donald McMorran

Listed grade II*, 24 April 1998

Like McMorran's smaller, contemporary Cripps Hall outside Nottingham, Devon County Hall is reassuringly undramatic, yet it is monumental in the simplicity of its detailing.

McMorran's buildings stand in the grounds of two earlier houses, including the grade II* Belair, which contains members' rooms. The council chamber and committee rooms occupy the adjoining range, its superior status and greater architectural complexity denoted by a broad clock tower. It is entered through a groin-vaulted carriageway that leads into an arcaded entrance hall. This space, with walls of polished Purbeck marble, echoes the staircase hall at Edwin Lutyens's nearby Castle Drogo. The Ionic columns of the staircase landing are the only explicitly classical elements, other detailing reflecting more recent Scandinavian design. The offices are arranged around courtyards, their long corridors developed as cloistered walks on the ground floor.

McMorran's characteristic round-arched arcading and blocky features such as the bell tower, contrasted with large areas of blank walling, display a confident use of classicism on a large scale.

Central Government War Headquarters

Corsham Mines

1957–70, Ministry of Defence

Various sections scheduled, 20 March 2013

The building of the Great Western Railway through Box in 1837–41 revealed rich seams of Bath stone. There were 96.5km (60 miles) of tunnels dug, but mining was in decline when in 1935 they were identified for a wartime ammunition store, and the bombing of the Bristol Aeroplane Company in 1940 encouraged the building of an underground factory. This monstrous conceit was purchased in 1954 to become Britain's emergency seat of government should London be destroyed. Access shafts were fortified and new ventilation, telephone exchanges, a radio room and a documentation system installed, as well as offices, kitchens and accommodation for government departments and the War Cabinet. Up to 4,000 personnel could be housed for 30 days.

Declassified in 2004, the headquarters remains an eerie embodiment of the Cold War, sealed behind thick blast walls. It remains legible thanks to the fittings and signage installed to ensure the smooth running of a meticulously detailed, strictly hierarchical plan. The mines' earlier history is also protected by scheduling, and wartime murals by Olga Lehmann are listed.

Neck Building

Boscombe Pier, Bournemouth

1958–60, John Burton, Bournemouth Borough Engineer's Department

Listed grade II, 8 December 2004

Boscombe Pier was built in 1888–9 for visiting boatmen and was acquired by Bournemouth Corporation in 1904. It was reconstructed after wartime breaching, and subsequently a new building was added at the 'neck' or landward end to promote the British seaside's revival. A bastion on the beach supports a line of kiosks at road level, boomerang-shaped and with a central entrance to the pier. Each element is expressed in a different material: concrete and stone for the bastion, a thin concrete slab roof supported on tapered piers, large areas of glazing over the shops and timber end canopies, with blue tiling facing the sea. A building at the seaward end has been demolished.

The sweep of the cantilevered roof is particularly joyous. This was a building despised (or simply ignored) by architectural critics as typical of the 'contemporary' style in the 1950s but which can now be celebrated. It is also a rare example of pier architecture from these years.

A £2.4 million restoration programme was completed in 2008.

Civic Centre and Civic Square

Armada Way, Plymouth

1958–62, Jellicoe, Ballantyne and Coleridge with H. J. W. Stirling

Listed grade II, 21 June 2007
Landscape registered grade II,
9 April 1999

Patrick Abercrombie replanned Plymouth with precincts bestriding an axis from the railway station to the Hoe. Perspectives showed a classical civic centre and guildhall separated by a great square, until in 1954 the city architect Hector J. W. Stirling designed a 14-storey curtain-walled tower inspired by Gordon Bunshaft's Lever House in New York.

But when Stirling then asked for more staff, an outside firm was brought in. Geoffrey Jellicoe and Alan Ballantyne made few alterations to his design save for introducing granite and slate spandrel panels, and finessing details. The office tower has a cantilevered butterfly roof and a mural by Mary Adshead; lower ranges hover on pilotis above reflecting pools. The two-storey council house alongside has etched glass by John Hutton and abstract panels by Hans Tisdall.

Jellicoe felt a combination of 'dignity and frivolity' was needed in the square. His curvilinear pools, seats and paving recalled the intricately informal style used at the Festival of Britain. The council is looking to sell the centre.

St George's Church

Darby's Lane, Oakdale, Poole, Dorset

1959–60, Potter and Hare

Listed grade II, 25 September 1998

St George's is a development of the ideas explored in Robert Potter's Church of the Ascension, Plymouth, within a more complex plan and on an unusually large scale for a post-war church.

Here the material is principally brick, but again there is variety with stone and concrete dressings, particularly for the large mullioned windows, and the canted tower is also reminiscent of the earlier church. The scheme was initiated by the Mothers' Union, so Potter designed a large Lady chapel within the single space. Short transepts give the semblance of a crossing, where a very early Anglican example of a central altar is placed on marble steps. The west end more closely resembles that of the Ascension, with a choir gallery reached by a sweeping timber stair to its rear, where is set the large, vase-like stone font. Here, however, the bright colour is not in the ceiling, but in the green granolithic piers that line the church; their tulip-like shape and the faceted timber ceiling they support are reminiscent of Coventry Cathedral.

City (formerly Pannier) Market

Market Avenue, Plymouth

1959–60, Walls and Pearn

Listed grade II, 25 March 2003

The central market, founded in the thirteenth century, was crucial to retail traders in Plymouth following the bombing of the central shops, with even Marks and Spencer taking a stall. This importance is reflected in the scale of the new market, the last phase of the city's rebuilding.

Shell concrete was first used to give large spans and natural top lighting to German market halls in the 1900s, and was developed further in Britain from the late 1950s. Engineered by Albin Chronowicz, Plymouth's market hall is 45.1m (148ft) wide and 68.2m (224ft) long, housing 144 permanent stalls and day benches. Portal frames were raised, which were infilled with seven conoid shells that were prestressed and separated by glazing, a more efficient construction process than shells alone. Shops surround the open market on three sides, some with street frontages, and there is a fish market on the fourth, all under lower, individual wavy roofs. David Weeks designed the lively entrance murals. It was renamed as City Market in 2008.

St Austell Library

Carlyon Road, St Austell, Cornwall

1959–60, F. Kenneth Hicklin,
Cornwall county architect

Listed grade II, 24 April 1998

St Austell's branch library is striking for its combination of granite rubble walling and patent glazing on a neat steel frame, a delightful juxtaposition of old and new materials with a quirky shape and an open-plan interior. The elegance of the steel frame coupled with the light flooding through the continuous clerestory roof lights enforces the building's modern character inside.

The library was designed as the first phase of a new civic centre. It was planned for 12,000 books, with the lending library in the main space and a reference collection in a small gallery that provides a lower ceiling to the children's library beneath. An extension was subsequently added to one side, which uses the same rubble walling and has the same strong cornice line.

St Austell Library exemplifies the fine-quality architecture designed by Hicklin's department in around 1960. It was followed by Saltash Library (job architect Royston Summers), a diminutive version of Le Corbusier's Palace of Justice at Chandigarh, now sadly too altered to be listed.

Salisbury Crematorium

Barrington Road, Salisbury

1959–60, H. Rackham, borough engineer; Brenda Colvin, landscape architect

Crematorium listed and landscape registered grade II, 22 August 2012

A total of 66 crematoria opened in the 1950s, when an Act of Parliament encouraged municipal provision, and another 53, more elaborate, followed in 1960–6. Colvin, already interested in the cremation movement, was commissioned here in 1956 and was assisted by John Brookes.

The buildings are set close to the southern boundary of the sloping, triangular site, adjoining a cemetery. Northwards, woodland is bisected by grassy glades. The central glade, aligned on the chapel, is enclosed by a beech avenue, yews and magnolias, while others are more informally defined by clumps of single species such as red maple.

The buildings form a close-knit group around a courtyard garden and pool enclosed by a colonnade. Their style is Scandinavian, jaunty in the flèche of the chimney with chequerboard flint and stone across the chapel's façade. The brightly lit chapel interior is finished in random Portland stone and white boarding, contrasted with exposed aggregate in the concrete frame.

Listing was prompted by refurbishment proposals for the chapel, since revised.

Parkham Wood House

Parkham Road, Brixham, Devon

1960, Mervyn Seal

Listed grade II, 5 March 2009

Mervyn Seal had newly moved to Brixham when he was commissioned by John Brady to design a three-bedroom house on the steep site adjoining his hotel. Seal was given complete freedom but little time; the basic design was made in a day.

The house has a large frontage, but is only 3.4m (11ft) deep because of the site and a wish to maximize views to the sea. It is cantilevered on a concrete slab, with brick cross-walls and timber façades. Le Corbusier inspired the eye-catching, easily drained butterfly roof, derived from his unbuilt Maison Errázuriz, and popularized after the war by Marcel Breuer. Local boatbuilders constructed staircases inside and out, their treads cantilevered off central spines. The double-height living space, which appears large despite its narrow width, was inspired by the Unité d'Habitation. Other internal features are 'contemporary' in style, including a rough limestone wall lining the snug at one end of the living room, boarded ceilings and an original chandelier.

Seal built many houses in Torbay but this is the most imaginative and complete.

Antenna no. 1 (Arthur)

Goonhilly Satellite Earth Station, Cornwall

1960–2, engineers Husband and Co. with the General Post Office

Listed grade II, 26 March 2003
Upgraded to II*, 19 December 2008

Antenna no. 3 (Guinevere)

Goonhilly Satellite Earth Station, Cornwall

1972, The Marconi Company

Listed grade II, 19 December 2008

Goonhilly was the birthplace of satellite communication, where GPO scientists John Taylor and John Bray first developed a 25.9m (85ft) open parabolic reflecting dish aerial. It can move 360° horizontally and 90° vertically, based on steel bipods and roller bearings. A parallel development to the dish at Jodrell Bank, the system was adopted internationally ahead of its French and American counterparts. In 1962, this Antenna no. 1 received and sent signals to the first active communications satellite, Telstar, and received the world's first live television pictures.

Antenna no. 3 by contrast is a 29.6m (97ft) dish supported on a tapering concrete tower with counterbalance weights, an unusual design and suited for higher-frequency observations.

By 2004 there were 64 antennae at Goonhilly, making it the largest satellite earth station in the world, but it was scaled down by the GPO in 2006. It is now run commercially.

RC Church of Christ the King

Armada Way, Plymouth

1961–2, Sir Giles Gilbert Scott

Listed grade II, 24 April 2009

Occupying a prominent site near the Hoe, this was Scott's last work, paid for by an anonymous female donor on condition that the design was simple yet eye-catching. It was constructed posthumously. Although conservative for the early 1960s, it sums up Scott's career as a church architect in both its stripped Perpendicular style and its plan of a short nave with a narrow sanctuary. There is no clerestory; instead, passage aisles or walkways rise almost as high as the nave under lateral vaults behind the high arcades. The spare composition is simple and light, yet its lack of ornament gives the interior cohesion and a heightened drama. The most unusual feature for Scott is the slender, square tower.

Sir Giles's son Richard Gilbert Scott added the attached presbytery and hall in 1963, using a complementary style that results in a harmonious ensemble which has remained little altered since its completion. Since 1988 the church has been used primarily as the Catholic chaplaincy to Plymouth University.

Upper Lawn (Solar Pavilion)

West Tisbury, Wiltshire

1961–2, Alison and Peter Smithson

Listed grade II, 14 February 2011

The Smithsons bought a kitchen garden in 1958, whose wall incorporated two tumbledown early eighteenth-century cottages that they rebuilt as a tiny weekend home. They retained the outer wall and the western cottage, including an end stack that became the supporting wall at the centre of the new house. A new bay was added beyond it that gave views towards the woods surrounding William Beckford's Fonthill Abbey.

The materials reflect the brutalist aesthetic set out by the Smithsons in 1955, the rough stone walls contrasted with plywood internally. Upper Lawn presents a sleek box to the courtyard, large areas of glass combining with folding teak window frames to the lower floor and aluminium cladding to the classically proportioned piano nobile – left partly blind on the road frontage and reached internally by a fixed timber ladder. The second cottage, including another stack, became an enclosed patio landscaped by Alison. Upper Lawn was immaculately restored in 2002–3 by Sergison Bates, who renewed the Smithsons' kitchen and bathroom.

Severn Bridge and Aust Viaduct

M48, South Gloucestershire

1961–6, Sir Gilbert Roberts of Freeman Fox and Partners with engineers Mott, Hay and Anderson Architect, Sir Percy Thomas

Listed grade I, 29 May 1998

Wye Bridge and Bleachey Viaduct

M48, South Gloucestershire

1961–6, Sir Gilbert Roberts of Freeman Fox and Partners with engineers Mott, Hay and Anderson Architect, Sir Percy Thomas

Listed grade II, 29 May 1998

A road bridge over the Severn was proposed in the 1930s to regenerate industry in South Wales and the project was revived after the war. In 1947 the Ministry of Transport built a wind tunnel to test the aerodynamics of suspension bridges, which first defined the vertical and torsional stresses to which they are subject. This research informed Scotland's Forth Road Bridge, built in 1958–64.

For the Severn Bridge a more sophisticated, steel-plated box structure was developed. Its stability depended on the aerodynamic shape of an extremely shallow deck only 3.05m (10ft) deep and an inclined suspender system to reduce vertical motion. The similarly elegant towers, though over 121.9m (400ft) high, used remarkably little steel. An early fully welded steel deck, the Severn Bridge was the first in the world to be streamlined and supported on inclined hangars.

The M48 continues across the Bleachey peninsula over a viaduct, whence a cable-stayed bridge carries it into Wales over the River Wye. It has a similar aerodynamically shaped deck.

St Aldate's Church

Finlay Road, Gloucester

1962–4, Potter and Hare

Listed grade II, 26 November 1999
Upgraded to II*, 3 December 2013

The sale, in 1927, of the city-centre St Aldate's Church was used to fund a new parish in the suburbs. It was resolved to build a permanent church only in 1958, however, when the diocese recommended Potter and Hare. Their model was St Agnes, Fontaine-les-Grès, France (1956), visited with the New Churches Research Group.

The design, finalized in 1961, is dominated by a timber hyperbolic paraboloid roof, which Potter considered gave the church its 'thrust' or dynamic. It contrasts with fine brickwork and large areas of glass, while the church's fan shape encompasses two eastern chapels, one now part of the vestry. For added drama there is a needle-like concrete spirelet over the prow-like west end, where internally a choir gallery repeats a favourite Potter and Hare feature. This was their first interior with a mature liturgical plan, which creates an unexpected intimacy. Potter wanted to line the lower walls with slate, but the congregation requested iroko hardwood, copied in later screens and furnishings, along with clear glazing.

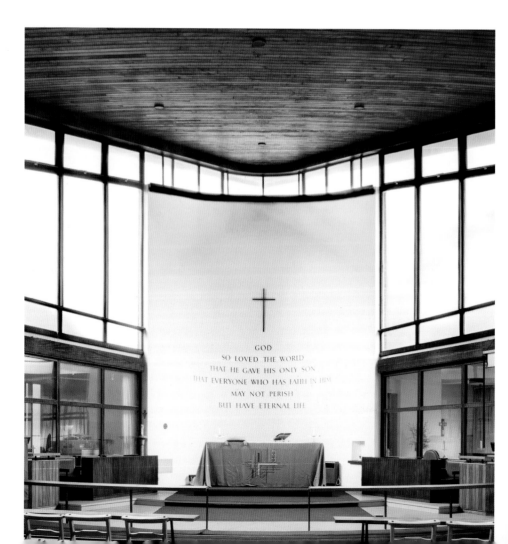

Lys Kernow/ New County Hall

Treyew Road, Truro, Cornwall

1962–6, F. K. Hicklin, county architect, with Geoffrey Jellicoe

Listed grade II, 24 April 1998

For years, Cornwall County Council struggled to build a new county hall in historic Truro until in 1959 it brought in Geoffrey Jellicoe, who found a site on the edge of the city and produced the initial design. Detailed by Hicklin, it resembles Le Corbusier's monastery of La Tourette enlarged and clad in granite aggregate panels. New County Hall hides its bulk through muted colouring, its articulation into smaller elements, and a colonnade of pilotis where the hillside falls away.

Closer inspection reveals still greater subtlety. It is built around a square terraced courtyard, landscaped by Jellicoe using local plants (just as he insisted on local aggregate) with a sculpture by Barbara Hepworth. The council chamber is cantilevered out on the east side over the entrance hall, and expressed as a solid wall on the courtyard side. It and the committee rooms were furnished by Interiors International, creating calm, sophisticated spaces, and hung with works by Cornish artists. Alterations to the building have been controlled to leave these spaces intact.

Taunton Deane Crematorium

Wellington New Road,
Taunton, Somerset

1963, Potter and Hare

Listed grade II, 25 September 1998

Potter and Hare came second in a competition for this crematorium, in 1956, but secured the commission. Characteristic of their style, rubble walling, concrete and copper roofs are blended harmoniously. The principal components are a high, light chapel, and a memorial chapel linked by a wide *porte cochère*.

The chapel contrasts rough walling with tall, narrow windows of coloured glass in muted greens and blues, deeply recessed and set in rough-textured aluminium frames. They were by the sculptor Geoffrey Clarke, who also produced the altar cross and candlesticks in textured aluminium. Across the driveway, the memorial chapel is as dark as the main chapel is light, a conical building lit only at clerestory level and with another cross by Clarke.

In a deceptively complex landscape by Peter Youngman, an open lawn to the front, with a cross reminiscent of that at Woodlands Cemetery, Stockholm, is balanced by a concealed sequence of gardens of remembrance either side of the memorial chapel; a cemetery was extended in 1969.

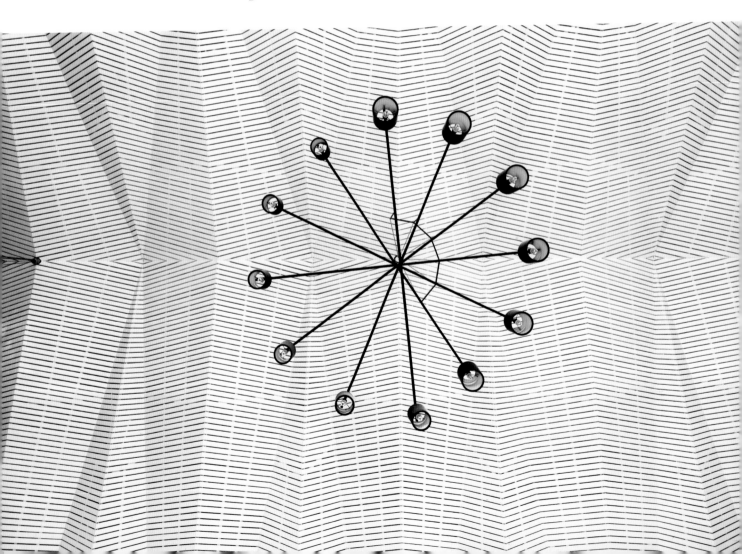

All Saints Church

Pembroke Road, Clifton, Bristol

1963–7, Robert Potter, to tower
of 1872 by G. E. Street

Listed grade II, 11 July 2001

All Saints was a powerful Victorian church by G. E. Street of 1863–72. Damaged by incendiaries in 1940, it could have been restored but instead a replacement was commissioned from W. H. Randoll Blacking, who died before work started on a scheme that retained only G. F. Bodley's narthex and F. C. Eden's sacristy.

Potter's solution to this mess was stunning. He linked the surviving fragments with a glazed cloister entered through Street's uncompleted tower and built a square church to the side. Street's church faced south, but Potter's is properly orientated. The altar stands beneath a baldacchino by Blacking with a piscina by John Skelton. The dominating feature is the vibrantly coloured Perspex glass by John Piper that fills the west and south windows, the latter set above a choir gallery. On the north side, Bodley's narthex became a chapel, where glass by Christopher Webb includes a window depicting the old church. All Saints stands opposite Clifton Cathedral and it is instructive to compare their contrasting forms of Catholic worship.

Stanton Guildhouse

Stanton, Gloucestershire

1963–73, Iorwerth Williams

Listed grade II, 11 June 1999

Stanton Guildhouse was created by Mary Osborn (1906–96), a devout Christian pacifist who met Mahatma Gandhi when teaching in London's East End in 1931. He encouraged her spinning lessons for the unemployed and later sent her a spinning wheel. She believed that there was a basic spirituality behind simple tasks and sought to create a semi-religious community supported by crafts and teaching.

In the war, Osborn moved to the Cotswolds, and her classes continued something of the area's crafts tradition at a time of technical change. She created a charitable trust, and a local architect experienced in restoration work produced a design using stone-faced concrete blocks with a stone slate roof. It was mainly built by volunteers, yet the workmanship is excellent. There is a central hall, with a weaving room, pottery workshop and dining room in the wings.

The Guildhouse, with its honest joinery and simple idealism, sits within the Cotswolds' Arts and Crafts Movement. It still provides courses in crafts and social work.

Creekvean

Feock, Cornwall

1964–7, Team 4 (Richard and Su
Rogers, Norman and Wendy Foster
with Laurie Abbott)

Listed grade II, 15 July 1998
Upgraded to grade II*, 9 May 2002

Creekvean was built for Marcus and René Brumwell, Su Rogers's parents and the founders of the Design Research Unit, who wanted a holiday home to indulge their passion for sailing. It demonstrates the architects' early enthusiasm for Frank Lloyd Wright, Louis Kahn and Alvar Aalto. The living and sleeping areas are divided by an external stair; its grassy treads resemble Aalto's Säynätsalo Town Hall and oversails the internal circulation areas.

Forticrete blocks and riven slate suited the unstable, rugged terrain high above Pill Creek, and quickly attracted lichens. The 'daytime' rooms on two levels form a low tower with slate stairs, including vertiginous steps to the grass-covered roof. The dining kitchen features an elegant free-standing steel unit by Su and full-height windows supported by neoprene gaskets. A gallery housed the Brumwells' exceptional art collection – its skylight all that remains from Foster's original designs for a cat-slide roof. The house's extended gestation turned the architects to steel construction. The house has been immaculately restored by sensitive new owners.

K8 telephone kiosk

1965, Bruce Martin

Listed grade II

The General Post Office held a competition in 1965 to find a successor to Sir Giles Gilbert Scott's iconic K6 kiosk of 1935, after Neville Conder's prototype K7 was abandoned in 1960. Unlike the K6, the new design was to have interchangeable components. It was also required to be easily maintained over a lifespan of at least 50 years, met by the use of cast iron and toughened glass. Martin's pedigree in designing series buildings was impeccable, for he had worked on the Hertfordshire schools and campaigned for modular coordination.

The K8 offered an unfussy contemporary approach, with clean lines and curves that eschewed Scott's neoclassical references, though its dimensions and appearance were respectful of its lineage. It was manufactured by the Lion Foundry and first installed in July 1968. A total of 11,000 had been introduced on to the United Kingdom's streets by 1984, but following privatization most were replaced by the utilitarian KX100, leaving Swindon as the K8's last stronghold. The photograph shows the kiosk at Langto Park.

Former Bath Cabinet Makers

Lower Bristol Road, Bath

1966–7, Yorke, Rosenberg and Mardall
Partner in charge, Brian Henderson

Listed grade II, 4 May 2007

Henderson had already designed office furniture for Bath Cabinet Makers when this factory was commissioned in 1964. It shows that Yorke, Rosenberg and Mardall could design sophisticated factories independently as well as in collaboration.

Henderson produced a flexible 5,295sq. m (57,000sq. ft) of space for storing furniture, as part of a linear flow from its manufacture in an adjoining factory (long demolished) to its dispatch at the opposite end of the new one. Its near-clear span is due to a Mero space frame, a lattice of short steel tubes that rest on just one line of columns to which tubes descend at 45° and are joined by spherical connectors. Mero, developed by Max Mengeringhausen from 1937, was the first space frame widely available in the 1950s; this was its first use in Britain. The cladding, chosen for easy maintenance, is made of asbestos sheets with a neoprene joint and anodized aluminium glazing on a black steel frame, making a consistent monochrome palette.

Closed in 2005, the factory was converted to a supermarket in 2014–15.

Valley Spring

Southstoke Road, Bath

1968, Peter Womersley

Listed grade II, 3 August 2011

John Womersley became the managing director of Bath Cabinet Makers and Arkana, furniture manufacturers, in c.1964 and in 1965 bought a nursery garden. The house built on its terrace was the third for him by his brother, in a romantic setting on the city boundary.

Peter Womersley's work for John charts the evolution of the post-war private house through contemporary, Miesian and brutalist styles. Valley Spring had to accommodate a family with teenage children, guests and an elderly mother, and to showcase modern furniture. Womersley had used a concrete frame for a house near Stratford-upon-Avon, which Valley Spring refines. In a three-dimensional or 'additive' approach on a proportional grid, he produced two dissimilar two-storey blocks and a single-storey range with its own entrance, linearly arranged around a central kitchen. Contrasting stands of hard, red brick walling include one concealing an open staircase, between which are areas of glazing between heavy timber sills and cornices.

The main spaces, with timber and tile finishes and built-in seating, survive.

Sheldon Bush lead shot tower

Temple Back, Bristol

1968–9, E. N. Underwood
and Partners, engineers

Listed grade II, 24 November 1995

Although its form was dictated by a precise industrial purpose, Bristol's lead shot tower is also a monument to local history. In 1782, the story goes, a dream showed Bristolian William Watts how to make lead shot by dropping molten lead mixed with arsenic from a great height into a vat of cold water. His technique is still used.

Watts's original tower in Redcliffe was demolished for road widening in 1968. Its replacement at a lead works 1.6km (1 mile) away was built to this exact principle, but the 42.67m (140ft) tower is made of raw, ribbed reinforced concrete and Y-shaped to separate the three components – lead 'drop', hoist and stairs, with a near-circular crucible room at the top and a pit at the base.

Closed in the 1980s, today the tower lies at the centre of an office development. The concrete has been cleaned and minor repairs undertaken, while most of the interior has been renewed; the crucible room can be hired for meetings.

Skip Shaft headframe

Geevor mine (Levant section),
St Just, Cornwall

c.1969

Listed grade II, 13 July 2011

The Levant mine occupies a valley running to the Atlantic Ocean and was worked between 1820 and 1930. In the late 1960s, a breach in the tunnel running under the sea was repaired and the Geevor mine expanded to work the Levant sections.

Thousands of timber headframes were once scattered through western Cornwall, but only three now survive, this being the best preserved. It stands on the cliff edge with two 1840s engine houses of the former Levant mine, one containing a unique steam-powered beam engine.

The headframe is a small wooden tower built over an access shaft through which miners were carried to and from their work; the winding wheel, the cage, and the furniture within the shaft all remain. Plywood cladding was applied when the shaft was employed, latterly, as part of the mine's ventilation system. It closed in 1990.

St Joseph's RC Church

The Square, Wool, Dorset

1969–71, Anthony Jaggard of John Stark and Partners

Listed grade II, 13 December 2013

The Welds are an ancient recusant family who built England's first post-Reformation Catholic church, in 1786–7, and in 1968 Sir Joseph Weld commissioned Jaggard to build in Wool, a village expanding thanks to nearby military bases.

St Joseph's is a small yet boldly massed rectangle composed of handmade brick and shuttered concrete, with a short pyramidal lantern built over the sanctuary. Stained glass was never commissioned, and the interior relies on the strength and quality of its materials, and the space frame roof engineered by L. G. Mouchel and Partners. The Space Deck system, developed in Somerset in the 1950s, was used for schools, offices and military buildings, but seldom for a church. The tile floor, solid benches and suspended strip lighting enhance the solidity and coolness of the space. The circular and oval forms of the Blessed Sacrament chapel and the baptistery to either side, the latter with the Weld family pew over, are separately expressed in brick.

RC Cathedral Church of SS Peter and Paul

Pembroke Road, Clifton, Bristol

1969–73, Sir Percy Thomas Partnership
Architects in charge, Ronald Weeks, E. S. Jennett and Antoni Poremba

Listed grade II*, 20 December 2002

A new cathedral was commissioned in 1965 to supersede Bristol's Pro-Cathedral of the 1830s. It claims to be the first cathedral in the world to accord completely with the new liturgy introduced by the Roman Catholic Church in the early 1960s. Its plan is more successful than that of Liverpool Metropolitan Cathedral because it places the top-lit sanctuary in front of a fan of seating for the congregation, so the celebrant can see everyone at once. The entrance is to the side, where a screen with glass by Henry Haig shields views of the main space and provides the one burst of colour. William Mitchell carved the Stations of the Cross in wet concrete, with just 1½ hours to complete each one.

Built in a remarkably short time to a limited budget, the rough, wigwam-like exterior does not prepare one for the quality of the interior, which combines serenity and simplicity with craftsmanship in the concrete detailing. Listing followed a grant from English Heritage.

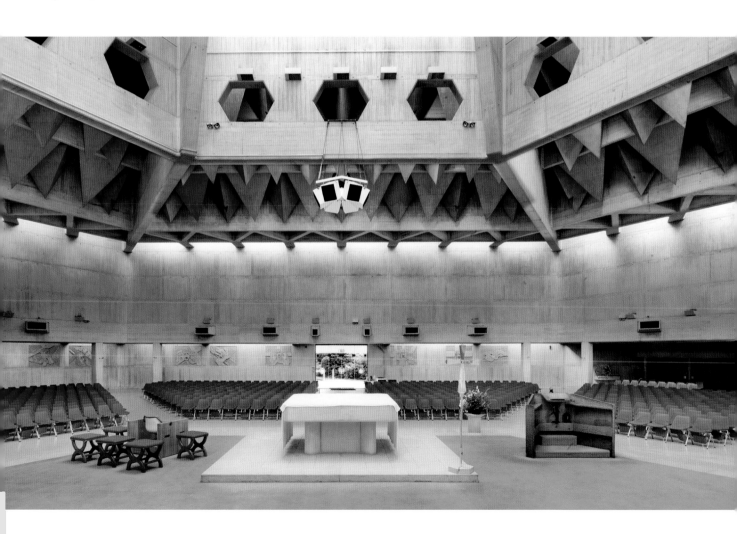

Rigg Side (Anderton House)

Goodleigh, Devon

1970–1, Peter Aldington
and John Craig

Listed grade II*, 24 July 1998

Rigg Side has strong affinities with Aldington's houses in his adopted Buckinghamshire, but it also responds to a different landscape and vernacular tradition. Here is a modern interpretation of the traditional Devon long house, with a carport at one end of its low, rectangular shell instead of a byre. The other end is clear-glazed, with doors to a patio.

The brief was refined over a year of meetings between Craig and the clients, Mr and Mrs Anderton. She was obsessively tidy, but her less tidy husband did not want to be shut away in a separate office, so Aldington designed a study in a low-walled pod that separates the kitchen from the living room on a lower level. The square pod is countered by a circular bathroom at the junction between the living areas and the more secluded bedroom wing.

The house was designed around the Andertons' traditional furniture, while featuring built-in cupboards and fittings by Aldington. It was restored by the Landmark Trust in 2002.

Lakeside, former head office of W. D. and H. O. Wills

Whitchurch Lane, Hartcliffe, Bristol

1970–5, Skidmore, Owings and Merrill, with Yorke Rosenberg Mardall

Listed grade II, 11 April 2000

The slick American image created by Skidmore, Owings and Merrill and Yorke, Rosenberg and Mardall for Boot's headquarters offices at Nottingham seemed right for the British arm of Anglo-American Tobacco in Bristol. The practices were commissioned in 1969 to design headquarters offices and an adjoining factory on the outskirts of Bristol. The factory was demolished in 1999, but the surviving office shell was acquired in 2003 by Urban Splash.

The buildings were constructed of CorTen steel, rich in manganese and vanadium, which rapidly oxidizes to a warm rust finish, and set in a valley landscaped by Kenneth Booth. Urban Splash have re-created Booth's lake, from which the main five-storey block rises on a broad podium, originally housing computers and social facilities. The podium roof itself is landscaped, its grid of paviours, gravel and planters mirroring the proportions of the architecture. The calm, flexible, neutral office spaces have given way to 273 flats reached from spectacular atria. The company village hidden in its own valley has been reinvented as a twenty-first-century housing community, completed in 2012.

Somerton Erleigh

Huish Road, Somerton, Somerset

1972–3, Stout and Litchfield

Listed grade II, 3 October 2012

Anthony Pretor Pinney had sold his ancestral home and wanted a new, small house when he saw Stout and Litchfield's house at Shipton-under-Wychwood (see p.341) illustrated in the *Architectural Review*. Approaching them in about 1968 with cuttings of Italian hill towns, he thought that a courtyard plan would suggest continuity with a nearby Roman villa. The site was determined by a large beech tree; otherwise the landscape sweeps up to the house, respecting planners' wishes that it sit lightly in its setting.

Tall stacks and blind walls in local lias rubble do suggest a miniature hill town. Shipton's lozenge-shaped units are repeated in mirrored pairs that conjure a complex roofscape with clerestories, and form a double-aspect living room and kitchen. These take up two sides of the courtyard, with bedrooms and utility rooms on the others, opening into it via sliding windows beyond a continuous circulation area defined by a timber arcade like a cloister. The result is a romantic confection of traditional elements in a modern guise.

Wildwood
(Courtyard House)

12A Western Avenue, Poole

1973–5, Richard Horden

Listed grade II, 1 February 2007

Horden designed Wildwood for his parents in 1970 when he was a student, because they had decided to sell their Edwardian family house. He had toured the United States by bus in 1968, and had admired the Californian Case Study Houses with their steel frames and open plans. His direct inspiration was Craig Ellwood's rigorously symmetrical house plans set across the whole width of the plot, as at the Daphne House of 1960 and Rosen House of 1961, both of which he visited. Other influences were Eliot Noyes and Robin Spence.

Wildwood is a rectangular house set in a walled courtyard surrounded by woodland, with an exposed, sturdy white steel frame that shields setback glazing incorporating sliding doors. Like Ellwood's best houses, there is a central double-aspect lounge and dining room, with bedrooms and a study in the corners. Horden not only transported a concept but American standards of detailing and finish. It secured him a job with Norman Foster, and informed his subsequent work in independent practice.

Herman Miller Factory

Locksbrook Road, Bath

1976–7, Nicholas Grimshaw
of Farrell and Grimshaw

Listed grade II, 16 August 2013

The American office furniture company Herman Miller established factories worldwide in the 1970s. It took over Bath Cabinet Makers (see p.304) and in 1975 held a competition for new premises across the river, won by Grimshaw with Jeff Scherer as chief assistant. The minuscule brief called for a welcoming and supremely flexible factory.

The structure is a steel frame on a regular, simple grid with just two rows of columns in the large, rectangular space. Its cladding is an interchangeable system of fibreglass panels, painted a stone colour, with curved corners, tinted glass and glass louvres. Entrances were also changeable, lavatories were constructed as pods that could be plugged into 16 locations, and other services were tucked into the roof behind its distinctive curved cornice panels. Grimshaw called it the 'Action Factory', acknowledging Herman Miller's 'Action Office' furniture manufactured here. The design evolved from earlier offices and warehousing in Tours, France, and enabled Grimshaw to define his own style. He founded an independent practice in 1980.

Renault Distribution Centre, now the Spectrum Building

Mead Way, Swindon

1981–3, Foster Associates

Listed grade II*, 18 September 2013

Pioneers of the hatchback, Renault aquired this greenfield site in 1979 for an enlarged parts distribution centre and after-sales training suite. The roofscape is the dominating element of Renault's signature yellow frame – corporate advertising without logos that endures despite the company leaving here in 2001.

All Foster's previous buildings had been elegantly sheathed clear-span sheds, but Renault responds to a widespread shift across High Tech architecture towards expressive structures. It has a grid of 42 linked columns or masts from which the roof hangs on tapered steel I-beams patterned with holes (to reduce weight), linked as portal frames and supported by high tensile rods, bolted for flexibility in high winds. An early piece of computer-aided engineering from Sir Ove Arup and Partners, it was a brilliant solution to the problem of wind uplift using traditional components; the membrane roof covering derives from the fabric technology of hovercraft skins. The columns are free-standing at the building's edge, and at its sharp prow one open module forms a dramatic *porte cochère*.

SOUTH CENTRAL

St Catherine's College
Manor Road, Oxford
1960–6, Arne Jacobsen

River Cherwell footbridge

off South Parks Road, Oxford

1949, Alfred Goldstein
of Travers Morgan, engineers

Listed grade II, 29 May 1998

This little portal frame footbridge crosses the tail of the Parson's Pleasure weir and now forms part of the Marston cycle track. It claims to be the first prestressed fixed arch bridge in the world, and was certainly the first statically indeterminate prestressed concrete bridge in Britain.

Most of the bridge was formed on site. The only precast elements were the prestressed concrete planks forming the walking surface, which have subsequently been replaced by an *in situ* concrete slab.

Due to the difficulties of securing a building licence, Goldstein designed the parapets using aluminium rather than steel, then novel.

Rhinefield Bridge

near Brockenhurst, Hampshire

1949–50, E. W. H. Gifford,
Hampshire County Council

Listed grade II, 29 May 1998

Rhinefield Bridge was among several little bridges built across the New Forest during the late 1940s, and carries a minor road over a stream. It was the first to be constructed of precast units, which were post-tensioned using the Freyssinet system and stressed together transversely. The bridge's slight vertical curvature made the longitudinal cables straighter, which reduced friction and produced a very attractive design that sits harmoniously in the landscape. The Freyssinet system of prestressing, first patented in England in 1938, reduced the amount of steel required at a time of shortages and licensing.

Gifford went on to enjoy a successful career in private practice, and worked extensively with the church architects Potter and Hare.

Nuffield College

New Road, Oxford

1949–57, Harrison, Barnes and Hubbard

Listed grade II, 30 March 1993

William Morris, Lord Nuffield, the Oxford car manufacturer, in 1937 proposed a postgraduate college in his name dedicated primarily to social sciences. The university's chosen architect, Austen St Barbe Harrison, produced a dramatic neo-Byzantine scheme in the style of his earlier work in Palestine, but Nuffield's demand for gables and pinnacles won out.

Harrison's revised design, following a cycle tour around Chipping Camden, was delayed by the war and subsequently became more austere as revised by Robert Hubbard. The distinguished tower – by Hubbard and containing a book stack – adds an impressive note to Oxford's skyline, its setbacks and spire reminiscent of Lutyens's St Jude's, Hampstead Garden Suburb, London (1915), but with Scandinavian-inspired fenestration.

The college consists of two long quadrangles, each with a pool and all the ranges have gables and hood-moulded windows. Imposing internal spaces include the dining hall with its marble floor and oak roof, and a chapel in the roof space with glass by John Piper and Patrick Reyntiens.

Former RAF Upper Heyford

Heyford Park, Oxfordshire

Nose dock hangars and control tower
1950–1

Squadron headquarters
late 1970s

Listed grade II, 7 April 2008
Site scheduled, 30 November 2006

A Royal Flying Corps station was first established at Upper Heyford in 1915. It was granted to the United States Air Force Strategic Air Command in 1950, and was used by B-47 Stratojets so large that special hangars were built that sheltered only their nose and engine sections. Similar hangars were built elsewhere for the American forces but these are unique in being of aluminium at a time when Britain led in the use of the material – the contemporary Dome of Discovery for the Festival of Britain was the world's largest aluminium structure.

The steel-framed control tower was built to a standard design as part of the base's remodelling for the Americans. More buildings followed in the 1970s when Upper Heyford was used for US F-111 bombers, with angled, windowless, hardened shelters of heavy reinforced concrete as a protection against attack. The squadron headquarters is most impressive as it retains its briefing room and decontamination facilities.

The site is important for its long aviation history and is now in commercial use.

St Crispin's School

London Road, Wokingham, Berkshire

1951–3, Ministry of Education
Architects and Building Branch

Listed grade II, 30 March 1993

In 1948 Stirrat Johnson-Marshall, mastermind of the Hertfordshire schools' programme, was headhunted by the Ministry of Education. His new development group expanded prefabrication into multistorey structures for secondary schools and revised layouts.

St Crispin's was the first of the Ministry's model 'secondary modern' schools, designed in 1949–50 by Mary Crowley and David Medd, recruited from Hertfordshire on their marriage, and Michael Ventris, decoder of the Minoan cypher, Linear B. They revised Hills's prefabricated steel-framed system used in Hertfordshire to the Ministry's near-metre module (3ft 4in). More innovative was the informal planning, particularly of single-storey art and technical areas that sought a distinctive character for the ill-defined training prescribed for secondary moderns under the 1944 Education Act. St Crispin's dispersed plan was repeated throughout England.

Fred Millett, a specialist in school murals, depicted the seasons through local rural activities. His *Summer* and *Autumn* in the entrance hall were restored in 2011–12 by the Perry Lithgow Partnership, who then re-created *Winter* in 2013.

Man-Carrying Centrifuge Facility

Building F49A, RAF Institute of Aviation Medicine, Royal Aircraft Establishment, Farnborough

c.1952–5, Air Ministry

Listed grade II, 16 August 2007

The Institute of Aviation Medicine (opened in 1945) developed a centrifuge to test the ability of pilots and equipment to withstand extreme acceleration and G-forces in high-speed jets and, later, space travel. It is set in a four-storey concrete drum, which is flanked by administrative, medical and research facilities.

Inside the drum, a cross-braced metal centrifuge arm rotates on a central shaft with a 9.14m (30ft) radius. It has a gondola at either end, each aping an aircraft cockpit, though only one is used at a time. Concealed above are two cranes for installing and servicing machinery. This gondola reaches nearly 30 revolutions per minute (9G) for manned experiments, and more when testing equipment. Tests on pilots are supervised by a doctor from a central observation station at the hub, and the 1950s control system remains substantially that used today.

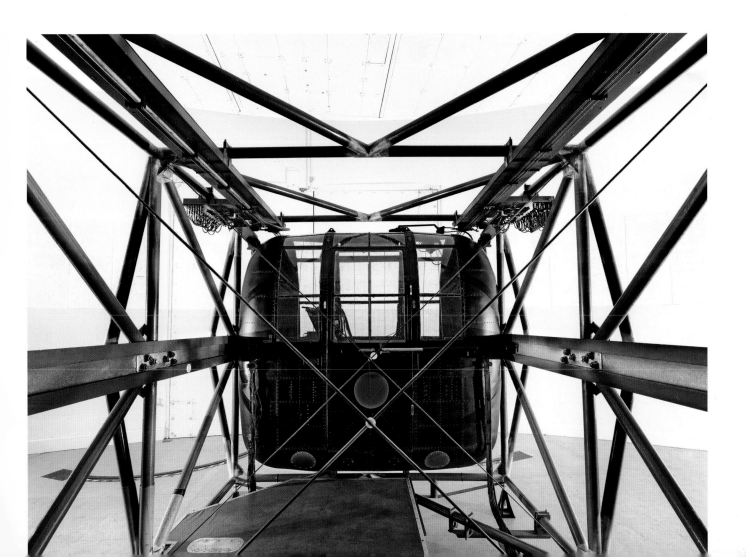

Church of St John the Evangelist

St John's Road, Newbury, Berkshire

1955–7, Stephen Dykes Bower

Listed grade II, 29 March 1988

A lone bomber in May 1943 destroyed William Butterfield's Tractarian church here. Dykes Bower's rebuilding reflects and enhances many elements of Butterfield's brash style at a time when Victorian architecture was still unfashionable and church polychromy painted over.

Dykes Bower's narrow red and grey bricks were handmade locally, and are more beautiful than their predecessors. The saddleback tower is derived from Butterfield's work here and at the Church of St Alban the Martyr, Holborn, but is loftier, as is the church itself. It appears taller still because of the painted ceiling, which incorporates built-in lighting. The east end has glass by Goddard and Gibbs that incorporates Victorian fragments, and a painted tester; it needed little decoration in addition to that supplied by the architecture.

Dykes Bower was a follower of F. C. Eden who worked at nearby Wash Common. He combined new churches with restoration work that confirmed his belief in a continuity between past and present, and is best known for his additions to St Edmundsbury Cathedral.

Queen Elizabeth II Court

County Hall, Upper High Street,
Winchester, Hampshire

1955–9, Cowles-Voysey,
Brandon-Jones, Broadbent
and Ashton

Listed grade II, 24 April 1998

Charles Cowles-Voysey, son of C. F. A. Voysey, was commissioned in the 1930s to build new offices, an art school and a library for Hampshire County Council. After the war only offices were required, so the scheme was redesigned as a quadrangle by John Brandon-Jones. He was instrumental in the post-war reappraisal of Philip Webb and W. R. Lethaby through his teaching at London's Architectural Association, while the influence of Dutch architects A. J. Kropholler and Hendrik Berlage suggests what might have been had Winchester been colonized by more recent North Europeans.

A Purbeck stone plinth and the use of small tiles in the roof eaves are deft local touches, while the dormers follow Webb prototypes. The Hampshire hog weathervane is by Laurence Bradshaw. The Arthurian influence is more clearly seen internally, where lean, neo-Saxon stone columns decorate the entrance halls. Art school staff created much of the decoration, including a map of Hampshire in the single committee room.

Woodside School

Mitchell Walk, Amersham, Buckinghamshire

1956–7, Ministry of Education Architects and Building Branch

Listed grade II, 30 March 1993

The first model schools erected by the Ministry of Education's development group looked at lightweight building systems in steel and concrete. But Amersham proved a turning point, where Mary and David Medd rationalized traditional brick construction to make it economical. This became a feature of their later work and that of Buckinghamshire, which ploughed a lone furrow for conventional construction in the 1960s.

Brick demanded thick, expensive cross-walls to support the roof. The Medds minimized these, pairing classrooms by age group and introducing more flexible planning. Woodside was the first Ministry school to address the specific needs of junior schools, offering more space for messy activities and science, while a central courtyard with a pond encouraged gardening and nature activities. Woodside also pioneered a range of furniture, and Dorothy Annan designed tiles around the sinks depicting fish, hedgehogs and snails, now gone.

The school has been carefully extended and modernized.

Provost's Lodgings

The Queen's College, Oxford

1958–60, Raymond Erith

Listed grade II, 30 March 1993

Erith's brief was for a house combining dining and reception rooms for college functions with accommodation for the provost's family. It assumes a different character on each elevation. To the south, Erith retained an abutting brewhouse as garages, and to the west is a driveway, and the garden elevation to the east has the simplicity of a Georgian vicarage although with a central belvedere lighting a first-floor lobby.

Still more austere is the frontage facing Queen's Lane. It is one of Erith's masterpieces and is deliberately formal, with few windows because it stands on the street. While the planning and top lighting of the upper floor owes something to John Soane and to Burlington's Chiswick Villa, this façade has more direct references to Palladio's Palazzo Thiene, Vicenza, of 1542. The ground floor is rusticated, with a central door under a broad fanlight, flanked by two empty niches and two tiny barred windows. Over it is another niche, two narrow windows and a cornice.

'The Beehives'

North Quad, St John's College, Oxford

1958–60, Architects' Co-Partnership (Michael Powers)

Listed grade II, 30 March 1993

The Architects' Co-Partnership (ACP) was commissioned in 1957, on the recommendation of the architect and historian John Summerson, after the college rejected plans by its ageing Honorary Fellow, Edward Maufe. ACP's brief was for a building 'which would not be disturbing' to its historic surroundings, and sketches developed into a distinctive sequence of linked hexagons that was chosen by the college fellows unanimously. It was the first truly modern design in Oxford, just as Cambridge University was reaching the forefront of architectural thinking.

Powers's design is a honeycomb in Portland Roach stone, three hexagons deep, with the centre units filled by three top-lit staircases and two bathroom units. The undergraduate study-bedrooms are arranged off half landings, giving three floors overlooking the President's Garden and two facing the quad over a semi-basement bicycle store. The building is firmly of its times: Powers wrote of Oxford's 'spiky skyline, in which suddenly to insert a flat-roofed, flat-faced building – it was 1957! – would have been wrong'.

Warsash Maritime Academy

Warsash, Hampshire

1959–61, Richard Sheppard, Robson and Partners

Listed grade II, 30 March 1993

Richard Sheppard and Geoffrey Robson specialized in the 1950s in college buildings for local education authorities, producing neat, well-planned buildings on low budgets.

Warsash trains officers for the merchant navy, from cadets aged 17 to senior personnel. The buildings were originally hierarchical, and this can still be felt in the duplication of some facilities.

The Moyana Building is the social centre of the college, with dining and common rooms overlooking the River Hamble. The quality of materials gives this building its distinction: its lowest part is faced in brick headers set at angles, reminiscent of Alvar Aalto, while inside the timber floors are inset with a coat of arms, and curved ceilings are emphasized by long clerestories.

The Shackleton Building, alongside, houses the cadets. The original dormitories have been subdivided into single and double rooms around three staircases. The larger windows on the first floor denote tutors' suites, while the fourth floor has common rooms, with balconies for watching ships. It has the same neat detailing and attention to materials as its neighbour.

Staircases 16, 17 and 18, Brasenose College

Radcliffe Square, Oxford

1959–61, Powell and Moya

Listed grade II*, 30 March 1993

Powell and Moya became masters of squeezing additions into historic Oxford and Cambridge colleges, beginning with a backyard, 18m (59ft) wide, at Brasenose. Here they contrived a five-storey block with a single-storey link, containing 32 units. The plan skilfully revises the Oxford staircase tradition, with a raised courtyard and ground-floor passageways that bisect the taller building.

That this was combined with some of the most forcefully modern architecture of its date in Britain is a still greater achievement, especially given Oxford's architectural conservatism hitherto. Early drawings show a functional composition with stone walling and a grid of windows, but in a delay while Brasenose reconsidered their budgets, Moya evolved the firm's mature style. Portland Whitbed and Roach stone is contrasted with exposed concrete floor plates and lead panels, and the proportions are traditional. There is a tension in the new geometry, however, from the battered plinth to the slight angle given to each tread of the tight timber staircases. Fellows' penthouse flats created a new skyline for Oxford.

North and West sides, Wolfson Quad, Lady Margaret Hall

Norham Gardens, Oxford

1959–61, 1963–6, Raymond Erith

Listed grade II, 30 March 1993

Lady Margaret Hall was founded in 1878, the year women were admitted for examination at Oxford. Erith inherited a tangle of Queen Anne-style buildings, mostly by Reginald Blomfield, which influenced the style with which he completed the main entrance quadrangle. First came the library, a double-height space with Diocletian attic windows, set over an arcaded ground floor containing the book stack. The overall form resembles Oxbridge buildings of the later seventeenth century, its starkness and lack of mouldings most reminiscent of Hawksmoor's demolished Christ's Hospital Writing Schools of 1692–5. Erith's interior is remarkable for its timberwork: wooden Tuscan columns support the gallery, where gentle settlement and dark varnish suggest a venerable age. He also designed the furniture.

For the western entrance block, Erith proposed 'a rest from windows'. He set a white pedimented portico in an almost blind brick wall that closes the end of Norham Gardens. It also suggests another Oxbridge tradition, that of the quasi-fortified gatehouse, but instead of medieval motifs the style is convincingly Palladian.

Past Field

Henley-on-Thames, Oxfordshire

1960, 1966, Patrick Gwynne

Listed grade II, 15 July 1998

Past Field was built for Dr Salmon, a GP, and his musician wife after Gwynne was recommended by a mutual friend, Geoffrey Rand. With a budget of just £8,000, a single-storey plan was adopted, while the boomerang plan with overhanging eaves gave shelter from the sun and screened what was then a treeless foreground. A high living room, with excellent acoustics for Mrs Salmon, was placed to one side of the near-circular central entrance, and bedrooms were lined up along the other. Sloping ceilings are separated by flash gaps from the grey brick and panelled walls. Gwynne designed the house to be extended at either end – and when in 1966 he added a master bedroom suite and a kitchen, the old kitchen became the dining room.

The house demonstrates Gwynne's attention to detail, with a love of timber veneers – seen in the house's panelling and built-in cupboards – and mosaics that create novel shapes and juxtapositions. One of his smallest surviving houses, it is less formal than his London work.

St Catherine's College

Manor Road, Oxford

1960–6, Arne Jacobsen

Listed grade I, 30 March 1993
Landscape registered grade II,
27 July 1998

St Catherine's is the quintessence of cool modernism, a demonstration to English architects by an international virtuoso of how it should be done. In Alan Bullock, the commissioning Censor (warden), Jacobsen had a perfect client, despite budgetary limitations rare in Oxford. More funding was available for the communal buildings, and the overall ensemble makes the contemporary, English-designed Churchill College, Cambridge, look insular.

Every detail is Jacobsen's, from the cutlery and furniture to the landscaping, the latter's studied textures and shades of green now swamping the yellow brickwork. Low courtyards of hedges and walls complement the simple plan: two ranges of study bedrooms flank separate central buildings for an auditorium, library and an L-shaped end block housing the dining hall and common rooms. The buildings' symmetry and expressed structure defines their cool formality, their long, low massing continued in linking pergolas and a canal. The bell tower and a cedar tree make vertical counterpoints, while the central lawn and the bike shed offer contrasting circular forms. The library features Jacobsen's Swan chairs, but for the high table in the dining hall and the senior common room he created the tall Oxford chair.

Since the college was listed, Stephen Hodder has reglazed the study bedrooms to reduce temperature extremes and added a large quadrangle to the north.

Spence House and studio

Beaulieu River, Hampshire

1961, Sir Basil Spence

Listed grade II, 10 December 1997

Spence built this house as a holiday home when he was working at Southampton University, on land acquired from the Beaulieu estate in 1958. Although it was originally small, there is a muscularity to the Scandinavian-inspired design. 'Powerful and resourceful', as Sir Nikolaus Pevsner described it, it is also efficiently and imaginatively planned. The large areas of glass and black timber cladding on the projecting *piano nobile* befit its location set high above one of England's most important yachting centres. The principal rooms are on this level for the views, with bedrooms leading directly off a large, open-plan living room lined in redwood cedar and warmed by a giant stove. The effect is reminiscent of an ocean-going schooner.

Spence also built a small studio in the woods behind the house, which is separately listed. The landscaping was by his regular collaborator Sylvia Crowe.

The house was given a free-standing extension in 1999–2000 by John Pardey; the additional rooms are reached via a glass bridge.

Askett Green

Askett, Princes Risborough,
Buckinghamshire

1961–2, Peter Aldington

Listed grade II, 8 July 1999

Aldington, well travelled thanks to National Service and a love of mountaineering, was one of the first architects to blend local vernacular traditions with the austerity of the Modern Movement, anticipating the greater humanism desired of housing by the 1970s. This is his first house, designed for mountaineering friends Michael and Celia White.

Askett Green was conceived as a rural cottage hugging the lane, in brick with only small windows to the street. The interior was made partially open-plan, because the Whites liked giving parties, but Aldington developed the walls with built-in seating and cupboards – a reflection of both men's expertise in timber. The kitchen fittings, sourced through Aldington's father (an executive at Hotpoint) were also built-in.

As the house neared completion, the Whites went to Nigeria for two years and the newly wed Aldingtons moved in. The experience prompted them to build their own house at Haddenham (see p.344). Askett Green, meanwhile, has proved adaptable for the Whites in their retirement.

Point Royal

The Green, Easthampstead,
Bracknell

1961–4, Philip Dowson
of Arup Associates

Listed grade II, 22 December 1998

New towns rarely experimented with tall flats, leading to accusations of wasted land and suburban sprawl. The exception was Bracknell, where the planner Sir Lancelot Keay conceived an 18-storey block in response to a land shortage.

The flats were intended for single professionals within a mixed development, their location determined by mature trees as at Harlow's The Lawn. An underground car park was created by scooping out the site and then creating pedestrian bridges leading to the entrance. The concave, hexagonal floor plan was chosen as requiring fewer internal walls than a rectangular block while giving each flat a dual aspect. Living rooms and bedrooms open on to a terrace enclosed by the peripheral frame of precast mullions, in a system developed by Dowson for his university work and which also takes part of the floor load.

Although alterations were made to the windows and balconies in 1992, Point Royal is so boldly modelled that it was still an obvious candidate for listing.

St Cross Libraries

Manor Road, Oxford

1961–4, Sir Leslie Martin

Listed grade II*, 30 March 1993

In its quest for modern architecture, Oxford University turned for advice to Leslie Martin, then gave him the job. The brief was for three libraries – for law, English and statistics – with shared seminar rooms and a lecture theatre, in which the law library with its large collection and better funding dominated.

The result is Martin's most successful independent work, enriched rather than sterilized by following Alvar Aalto's advice to serialize the library plans. They are reached at different levels from an outside staircase, the centrepiece of the design and which leads to a raised courtyard – both motifs derived from Aalto's Säynätsalo town hall. The English and law libraries are similar, each one square and entered on a corner, with central seating under top lighting and galleries on two sides, but the English library has windows to the sides and central columns were omitted. These libraries are little altered but that for statistics has been converted for teaching. A handsome internal stair highlights the cleverness of the complex section.

Wolfson and Rayne Buildings, St Anne's College

Woodstock Road, Oxford

1962–4, 1966–8
Howell, Killick, Partridge and Amis

Listed grade II, 30 March 1993

St Anne's began as a society for women students living at home or in lodgings, and became a college only in 1952. It then rapidly outgrew the other women's institutions.

Following their highly praised entry for the Churchill College competition in 1959, Howell, Killick and Partridge were commissioned to design a necklace of six linked buildings that could be erected as funding permitted. In practice just two were built, funded by bequests from Sir Isaac Wolfson and Max Rayne respectively.

The convex curved blocks with their concave covered link sit well in a mature setting of nineteenth-century houses and trees. The curves make the short corridors seem less institutional, and give interesting shapes to the 45 study-bedrooms within each block. They also create a larger, cigar-shaped core, which contains staircases, kitchens and bathrooms, and two common rooms. But the façades are the most memorable features, with crisply finished, storey-high precast panels that incorporate canted, projecting bay window units, a pioneering use that became Howell, Killick, Partridge and Amis's trademark.

15–17 Blackhall Road

Oxford

1963, Michael Powers
of Architects' Co-Partnership

Listed grade II, 15 July 1998

Following the success of the 'Beehives' (see page 328), Michael Powers was invited to design three fellows' houses on a site adjoining the main college. Domestic work is rare within ACP's extensive oeuvre.

Largely hidden behind high walls, the houses consist of one mirrored pair and one smaller detached house, built of almost white brick as a counter to their red-brick Victorian surroundings. There are bands of concrete where floor slabs and ring beams are exposed. No. 16 has a small rear extension, added sympathetically by Cluttons in 1973.

However, it is the interiors that are most impressive, with fashionable exposed brickwork and built-in timber fittings. The top-lit semicircular stairwells are particularly dramatic. Perhaps it is because fellows are expected to have relatively few possessions, save for books, that these houses make such strong architectural statements without the need for personal embellishments. They were recently restored and refurbished by Alan Berman Associates.

Synagogue and Amphitheatre

Carmel College, Mongewell, Oxfordshire

1963, 1965, Thomas Hancock

Listed grade II, 25 November 1999

Carmel College was founded as England's only Jewish boarding school in 1948 by Rabbi Dr Kopul Rosen, and in 1953 moved to a mansion by the Thames. Thomas Hancock produced a master plan c.1960, though it was not strictly followed.

The synagogue is Hancock's centrepiece. It is wedge-shaped, its roof supported by wooden beams that soar upwards from the low entrance to the east wall, 15.2m (50ft) high, that housed the Torah. To either side are panels still filled with *dalle de verre* by Nechemiah Azaz, an Israeli sculptor who also made glass for the low entrance wall and a sculpture of the burning bush. A contrast to the height of the synagogue is the sunken amphitheatre behind it, formed of concrete and engineering bricks.

Carmel College closed in 1997, and proposals for housing were approved in 2014, with the synagogue being converted into a leisure centre. Azaz also worked at Belfast Synagogue (1964).

New House

Shipton-under-Wychwood,
Oxfordshire

1963–4, Stout and Litchfield

Listed 15 July 1998; upgraded to II*,
12 July 2012
Landscape registered grade II*,
12 July 2012

This is one of the most magical post-war houses, thanks to its hidden setting and Japanese water garden. Stepping across stones over raked gravel is to enter a serene other world.

   The house was built for the barrister Milton Grundy as a weekend retreat. Cotswold stone and pitched roofs were a planning requirement, and Stout and Litchfield developed a series of linked pavilions that broke down the house's components, with the largest, central one housing the kitchen and dining area, and three to the east each containing a bedroom and bathroom, garden door and view. Splaying the walls to make each unit a parallelogram created slightly canted roofs like old farm buildings. This was Stout and Litchfield's first work and elements reappeared in their subsequent houses. The garden was designed by Viacheslav Atroshenko after he and Grundy visited Kyoto's Ryoan-Ji garden, working with Mr Kasamoto and incorporating mature trees. Atroshenko added a mural in 1971.

Upper Exbury

Exbury, Hampshire

1964–5, James Dunbar-Nasmith

Listed grade II, 29 April 2013

Dunbar-Nasmith was a college friend of Leopold de Rothschild (1927–2012), a passionate music-lover who wanted a weekend house for entertaining. They created a country house in a modern idiom, whose quality of finishes and detailing suit its traditional furnishings and grand piano.

The house bestrides a slope, concealing garaging and a service wing behind a double-height music room and living area that faces south overlooking the garden. The levels within this elegant yet comfortable space are connected by steps that curl around the fireplace up to a gallery under an open timber ceiling. Dunbar-Nasmith recognizes the importance of materials in his work, preferring brick to concrete and paying attention to door handles and balustrades that are 'nice to feel', considering such pleasures more important than style. This is evident in the aluminium balcony balustrade supports by Ann Henderson and crunchy crystal doorknobs by Helen Weir, as in the sculptural glass light fittings.

Dunbar-Nasmith formed a partnership in Scotland with Graham Couper Law.

The Kenyon Building

St Hugh's College, Oxford

1964–6, David Roberts, with
Geoffrey Clarke and Peter Hall

Listed grade II, 7 October 2008

St Hugh's became a full college for women in 1959. Named for its long-serving warden, the distinguished archaeologist Dame Kathleen Kenyon, this addition contains study-bedrooms for 47 undergraduates, three flats for fellows and a caretaker, plus a common room.

Although more powerfully built than Roberts's Cambridge buildings (see p.213 and p.243), with exposed concrete balconies and fascias that create drama on its staggered, V-shaped plan, the interior is nevertheless surprising. The entrance leads to a top-lit central stairwell that rises straight through the building through three floors, its exposed concrete flooded with natural light and with a fat, board-marked boiler flue for added drama.

David Roberts had established his reputation as the first university architect to design in a modern idiom at Cambridge, where he had already used a stepped profile to give a dual aspect to study-bedrooms. The Kenyon Building is more accomplished, suggesting inspiration from the American architect Louis Kahn in its use of brick and pit-marked concrete.

The Turn, Middle Turn and Turn End

Townside, Haddenham, Buckinghamshire

1964–8, Peter Aldington

Listed, 15 July 1998
Upgraded to grade II*, 19 May 2006

Turn End is Peter Aldington's Taliesin, hand built by him and his wife Margaret as their home and studio, subsidized by two smaller houses in its entrance yard. These loose-knit, single-storey dwellings, with high pantiled roofs and dormers, have the rambling quality of Frank Lloyd Wright's houses, but the aesthetic is a more complex mix of modern and vernacular sources.

The site lies at the heart of a village noted for high walls of kneaded chalk and straw, called wychert. Two remain happily here amidst painted concrete block walls and lacquered timber. Enclosing walls and a complex plan provide privacy and tranquillity where everything has its special place; Aldington's typically big joinery details, with every possible bench, cupboard and appliance built in, extend at Turn End to a concrete bed base. Folding windows here overlook a courtyard and pool, paved and planted as carefully as the house. To the rear a curving glade leads to further garden rooms, the result of later land purchases and each given its own character.

Clayton House

Green Lane, Prestwood,
Buckinghamshire

1965–6, Peter Aldington
and John Craig

Listed grade II, 8 July 1999

While still living at Askett Green in 1964, Aldington was commissioned to design a house for Howard and Liz Quilter, offal merchants. It enabled him to set up in private practice, and it was the first house where Craig assisted. It is more opulent than Aldington's earlier works, although the cost was only £25,000. With no local references to be made, it owes something to Frank Lloyd Wright while remaining distinctively Aldington's work, with enclosed volumes in brick and an open-plan first floor in timber, stained black externally.

A low wing at the entrance provided independent accommodation for the Quilters' four children. The adult area, at right angles, has a spacious living room, bedroom and study reached by a circular stair from the dining area and entrance below. Large windows open on to a garden pool resembling that at Turn End, and to a first-floor balcony. Paul Collinge, Aldington's one-time partner, added a swimming pool in 1992.

Christ Church Picture Gallery

off Oriel Square, Oxford

1965–8, Powell and Moya

Listed grade II*, 24 April 1998

If Cardinal Wolsey could conceal a cathedral behind Tom Quad then, figured Philip Powell, his practice could conceal an art gallery. Entered through an eighteenth-century basement, this was Powell's favourite building, partly because it was hidden in the deanery garden and roofed in grass. A ramp was inspired by Le Corbusier's at the Villa Savoye.

Inside, the eye is led to a glazed cloister overlooking a courtyard. There are two top-lit galleries for displaying the college's collection of Italian and Flemish paintings and a sequence of smaller spaces for showing and storing its large collection of drawings. Powell and Moya experimented with plyglass, the only glazing then available that controlled ultraviolet rays, and tungsten filaments to make the fluorescent lighting more natural. The unpainted rendered finishes reflect contemporary Italian practice in museums.

Very few art galleries were built or extended in the immediate post-war years. Christ Church was one of the first examples of what has become the quintessential building type of recent decades, and still works as intended.

Blue Boar Quad

Christ Church, Oxford

1965–8, Powell and Moya

Listed grade II*, 10 October 2006

Following their Brasenose triumph (see p.330), Powell and Moya were commissioned in 1963 to squeeze accommodation into Christ Church's backland site, but were then asked to produce the picture gallery first.

The irregular-shaped quadrangle, defined by simple grass and paving at the insistence of the architects, is concealed behind older buildings that provided the only access until 2008. An amalgam of their earlier Oxbridge schemes, 61 study-bedrooms were strung between thick, stone-clad buttresses with bands of anodized aluminium glazing, concrete transoms and lead panels. Four staircases interrupt the regular rhythm. But whereas each range of the Cripps Building at St John's, Cambridge (see p.249), has two elevations, here there is only one, as the scheme backed on to a thick wall to Blue Boar Lane, saved from demolition for road widening. As at Brasenose, there are penthouse sets for tutors with overhanging roofs, here partly sloping, that offer views across the city – always important for Powell.

The quad was renovated and remodelled by Purcell Architects in 2007–8.

Wolfson Building, Somerville College

Woodstock Road, Oxford

1966–7, Philip Dowson
of Arup Associates

Listed grade II, 12 March 2009

Janet Vaughan, Somerville's warden from 1945–67, launched Dowson's career with a series of accommodation blocks, of which Wolfson was the last and finest. It is one of several buildings in which Dowson explored precasting and weathering techniques around a simple grid plan. A precast concrete structure was installed in six weeks, with square bay windows that look spectacular viewed from the curve of Walton Street behind. Each denotes a fellow's set of rooms (study-bedroom), reached from entrances in older buildings to either side.

Dowson was one of the first architects to plan against loneliness in university accommodation, and his carefully planned bedsits included large window seats in the bays to encourage neighbourliness and self-expression. His university work was always designed with intelligence and an attention to structure that makes the buildings easily interpretable and distinctive.

The ground floor, containing a hall, was extended towards the college's quadrangle by Niall McLaughlin in 2012, when windows were also renewed.

Diggs Field

Haddenham, Buckinghamshire

1966–7, Aldington and Craig

Listed grade II, 19 March 2010

Diggs Field was built for a retired couple, Dr and Mrs Leslie, and their young friend Diana Alderson, who had lodged as their land girl in the war. Alderson inherited a Victorian house in Haddenham, but admired Aldington's Turn End and so commissioned a new house in brick and cedar. It was conceived as two autonomous units, with a shared kitchen and a high timber conservatory or sun lounge housing an elaborate staircase. Based on the Victorian conservatory in Alderson's old house and making a pleasant place to read on winter days, this forms a link between the two sections. The two-storey range served as Alderson's living room and bedroom over garaging, while the long, single-storey range housed the Leslies. The detailing is softer than in Aldington's earlier work, a response to the trio's antique furniture.

The house exemplifies Aldington's skill in designing to the complex briefs developed by John Craig in lengthy consultation with the clients.

Wyndham Court

Commercial Road and Blechynden Terrace, Southampton

1966–9, Lyons, Israel and Ellis

Listed grade II, 22 December 1998

Lyons, Israel and Ellis worked extensively for Southampton City Council, building a catering college and several housing schemes. Wyndham Court was an extremely sensitive site, for it was next to the railway station and close to E. Berry Webber's dominating Civic Centre of 1929–39. The latter dictated a low-rise design, and the choice of a complementary white concrete. Wyndham Court was targeted at professionals, with rents well above those for normal council housing, and brought population back to the city centre.

There are two floors of flats and four floors of two-storey maisonettes raised above an open ground floor on a sloping site, with shops on the higher elevation facing Commercial Road. The plan comprises a private courtyard development, with a basement car park, and an eastern spur set under pilotis. The design is so strong that it has withstood reglazing in uPVC.

Oaklands

Bulmershe Road, Reading

1967, Diamond, Redfern and Partners

Listed grade II, 4 February 2013

A Victorian villa in extensive grounds was replaced by five blocks of flats, retaining old garden walls, a gazebo and mature trees within a landscaping scheme by Sheila Hayward. The development was unusual in that the promoter was the owner, J. A. Spurgeon, a descendant of the famous Nonconformist family, who designated one block for letting to retired Baptist ministers and their families. The other blocks are managed by covenants and a residents' association similar to those established by Span Developments Ltd, and Oaklands exhibits a similar care in its design and landscaping.

The five blocks, designed by Frank Briggs and Peter de Souza for the Midlands practice, are similar. The ground floor comprises one- and two-bedroom flats with patios, and above are larger maisonettes with balconies, making 21 flats and 29 maisonettes in all. They are built of brick with heavily raked joints, their upper storeys clad in horizontal white boarding (now renewed) that contrasts with all black vertical boarding and window surrounds.

Templeton College

Kennington, near Oxford

1967–9, 1974, 1986,
Ahrends, Burton and Koralek

Listed grade II, 15 April 1999

England's first business schools were founded in 1965. Oxford's first director, Norman Leyland, had commissioned Powell and Moya at Brasenose, where Richard Burton had been job architect. Now he requested a phased scheme of teaching facilities and superior accommodation for middle managers on six-month secondments. Burton set the classrooms around an atrium library, placed centrally to encourage the managers to use it, and with a 'tartan' grid, each square unit supported on four corner columns, enabling services and partitions to be set between them at the junctions and extensions to be added rapidly.

Burton chose zinc as the principal facing, after problems with lead at Brasenose. Because of the nearby major road, the bedroom windows face inwards, with a sloping profile. There is a close interplay between the buildings and James Hope's landscaped courtyards, with unexpected vistas between blocks and bridges over a stream. The entrance was designed around a tree, with a narrow rill between the steps. Only the earliest phases and the library extension are listed.

Hilda Besse Building

St Antony's College, Oxford

1967–70, Howell, Killick, Partridge and Amis

Listed grade II, 28 September 2009

St Antony's College was founded through the generosity of Antonin Besse, a French shipping merchant who sought a college dedicated to international relations.

When the Nuffield Foundation declined funding for a complex that included living accommodation, commissioned in 1960, the college resolved that a hall and common rooms were its priorities. John Partridge determined that his revised building should be complete in itself, resulting in an exquisite box of two halves distinguished by its projecting staircases. On one side is the double-height dining hall; on the other are common rooms over the kitchen. Natural and artificial light are controlled from the sides and from above, enhanced by timber linings to the faceted concrete cladding and diagrid roof. At night, light and dark areas are transposed. The structure is based around octagonal columns, the one blocking the entrance inspired by Chartres Cathedral. The simple spaces lend themselves to the display of artefacts from Persian kilim rugs to Japanese sculpture.

Bennett Associates' Gateway Buildings, opened in 2013, now partly obscure the block.

Garden Building

St Hilda's College, Oxford

1968–70, Alison and Peter Smithson

Listed grade II, 12 November 1999

St Hilda's is a women's college, and the Smithsons sought a design that was recognizably a 'girls' place'. It is a square building, with big windows set behind a timber screen to reduce glare and suggest greater security, which they described as 'a kind of yashmak'. The dressing lobbies in each bedroom were designed to hide a 'cascade of washing powder and stockings', and provided sound insulation from the central core of service rooms and corridors. Not only is the building practical, it is also exquisitely detailed with thick timber joinery inside and out.

This is the Smithsons' only university building. With its central service pod, it resembles the towers of their 1959 Churchill College design and The Economist Group building (see p.524) on a small scale, a development of an idea first explored in their 1956 House of the Future. It also reflects their growing concern to treat façades as a series of skins in a gentler approach to architecture, which they saw increasingly as a framework for its users to personalize.

Florey Building

St Clement's Street, Oxford

1968–71, James Stirling

Listed grade II, 12 March 2009

Howard Florey, provost of The Queen's College, sought a memorial both to himself and to attract good students; his sudden death in 1968 cost the project its leader. The brief was only for study-bedrooms and a breakfast room, as other meals would be served on the main college site.

Stirling was a compromise choice, other candidates having divided the building committee. He ignored the immediate neighbourhood, earmarked for demolition, and faced his accommodation towards the river, where the council sought a public path. Instead there is an awkward junction between the river and Stirling's steps, outweighed by a top-lit breakfast room with its striking ventilator. Otherwise Stirling reworked the traditional Oxbridge quadrangle down to the covered arcades, but as an amphitheatre of glass, brick and tile with each storey jettied over the other in the manner of Marcel Breuer's Elberfeld Hospital project of 1928–9.

Wolfson College

Linton Road, Oxford

1968–74, Powell and Moya

Listed grade II, 20 June 2011

Wolfson is a complete college, designed in a single building campaign for graduate students and their families. It was one of two graduate colleges founded by Oxford University in 1965, and is the largest in Britain. Isaiah Berlin was appointed president, the title chosen as most appropriate for a college with strong egalitarian principles. Wolfson has no high table, and only one common room.

Powell and Moya were invited to design the buildings after fellows had admired their work at St John's, Cambridge (see p.249), although Berlin himself suggested the curved form of the riverside quad by means of a sequence of postcards of the harbour at Portofino, Italy. This answers the form of the punt dock, and makes a visual link between the main quadrangle of communal accommodation more typical of Powell and Moya's style and the range for married students beyond. The housing for students with children is set back, their three ranges set on a plinth over the nursery and reminiscent of hostels at their Swindon hospital (now demolished).

Former Blackwell's Music Shop and Wadham College housing

Holywell Street, Oxford

1969–70, Isi Metzstein and Andy MacMillan of Gillespie, Kidd and Coia

Listed grade II, 4 December 2000

Metzstein and MacMillan were consultant architects to Wadham College, which owned a garage on Holywell Street. They replaced it with a shop that extended the depth of the site, with student accommodation above. A quadrangle for fellows was also tucked behind the adjoining King's Arms public house.

The street frontage is a pastiche in concrete of the jettied buildings found along the historic street, though the two-stage roof with a clerestory and the setback splays to the shopfront are very distinctive. The firm fitted out the interior with bookshelves, while two light wells bring natural light into the basement trading space and provide a visual link from the college behind. The single-storey Fellows' Court is lined in zinc sheeting and is deliberately minimal in design.

Metzstein and MacMillan also remodelled the King's Arms, after spending many happy hours there. It is ironic, then, that proposals to expand the pub's restaurant into the bookshop should have prompted the listing. Further refurbishment was undertaken in 2012–13.

Julius Gottlieb Boathouse, former Carmel College

Mongewell, Oxfordshire

1969–70, Sir Basil Spence, Bonnington and Collins
Job architect, John Urwin Spence

Listed grade II*, 25 November 1999

Spence and his son were commissioned in 1966 to produce a memorial to Julius Gottlieb, a wood designer and patron of the arts buried nearby, whose son was a governor at Carmel. Gottlieb's and Spence's grandsons were at Hampstead School together.

The building's lower section is a boathouse, set off an inlet of the River Thames. Its roof is a sculpture terrace to an exhibition gallery for art and industrial design created within a concrete pyramid at the other end. Gargoyles feed rainwater to pools below, and wedges of primary colour denote triangular windows. Inside, the concrete is board-marked and there is an enclosed area for sculpture and other free-standing exhibits. The manner in which even the holders for gallery spotlights are of shuttered concrete shows a remarkable consistency of vision.

The striking form of the gallery and boathouse are perhaps the ultimate expression of the increasing interest in geometry in the 1960s by Spence and his design team. Proposals made in 2014 included adapting the gallery into a restaurant.

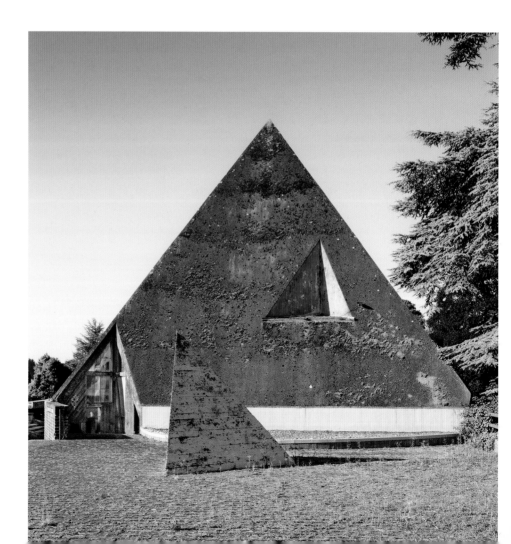

Youlbury House

Wootton, Oxfordshire

1969–71, Hal Moggridge

Listed grade II, 28 July 2009

Youlbury was built as a weekend house for William Goodhart QC and his family. It is one of only three houses designed by Moggridge, the brother-in-law of Goodhart's wife Celia and partner of the landscape designer Brenda Colvin. It replaced a Victorian house, previously owned by the archaeologist Arthur Evans, who had planted extensive woodland gardens that Goodhart had loved since boyhood in their romantic semi-dereliction. The new house perches dramatically over a precipitous slope, and the principal space is an airy upper-floor living room that appears to project over the hillside. It is reached by cleverly skewed stairs, angled to get extra light and to invite exploration, after plans for a regular hallway were revised; a full kitchen was added only as building began. Fittings are of ash, with a floating pine ceiling to the living room.

The collaboration between client and architect created a house of individuality and refinement, with an exceptional relationship to its remarkable Edwardian setting.

Hill House

Hampshire

1970–2, Denys Lasdun and Partners

Listed grade II*, 19 December 2012

This is Lasdun's one post-war private house, commissioned by Sir Timothy Sainsbury after they met at a conference on urban planning. He and Lady Sainsbury were looking for a country home that combined family accommodation with rooms for entertaining and their collection of English paintings. Lasdun first proposed a ziggurat design set into the hillside, but Sir Timothy felt the main half landings to be impractical. Architect and client worked closely with the conscious aim of creating a classic house and the result celebrates the temple-like qualities found in Lasdun's post-and-lintel construction. The plan is almost cruciform, with a largely double-height stair hall and drawing room on a central axis, connected by a gallery at the upper level and flanked by family rooms.

Lasdun added a swimming pool in 1984–5 and his last designs were for a library, completed in 2001 after his death. It is arguably the only house in Britain that combines the qualities of a country house with a thoroughgoing monumental modernism.

Maidenhead Library

St Ives Road, Maidenhead

1970–73, Ahrends, Burton
and Koralek

Listed grade II, 11 June 2003

The Roberts Report in 1959 recommended that small boroughs should lose their status as independent library authorities. Redcar and Maidenhead, growing fast, objected and developed new buildings with the Department of Education and Science in an initiative to make libraries more welcoming to the public.

Ahrends, Burton and Koralek came to prominence when, in 1961, Paul Koralek won a competition for a library at Trinity College, Dublin. This smaller building, also with Koralek as lead partner, is similarly a top-lit flexible space with balconies arranged around fixed staircases. However, like much of ABK's work of the 1970s, it uses a greater variety of materials.

Maidenhead's new library was built alongside the old, which was then demolished and a garden made on the site. It adopts a steel space frame to create a column-free interior and a high clerestory. Hard red brick, inspired by the Victorian town, gives a semblance of weight to the lower structure, even though it is not load-bearing, and extends to a surrounding plinth.

St Anne's RC Church

Fawley Court, Marlow Road, Fawley

1971–3, Władysław Tadeusz
Jeorge Jarosz

Listed grade II, 28 September 2009

St Anne's was of importance to the Polish community in Britain and beyond. It was conceived as a college chapel and church for the Congregation of Marian Fathers, a Polish religious community based at the adjacent Fawley Court until 2008. The patron was Prince Stanisław Albrecht Radziwiłł (1914–76), who is buried in the crypt, and was built in memory of his mother Anne. There were many other memorials.

Externally the church is tent-like in form, with an angular and beautifully crafted copper roof sweeping down to ground level. This belies a greater irregularity of the church's massing and plan, which are striking and inventive. Inside, its timber ribs and boarded ceiling create an impressive yet warm and welcoming worship space, cleverly lit with limited natural and electric light. Exposed brick walls provided an angular altar backdrop and a foil to the fittings, now gone. The church closed in 2009.

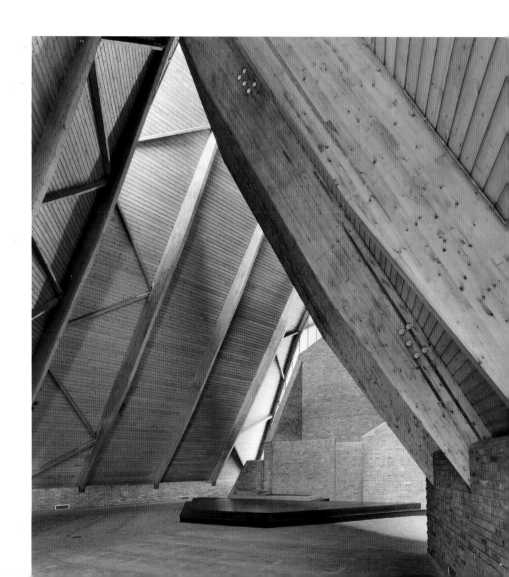

De Breyne and Hayward Buildings

Keble College, Oxford

1971–3, 1975–6; Ahrends, Burton and Koralek

Listed grade II*, 4 October 1999

Ahrends, Burton and Koralek (ABK) were commissioned in 1969 to build study-bedrooms, two flats and a common room following a master plan by Casson and Conder. The difficulty was to design a building that could stand up to Butterfield's apotheosis of Victorian Gothic brutalism.

Their solution was a snake-like building, which falls in height as it uncoils down Blackhall Road. A circular staircase forms its eye. Curved forms became a hallmark of Peter Ahrends's designs, for whom a honey-coloured brick and angled black glass offer a sophisticated coolness juxtaposed with Butterfield's fireworks, while limiting solar gain. The pairs of rooms are reached by staircases connected by a sunken glazed walkway, first suggested by Ahrends as a means of retaining the old houses on the site. The former common room adds another curve.

Listing was hastened when a new block by Rick Mather required the demolition of the tip of the snake's tail on Blackhall Road, and ABK's common room interior has now also gone.

7-23 Silver Street

Stony Stratford, Buckinghamshire

1973–6, Milton Keynes
Development Corporation
Chief architect, Derek Walker
Project architect, Wayland Tunley

Listed grade II, 30 May 2012

Milton Keynes was England's largest and most ambitiously planned post-war new town, and a centre of debate between modernism and vernacular styles.

This terrace of red-brick town houses was designed as the southern boundary and entrance to Cofferidge Close, the first new development by the Corporation within the existing market town of Stony Stratford. A commercial and retail scheme with Development Corporation offices, Cofferidge Close was inserted delicately behind the historic high street. Square brick colonnades are its defining feature, while new landscaping acknowledged an earlier orchard and retained existing trees.

The houses all echo carefully observed details from the town's vernacular buildings and traditional street signage, with modern patent glazing to bedroom windows in the roof. Flexibly planned living rooms are on the first floor, where full-height windows open on to balconies, while on the ground floor, kitchen/dining areas lead into a secluded courtyard. Listing was prompted by redevelopment proposals for the shopping centre that were rejected in 2013.

Lyde End

Church End, Bledlow,
Buckinghamshire

1975–7, Aldington and Craig
Project architect, Paul Collinge

Listed grade II, 20 August 2009

Lyde End is a group of six linked cottages clustered around three sides of a courtyard with a carport on the fourth. They were built for the future cabinet minister Lord Carrington, who wanted low-cost housing for the village, an early response to the shortage of affordable housing in rural parts of the south-east.

Carrington stipulated that the houses should nestle into the village and give a feeling of protection and homeliness. He expressly did not want a neo-Georgian pastiche. Aldington repeated the form of his development at Haddenham, with a nod to John Weeks's Rushbrooke in the high mono-pitched roofs, while Paul Collinge acknowledged Alvar Aalto's influence.

There are five bungalows, with a two-storey house at the rear for Carrington's estate foreman. French windows in the open-plan living areas give on to partly covered yards, while inside there are unplastered brick walls and exposed sloping timber ceilings. While extremely compact, they are carefully detailed; they remain practical and are popular with their inhabitants.

Shopping Building (thecentre:mk)

Midsummer Boulevard, Milton Keynes

1975–9, Milton Keynes
Architect's Department,
Job architects, Stuart Mosscrop
and Christopher Woodward

Listed grade II, 16 July 2010

The centrepiece of the new town, the design was based on the word picture painted in Milton Keynes's master plan and on nineteenth-century gallerias, in reaction to American shopping malls with expensive underground services. This is an indoor mall, but is naturally lit and incorporates two squares, one outdoors, for shoppers enter at ground level while deliveries are made from rooftop parking accessed by a road spanning the building. The long, luminous arcades have travertine benches and planters, and artworks include Liliane Lijn's hanging *Circle of Light*.

Steel was expensive, but saved time and interest payments. Woodward admired Cesar Pelli's mirror-glass town hall in Los Angeles and Norman Foster's IBM building at Cosham, so adopted a similar steel section and windscreen gasket fixing for the symmetrical elevations. Mirror glass equally suited shops wanting windows at the upper level and those seeking enclosure.

The centre was initially protected by complex management agreements rather than listing. It was extended in 2000, but proposals for further works in 2012 were withdrawn.

Former RAF Greenham Common

Berkshire

Cruise missile complex
1980-3
Scheduled 3 March 20013

Control tower
1951-3, with 1980s allocations
Listed grade ll, 13 January 2012

Combat Support Building
1984-5
Listed grade II, 2 September 2014

Former Wing Headquarters Building
c.1985
Listed grade II*, 1 September 2014

The ground-launched cruise missile alert and maintenance area (GAMA) here was perhaps the most famous symbol of the Cold War in Britain, as the focus of women's peace protests.

A wartime airfield, Greenham was substantially rebuilt in 1951 for US B-47 Stratojets, with one of the longest military runways in the world and a bomb store for nuclear missiles. The control tower was built at this time.

The iconic structures, however, are on the GAMA site. From 1980, six monumental cruise missile shelters were built in two rows of earth-covered reinforced concrete with massive concrete and steel blast doors. The 'quick reaction alert' shelter was designed for immediate retaliation to attack and manned constantly; all could house 16 missiles on mobile launchers. The complex was surrounded by a triple fence including a guardroom, watchtower (demolished) and other support buildings. It was designed to stand alone if the rest of the base had been compromised. The missiles were removed in 1989–91 and the base closed in 1992.

University of Sussex,
Falmer, Brighton,
1960 onwards, Basil
Spence and Partners

Fort Halstead

Dunton Green, Kent

Buildings F16 and F17
1947
Listed grade II*, 21 March 2012

Building Q14
c.1948–52
Listed grade II, 25 February 2011

Fort Halstead, built in 1895–7 as a centre for volunteer forces, was used for rocket development in the Second World War. In 1947 it became a top-secret research establishment where scientists, guided by the physicist William Penney in close cooperation with the RAF, developed Britain's first atomic bomb. New structures were erected to manufacture, test and assemble the weapon, particularly its electronic detonators. Buildings F16 and F17 were built for this testing, largely of heavy reinforced concrete, F17 with a large and prominent T-shaped funnel to its roof. Building Q14, of brick and steel, was the building in which the prototype warhead and its ballistic casing here assembled in a double-height workshop, although wooden models stood in for the live explosive components. A plaque commemorates the importance of the work undertaken here.

Britain exploded her first atomic bomb on the Monte Bello Islands, Australia, on 3 October 1952. Atomic weapons research and development continued at Fort Halstead until 1955, since when it has concentrated on conventional explosives.

Church of St John the Evangelist

Upper Maze Road,
St Leonards-on-Sea,
East Sussex

1950–2, 1955–7,
H. S. Goodhart-Rendel

Listed grade II*, 25 September 1998

Goodhart-Rendel truly hated pointed arches, but here had to incorporate Arthur Blomfield's baptistery and tower of 1883–4, which survived war damage in 1943. Externally the old and new work meshes together beautifully, Goodhart-Rendel demonstrating his love of diaper brickwork without sacrificing originality. The stepping of the transepts on the falling site is masterful.

The nave and transepts were rebuilt first, with round arches in the lower arcades and pointed arches above. The double chancel arch that dominates the interior was designed to support the concrete vault and carry the organ, as shown in a drawing in the south transept. The present organ in the north transept was brought from St Catharine's College, Cambridge, in 1974. The tall, painted chancel fittings are by Goodhart-Rendel save for the choir stalls, where Blomfield's work was salvaged and remodelled. The aisle and clerestory windows are by Joseph Ledger, the former inspired by Romanesque painting while the latter are outlines of saints in clear glass. baptistery windows are by Margaret G. Thompson.

Air Forces Memorial

Cooper's Hill, Englefield
Green, Surrey

1952–3, Edward Maufe

Listed grade II*, 5 September 1998

The location where the Magna Carta was issued, Runnymede encapsulates the mid-century's sentimentality for English history, and makes an ideal location for a monument to Britain's 20,000 Second World War airmen and ten women who have no known grave. Its humility contrasts with the American cemetery at Madingley.

Maufe's scheme resembles a memorial quad at a public school, and made good use of a dramatic setting. In the entrance cloister, wall tablets recording the names of the fallen have an impressive rippling effect. On the furthest side a tower, embellished only by Vernon Hill's figures of Justice, Victory and Courage, forms a shrine, its limed oak fittings familiar from Maufe's churches. There are unexpected vistas across the Thames from Windsor to London. The etched angels on the picture windows are by John Hutton, ahead of those at Coventry Cathedral.

Heathrow planes circulating overhead make an appropriate tribute from the modern world.

St Mary's Church

Decoy Drive, Willingdon,
Eastbourne, East Sussex

1952–4, Edward Maufe

Listed grade II, 25 September 1998

One of Maufe's most charming designs, it replaced a mission church of 1908 destroyed in the war.

St Mary's hugs a low rise overlooking Hampden Park, its glistening, white-painted brick the first clue to its authorship. The big-roofed nave has a barn-like quality, from which emerge a narrow bell turret and a stubby tower over the chancel. The memorial clock commemorating Revd Donald Carpenter, who supervised the rebuilding, is an appropriate addition.

Inside is quintessential Maufe. The pointed concrete arches, defining narrow aisles, are refined from details at the Church of St Thomas the Apostle, Hanwell (1934) and subsequent buildings. The cushion capitals and their corresponding stepped window section, particularly noticeable in a squint between the chancel and the Lady chapel, are other Maufe signatures copied from his favourite Stockholm buildings, Ivar Tengbom's Högalids Church and Ragnar Östberg's Stockholm City Hall. Grey-white render and blue ceilings provide tranquillity in a sea of modern chairs. The east window is by Moira Forsyth.

23 St George's Street

(formerly David Greig's, now Superdrug), Canterbury

1953–4, Robert Paine and Partners

Listed grade II, 24 November 1995

Shops are among the most ephemeral of building types, and this is a rare survival from the 1950s. It was built for a family firm of butchers and grocers, who are commemorated by an engraved inscription, and replaced a shop destroyed in the Blitz. It was conceived to challenge the self-service stores then beginning to appear.

The double-height shop is backed by a higher range, originally housing cold stores, offices and flats. It was developed as a pavilion at the end of a terrace of larger premises overlooking a square, so emphasis was given to the side elevation facing Canterbury Lane. Here, mosaic-clad columns support a folded concrete slab roof and glass panels shield a lower arcade lined with plywood advertising panels, sadly now painted. The roof was originally exposed internally and this feature was partly restored in 1999. A yard at the rear of the building has been replaced with a new block that repeats the triangular motifs of the main building.

Equatorial Group

Herstmonceux Castle, East Sussex

1953–8, Brian O'Rorke

Listed grade II*, 26 March 2003

The Royal Greenwich Observatory moved in 1953 to Herstmonceux. Equatorial telescopes are those mounted parallel to the Earth's rotational axis.

O'Rorke was bathing when he conceived the layout of the six observatory domes, known as the Equatorial Group, placing them on a raised bastion of flint and brick that recalls an eighteenth-century garden feature. The three at the rear were intended for reflective instruments and are linked by workshops. The largest domes, for refractors, are set beyond the bastion across short bridges, one overlooking a staircase entrance. The smallest dome has stone seats on globe-shaped feet, found also on the workshop steps. All have rotating roofs so that the motorized telescopes could track the stars; the largest, housing the Thompson telescope of 1896, also has a rising floor so that an astronomer can tilt the telescope down to the horizon without climbing ladders. The group's centrepiece is a canal into which a distracted astronomer might easily have slipped. The Observatory moved in 1990, leasing the Equatorial Group to a trust.

St Leonard's Church

Undercliff, St Leonards-on-Sea,
East Sussex

1953–61, Adrian Gilbert Scott

Listed grade II, 25 September 1998

James Burton's Gothic chapel of 1831–4 was destroyed in 1944. The War Damage Commission insisted that the church be rebuilt on the its historic site behind the seafront despite subsidence problems that continue today.

St Leonard's is similar to Scott's church in Lansbury (see p.426), and he probably worked on both schemes simultaneously after an initial proposal for St Leonard's devised with his brother, Giles, was deemed too expensive. Both feature parabolic or catenary arches and a blue stone dado with a continuous wave motif. The difference is that here Scott stressed a single axis towards the sea, inspired by a site he termed 'romantic', enforced by the chunky tower added in 1960–1.

The incumbent, Canon Griffiths, determined the interior's maritime iconography. The green marble sanctuary floor is decorated with loaves and fishes of white marble, including reliefs of locally caught skate and herring. The pulpit is a prow of a fishing boat made in Galilee and transported by the Prince Line Shipping Company, which also presented its ship's binnacle as a lectern. The glass is by Patrick Reyntiens from 1957.

Martin's

Toys Hill, Brasted, Kent

1954, Powell and Moya

Listed grade II, 23 April 2007

Early in their careers Powell and Moya built several private houses, but most have been altered or demolished. The exception is fortunately the finest, built for Monica and Muriel Anthony, spinster sisters who wanted a weekend retreat. The architects were recommended by Monica's friend Ian McCallum of the *Architectural Review*.

The site slopes steeply southwards. A garage and box room (later extended) were built on the road front, where cedar boarding gives dignity to their unusual prominence. The rest of the house appears to tumble down the hillside, but is essentially two linked single-storey pavilions that follow the contours. One houses the large living area, given added height by being set down steps from the dining room and kitchen under a common flat roof. Built-in bookcases resemble those installed by Powell in his own house. The bedroom wing permitted each sister to enjoy a room with a view. The house is simple, built while licensing restricted building materials, but gains interest from its disjointed, constructivist profile and fine internal finishes.

Friary Church of St Francis and St Anthony

Hasslett Avenue West, Crawley

1958–9. H.S. Goodhart-Rendel

Listed grade II, 2007

Italian Capuchin friars were invited in 1859 by Mrs Alfred Montgomery to Crawley, where a church was built in 1861 on land donated by her cousin Francis Scawen Blunt. The founding of the Guild of St Anthony of Padua there led to the double dedication.

The development of Crawley new town encouraged the community to commission a new church in 1955. An early project shows a flat patterned frontage but the final design is splayed, with attenuated Romanesque figures to the door-jambs. A saddleback tower denotes the central crossing. The interior has a low nave dominated by a painted concrete vault, while beyond the altar glistens, thanks to light from concealed windows in the tower. The chapel of St Anthony was moved from the old church, and there are monuments to the church's founders, here and in the graveyard.

The friars left for Canterbury in 1980 and the friary was demolished. In 1993–4 the crossing arch was removed, opening up the interior, and a Blessed Sacrament chapel was added.

Jellicoe Roof Garden

House of Fraser (formerly Harvey's),
High Street, Guildford

1956–7, Geoffrey Jellicoe

Landscape registered,
30 August 2000

The Festival of Britain saw the emergence of a new garden style, featuring curving drifts of plants, amoebic-shaped rock pools, and planters. Inspired by Roberto Burle Marx in Brazil and Thomas Church in the United States, small, dense gardens offered lungs in the busy exhibition and controlled pedestrian flows.

A later version appeared on the roof of Harvey's, a flagship of the Army and Navy Stores' post-war provincial expansion. An L-shaped water garden, it serves the adjoining café terrace and there was originally also a viewing platform above. Jellicoe called it his 'sky garden' because the ever-changing sky was reflected in the shallow water and because he designed it during the first Sputnik flight. Carved out of the water are abstract-shaped islands formed in cobbles and reached by stepping stones, which Jellicoe likened to 'planets spinning through space'. He wrote in 1966 that 'the underlying idea has been to unite heaven and earth; the sensation is one of being poised between the two'. Three willow trees have long disappeared, but fountains remain.

St Richard's RC Church

Cawley Road, Chichester

1957–8, Tomei and Maxwell

Listed grade II, 13 November 2007

A new church was built to replace that of 1855, deemed inadequate a century later, with half the money coming from football pools run by the priests. The extensive building is a simple, portal-framed structure infilled with brick, which was typical of Tomei and Maxwell's extensive church practice, save for its prominent campanile. The T-shaped plan has a large sanctuary in the crossing.

However, in 1962 Fr Langton Fox, who had close ties with Chartres, commissioned 62 *dalle de verre* windows from Gabriel Loire, among the first artists to develop the technique on a large scale. There are full-height windows in the gable ends of the nave and transepts, with smaller clerestory panels depicting scenes from the Bible and of Chichester life, past and present. David O'Connell painted the altarpiece depicting the Crucifixion and the Stations of the Cross, and designed the baptistery fittings. Reordering in 2008–10 included moving his font, with its base of gold mosaic and Sicilian marble, and installing an ambo in a complementary style.

RC Church of The Divine Motherhood and St Francis of Assisi

Bepton Road, Midhurst, West Sussex

1957–66, Guy Morgan and Partners

Listed grade II, 14 October 2011

This prominent, fan-shaped church – innovative in 1957 – was built to replace a smaller one in Rumbolds Hill. Built of Sussex sandstone and stock brick, its outer face is largely glazed except for its centrepiece, where a Madonna and Child by Richard Guyatt fills the wall above the porch.

These windows bathe the interior in light, with additionally an oculus over the altar. The steel frame supports a suspended timber ceiling, and two sets of sweeping stairs serve a balcony. A continuous stone band is carved with the Stations of the Cross, while the figure of Christ over the altar is by Michael Clark. These fittings were commissioned in 1962 by a new incumbent, Fr Waller, who also secured the redesign of Guyatt's sculpture in higher relief – to the consternation of Morgan, then grieving the death of his son.

The church was completed in 1962 but a short open colonnade and a soaring campanile, both part of the original design, were realized only in 1966.

Sunley House (formerly Barclays Bank)

14–19 Middle Row, Maidstone, Kent

1958–62, Sir William G. Holford

Listed grade II, 17 September 2010

Holford's career as an architect and planner spanned the war and he developed a large practice responsible for many controversial master plans such as London's Paternoster Square. Sunley House was a rare building commission, and shows his personal hand in the use of decoration.

Designed in 1956 and built in two phases as a regional office for Barclays Bank, Sunley House has a wedge-shaped site. Its design is unusual for a bank in having an exposed concrete frame, although one of narrowly spaced trusses infilled with black bricks and knapped flint – a modern interpretation of a local tradition that contrasts with smooth Portland stone dressings and a plinth of Belgian fossil marble. Marble pilasters and downlit, bronze-lined recesses between the ground-floor windows provide colour, pattern and modelling. Elsewhere are reliefs related to money and prosperity, including pound and shilling coins from the time of Charles I, a farthing, and a halfpenny dated 1962, as well as the Barclays Griffin.

Arundel Park House

Arundel Park, West Sussex

1958–62, Claud Phillimore

Listed grade II, 22 October 2013

Lavinia, Duchess of Norfolk, requested a relatively small secluded house after opening Arundel Castle to the public. It was also intended as a dower house for herself and her daughters as, following her husband's death, the title would pass to a cousin. She had been impressed in the 1930s by Ditchley House, whose tripartite plan made a small house appear impressive.

The Duchess had selected the site before by chance she met Phillimore, who was recovering from tuberculosis at Midhurst Sanatorium, a charity she supported. The second son of Baron Phillimore, he read architecture at Cambridge, then set up in practice before completing his training. He specialized in building or remodelling country houses, of which this is the finest, featuring the bowed end walls of which he was fond. Inside, the L-plan staircase has a wrought-iron balustrade with the Norfolk monogram, and a crystal ball newel finial. Otherwise the rooms were grand yet simple, designed to hold the family art collection.

The Beach House

Pett Level Road, Pett, East Sussex

1959–60, Michael Pattrick

Listed grade II, 26 November 2001

Michael Pattrick built this house as a holiday home for his friends Richard and Phoebe Merrick, members of a prominent local family interested in modern design. It is raised on pilotis to give views of the sea across the high sea wall built following the floods of 1953. The ground floor has a small entrance and more recent galley kitchen, but most of it is left open as a carport. The upper floors are set in a prestressed timber frame designed to withstand gales and clad in timber.

Inside, the first floor has four tiny bedrooms with built-in bunks. At the top is the living area, with wonderful views. This room is nautical in feel – streamlined, compact and with varnished timber floors, cabinets and stairhead. Steps from the balcony lead down to the beach.

This is a magical house, intended as a beach house for a family who lived nearby, but adapted with minimal intervention for longer-term living.

Dungeness lighthouse

Dungeness, Kent

1959–60 (opened 1961)
Ronald Ward and Partners

Listed grade II*, 26 March 2003

Britain's first major new lighthouse for 50 years superseded that built at Dungeness in 1904, whose light was to be obscured by the atomic power station nearby. The 43m (141ft) tower was constructed of 21 concrete drums, each only 15cm (5½in) thick, which were lifted into position by a special crane and post-tensioned to withstand gales of 129km/h (80mph). Prestressing at the bottom means that there is no need for it to be tapered like other lighthouses. Traditional black and white banding was created using coloured aggregates, though it is now also painted. The perforations originally contained loudspeakers for the fog signal.

There has never been any living accommodation here, and all the machinery and electronics are housed within the concrete spiral ramp at its base. The light, run automatically since 1991, is reached by a cantilevered spiral staircase, slightly kinked and with a steel handrail.

Dungeness is a modern response to a traditional building type, built just when industrial architecture was becoming admired for its functionalism.

Sorrell House

Bosham Hoe, near Chichester

1960, Peter Foggo and David Thomas

Listed grade II*, 15 July 1998

Architects always recognized the possibilities of timber as a flexible and lightweight building material ideal for small houses, but it began to be used in more interesting ways around 1960.

This weekend cottage, designed by two young architects in their spare time, is a supreme example. Thomas likened it to 'making a piece of furniture'. It was erected on stilts to give views over the countryside, and to permit boat storage underneath. Access is by stairs to a verandah, from which the rooms can be entered separately. A continuous wall of windows overlooks the sea. Some of the nautical details were by the shipbuilder contractor; others were simply and carefully detailed by the architects to give the impression that the house is created from a kit of parts.

Foggo and Thomas added a wing in 1965, and a second followed in 1998 by Richard Constable of Foggo Associates, working with Thomas. Nevertheless, the house remains tiny compared with the office buildings with which the architects later made their reputations.

University of Sussex

Falmer, Brighton

1960 onwards, Basil Spence
and Partners

Falmer House
Listed grade I, 30 March 1993

Other buildings in Fulton Court
Listed grade II*, 30 March 1993

The seven new universities built in England in the 1960s marked the culmination of post-war public patronage, and offered exceptional opportunities for architects to create new urban communities. Earlier, Keele had in 1950 challenged traditional course structures but produced little architecture. Its successors were more image-conscious.

Sussex was the first. Brighton Council offered a picturesque site near Stanmer House, and subsequent universities repeated its campus model. Spence was appointed in 1959, and combining local brick and flints with concrete segmental arches he developed a style reminiscent of Le Corbusier's Maisons Jaoul, grand yet respectful of the surrounding Downs. His masterstroke was first to design a courtyard building, Falmer House (1960–2), which made an inward-facing centre while the rest of the campus was constructed. Gaps in the structure allowed views of the countryside and Ivon Hitchens gave a mural to the refectory.

Spence's subsequent buildings ring a greensward behind Falmer House. To the east Physics (1960–6), Chemistry (1963–5), and Engineering and Applied Sciences (1964–6) repeat its brick and concrete idiom with a long, covered arcade, from which steps rise to lecture theatres. To the north is the Arts Building (1962–8), a series of semi-open courtyards where much of Sylvia Crowe's landscaping survives. The west side is dominated by the Library (1962–71, subsequently extended), while to the south-west is the Attenborough Centre of 1968–9. More distinctive is the non-denominational Meeting House (1965–7), shaped like an oast house; glass and fittings in the chapel are by Spence. The result is a small town in the heart of the Downs.

Gerald Askew Wildfowl Reserve

Bentley Farm, Terrible Down,
East Sussex

1960–71 extensions, car lodge
and gate piers, Raymond Erith

Erith's work listed grade II,
15 July 1998 and 7 February 2002

Gerald Askew began collecting wildfowl paintings in 1960 and by 1966, when Bentley Farm was opened to the public, it was England's largest private holding. A wing to the eighteenth-century house was added in 1960–1 as a drawing room, the same height as the house but only one storey, with flintwork on the front elevation, a Venetian window, and niches marking the junction with the earlier house. Erith also created a first-floor octagon room within the old house, deploying Tuscan columns. He then added, in 1969–71, a balancing west wing to form the Bird Room picture gallery, with a stone fireplace based on those by Palladio at the Villa Barbaro.

Although it has been long listed for its Georgian elements, Bentley Farm has been given greater distinction by Erith's work. He also built a car lodge or barchessa, with Tuscan columns supporting a big tiled roof, and in 1965 added brick gate piers to a deliberately skewed plan.

Askew's collection is now administered by East Sussex County Council.

Ewell Honda

Ewell Bypass, Ewell, Surrey

1961, William H. Arend and Son

Listed grade II, 11 October 2012

As car dealerships swelled in the late 1950s, so more showrooms appeared at busy road junctions on the edge of town, many adopting a circular plan. Dawnier Motors, dealers in Triumph cars, commissioned a fan-shaped showroom, based on ten portal frames set radially to give a clear span of nearly 12m (39½ft). Truscon, specialist concrete engineers, used a special formwork to give a smooth finish that was then painted. Outside, deep cantilevers support a broad, upswept canopy that shelters inclined full-height windows, allowing a good view of the cars, and creating a futuristic, UFO-like appearance especially when the showroom is lit up at night.

Sadly, though this exciting structure is intact, the horizontal elements of the portal frames and the fascias have been overclad. Nevertheless, it is rare to find a 1960s showroom still in use.

Chichester Festival Theatre

Oaklands Park, Chichester

1961–2, Powell and Moya

Listed grade II*, 12 June 1998

Retired councillor Leslie Evershed-Martin saw Tyrone Guthrie's Shakespeare Festival Theatre at Stratford, Ontario, on television, and resolved to build a similarly large but novel theatre to attract actors and visitors to Chichester. He envisioned a Glyndebourne-like festival theatre.

Evershed-Martin was introduced to Powell and Moya through Powell's father, a cathedral canon. The hexagonal, tent-like plan is theirs but the amphitheatre seating which swells out above the foyer has Greek sources, while the tongue-like stage of Canadian maple is Guthrie's, with a Juliet balcony and minstrel gallery. Such combinations of new and historically based ideas on theatre staging abounded in the early 1960s. Chichester's lack of flexibility was deliberate as well as cheap. Projecting staircases anchor a circular beam that anchors the open-truss roof. The theatre was wholly funded by donations, and for many years had no backstage workshops.

Sir Laurence Olivier was invited to be Chichester's first director, leading to comparisons with the Olivier Theatre at the National Theatre, his next appointment in 1962.

Turnpoint

Onslow Road, Burwood Park,
Walton-on-Thames, Surrey

1961–2, Rodney Gordon

Listed grade II, 6 December 1996

Rodney Gordon was Owen Luder's design partner, headhunted from the London County Council after designing the Faraday Memorial (see p.577). He found speculative work invigorating, for he had complete freedom so long as he maximized plot ratios and kept down costs. Their collaborations included Eros House in Catford, Portsmouth's Tricorn Centre and Gateshead's Treaty Centre, among the most monstrously brutalist buildings of the 1960s.

Meanwhile Gordon built himself a house. The contrast between his shopping centres and tiny Turnpoint could not be greater. Yet Gordon was detailing pine shuttering for concrete, and gained a parallel interest in timber. Turnpoint has a light steel frame, including stilts that raise the house over excavated car parking, which is clad in cedar boarding. The constructivist aesthetic continues in the way the walls and eaves are extended, with chains to carry rainwater to the ground. All the standard-sized windows were double-glazed, with a blind set between the layers of glass. Listing was prompted by a threat of demolition. It has since found sympathetic owners.

Walton Court

Station Avenue, Walton-on-Thames, Surrey

1961–2, 1967–8, Gordon Tait of Burnet, Tait and Partners

Listed grade II, 24 November 1995

Bird's Eye was one of the first companies to move its offices out of London as car ownership became general, bringing staff from several locations to a single site near Heathrow. It wanted a four-storey building, and although planning permission was only granted for three storeys, the projecting rooftop services and tall serrated fascia – identical to the lower spandrels – optimistically envisaged a future extension; instead, a small addition was made to the side.

Most memorable is the image created by the anodized aluminium curtain walling, whose projecting half hexagon panels create movement along the façades, an early example of 1960s op art. Their form is reflected in the pool that runs the length of the building. The sculpture of flying birds is by John McCarthy.

The office accommodation is set around two internal courtyards landscaped by Philip Hicks. One is Japanese in feeling, the other has sculpture by Allen Collins. The second-floor canteen was, appropriately, one of the first to be supplied with pre-packaged meals.

Congress Theatre

Carlisle Road, Eastbourne,
East Sussex

1961–3, Bryan and
Norman Westwood

Listed grade II*, 12 June 1998

Eastbourne Borough Council commissioned a large auditorium for opera, ballet and conferences to complement its Victorian theatres and Winter Gardens. Few halls respond successfully to so mixed a brief, because of conflicting staging and acoustic requirements. The Congress Theatre, now mainly used for one-off shows, is the exception.

It is a square hall seating 1,680 people, with balconies and side slips, and has a giant stage with flying facilities. Side windows have been blocked, and the mass of seats and delicately coved ceiling impart a sense of true theatre. The floor can be lowered to form an orchestra pit or raised for an apron stage. The acoustics best suit speech, but are adequate for music.

The Congress comes to life externally at night, when light pours from the foyer that runs under and around the auditorium. The curtain-wall façade is an early use of butyl gaskets holding the glazing, while to the rear, patterns of coloured brick, cut brick, tile, three concrete facings and slate hanging lessen the building's bulk.

Holy Trinity Church

Twydall Lane, Gillingham, Kent

1963–4, Arthur Bailey

Listed grade II, 29 October 2009

Holy Trinity stands on a prominent corner plot in the post-war suburb of Twydall. Arthur Bailey was appointed in 1962, and despite a limited budget applied a striking ambition to the project. Though best known for traditional churches and restoration work, in his later years he produced more innovative designs, of which this was the only one to be realized.

For the multifaceted walls, Bailey chose cheap yellow stock bricks, laid crudely to produce a rough, uneven finish. Above soars a tall roof, cruelly likened for its black shingle cladding to a witch's hat. Inside, its steel construction is exposed. The interior fittings are also by Bailey, who created a diagonal axis across the square space with beautiful hardwood pews and set the sanctuary across one corner; a Lady chapel is tucked behind. The egg-shaped font is brought close to the altar and lectern, drawing together the elements of Christian worship. The aesthetic is brutalist in its honest construction, but expressive in its use of materials.

Swanscombe footbridge

A2 at Swanscombe Park, Kent

1963–4, John Bergg and H. Bowdler
of Kent County Council

Listed grade II, 25 May 1998

This is a particularly elegant bridge, closing the notch that the cutting of the road makes in the skyline. It is a graceful, three-hinged concrete arch spanning 48.7m (160ft), with a prestressed tendon through it.

Motorways and trunk roads need more than twice as many bridges per kilometre as older roads, and some 3,000 were built in the 1950s and 1960s. Bergg went on to design other bridges, in Kent and elsewhere, but never bettered this simple but inspired response to the beautiful setting of the North Downs.

Yvonne Arnaud Theatre

Millbrook, Guildford

1963–5, John Brownrigg
of Scott, Brownrigg and Turner

Listed grade II, 11 October 2012

Changes in theatre design towards a closer relationship with the audience were a response to more realistic acting and the artificiality of cinema and television. The first new-style auditorium for professional actors was at Chichester (see p.390), but elsewhere many theatres adopted an end stage and flexible apron forestage. The Yvonne Arnaud Theatre epitomizes the genre, its site by the River Wey donated by Guildford Council, which also gave £20,000; other funding came from public subscriptions. Its name commemorated a local actress and pianist.

This circular auditorium seats 560 people, with a revolving stage and cyclorama that offers alternatives to traditional painted scenery. Ribbed concrete walls and a reflective timber soffit over the stage provide rich acoustics. Encircling open foyers on three levels overlook a riverside terrace, their full-height glazing continuing between narrowly spaced vertical fins round to the lift tower and entrance, where their shadows are countered by an upswept canopy.

Former Gillett House

Chichester Theological College,
now Marriott House Nursing Home,
Chichester

1963–5, Ahrends, Burton and Koralek

Listed grade II, 31 January 1996

This former hostel for theological students was Ahrends, Burton and Koralek's (ABK) first English work. The brief sought 35 study-bedrooms, three staff flats, a library and a lecture room, which Richard Burton set around a courtyard, bridged at first-floor level over covered ways. It also had its own tiny chapel on the first floor.

The building is largely built of local red brick, with hefty concrete bridges and baffles. In addition to a window, each room has a skylight to give extra light to a desk beneath it. A library at the rear is also top-lit. It is the most brutalist of ABK's buildings with its expressionistic use of brick, concrete and tiles, and in its Corbusian waterspouts, but it already demonstrates the very precise, three-dimensional geometry that became the firm's signature.

The college was closed in 1994. Listing ensured its preservation, although in its conversion to a nursing home, part of the courtyard has been infilled and alterations made to the interior.

White Fox Lodge

Udimore, near Rye, East Sussex

1964–5, John Schwerdt and Partners

Listed grade II, 5 May 1999

Sidney Horniblow was a successful advertising manager who proposed a neo-Georgian bungalow for his collections of modern art and antique furniture. Instead, Schwerdt persuaded him to study Frank Lloyd Wright's houses while he was working in the United States.

The final design makes references to Wright's houses of the 1930s, to De Stijl designs and Mies van der Rohe's theoretical concept for a brick country house of 1924. These include its overhanging timber eaves and projecting brick walls, which emphasize the pinwheel plan and integrate the house with a garden by Sylvia Crowe and views across the South Downs. Each wing serves a different function, with living, sleeping, guest and service accommodation carefully separated. The internal finishes are simple but well crafted, with special attention being given to the full-height doors and fitted cupboards.

Details of the house were never published and it was unknown until Mrs Joan Horniblow requested it be listed shortly before her death. John Schwerdt trained in Brighton and worked around Lewes; this was his most ambitious work.

Church of the Resurrection

St Mary's Abbey, West Malling, Kent

1964–6, Maguire and Murray

Listed grade II*, 18 February 1999

The ruined convent of St Mary's Abbey, founded c.1090, was the setting for a Gothick house in the eighteenth century, when the surviving twelfth-century front and south transept were landscaped. The order was revived in 1892, and in 1916 Anglican Benedictine nuns moved here.

Maguire and Murray first rebuilt the fifteenth-century cloister, with a lounge for the nuns' visitors. For the new church Maguire gave himself greater freedom, because it is free-standing save for a link to the south transept. It is the most powerful expression of his belief, inspired by Rudolf Wittkower, in building the house of God in accordance with fundamental geometry – here a bold rectangle rising to a cylinder, with a conoid roof likened by Maguire to 'two half oasthouses'. The concrete block walls have the colour of medieval ragstone, but a smoothness that highlights their shape. Ring beams carry the weight of the roof to the walls, although internal columns were inserted in 1972.

The interior has recent fittings, save in a low side chapel for guests.

Long Wall

Golf Club Road, Weybridge, Surrey

1964–8, Leslie Gooday

Listed grade II, 15 July 1998

As work began on Gooday's swimming pool in Richmond, he designed a new house for himself outside Weybridge. There are similarities between the two buildings, notably in the way Long Wall is built up of differentiated volumes, some with flat roofs and others with a copper-clad mansard. Although quite large, this broken roofline ensures that the house slots demurely into the side of a wooded hillside. The different roof levels are expressed internally in a series of double-height and lower spaces. This is the second house that Gooday built for himself, and it owed something to Frank Lloyd Wright's Usonian houses but with a more complex, picturesque plan and use of contrasting materials.

Gooday came to prominence as staff architect to the Festival of Britain under Hugh Casson, from which he developed a specialism in industrial and exhibition design. This influence can be seen in the neatness of his architecture, and in his attention to details and finishes.

Church of Our Lady Help of Christians

Worth Abbey, Turners Hill,
West Sussex

1964–89, 2001, Francis Pollen

Listed grade II, 16 November 2007

Worth Abbey was founded in 1930 as a boys' boarding school. Pollen's first scheme, in 1957, was for an oval church, but in 1962 he produced a circular design in the centre of buildings for 50 monks and ten novices; a pyramidal roof was suggested, but a dome was preferred. Such geometry placed Worth in the vanguard of liturgical thinking, inspired by Rudolf Wittkower's *Architectural Principles in the Age of Humanism* – a key brutalist text – as well as Le Corbusier.

Worth Abbey was constructed austerely yet powerfully, with powerful brick columns and concrete beams. Local contractors would not give a price so John Lyles, the school's carpentry master, acted as contractor. The first service was held in 1970 and the church was consecrated in 1975. More vernacular elements followed for the monks' accommodation, only completed in 2001. Thomas Heatherwick designed fixed pews, monastic stalls and confessionals in a remodelling undertaken in 2011.

1 Leycroft Close

Canterbury

1966, Walter Greaves, construction overseen by E. Morton Wright

Listed grade II, 5 November 2010

When he joined the new University of Kent's English department, Morris Shapira commissioned Walter Greaves to design a modern house nearby. Greaves had assisted Peter Moro on the Royal Festival Hall and in private house work before establishing a small domestic practice of his own. When he moved to Sussex, Greaves handed Shapira's house to E. Morton Wright, who produced the working drawings and saw it through to completion.

Greaves's spatial ingenuity and an immaculate attention to detail are evident in this compact gem. From the road the house is enigmatic, with limited fenestration and a front door tucked out of sight. Once inside, however, views into the garden draw one through an unfolding sequence of hallway, dining area and living room, the latter using a fall in the land to gain added height. A study and a bedroom wing on half levels sit to one side. Neatly detailed, built-in furniture designed by Morton Wright survives throughout the house.

RC Chapel of the Most Holy Name

Sir John Moore Barracks,
Shorncliffe, Kent

1966–8, Zbigniew Jan Piet
of Brian and Norman Westwood,
Piet and Partners

Listed grade II, 25 January 2000

The Army only built a Roman Catholic chapel where there were many young trainees, as at the John Moore Barracks, built from 1961 for 750 school leavers. Its design was by Zbigniew Jan Petruszewski, who came to England in 1945 and studied at the Polish School of Architecture in Liverpool. He abbreviated his name on qualification.

The chapel is roughly triangular, with one curved wall to the sanctuary at the narrow end. Partly submerged in the ground, its concrete foundations are exposed internally as low walls formed in shuttering lined in polythene. Above soars the roof, where concealed lighting is reminiscent of Frank Lloyd Wright's Unitarian church at Shorewood Hills, Wisconsin, but built of Polish timber and inspired by boyhood Scout camps. For Piet, the building combined this nostalgia for the Poland of his youth with a deep gratitude for what Britain had given him.

Listed when it faced redundancy, the chapel – minus its fittings – is now a Gurkha museum.

South Downs House

Near Chichester

1966–8, Edward Cullinan
with Alice Milo

Listed grade II, 16 November 2007

Cullinan's first substantial house came through Denys Lasdun, who passed on this commission from Peter and Anne Law. The steeply sloping site had stunning views, and Cullinan raised and extended an Edwardian keeper's box in buff brick and concrete, with timber eaves and exposed end beams. A flat and partially grassed roof suggests that the house is emerging from the hill.

Most of the principal rooms are on the new upper floor, around a diagonal axis leading from the near-blind entrance front to the garden terrace facing the view, at first-floor level as the land falls away behind the house. A living room, with a feature fireplace, is linked to a dining room on the smaller lower floor set into the slope. Built-in fittings are designed with extraordinary attention to detail, down to doorknobs and switches, and demonstrate Cullinan's interest in storage as well as materials. His practice added an annexe in the 1970s.

Forest Lodge House

Epsom Road, Ashtead, Surrey

1967, Michael Manser

Listed grade II, 12 August 2003

Michael Manser's interest in steel began while he was a student, when Ove Arup introduced him to the work of Philip Johnson. It developed further when, in 1961–2, he built a house overhanging a cliff with the engineer Jack Dawson, with whom he designed more than 30 houses.

Forest Lodge House is a typical example, with its classical proportions and rectangular plan, but is exceptionally well detailed thanks to the close involvement of the client, John Vickers. Full-height glazing and opaque panels were interchangeable in the frame. The living area and cellular sleeping accommodation are divided by a spine of bathrooms and cupboards. Vickers supervised many of the details, including the excellent joinery. Sliding walls in the living areas could be partly opened up, which proved useful when Mrs Vickers was later confined to a wheelchair. Manser also advised on the addition made following the house's listing.

Thorndike Theatre

High Street, Leatherhead, Surrey

1967–9, Roderick Ham

Listed grade II, 8 July 1999

Leatherhead had a flourishing repertory company, established by Hazel Vincent-Wallace with support from Dame Sybil Thorndike and her husband Lewis Casson. Ham built a new theatre within the shell of the old Crescent Cinema, the frontage of which was sold for redevelopment as shops; the theatre has only a narrow entrance under a boldly lettered canopy.

The auditorium established Ham's reputation as a theatre specialist. It holds 526 seats in a single, steep tier; its 'Continental' arrangement without a central aisle has since been widely adopted. There was space for wheelchairs, served by a lift, long before disabled access became a requirement. The stage has a traditional fly tower and defined curtain line, but there is no moulded proscenium making a frame between the actors and audience. Foyer bars and cafés on three levels were designed with broad staircases and balconies under dramatic top lighting, where the audience became the stars. Listing saved the theatre from demolition, and it has since reopened.

Teesdale

Westwood Road, Windlesham, Surrey

1967–9, Ernö Goldfinger

Listed grade II*, 11 January 1999

Although Goldfinger is best remembered for his Balfron and Trellick towers in London, he also designed private houses, of which this is the best preserved after his own. It is quite different from Goldfinger's big blocks, though it was designed to a strict grid, with a timber frame and a monumentality that belies its tiny scale. The design evolved from a two-storey courtyard to the present linear arrangement to maximize the superlative view.

Teesdale is divided into two angled sections by a conservatory, rebuilt before the house was listed and again by engineers Malishev Wilson in 2006–7. One wing houses open-plan living areas; the other the bedrooms. The full-height windows are set back behind the overhanging roof, so that the thick timber columns frame the spectacular views. As requested by the client, all the rooms are lined in Western red cedar while a fireplace is set in a free-standing wall that defines the living room and study areas and is clad in white marble.

Capel Manor House

Grovehurst Lane, Horsmonden, Kent

1969–70, Michael Manser
Engineer, Jack Dawson

Listed grade II*, 18 September 2013

This is Manser and Dawson's finest house, designed in 1966–7 for John Howard MP, parliamentary private secretary to Edward Heath, to replace a villa of 1859–62 by T. H. Wyatt. They found that the raised terrace and cellars of the old house remained sound, and perched the new one on top to maximize views over the Victorian landscape. The colonnade of the adjoining winter garden was also retained, to screen a swimming pool, and Wyatt's proportions below determined Manser's 0.91m (3ft) by 1.22m (4ft) grid.

The house is remarkable for its transparency. This is the lightest of structures, with full-height glazing that has no mullions at the corners and sliding windows instead of doors. Deep boarded eaves enhance the relationship between indoors and outdoors, framing views, while internal walls of exposed brick define but do not enclose the sunken living area and create a pod for bathroom areas. The house has been immaculately restored by the current owner, who has created guest accommodation in a separate pavilion.

Vista Point

Tamarisk Way, Angmering-on-Sea,
West Sussex

1969–70, Patrick Gwynne

Listed grade II, 31 July 2006

Many of Gwynne's houses were designed for close friends, and Vista Point was commissioned by his quantity surveyor, Kenneth Monk, who wanted a weekend house overlooking the sea. Its principal rooms are set on the first floor behind a large balcony to enjoy the view, with bedrooms below.

As in many of Gwynne's houses, the accommodation is arranged around a top-lit spiral staircase, and Vista Point exemplifies the movement in his work towards more amoebic shapes. Its softly curved elevations splay out towards the street and still further on the taller elevation facing the sea. The sloping roof was likened by Stanley Holloway, a one-time neighbour, to a ski slope. Gwynne clad the stair hall in timber and lined other walls in his favourite textured grass paper. He enjoyed creating built-in furniture for his clients, at Vista Point creating orange kitchen fittings and two large hatches to the dining and living areas, for food and drinks respectively.

Branksome Conference Centre, formerly Olivetti

Hindhead Road, Haslemere, Surrey

1970–2, James Stirling

Listed grade II*, 21 January 1997

Edward Cullinan altered and James Stirling extended a house of 1901 by E. J. May as a training centre for Olivetti, major post-war architectural patrons. Stirling's work occupies a pivotal place between his brutalist, neo-Victorian aesthetic and later post-modernism. Colin Rowe claimed Thomas Hope's nearby Deepdene as an inspiration, with its similarly angled extension and glazed link. Stirling had begun collecting Hope artefacts, and Olivetti suggests affinities with late Georgian explorations of new materials, historic styles and the interplay between space and light.

Stirling's glazed ramp gives on to classrooms and a lecture theatre with sliding screens. They are formed of glass-reinforced polyester, introduced as a building material around 1964, which lent itself to the soft curves of Stirling's architecture just as it did to Olivetti's adding machines and typewriters. The building would have been more startling had he been allowed to use green and purple cladding panels outside instead of buff; his vibrant greens and yellows nevertheless dominate the interior.

Christ's Hospital Arts Centre and Music School

Horsham, West Sussex

1972–4, Bill Howell of Howell, Killick, Partridge and Amis

Listed grade II*, 4 December 2000

Christ's Hospital heralded the revival of the courtyard theatre in England, anticipating the Cottesloe (now Dorfman) auditorium at the National Theatre complex in 1973–7, and the Swan Theatre, Stratford-upon-Avon (1986). It also has architectural panache, with a tough timber structure, in brilliant red, to the galleries that ring a central flat space. The stage can be set centrally or at one end using the plentiful student labour.

Howell's building surrounds a music block built c.1910 on the axis of Aston Webb's neo-Baroque main hall. The school band marches the pupils into dinner twice a week, and Howell created a covered space where they can form up below a small recital hall raised on stilts. Spiral timber staircases to either side are in Howell, Killick, Partridge and Amis's chunky constructivist style. The hall and practice rooms form a symmetrical composition, to which the theatre is an adjunct. Howell was killed in a car accident and is commemorated in the foyer.

Thorncroft Manor

Leatherhead, Surrey

1974–6, Michael Manser
and Partners

Additions listed grade II*,
18 April 2002

Thorncroft Manor is a compact villa of 1772 by Sir Robert Taylor. It was converted to offices in the 1970s for a firm of engineers, who commissioned an extension. Faced with the problem of adding to a distinguished full-square house in a 'Capability' Brown landscape, Manser and his team devised a set-back, three-storey block clad entirely in mirror glass.

The mirror-glass building was the ultimate minimalist statement, making only subliminal use of classical proportions. The first example was the Bell Telephone Center at Holmdel, New Jersey, of 1962 by Eero Saarinen, and was followed in Britain by Norman Foster's offices for IBM at Cosham, Hampshire. Manser's building is neatly detailed and the top floor, originally a restaurant, is angled to reflect the sky. It took two years for the scheme to be approved by local planners. It was Manser's first major office building, tactful and yet confidently modern.

Severels

Runcton Lane, Runcton,
West Sussex

1980–1, Walter Greaves

Listed grade II*, 29 August 2013

Walter Greaves met his wife Annabel when he and his boss Peter Moro designed a house for her parents in Chichester. The couple returned to the area in the late 1960s, and once their four children had grown up they built a house in the grounds of their former home. A stream canalized by Greaves creates the boundary and a picturesque setting.

The new house evolved slowly as a labour of love. It is a series of amorphous modules with rounded corners linked by a broad central corridor. They are built of timber and are boarded in mellow cedar, prone to attack by woodpeckers. Most are single storey, as Greaves developed multiple sclerosis, and a ground-floor bedroom suite lies immediately below that on the first floor, whose stair is lit by an oriel window that dominates the main façade. The tall living room has open rafters, a brick chimneypiece and built-in window seats that continue into the adjoining kitchen. This is a generous yet carefully detailed house with subtle yet beautiful features.

Sutton Place

near Guildford, Surrey

1980–3, Sir Geoffrey Jellicoe

Landscape registered grade II*,
8 August 2001

Jellicoe was considering retirement in 1980 when he was commissioned by the American Stanley Seeger to develop a complex of gardens around a Tudor mansion, within informal nineteenth-century grounds and more formal enclosures south of the house that had been laid out after 1900.

Jellicoe and Seeger shared a belief that landscape art should be a continuum of past, present and future, and have allegorical meanings. North of the house, Jellicoe created a foetus-shaped lake in the open landscape, adjoining hills that represented the ages of man. Garden rooms adjoin the house, including the Paradise Garden to the east, reached by stepping stones across a moat. More famous is the garden sequence to the west, where a former swimming pool was remodelled and a long, narrowing walkway adjoining the kitchen garden was lined with urns from Mentmore in an optical illusion inspired by René Magritte. Most remarkable is an older hedged enclosure with a reflecting pool, into which Jellicoe inserted Ben Nicholson's giant *White Relief* in Carrara marble, his last major work.

Desert Quartet, Montague Shopping Centre

Alexander Terrace, Worthing

1989, Dame Elisabeth Frink
on a loggia by Graham Excell

Listed grade II*, 11 May 2007

In 1985, a new shopping centre was designed opposite Liverpool Terrace, at the heart of Regency Worthing. In recompense, the developers engaged Excell to produce a sympathetic design for the façade opposite, which included bespoke sculpture. Elisabeth Frink (1930–93) was commissioned that year.

The solution was a stuccoed, neo-classical loggia, which supported four monumental heads. They were called the *Desert Quartet* because they were inspired by ancient monuments that Frink had seen in the Tunisian desert. Cast in bronze, but with a textured surface that reveals her method of first carving a plaster model, they are the culmination of a long exploration of the male head — one of a handful of subjects that fascinated Frink throughout her career. The *Desert Quartet* is unusual in combining four such massive heads in one piece, each with a subtle individuality of expression. It was one of her last public works. Listing led to the retention of the sculpture, and in 2015 it and the loggia remain England's youngest listed structure.

School of Oriental
and African Studies,
1970–3, 1970–6,
Denys Lasdun and Partners

E. Pellicci café

332 Bethnal Green Road,
Bethnal Green

1946

Listed grade II, 13 January 2005

Bolotonno Fabrizi acquired a confectioner's shop here in 1908, and passed it to the Pellicci family in 1915. Mrs Elide Pellicci turned it into a café in 1939, but it was only in 1946 that she could undertake its remarkable remodelling. Many Italian immigrants made the transition from ice-cream manufacturing to running cafés and coffee bars, aided in the 1950s by the arrival of Gaggia coffee machines. Mrs Pellicci's shopfront was of Vitrolite, an American opaque glass developed in Britain by Pilkington's and here an unusual primrose yellow – a welcome antidote to the drab war years. The fascia proudly announces her business in shiny steel letters.

The tiny interior is richly decorated with elaborate Art Deco marquetry by Achille Capocci, including sunbursts and Egyptian capitals. It provides stylish, if old-fashioned, surroundings for fry-ups and steaming espressos.

Elide's son, Nevio Pellicci, was awarded the Medallio d'Oro for services to the promotion of Italian culture abroad soon after the building was listed.

Spa Green Estate

Rosebery Avenue, Islington

1946–50, Francis Skinner
and Berthold Lubetkin
(succeeding Tecton)

Listed grade II*, 22 December 1998

Berthold Lubetkin was commissioned in 1938 to design housing for the Borough of Finsbury, following his progressive health centre there. Bomb damage expanded the site, and the *County of London Plan* prescribed a density of 200 persons per acre.

By 1942 the engineer Ove Arup's experiments at Lubetkin's Highpoint II (1936–8) had evolved into a building structure of reinforced cross-walls and floors called a box frame. It was economical of materials while, unlike conventional cross-walling, it permitted varied plans and for the lowest block to have a serpentine curve. It also freed Lubetkin to orchestrate the façades in syncopated patterns of brick, tiles and balconies based on Caucasian carpets.

With generous government loans in 1945–7 there was money for decent lifts, wood block floors and a Garchey refuse disposal system, making the blocks lavishly equipped as well as looking lively. The rooftops of the two taller blocks have aerodynamic enclosures for drying clothes, while the low block incorporates the estate office.

Barn Field and Wood Field

Parkhill Road, Hampstead

1947–9, Farquharson and McMorran

Listed grade II, 22 December 2000

Hampstead Borough Council commissioned these two blocks of flats (named after old fields) to replace buildings lost to war damage. Encouraged by its architect councillor, Oswald Milne, it determined that they should reflect the area's eighteenth-century character, and in Donald McMorran found a sympathetic yet inventive designer.

These, his first and most lavish flats, combine references from John Soane and Scandinavia to create a lean, spare but well-proportioned classicism. The grouping of windows is distinctive, as is the device of setting little tiled gabled roofs behind a high parapet – here stepped down the sloping site. The dwellings are well equipped with lifts – exceptional for a four-storey block – set in a slight projection on the outer face of the staircase halls. Many flats retain original fireplaces and cupboards. The semi-basement has a store for each flat and a covered play area.

Listing was prompted when residents opposed the council's scheme to replace McMorran's finely detailed sash windows with uPVC units.

Newbury Park bus station

Eastern Avenue, Ilford

1947–9, Oliver Hill

Listed grade II, 19 March 1981

In 1937 Oliver Hill was commissioned to rebuild Newbury Park Station as a transport interchange, as part of the electrification of what became the Central Line. Frank Pick, London Transport's design patron, had met Hill at the Council of Art and Industry. However, the war intervened, and in 1947 only the bus station and a canteen were deemed sufficiently important to secure a building licence.

The simplicity of Hill's bus station symbolizes post-war austerity. It is a concrete barrel vault of painful thinness, cast on seven round-arched ribs and sheathed in copper. The primitive shell construction, with no prestressing, indicates the work of an architect rather than engineer, and perhaps its pre-war origins. The building was a popular winner of a Festival of Britain Merit Award in 1951, whose distinctive Poole Pottery blue plaque faces the road.

It is such a striking local landmark that it was quietly listed as early as 1981, in a resurvey of older Redbridge buildings, as a 1930s design. It was restored in 1994–5.

Woodberry Down Primary School

Woodberry Grove

1949–51, London County Council Architect's Department

Listed grade II, 23 January 2007

In 1947 the London County Council (LCC) prioritized building primary schools for its new housing estates, including the Woodberry Down neighbourhood. The most sophisticated school of the programme, it was built of yellow brick and blue tiles to a Scandinavian-inspired design with shallow pitched roofs.

The entrance is on a narrow, sloping site adjoining the New River. It retains its LCC plaque and script lettering for 'Infants' and 'Juniors', also tiled. The long finger plan and blocky massing are characteristic of the 1940s, with the assembly and dining halls stacked – juniors above infants – taking advantage of the slope. The interior features a sgraffito mural in cement by Augustus Lunn, salvaged from the Festival of Britain's South Bank exhibition in 1951. It depicts youths woodworking and reading, with a bee above a microscope and violin.

Brick schools proved slow and expensive to build and the LCC turned to prefabrication, so the durable, careful construction of Woodberry Down was not repeated.

John Scott Health Centre

Green Lanes, Woodberry Down

1949–52, W. J. Durnford and
A. E. Miller, London County Council

Listed grade II, 23 January 2007

The National Health Service Act (1946) promoted comprehensive health centres for the whole family, and the London County Council began acquiring sites, starting at its flagship estate at Woodberry Down. Durnford and Miller prepared designs with the council's medical officer, Dr John A. Scott. But then the Ministry reneged on its promise and the centre was built only after a personal appeal to Aneurin Bevan, who turned the first sod on the site. Elsewhere, Bevan pushed his limited building resources into housing.

As Britain's first health centre, Woodberry Down was unique for its scale and opulence. The brick exterior is simple, though it makes references to the seminal 1930s Finsbury Health Centre in its use of glass bricks. Inside there is a panelled entrance hall, a doctors' common room with a stone fireplace and luncheon facilities, and the café and meeting hall are also original. Most elaborate are the staircase balustrades, made of mild steel and etched glass like those at Simpson's of Piccadilly, a model of pre-war modernist luxury.

Lansbury Lawrence School

Cordelia Street, Poplar

1949–52, Yorke, Rosenberg and Mardall

Listed grade II, 5 March 1998

The two-storey primary school was the first and most admired building in the Lansbury Neighbourhood, the 'Live Architecture' exhibition of the Festival of Britain where a real piece of the East End was rebuilt. It was named after Susan Lawrence and Elizabeth Lansbury, local campaigners against working-class poverty in Poplar in the 1920s.

Yorke, Rosenberg and Mardall (YRM) were an international team experienced in prefabricated construction, and there is a steel frame of 2.51m (8ft 3in) by Hills of West Bromwich under the stone, brick and concrete cladding. Infants are on the ground floor and juniors above, their assembly halls set prominently one above the other. YRM's innovation was to introduce roof lights into the infants' corridor by placing that for the juniors upstairs to one side, with glazed spurs linking it to paired classrooms. Vivid geometric tiles by Peggy Angus enliven the dining hall and entrance hall – the latter carefully restored in 2007. They also feature in the single-storey nursery added alongside in 1952, the first built by the London County Council after the war.

Greenside School

Westville Road, Hammersmith

1950, Ernö Goldfinger

Listed grade II*, 30 March 1993

Brandlehow School

Brandlehow Road, Putney

1950, Ernö Goldfinger

Listed grade II, 30 March 1993

Greenside and Brandlehow schools were designed by Goldfinger using the London County Council's budget for temporary buildings, and cost £131 and £124 per place respectively. Goldfinger achieved this economy by developing his own concrete-framed system, a contrast to the two-storey steel frames being adopted at Lansbury Lawrence and elsewhere.

Goldfinger's portal frames were erected in four weeks, and were then infilled with brick and large windows, some with canted glazing. The corridor planning is very simple, and sinks for messy work had later to be added, but his design has a strength and architectural presence. Both schools have been sympathetically extended, and the caretaker's house at Brandlehow has been rebuilt as maisonettes after it was demolished illegally.

Though little different apart from Brandlehow's red bricks and Greenside's gentler yellow stocks (see photograph), the latter is listed grade II* for its exceptional mural by Gordon Cullen, urban designer and artist to the *Architectural Review*, with cameos restored in 2011 that include the Comet aeroplane and a modern locomotive.

Calvary Charismatic Baptist Church

East India Dock Road, Poplar

1950–1, Cecil Handisyde
and Douglas Rogers Stark

Listed grade II, 25 September 1998

Trinity Congregational Church was destroyed by a rocket in 1944. Stark's father, a prominent member of the congregation, was an architect but passed the job of replacing it to his son at the London County Council. The younger Stark brought in Handisyde, and obtained the building licence by securing its admission into Lansbury's 'Live Architecture' exhibition. The council dictated the choice of brick.

Trinity was the first post-war 'church centre', with community facilities and schoolrooms as well as a church. It was imitated in new towns and on estates where social facilities were limited. The church itself has an external portal frame from which the roof is suspended; concentrating light sources in the roof reduced traffic noise. Sloping side walls were designed for good acoustics, with balconies for overflow congregations on special occasions. There is etched glass from the old church. A surviving bell prompted the tall tower, its Scandinavian styling by Handisyde.

Trinity became a Methodist church in 1976 and a charismatic Baptist church in 2006.

YMCA Indian Student Hostel

Fitzroy Square, Camden

1950–2, 1962–4, Ralph Tubbs

Listed grade II, 6 March 1996

This hostel is a gallant symbol of a newly independent nation, built as a base for Indian students in London. It replaced a hostel founded in 1923 in Gower Street, which after wartime bombing was acquired by University College, who presented this site in return.

Tubbs was anxious to avoid parallel lines where possible – hence the main stair's acute angles and the basement hall's raking rear windows. The Festival of Britain styling is a reminder that Tubbs was the architect of its 'Dome of Discovery'. The large first-floor windows light reading and television rooms, while a rooftop non-denominational prayer room gives weight to the corner of the square. The building has a close relationship with Fitzroy Square. It sits between Robert Adam's two terraces, which governed its height and massing, but not its style.

Tubbs extended the block in 1960–2, and more additions were made in 2002–4. The hostel remains an important cultural centre, with a popular ground-floor restaurant and the basement Mahatma Gandhi Memorial Hall.

RC Church of SS Mary and Joseph

Upper North Street, Poplar

1950–4, Adrian Gilbert Scott

Listed grade II, 5 March 1998

Of all the buildings erected within the 'Live Architecture' exhibition at Lansbury, this was the most traditional and was thus reviled. Yet in 1951 only its foundations had been laid. Now we can admire it as one of the most powerful church compositions of the 1950s.

The funder, the War Damage Commission, insisted that the new church should be the same size as its bombed predecessor, although many of the congregation had left the area. A Greek cross plan was adopted for the tight site, which proved easy to adapt to post-Vatican II liturgical requirements by bringing Scott's baldacchino forward.

Most powerful is the brick exterior, which steps up to a broad central tower, each level topped with a cornice and pantiles. Parabolic arches, within and without, derive from a scheme of 1946–7 by Scott's brother Sir Giles for Coventry Cathedral, and became a feature of Adrian's work. Inside, the stone dado, with Stations of the Cross by Peter Watts, was also much repeated.

St Columba's Church

Pont Street, Kensington

1950–5, Edward Maufe

Listed grade II, 29 March 1998

Thanks to its central location and some remarkable ministers, St Columba's, founded in 1883, became London's pre-eminent Scottish Presbyterian church before it was destroyed in 1941. Maufe exhibited designs for a new church as early as 1944, which the realized building closely followed.

The design features a Scandinavian-style tower and simple Portland stone walling. Maufe also suggested seventeenth-century Scottish churches as an inspiration for one of his most inventive exteriors. Heavily moulded capitals grace the columns of its entrance hall and stairs leading to the first-floor church. Worship extends to a Sunday lunch in the ground-floor hall, where services were held before the church was finally completed.

The church has the narrow passage aisles characteristic of Maufe's Anglican designs, but it is otherwise wider and lighter. The simple round-arched arcades lack any Gothic traits, and heraldic panels provide the principal decoration. Maufe's favourite collaborators provided decoration, including a rose window by Moira Forsyth and a figure of St Columba by Vernon Hill.

Technical Block A

Heathrow

1950–5, Sir E. Owen Williams
and Partners

Listed grade II*, 2 April 1996

Heathrow was acquired in 1943–4 with the intention that it should become a civil airport after the war, and Williams was commissioned to design a hangar, maintenance and office complex in 1950. He created an unusually egalitarian building for 4,000 staff under a single roof – a simple yet logical piece of rectangular geometry with a hangar in each corner. A spine of engineering workshops runs the length of the building and offices form a cross-axis and entrance façade.

Williams demonstrated that concrete was cheaper than steel. He placed great cantilever arches at the entrance to each hangar, each with a span of 102.4m (336ft), and counterbalanced by ear-like protrusions revisiting those over his Empire Pool of 1934. Suspended between them is a beam 2.74m (9ft) deep, in a technique adapted from bridge-building, which supports the folding doors and braced concrete roof. All these entrances survive, but three of the hangars were extended in 1980 to take longer aircraft; the south hangar survives with its original doors.

All Saints Church

Uxbridge Road, Hanworth

1950–1, 1956–7,
N. F. Cachemaille-Day

Listed grade II, 15 April 1991

A church for this new neighbourhood was postponed by the war and shortages of materials. Cachemaille-Day produced a design that was built in two phases, with the low entrance range being consecrated in 1951 and the main church in 1957. The relief over the main entrance is by Bainbridge Copnall.

The square church is spanned by two reinforced concrete arches, which support a central glazed corona. A wide, shallow apse lined in gold leaf exemplifies Cachemaille-Day's interest in rich colours and contrasts of light and shade. He wrote in 1946 of the need to bring celebrant and congregation closer in worship, and experimented with liturgical ideas when clients allowed. He often put the choir into a gallery at the west end, and here the choir was briefly in the centre of the congregation before being moved to the back.

Abstract glass in the cupola adds warmth and mystery, while figurative glass is sandblasted.

The Phoenix School

Bow Road, Bow

1951–2, Farquharson and McMorran for London County Council

Listed grade II*, 30 March 1993

The Phoenix School was built as an open-air school for delicate and asthmatic children, replacing a school created in 1921–2 out of First World War army huts, which was destroyed in 1940. Earlier open-air schools were formed from lightweight timber shelters, but here a more substantial hall and two-storey classrooms were proposed – although heating was minimal. Children received three substantial meals a day, were expected to rest in the afternoons and had many lessons outdoors in the tree-lined courtyards.

Donald McMorran is best known for his neo-classical architecture. Here he produced a simple yet elegant design of brick and glass, cladding a precast concrete frame without extraneous ornamentation. Covered walkways, now glazed in, link the central hall with its commanding bellcote to two-storey classrooms to the north, and a lower housecraft room, now the dining hall, to the south. Sympathetic extensions have created a courtyard for primary school children.

Phoenix is now a Supported National Curriculum school, serving students aged 2–16.

15, 17 and 19 Aubrey Walk

Kensington

1951–2, Raymond Erith

Listed grade II, 29 March 1988

That the late Georgian terrace had affinities with those of the austere 1950s is nowhere better demonstrated than in this example by the master of the genre. Erith massed blank walls either side of round-headed relieving arches and blind windows; the paved forecourt and simple railings are integral to the composition. The houses have few windows facing the street because Erith introduced a contrastingly vivacious Regency style of bow windows and verandahs to the rear elevations, where the houses share a secluded rear garden. Internally, the small scale is resolved by tightly planning the staircases and by Erith's restrained detailing. The houses have since been combined into one.

The design was suggested by nearby terraces (Nos. 2–26) of c.1826, but Erith's is a more inventive composition. It was admired by no less a person than the modernist Ian Nairn, who called it 'not a copy or a pastiche, but the real thing . . . It shows up the fussy modernity of the houses opposite, something I wish that I did not have to admit.'

Bevin Court

Cruickshank Street, Islington

1951–4, Skinner, Bailey and Lubetkin

Listed grade II*, 22 December 1998

Lubetkin first erected a memorial here to Lenin, who stayed nearby in 1902–3. When it was vandalized, the remains were buried under this new housing for Finsbury Borough Council, surprisingly named after Labour's anti-communist Foreign Secretary; Francis Skinner quipped that only two letters needed changing.

Early plans for staggered blocks around a traditional square were frustrated by cuts in August 1947, and Lubetkin found that one seven-storey block was cheaper. Bevin Court has a 'Y' plan giving maximum sunshine. Lubetkin devised chequered elevations of brick and precast panels that show the alternating floor plans permitted by the block's rigid box frame construction.

The climax is the central stairwell, within which stairs are cantilevered from half landings within a circular open well. Their plan repeats every third floor, in an evolution from the ramps of Lubetkin and Tecton's penguin pool at London Zoo – but for humans – and the most baroque example of Lubetkin's obsession with pattern and movement. The entrance mural incorporating heraldic symbols is by Peter Yates of Ryder and Yates.

Church of St Mary the Virgin

Worton Road, Isleworth

1952–5, H. S. Goodhart-Rendel

Listed grade II, 16 November 2007

Designed in 1937 and built without major revisions, St Mary's is transitional between Goodhart-Rendel's pre-war and post-war work, and his last new Anglican church. The exterior features the brick diapering typical of his buildings, which after the war combined traditional Arts and Crafts motifs and modestly painted interiors with innovation in construction. The plan is simpler than it looks, a central crossing with broad transepts and nave spanned economically by cleverly intersecting brick arches of deceptively different widths, a concept developed from Eric Gill's St Peter's, Gorleston, Norfolk, of 1938–9. The Diocletian windows in the crossing are a more typical Goodhart-Rendel feature. The sanctuary area was extended in 2006, when the church was painted pink.

The large faience-tiled reredos behind the altar was designed by Goodhart-Rendel's favourite artist, Joseph Ledger, and made by Carter and Co. of Poole.

Trades Union Congress Memorial Building

Great Russell Street

1953–7, David du Rieu Aberdeen

Listed grade II*, 29 March 1988

Congress House combines the functions of war memorial, public hall, offices, council chamber and education centre on a confined site adjoining Lutyens's YWCA hostel. A competition was held in 1948, but building was then delayed. When it was finally completed, it merited a special issue of the trendsetting *Architectural Design*, such was its importance as late as 1957.

The main façade is an honest curtain wall fronting offices that is dominated by Bernard Meadow's giant bronze figures of workers. The side elevation, by contrast, contains a surfeit of contrasting volumes that define the cantilevered horseshoe staircase, projecting library and garaging. The interior is a demonstration of quality finishes and model working conditions, with panelled offices, while the basement conference hall is top-lit above a space frame roof. The interior has been substantially upgraded while retaining the major features.

The central courtyard contains the memorial. The wall of the YWCA was faced in marble (since renewed) and Jacob Epstein's giant pietà of a worker was unveiled early in 1958.

Bousfield School

South Bolton Gardens, Kensington

1954–6, Chamberlin, Powell and Bon

Listed grade II, 30 March 1993

Bousfield School is full of humour and humanity as well as architectural invention. It replaced several large houses damaged in the Second World War, including one lived in by Beatrix Potter, commemorated by a plaque. The entrance from The Boltons has a water jump instead of fencing – to deter school inspectors, Powell quipped. Slits in the wall alongside give views over an open-air theatre.

The plan comprises a single-storey infants' department and two-storey junior school on either side of paired assembly halls. On the first floor are twin dining halls with a shared servery set over the kitchen. The architects designed a steel frame on a near-metre grid (3ft 4in), left exposed and infilled with aluminium-framed curtain walling similar to that at Great Arthur House, Golden Lane (see p.504). Early Chamberlin, Powell and Bon schemes use brilliant colours: the yellow verticals and blue horizontal panels, with green where they meet, are a youngsters' guide to colour theory. The water tank in the playground resembles a giant lollypop or Belisha beacon.

10 Regent's Park Road

Primrose Hill

1954–6, Ernö Goldfinger

Listed grade II, 22 December 1998

These small flats replaced a bombed house, and were built for ten friends who had formed a housing association. Goldfinger had to make the proportions of his building fit with those of its neighbours, which are not in line, so while the front wall adjoins that of the house to the right, the balcony fronts align with that to the left.

There were originally two flats per floor (some are now knocked together), with rooftop studios hidden behind a terrace and parapet so that the building appears no taller than its neighbours. They are compact, with folding partitions and timber fittings. The entrance, over a communal basement laundry and garden room, has square-paned surrounds reminiscent of Goldfinger's own Willow Road house. A cantilevered staircase with open risers was much repeated.

The exposed, wire-brushed concrete and red brick were Goldfinger's first exploitation of the sculptural possibilities of a frame and infill composition, as inspired by Auguste Perret.

Sulkin and Trevelyan Houses

Usk Street and Morpeth Street, Bethnal Green

1955–8, Denys Lasdun
of Fry, Drew, Drake and Lasdun

Listed grade II, 22 December 1998

From Columbia Market to the first London County Council flats, the early history of charitable housing can be told within Bethnal Green. Peter Benenson, deputy head of the borough's housing committee and founder of Amnesty International, was anxious that local people should be rehoused within the borough rather than out in the suburbs. Lasdun's was one of four modern practices commissioned in 1951.

The area granted Lasdun was bisected by old roads and retained buildings. Sulkin House replaced a Victorian church, and contains the boiler house for the entire scheme of three slabs and two towers. The two listed towers have a butterfly plan, with 12 maisonettes set either side of a central lift and staircase in a separate core. They thus pioneered his 'cluster' concept, separating noisy services from flats, as Goldfinger later did at Balfron Tower (see p.474), while the facing lines of balconies on either side were a rare encouragement of neighbourliness in the air. Lasdun was limited to eight storeys here but developed these ideas further at Keeling House (see p.443).

BBC Television Centre

Wood Lane, Hammersmith

1955–60, Graham Dawbarn
and Walton H. Lindsay
of Norman and Dawbarn

Listed grade II, 9 July 2009

The BBC made the world's first regular television broadcasts, and quickly realized the need for purpose-built studios. It acquired land in 1949 and commissioned Dawbarn, who first sketched a drum of offices surrounded by studios and workshops on the back of an envelope. Corridors and driveways separated artists, administrators and technicians save on the studio floor. The plan was compact yet extendable, and was essentially the one that was realized after long funding delays.

The distinctive core or 'doughnut' remains little altered. Offices surround a courtyard, where a central sculpture depicting Helios radiating light around the world by T. B. Huxley-Jones is set over semi-submerged sound laboratories. A glazed entrance hall features John Piper's giant mosaic mural, an abstract integration of architecture and design. This core was surrounded by seven studios, dominated by Studio 1 with its dotted façade. Television Centre closed in 2013.

Our Lady of Mount Carmel and St Simon Stock RC Church

Kensington Church Street, Kensington

1957–9, Sir Giles Gilbert Scott

Listed grade II, 25 September 1998

A Carmelite church was established in Kensington by Father Hermann, a Jewish convert who came to England in 1862. The church built by E. W. Pugin in 1862–3 was gutted in 1943 and totally destroyed by a rocket in 1944.

Scott's replacement is built of pale brick. It has a luminance reminiscent of his first parish church – the Annunciation, Bournemouth (1906) – for the sanctuary, with its gilded reredos, is lit by concealed windows hidden behind the chancel arch; they also make the church seem taller than it is. A series of arches form trusses that span the passage aisles (incorporating Stations of the Cross) and broad nave. They stop short of the roof, so that light can freely enter from the clerestories above – for there are no windows in the nave walls.

The original church was noted for its Cavaillé-Col organ, and a new organ was installed in 1965 by Ralph Downes, who had designed the organ in the Royal Festival Hall.

6 Bacon's Lane

Highgate

1957–9, Leonard Manasseh

Listed grade II, 10 August 2009

Manasseh built three houses on the site of a Victorian villa, on one side of a street of architect-designed houses. He secured the plot overlooking Highgate Cemetery for himself and his large family, and remodelled the kitchen garden to incorporate Daphne Hardy-Henrion's sculpture *Youth*, rescued from the bar he designed for the Festival of Britain's South Bank.

The steep, unequally pitched roof overcame a covenant on the site that restricted new building to two storeys, and incorporates a gallery to the double-height living room. The main entrance is at half-landing level, between the adults' rooms on the first floor and the ground-floor kitchen-diner, a playroom and children's bedrooms. Manasseh co-designed the built-in dresser. Most distinctive are the materials: salvaged stock bricks are contrasted with exposed concrete floors externally and are unplastered within, while Manasseh bought 74 marble washstands to make the living room and bathroom floors. A personal response to the 'as found' aesthetic extolled by the new brutalism, the house signalled a greater toughness in Manasseh's work.

Keeling House

Claredale Street, Bethnal Green

1957–9, Denys Lasdun
of Fry, Drew, Drake and Lasdun

Listed grade II*, 23 November 1993

Here Lasdun fulfilled his ambition to build a tall 'cluster block', inspired by a visit to the United States and Kevin Lynch's theoretical writings. He identified a cluster as a unit of size and grain equivalent to an East End street, and conducted a survey of local needs.

Keeling House required the demolition of just six houses. At 16 storeys, it was London's second tall block (after Golden Lane), four pairs of maisonettes around a separate central lift and stair tower offering sound insulation yet neighbourliness. The staircases have storage lobbies on alternate levels. On the fifth floor, the maximum height for firemen's ladders, there are bedsitters. The flats, built around precast end panels that acted as shuttering, have the clean proportions found in 1930s modernism.

In 1992 the block was set for demolition because of spalled concrete, but following listing it was sold for £1.3 million and restored by Marshall and Munchenback, who later added penthouses. Lasdun's unlisted slab blocks and pensioners' bungalows alongside have been demolished.

The Firs

Spaniard's End, Hampstead Heath

1958, Patrick Gwynne

Listed grade II, 28 November 1996

Gwynne was introduced to Mr and Mrs Otto Edler by the builder Leslie Bilsby, and produced a house that is rich in its materials and playful in its curvaceous plan and detailing. The Edlers wanted all the principal rooms to face south across the garden, so Gwynne made this elevation wider, with bowed brick walls to either side as he later repeated at Vista Point (see p.409). A mosaic-clad fascia supports the roof, which similarly tilts up towards the garden, where it is supported on steel columns that also carry a balcony.

This richness of shapes and materials continues inside, with a strong 1950s character. The living room has big steel windows, a sliding screen to separate it from the study when a single space is not required, and cupboards that revolve to conceal the television. The fireplace wall is lined in marble. The circular stairwell is another distinctive feature that Gwynne repeated subsequently. His sense of shape and proportion extended to the kitchen, where he installed a kidney-shaped island table.

St Mary's Church

Brentmead Gardens, West Twyford

1957–8, N. F. Cachemaille-Day

Additions listed grade II,
25 February 2010

A church was recorded at West Twyford in the Domesday Survey, but by the eighteenth century it served little more than the adjoining manor house. In 1807–9 William Atkinson rebuilt both in the Gothick style, when the house was renamed Twyford Abbey.

West Twyford expanded rapidly with the building of the North Circular Road in 1930, but it was not until 1956 that Cachemaille-Day designed a parish church as an addition to Atkinson's work, which became the Lady chapel. A west choir gallery was omitted from the final design, although the simplified adjoining tower was enlivened by Kathleen Parbury's sculpture, *Madonna and Child*. Instead, the west end has tiny windows containing abstract glass by A. E. Buss, who also designed the east window in the old chapel. The greatest features are mushroom-like columns resembling those of Frank Lloyd Wright's Johnson Wax factory.

The new church was built over a stream and faced demolition when its foundations slipped. Instead its church fittings have been removed and it has become a hall to Atkinson's chapel.

St Paul's Church

Burdett Road, Bow Common

1958–60, Robert Maguire
and Keith Murray

Listed grade II*, 29 March 1988

St Paul's is the vanguard of the Liturgical Movement in the Church of England, the vision of its long-serving incumbent Father Gresham Kirkby. He admired the free-standing altar at the nearby Royal Foundation of St Katharine by the silversmith Keith Murray, who introduced him to Maguire. Their partnership and the New Churches Research Group were founded in 1957–8.

St Paul's is a stepped cube centred on an altar set under a glazed pyramidal roof. It is raised up two steps beneath a baldacchino of black steel. The congregation sit all around on benches, and around them in turn the processional route runs behind a segmental arched arcade later decorated with mosaics by Charles Lutyens. There are projecting side chapels and an entrance porch, where – symbolically – sits the font, formed from an off-the-peg industrial vat.

Maguire brought to church-building the interest in natural materials and Wittkower that had inspired the Smithsons. The building of St Paul's coincided with Peter Hammond's campaign for liturgical planning and his influential book *Liturgy and Architecture*.

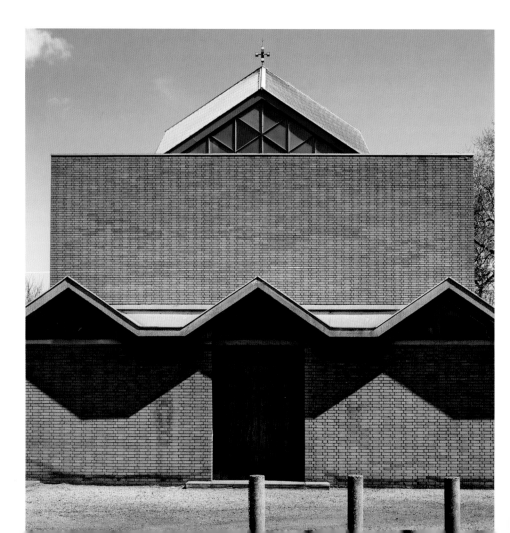

Kensington Central Library

Hornton Street, Kensington

1958–60, E. Vincent Harris

Listed grade II*, 24 April 1998

Vincent Harris claimed that Kensington did not want a modern design for its library. Today it is celebrated as perhaps his last great work, but in February 1959 art and architecture students opposed to traditional or bland new buildings led an 'Anti-Ugly' protest outside it.

The design, with its end pavilions pierced by arched openings, is characteristic of Harris. Such pavilions first appear in his county hall competition entry of 1907 and were built at Bristol Council House (1939–57). Here they support busts of Chaucer and Caxton, and the parapet is surmounted by a figure, *Genius*, by William McMillan, who also did the mighty stone lion and unicorn pylons that symbolize the borough's Royal status.

The internal planning is spacious. The end pavilions – one is the entrance, the other the children's library – are lined with Doulting stone; between them the lending library is simply finished, but the lofty proportions and columns give great dignity. The first-floor reference library has sumptuous walnut panelling, and both spaces retain original mahogany bookcases.

30A Hendon Avenue

Finchley

1959, Geoffry Powell
of Chamberlin, Powell and Bon

Listed grade II, 28 November 1998

Dr Erich Rossdale was a German Jewish refugee who requalified as a doctor in Britain while his wife went out to work, prospered and supported him. Why they chose Chamberlin, Powell and Bon to design a small house for their retirement is unknown, but they proved to be the firm's most contented clients. They sought a modern house, even though it was always to be filled with traditional furniture.

The house is raised on stilts so that it nestles amidst the treetops of its orchard setting. A large terrace is reached via steps, with the area beneath serving as a store, and the house is largely timber-framed save for a central core housing the ground-floor garage and chimney stack. Powell suggested that this also contain a snug inglenook within the large, open-plan living room, to give a choice of spaces appropriate to the changing seasons.

More trees now surround the house, but Powell's expression of materials and clever plan remains intelligent and logical.

RC Church of St William of York

Du Cros Drive, Stanmore

1959–60, Hector Corfiato

Listed grade II, 19 July 2006

The Roman Catholic parish of Stanmore was created in 1938, but building was delayed by the war. The dedication reflects a movement to celebrate English saints.

Corfiato studied in Paris before coming to teach at London's Bartlett School of Architecture, which in the 1950s became a last bastion of neo-classicism. One of three churches by him, St William of York has a remarkably complete and refined interior that cost £81,000 instead of the intended £54,000. The bricks lining the interior are narrow and beautifully laid, with circular columns to the single aisle reminiscent of those Corfiato had adopted at Notre Dame de France (see p.504). Classical details appear in the pews, the confessionals and the altar rails; a forward altar has been installed without disturbing the older fittings. Dominating the Byzantine interior is the soaring baldacchino with black and gold columns, its canopy swathed in gold cloth and hung with tassels. At Corfiato's death in 1963, his work was described as 'sensitive and beautiful', aptly describing this harmonious design.

St Michael and All Angels Church

Lansdowne Drive, London Fields

1959–60, N. F. Cachemaille-Day

Listed grade II, 28 March 2006

St Michael's is the most ambitious of a series of churches and restorations by Cachemaille-Day in Hackney. It is one of his last churches, funded by compensation for a war-damaged church on the other side of London Fields.

The brick exterior is austere, but the interior is wonderfully colourful and light. It has a high, curved shell roof, and after a design for a baldacchino was rejected, Cachemaille-Day created a simple octagonal frame for the central altar. Rather than the strong chiaroscuro of his pencil drawings, there is vibrant stained glass made to his designs by Goddard and Gibbs.

The joy of the church is its fine works by John Hayward: the dramatic aluminium sculpture of St Michael slaying the dragon over the entrance, stained-glass figures of the apostles, and striking murals depicting Old and New Testament scenes and the Baptism of Christ, presented in 1962. These were painted on large canvases applied directly to the wall.

Commonwealth Institute

Holland Park, Kensington

1960–2, Robert Matthew,
Johnson-Marshall and Partners

Listed grade II*, 12 October 1988

The Commonwealth Institute replaced T. E. Collcutt's Imperial Institute of 1887–93, and was designed as an exhibition centre where each Commonwealth nation devised a display about itself. Its youth-centred approach was important to Stirrat Johnson-Marshall, previously architect to the Ministry of Education. The concept of a 'tent in the park' was his, as was the desire for an uninterrupted central space. Served by a central, circular ramped platform, this was reminiscent of that inside the 'Dome of Discovery' at the Festival of Britain in 1951, and James Gardiner served as exhibition designer to both.

The clear span was devised by Johnson-Marshall's assistant, Roger Cunliffe, and the engineers Alan Harris and James Sutherland, who turned to the anticlastic or double-curved roofs then being made fashionable by Félix Candela. This is the outstanding English example of the hyperbolic-paraboloid roof, clad in copper presented by Rhodesia and Malawi. It is being retained as part of the new Design Museum by John Pawson, while the OMA Partnership has designed luxury flats to replace the administrative block and landscape.

Royal College of Physicians

Outer Circle, Regent's Park, London

1960–4, 1994–6, Denys Lasdun and Partners

Listed grade I, 24 April 1998

The building that brought Lasdun to prominence was an exceptional commission: a modern ceremonial building constructed to an ample budget. The Royal College of Physicians, founded in 1518, evolved as a regulatory and educational organization until its premises off Trafalgar Square became too small. It asked for a reception hall, lecture theatre, dining room and library, with a controlling Censors' Room incorporating panelling from an earlier building by Robert Hooke. Lasdun pushed a grand staircase through the reception hall to make it the centre of the college, up which the Censors marched in their robes to meetings in the first-floor library. The building is also defined by its materials: mosaic-clad concrete for the structural elements, with brick for infill walls and ancillary accommodation. Lasdun made more delicate additions in 1994.

The building owes something to Frank Lloyd Wright, who Lasdun admired. The planning has also been likened to the seventeenth-century images of blood circulation in the hall.

Barking Station booking hall

Station Parade, Barking

1961, John Ward of British Railway's Eastern Region

Listed grade II, 24 November 1995

The electrification of Eastern Region's suburban lines was an important part of British Railways' modernization plan of 1955. A team of dynamic young architects was headhunted, with Ward becoming a group leader. Several new stations and signal boxes were realized, but at Barking only a new booking hall was constructed, set on the bridge over the tracks to advertise the railways' new, modern image.

Ward's design resembles 'on an English smaller scale' – as *The Builder* magazine explained condescendingly in 1962 – the frontage then recently added to Rome's Termini Station. With its thin, concrete beams creating a dramatic canopy and upsweeping roof, and large clerestories, Barking – like Rome – entices the traveller with an expressionistic image of light and speed while keeping the actual locomotives and tracks out of view underneath. There is great liveliness despite its small scale and the infiltration of shops into the concourse.

4 Beechworth Close

Hampstead Heath

1961, Patrick Gwynne

Listed grade II, 26 April 1999

Max and Anne Bruh wanted a house that was easy to run, 'with a certain toughness to withstand the mild ravages which even the nicest teenagers are liable to perpetrate'. They inspected The Firs (see p.444) nearby and appointed Gwynne, a master of hard finishes.

The plan resembles that of four houses Gwynne had built near Kingston-upon-Thames a year before (now mutilated), but here the larger scale enabled him to set back the upper storey, emphasized by contrasting grey-black bricks and white render, and add a service entrance. The Bruhs had acquired a site with fine mature Victorian planting, but the garden faced north, so Gwynne placed the living room across the house to give it both north and south aspects. The dominant feature is an elegant central stairwell, generously scaled and lit by a circular skylight. Built-in cupboards and finishes of timber and grass paper create homogeneity. The intricacy and clever contrivance of these fittings demonstrate Gwynne's sense of the exquisite.

BT Tower (formerly Post Office Tower)

Cleveland Mews,
off Tottenham Court Road

1961–5, Ministry of
Public Buildings and Works
Chief architect, Eric Bedford
Job architects, G. R. Yeats,
F. G. Micklewright and
C. A. E. Thatcher

Listed grade II, 26 March 2003

The Museum Exchange was London's telecommunications hub, serving Broadcasting House and a television transmitter, when in 1952 it was chosen to be the centre of a national aerial network. As tall buildings appeared in London, the design was heightened twice, eventually reaching 176.8m (580ft) – plus a 12m (39½ft) mast. Stability was crucial to the accuracy of the narrow-beam transmitters, which were mounted on circular galleries for maximum flexibility and to reduce wind resistance.

Only a small public observation platform was planned at first, but this was reconsidered in 1960 following the success of the world's first tower restaurant at Stuttgart in 1956.

The Post Office Tower symbolized the space race, the panoramic globe topping the tower resembling an artificial satellite, while the lifts were Britain's fastest. The observation decks attracted 4.6 million visitors before a bomb attack in 1971 prompted their abandonment; the revolving floor survives from the restaurant, which closed in 1980.

Centre Point

New Oxford Street

1961–6, George Marsh
of Richard Seifert and Partners

Listed grade II, 25 November 1995

Centre Point evolved out of a proposal for a roundabout at Tottenham Court Road, when the developer Harry Hyams offered land in return for 29-storey offices and an eight-storey block of shops and flats, linked by a bridge over the new road.

The design was refined, with the tower becoming narrower but taller, and the top floors were planned as a restaurant and open gallery. The elevations were among the first in England formed of precast sections, each shaped like an inverted 'T', with a gently curved plan and an entasis. When the sun touches them there is a ripple of Op Art movement worthy of the artist Bridget Riley or designer Mary Quant. Marsh also introduced mosaic floorings and artworks by Jupp Dernbach-Mayen, whose fountains were removed in 2010.

Centre Point was initially admired as the symbol of 'swinging London'. It acquired notoriety when Hyams set an unrealistically high rent, and it remained empty until the late 1970s.

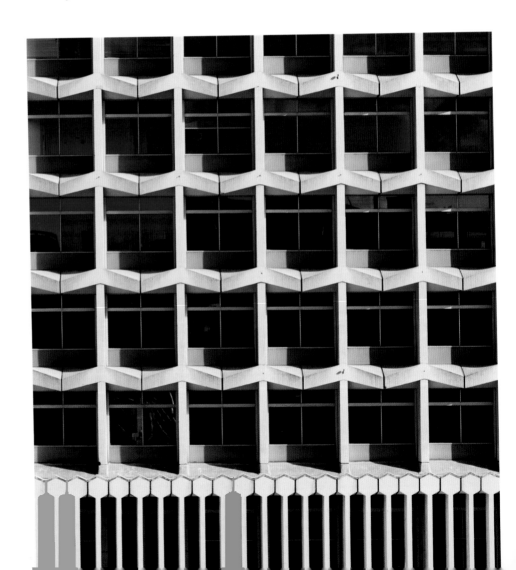

Twelve Cranes

Royal Victoria Dock, West Ham

1962, Stothert and Pitt

Listed grade II, 17 November 2009

This is the most concentrated ensemble of cranes surviving in London's Docklands. They are early examples of Stothert and Pitt's DD2 dockside crane, an all-welded tubular steel design introduced in 1959 to critical acclaim and commercial success.

The Royal Victoria Dock was the largest in the world when it opened in 1855. After the Second World War it experienced a brief resurgence in trade, followed by a rapid decline as the shipping industry adopted containerization. When the dock closed in 1980, the cranes were stored and later fixed along the vast dockside as part of the regeneration of the area. Their arrangement in pairs is visually arresting, both for the rhythm they create and their reflection in the dock's huge expanse of water. The cranes have an almost sublime quality, particularly in silhouette, and a symbolic interest as representing the swansong of a vanished industry. Two more cranes sited alongside date from the 1920s and are also listed.

The Chapel, St Mary's University College

Waldegrave Road, Strawberry Hill

1962–3, Sir Albert Richardson, Houfe and Partners

Listed grade II, 17 February 2006

This powerful late work by Richardson, assisted by S. P. A. Holland, marks the end of a long English tradition of tall brick churches inspired by Albi Cathedral, and of college chapels. It is raised over the former library to give it still greater height. Deep buttresses within the church, cut by passage aisles and a balcony, leave sheer elevations interrupted only by narrow windows.

The impressive interior features *dalle de verre* by Gabriel Loire of Chartres, an abstract ensemble strong in blues and reds based on the mysteries of the rosary. Peter Gallichen and Albert Rose's tall reredos, which depicts Richardson in its bottom corner, was added in the 1970s, when the simple forward altar and steps were remodelled. Stained glass in a projecting spiral staircase by Lavers and Westlake is dated 1901.

St Mary's evolve from a Roman Catholic teacher training college founded in 1850, which moved in 1925 to Strawberry Hill.

Heinz UK headquarters and former laboratories

Hayes Park, Hillingdon

1962–5, Gordon Bunshaft of Skidmore, Owings and Merrill

Listed grade II*, 24 November 1995

Although best known for designing New York skyscrapers, Bunshaft also pioneered the design of low, luxurious, greenfield headquarters buildings. For his one English building, on a green-belt site, he also explored precast concrete techniques.

The two buildings are set in echelon, the laboratories subordinate to the headquarters. A condition of the planning permission was that they should appear only two storeys in height, so the ground floors were sunk into the sloping hillside, and the open-plan offices are mainly lit from an internal courtyard. Contemporary critics were astounded that all the ceiling lights were symmetrical; in Bunshaft's work no duct or extractor is out of place. The external shell has darkened but remains crisply finished, and its elegantly waisted concrete stanchions frame every view out – a tough test of their precise casting.

There is a purity to Heinz's headquarters appropriate to its product. It originally sat amid giant elms; since their destruction it has appeared to float over the landscape.

62 Camden Mews

Camden Town

1962–5, Edward Cullinan

Listed grade II*, 15 May 2007

Mews plots around Camden Square were released by the local council in the 1960s and became fashionable among young architects for their own homes. This pioneering example was built by Cullinan and his wife Ros for themselves and three children, largely at weekends. The tiny house is supported on the party wall on its northern boundary, and set sideways to the street to secure maximum sunlight without being overlooked. A concrete beam on timber posts supports the roof on this glazed south elevation. This carriage-like form informed many of Cullinan's later buildings, while its chunky timberwork was inspired by a year's study in California, with lapped details befitting his limited carpentry skills. The open-plan living space is on the first floor, with a built-in kitchen and shelving by the Cullinans, and tiny bedrooms are on the brick ground floor.

Cullinan was then working for Denys Lasdun, and the brick forecourt paviours came from the Royal College of Physicians. Widely published, the house introduced a novel yet personal rough-hewn, even brutalist, vernacular.

Jack Straw's Castle

North End Way, Hampstead

1963–4, Raymond Erith

Listed grade II, 14 May 1974

Such was Erith's success in re-creating a historic landmark that in 1974 his building was listed as a partly Georgian building. Yet the pub had been largely rebuilt even before a landmine damaged it in 1941. By 1961, Charrington Brewery wanted a smart restaurant and brought in Erith, then just completing his remodelling of No. 10 Downing Street. He had long nursed an ambition to build in timber, as a response to the precast systems then dominating architectural fashion; his planning application coincided with that for Centre Point's elevations. The Royal Fine Arts Commission and local architects approved, although dourer residents agitated for more sober Georgian proprieties. Frivolity prevailed. The frame took eight weeks to erect, then the roof was completed before the walls were weatherboarded.

Jack Straw's is a stylistic palimpsest. A seventeenth-century cornice lurks between Gothick glazing and crenellations, while the canted bays, courtyard verandah and towers suggest early nineteenth-century additions. It was converted to flats in 2003–4.

Swiss Cottage Central Library

Avenue Road, Camden

1963–4, Sir Basil Spence, Bonnington and Collins

Listed grade II, 2 December 1997

The library and adjoining baths were all that was built of a civic complex for the Borough of Hampstead, a scheme aborted by London government reorganization. The library became a memorial to Conservative Hampstead, now part of Labour-dominated Camden.

The public areas are set around a double-height exhibition space on the upper floors, entered at ground level at the top of the falling site. At either end are the lending and reference libraries, both with spiral stairs serving galleries that house most of the books. Spence planned the interior to appear as open as possible and this was reinforced in the remodelling by John McAslan and Partners in 2001–3, which removed many of the internal screens.

The library's cigar shape is emphasized by the projecting concrete fins on the public upper floors. This verticality was a contrast to the strong horizontals of Spence's swimming baths next door, which were rejected for listing against English Heritage's advice and demolished.

Mural at City of London Academy

Packington Street, Islington

1963–4, William Mitchell

Listed grade II, 27 November 2008

This is a semi-abstract mosaic made of broken china, tiles and glass. A large pair of compasses with a circular hinge bears the image of a face surrounded by the words 'James I made a river from Hertfordshire to Islington Pond', referring to the New River of 1609–13 that once flowed past here. A fish surrounded by circular patterns evokes river life and plants.

William Mitchell and Antony Hollaway were employed by the London County Council in 1957–65 to produce decorative finishes and artworks, mainly for its new schools and housing estates. The costs of materials, usually concrete in Mitchell's case, were absorbed into normal building expenses. This mural was constructed at the same time as the (now demolished) Islington Green School by Scherrer and Hicks, and was originally one of a pair. The council's art programme was short-lived, surviving only a year after the council was disbanded in 1965. By the end of the 1960s, London's budget for public art had been cut by three-quarters.

Schreiber House

West Heath Road,
Hampstead

1963–4, 1967, James Gowan

Listed grade II, 15 July 1998

It was Gowan's commission from C. S. Schreiber, the furniture manufacturer, which prompted him to leave James Stirling. It is a home of monumental proportions, clean and light, revealing similarities with his Ham Common landings but realized in the finest concrete with marble floors and bronze fixtures – notably in the interwoven staircase balustrading.

The vertical bands of aluminium windows and grey Staffordshire brick are the abiding image, making the four-storey home resemble a Norman keep. Most of the rooms run right through from south to north, so that they can enjoy both the sun and views of Hampstead Heath. They were designed on a rigorous grid of 0.9m (3ft), which determined the wall thicknesses, the troughs of the concrete ceilings and the fine panelling. Money was spent not on ornament but on high-quality materials, with built-in furniture designed by Gowan and made by Schreiber's factory.

In 1967 Gowan designed a sunken pool house that complemented the angularity of the house, but this was sold and incorporated into a new house in 1992–2000.

190 Sloane Street (former Sekers)

Knightsbridge

1963–5, Harry Teggin
of Brett and Pollen

Listed grade II, 24 November 1995

Lord Esher was architect/planner to the Cadogan Estate, which includes Sloane Street, and the showrooms for Sekers Fabrics Ltd were conceived as part of a larger redevelopment. Designed by his former assistant, the overhanging upper office floors were a compromise as part of a street widening scheme.

This is the earliest of three sophisticated buildings by Harry Teggin. It is supported on just four main columns, with all the services placed against the party wall to the north. The west and south elevations are thus remarkably open and light. The setback mezzanine floor enables a double height entrance, while the upper floors have curtain walling of black aluminium.

Opening the showroom, which originally had interiors by Dennis Lennon and fixtures by the sculptor Robert Adams, Sir Basil Spence pleaded for a 'warm humanity, richness and quality' in the London scene. He admired Sekers's shop for the extrovert mechanistic glass and concrete frame, very different from Miki Sekers's Rosehill Theatre (see p.20).

Hornsey Library

Haringey Park, Crouch End

1963–5, Ley and Jarvis

Listed grade II, 23 March 2001

Like that at Swiss Cottage, the opulent Hornsey Library was a last stand by an authority abolished by local government reforms in 1965. But its architects were local, and it was praised in librarians' periodicals rather than the architectural press.

The building's interest lies inside. It is a building of two halves, separated by an entrance under the projecting first-floor reference library. To the left is the adults' lending library, a double-height space with a gallery on two sides inspired by the slightly earlier Holborn Library. More stairs lead to the reference library, with patterned shelving, fixed desks and a meeting hall with its own foyer and coffee bar overlooking a courtyard.

Works of art recall Hornsey's history. The fountain behind T. E. Huxley Jones's attenuated bather has plaques depicting the borough and its medieval church. Frederick Mitchell engraved a map of the borough on the staircase window, with a vignette of the new library at its centre.

1 Colville Place

Fitzrovia

1964, Max Neufeld

Listed grade II, 13 April 2000

Max Neufeld was an architect with the London and Greater London councils for 25 years, working in Covent Garden after an early specialization in old people's homes. He and his wife loved central London and found a 4.57m (15ft) gap site left by a stray bomb, where Neufeld secured permission to build a gallery or studio with a maisonette and roof garden on top.

The construction consists of timber joists on hangers spanning the party walls, with beams to front and back taking the external walls. A spiral staircase has its own brick drum at the rear. There is a precision to every detail of the built-in timber fittings and particularly the staircase, all by Neufeld. They make for a calm, minimal interior, which was rejected for publication by the *Architectural Review* because it had so little furniture.

Had it been built, the Smithsons' brutalist so-called 'House in Soho' would have been in the same street. Neufeld's design is less well known but infinitely more elegant.

1 Aylmer Close

Stanmore

1964–5, Edward Samuel

Listed grade II, 19 August 1996

Basil Spence passed on a commission for a house to Samuel, then his assistant, which enabled him to start his own practice. Aylmer Close, his best-known work, followed, erected next to a Georgian house that survives as flats and incorporating much of its garden, including a small lake.

The house is long and rectangular, with a small projecting study to the rear. The plan comprises two parts: the adults' area includes an open-plan living and dining area, master bedroom and study, and a children's wing with its own playroom and eating area. It was built using a timber frame on a brick plinth, with chunky timber cladding. This aesthetic continues inside, with the frame expressed in varnished timber and with timber cupboards and room dividers. Samuel claimed inspiration from Japanese architecture, Frank Lloyd Wright and above all the exceptional landscape, yet the house also exemplifies the tougher architectural mood of the early 1960s. Samuel later marketed the timber system as the Oliver Unit House.

Ventilation towers

Blackwall Tunnel, between Poplar and Greenwich

1964–7, Terry Farrell
of London County Council
Architect's Department

Listed grade II, 20 December 2000

When the young graduate Terry Farrell worked for the London County Council in 1961–2, its Special Works Division was engrossed in the South Bank Centre. He was therefore put to design the ventilation towers urgently required for the second Blackwall Tunnel unaided.

The two structures, one either side of the river, were originally almost identical. Each houses shafts containing exhaust and blower fans to discharge foul air. Farrell also designed a small supervisor's office at the northern end of the new tunnel, and worked on the tunnel lining. He admits that although the shafts' curvilinear funnel shape was hailed as aerodynamic and functional, it was actually inspired by Oscar Neimeyer. It was made possible by the use of sprayed concrete or Gunite, pioneered in Britain by the engineers Flint and Neill and then beginning to be used for electricity cooling towers. Long distinctive local landmarks, the southern tower was in 1998–9 partly enveloped by the Millennium Dome.

Haggerston School

Weymouth Terrace, Hackney

1964–7, Ernö Goldfinger

Listed grade II, 18 June 2004

Ernö Goldfinger's only secondary school was built for girls in the muscular style of his maturity, a series of strong shapes and proportions based on the Golden Section. It has the long, four-storey teaching slab (completed in 1965) customary in secondary schools built by the London County Council on tight urban sites, with linked blocks housing the hall and gymnasia. The first of these is perhaps Goldfinger's finest public space, housing an assembly hall, music room and first-floor offices off a double-height entrance foyer with coffered ceilings and paved floors. The bold concrete door surrounds are particularly impressive, as is the handsome stair and timber balcony balustrading.

The teaching block was remodelled in 2010–12 with new circulation and fenestration by Avanti Architects, who as part of the conversion to co-educational use added an elegant new block inspired by Goldfinger's caretaker's house, a carefully proportioned grey-brick box with a concrete slab roof. Nick Goldfinger has since restored some of his grandfather's furniture here.

Fulwell Cross Library

Fairlop

1965–7, Frederick Gibberd

Listed grade II, 23 April 2007

When a scheme by the borough engineer was rejected by planners at Essex County Council, Ilford councillors commissioned Frederick Gibberd to design a borough library and a swimming pool on the strength of his work at Harlow. He agreed to produce plans and elevations in September 1958, but changes to the brief for the baths and local government reorganization caused delays.

The library's circular plan resembled in miniature Gibberd's Liverpool Cathedral, also designed in 1959, with an axis from the entrance through the central lending hall to a lower reference room beyond. Offices, a children's library and a clinic formed an outer ring, now in a variety of uses. The visual impact comes from a ribbed concrete dome over the main lending library, sheathed in copper and raised over round-headed clerestory windows. The building's simple geometric shapes and crisp, precast panels are typical of Gibberd's mature style, and this is one of the finest examples of his later work.

8A Fitzroy Park

Highgate

1965–7, Hal Higgins
of Higgins and Ney

Listed grade II, 25 November 1999

The engineer Peter Epstein liked a house by Higgins in Hampstead, and commissioned a larger one for himself.

The house's complex plan comprises five pavilions set around a large living room built over a swimming pool on the lowest part of the site, away from the road. By exploiting the steep hillside, Higgins fitted in several circulation levels, with movement between the pavilions independent of the living room. The pavilions are constructed of brick, but are linked by bridges of black steel and glass, also used for the principal garden elevations and a terrace adjoining the living room. Each pavilion has a different function: one has the master bedroom and a study; one the children's rooms, linked to that for the nanny over garaging; there is one for guests, while that to the rear contains the kitchen, housekeeper's quarters and a projecting dining room. The result is a rare 'luxury' modern house surviving from the 1960s, and a distinguished example of the enthusiasm for geometrical 'pods'.

Lecture theatres, Brunel University

Uxbridge

1965–7, John Heywood of Richard Sheppard, Robson and Partners

Listed grade II, 23 June 2011

Acton Technical College expanded after 1945, until in 1957 its prestigious university courses were separated into a new Brunel College. On the recommendation of the Robbins Committee, Brunel secured university status in 1966, and a new campus outside Uxbridge was planned as a major complex for studying engineering.

Richard Sheppard, Robson and Partners were commissioned to prepare a development plan and design the non-departmental buildings, including a lecture theatre block inspired by that opened at the University of Manchester Institute of Science and Technology in 1959, the first of the genre. Six lecture theatres and smaller teaching rooms are gathered on three levels. The building's *in situ* concrete structure is most expressive on the north elevation, where the two tiers of raked lecture theatres project, the largest on top and with escape stairs between them. It was rare that the technical universities founded in the late 1960s produced distinctive buildings, and Brunel featured as a location for the film *A Clockwork Orange*.

Brownfield Estate

St Leonard's Road, Bromley-by-Bow

Balfron Tower
1965–7, Ernö Goldfinger
Listed grade II, 14 March 1996

Carradale House
1967–8, Ernö Goldfinger
Listed grade II, 4 December 2000

Housing shortages prompted the London County Council (LCC) to commission many private architects to design its smaller schemes. Balfron Tower, a 26-storey block of 146 flats with a taller service tower, looks tough – and Carradale House, at right angles, its 11 storeys bisected by a lift tower, seems still stranger. Their façades reflect Le Corbusier's plan for Algiers as well as earlier unrealized projects by Goldfinger. But their concrete is perfectly finished, Balfron Tower's entrance hall is lined in marble, and the flats are generously planned. The lifts serve every third floor, for speed, and doors off the connecting galleries lead up or down to larger flats and to small ones on the level. Balfron Tower also has maisonettes. Goldfinger placed the boiler house at the top of Balfron's service tower away from the ground-floor gardens and playground; as construction began, the LCC decided that it should also serve Carradale House, so its exaggerated sculptural form was accidental. Goldfinger lived in Balfron Tower briefly in 1967.

23 Kensington Place

Kensington

1966–7, Tom Kay

Listed grade II, 27 February 2013

Tom Kay was invited by the photographer Christopher Bailey and his wife, opera singer Angela Hickey, to convert a narrow end-of-terrace house, but persuaded them that a new house would best suit their detailed brief. They wanted a large living room for Hickey's grand piano, so Kay placed the stairs in a 1.83m (6ft) tower to the side.

Kay maximized the site by excavating a large basement for the kitchen (set underneath the attached garage) and dining room. The house is entered from Hillgate Street by a ramp or down an external stair through the kitchen garden. The double-height living room was placed on the first floor to maximize light, with a balcony study behind a sloping north window.

There are some similarities with Jan Duiker's house at Aalsmeer (1924). Otherwise the severe forms are of their times, the Staffordshire blue brick striking in red brick Kensington and exposed internally, including as paviours in the living room.

Bromley Hall School

Bromley Hall Road, Bromley-by-Bow

1967–8, Bob Giles
of GLC Architect's Department

Listed grade II, 9 January 2012

London was a pioneer in special education, building detached centres for blind and deaf children and open-air schools for 'delicate' and tuberculoid children before the First World War. In this progressive tradition lies Bromley Hall School, designed for 120 physically disabled children aged 5–16. The noisy, unappealing site, wide age range and need for seclusion suggested a sheltering, introspective and heavyweight building on a single level.

Bob Giles devised a cellular plan of alternating pavilion classrooms and courtyards giving each year-group its own space, influenced visiting Arne Jacobsen's Munkegård School of 1948–57 and Vangebo School by his assistants Gehrdt Barnebusch and Henning Larsen near Copenhagen. Each pavilion is lit by a canted skylight set in a pyramidal roof, which recall nearby Three Mills and Erich Mendelsohn's Hermann hat factory in Luckenwalde, Germany (1920). A tough interior of tiles and bricks stood up well to lively children in wheelchairs.

The building was listed after demolition was proposed by the local authority.

25 Montpelier Row

Twickenham

1967–9, Geoffrey Darke

Listed grade II, 5 October 2007

Built by Geoffrey Darke as his family home in the middle of a fine 1720s terrace, this is a rare example of a post-war house in an eighteenth-century context. It reflects the ethos of the existing houses, and structurally buttresses that next door.

The Richmond-based practice of Darbourne and Darke specialized in building integrated, medium and low-rise social housing, using high-quality materials that extended to street furniture and brick planting boxes. Here, the brown brick and rich, dark timber – exposed inside and out – complement without mimicking their neighbours.

The plan echoes that of the eighteenth-century town house, with a bow to the rear and a small wing (Darke's office) denoted by a large oriel window annexed to the front. It is also a personal statement, well seen in the staircase joinery. The principal rooms are surprisingly high and open, with a ground-floor kitchen and dining room, and a first-floor living room giving on to a terrace. Bedrooms are tucked under the exposed, inward-sloping roof.

81 Swains Lane

Highgate

1967–9, John Winter

Listed grade II*, 10 August 2009

This is one of the best-known and most influential steel houses in England, a pioneering use of Cor-Ten steel cladding in domestic construction. Winter was inspired by *Art and Architecture* magazine to head for California in the 1950s, where he learned about steel construction working for Skidmore, Owings and Merrill and for Charles Eames. This was designed as the architect's family home, maximizing a tight plot adjoining Highgate Cemetery.

The house is defined by its module of 2.44 x 3.66 x 6.01m (8 x 12 x 20ft), with regular areas of glazing between the frame and discreet ventilation ducts. The minimal detailing carefully allows rainwater to wash over the Cor-Ten without making streaks or stains.

The top floor is a 'quiet' open-plan living room and study, set round a central fireplace and stair core that runs through the house. Here the internal steel frame is clearly exposed. The bedrooms are on the middle floor, with a family room-cum-kitchen on the ground floor that has built-in fixtures by Winter.

The Brunswick Centre

Bloomsbury

1967–72, Patrick Hodgkinson

Listed grade II, 24 September 2000

Patrick Hodgkinson pioneered interest in low-rise, high-density housing, and developed this scheme working for Leslie Martin after one for St Pancras Council was not realized. LB Camden, successors to St Pancras, became the clients for the housing here in 1965.

The Brunswick Centre is a classic 'megastructure', integrating many functions within one coherent concept. Two long, stepped terraces of flats are aligned either side of a shopping piazza, with car parking below. Each block has an A-section, the inner circulation space tapering upwards in a powerful composition of soaring columns threaded with walkways. Housing and shops are equally important to the scheme. Opposite Brunswick Square, the flats are omitted and columns stand proud around the glazed entrance to a basement cinema; their scale is reminiscent of Antonio Sant'Elia's project for Milan Central Station (1914).

Hodgkinson resigned in 1970 and the centre was finished cheaply, with the concrete never painted as intended; since listing the centre has realized his intended sophistication.

38 Millfield Lane

Highgate

1968–9, Philip Pank
and Robert Howard

Listed grade II, 1 February 2007

This house, originally with a separate staff flat, was built for the literary agent Harvey Ünna, who had admired Pank's own house in Kentish Town. This is a larger and more luxurious house, but is similarly built of brick and exposed timber, set at the rear of the sloping site with views across Hampstead Heath. The slope allows the main entrance to be at first-floor level, which is fully glazed towards the Heath behind a substantial sheltered paved terrace, its canopy apparently suspended from the extended box beams above. In the large living room and dining room behind, lined in fair-faced brick, the powerful wooden roof structure is exposed, with high-level windows between the box beams. Finishes and built-in fittings are of a very high quality. A clever addition linked the main house and staff flat while the property was under consideration for listing.

Philip Pank (1933–91) was an artist as well as an architect.

St Margaret of Scotland Catholic Church

St Margaret's Road, Twickenham

1968–69, Austin Winkley
of Williams and Winkley

Listed grade II, 25 March 1999

Winkley had studied under Robert Maguire and was one of the first Roman Catholic members of the New Churches Research Group of architects investigating liturgical church planning. Father Sidney Thomason, who commissioned St Margaret's in 1965, wanted a building which expressed the modern spirit that swept the Roman Church in the 1960s.

There is a weekday chapel and a hall, with the main church behind. This is diamond-shaped, entered from the side under a low entrance, with higher roofs over the baptistery and the altar placed in opposite corners. The use of concrete blocks follows that by Maguire and Murray, which with the opaque patent clerestory glazing impart a calming, silvery coolness. This is enforced by the church's hidden position, its cool timber furnishings, and stained glass by Patrick Reyntiens in which greys and blues predominate. Steven Sykes's hanging altar cross is of gold mosaic.

Cheltenham Estate

Golbourne Road, Kensington

Trellick Tower
1968–73, Ernö Goldfinger
listed grade II*, 22 December 1998

Edenham Way
1968–73, Ernö Goldfinger
listed grade II, 13 November 2012

Trellick Tower is the landmark within a low-rise estate of flats and houses subsequently also listed, which continued the London County Council's tradition of mixed development, their tough brick walls featuring curved corners and timber panels.

Trellick Tower has 217 flats and maisonettes in a 31-storey tower and seven-storey wing. There is a ground-floor community centre (originally a nursery), shops and a doctor's surgery. An intended public house became Goldfinger's office and is now an advice centre. Trellick thus approaches the aims of Le Corbusier's Unités d'Habitation to fulfil all a neighbourhood's needs in one building. The arrangement of a separate lift tower, giving access to every third floor of flats, with the 23rd and 24th floors combined as maisonettes, is repeated from Balfron, but the surmounting boiler house is more exaggerated. The building is constructed of scrupulously finished concrete on a cross-wall frame, with cedar panelling to the balconies. The foyer has an abstract glass panel, re-created by residents after the listing.

2 Carson Terrace

Kensington

1969–70, Peter Aldington
of Aldington and Craig

Listed grade II, 10 September 2003

This two-storey mews house was built over garages and a basement darkroom for Tim Rock, editor of the *Architectural Review*. Although the building is tiny, only 4.5m (14ft 9in) deep, Rock wanted the possibility of letting the first floor separately. The one-bedroom flat and top-floor studio therefore have separate, back-to-back staircases from a shared front door, and a galley kitchen was placed in the studio. Projecting oriels gave greater space to the first floor, while the studio gains greatly from its open-truss roof lined in Douglas fir, and a built-in table and shelving by Aldington repeats the heavy, sectioned joinery found in his first house, Askett Green (see p.335). This is in many ways a refinement of that tightly planned little house, with the similarly steep stairs and big cupboards, but the exposed concrete structure and smart stock brick infill is better finished. It is Aldington's only work in London.

22 Murray Mews

Camden

1970–3, Tom Kay

Listed grade II, 11 January 2013

Camden and Murray Mews were never fully developed, until in 1962 St Pancras Council sold plots and they became a haven of architect-designed houses. This house was designed in 1967–8 when Kay was unsure of the future size of his family and his practice, so the ground floor was planned flexibly. The structure is partly supported on Richard Gibson's house next door, though Kay won an appeal to build up to the street frontage, where steps rise to the first-floor entrance. Constructivist planes and geometric shapes relate this archetypal mews house to its neighbours.

The upper floor contains the kitchen, bedrooms and living room, maximizing natural light in the deep plan without being overlooked through toplighting. Stairs lead to a downstairs design studio and flat. Kay employed a building firm for the main construction, but made much of the internal joinery himself. Warm tiled floors and exposed brickwork make a fitting space for the Kays' collection of modern furniture and kilim rugs.

School of Oriental and African Studies

Woburn Square, London

1970–3 Denys Lasdun and Partners

Listed grade II*, 20 May 2011

Institute of Education

Bedford Way, London

1970–6, Denys Lasdun and Partners

Listed grade II*, 4 December 2000

While the University of London was discouraged from expansion after 1945, smaller departments needed more facilities. Lasdun was appointed in 1960 to develop earlier proposals by Leslie Martin and Trevor Dannatt. His scheme created a new square between a long teaching spine and a major new library for the School of Oriental and African Studies (SOAS), whose spectacular interior comprises three levels of balconies in a top-lit cuboid space spanned by a diagonally set grid of slender concrete trusses.

A teaching building on Bedford Way was to be shared by the Institute of Education with other users. Its long elevations demonstrate Lasdun's mature language of horizontal strata and towers, their concrete contrasted with bronze anodized aluminium. His library, added in 1990–3, is denoted by pyramidal roof lights. There is one great spur wing with a deliciously over-scaled escape stair; five were originally intended, and Lasdun long wished to build two so as to embrace the SOAS pavilion. Inside, the stairwell descending to basement lecture theatres is a simplified version of that at the Royal College of Physicians.

Dunboyne Road Estate

Mansfield Road, Gospel Oak

1971–7, Neave Brown of Camden Architect's Department

Listed grade II, 9 August 2012

Camden had the highest-rate income per person outside the City and Westminster, and a team of bright young architects. Their inspiring leader, Sydney Cook, inherited several schemes for tower blocks in 1965, but preferred low-rise, high-density solutions. One was Dunboyne Road, given to Neave Brown, who had already built a tightly planned terrace for himself and friends.

Brown's sources included Le Corbusier's Rob et Roq project and Atelier 5's Siedlung Halen outside Berne, but also home-grown Victorian terraced housing and Patrick Hodgkinson's early projects in St Pancras. There are three pairs of terraces with a pub and shop, in stark white concrete with dark joinery, linked by a walkway and underground parking entered at the bottom of the site. Each pair comprises a maisonette set over a smaller unit on one side of a pedestrian walkway, and a maisonette on the other. Living rooms are above bedrooms to ensure better light, and all units have terraces, with additional gardens on the roof of the lower blocks.

29½ and 28½ Lansdowne Crescent

Kensington

1972–3, Jeremy Lever

Listed grade II, 23 November 2012

These two maisonettes, the larger upper one built as Jeremy and Jill Lever's family home, fill a tiny gap in a Victorian terrace. This was narrower at the front than at the rear, where the land falls sharply. Built of reclaimed stock brick, the front is rendered to match the existing buildings.

A modern interpretation of the town house, there are six floors, seven at the back – where terraces overlook a shared garden, reached via steps. The larger unit features a double-height living room, lit by full-height windows and overlooked by a gallery. Built-in furniture – notably in the attic library – and finishes in British Columbian pine contrast with white-painted surfaces and quarry-tiled floors.

Lever was a partner in the firm of Darbourne and Darke, and the house follows a similar aesthetic while demonstrating his skill in integrating housing and landscape. The house won a RIBA award in 1974, gaining praise for 'the section and the consistency of detail'.

Alexandra Road Estate

Swiss Cottage

1972–8, Neave Brown, Camden Architect's Department

Listed grade II*, 18 August 1993

Former Jack Taylor School
Listed grade II, 17 July 2013

Camden Council acquired Alexandra Road after turning down proposals by the Eyre Estate for a tower block there. Sydney Cook brought in Neave Brown, and his complex stepped terraces with their balconies assumed a grandeur akin to Georgian town planning in modern dress.

Two terraces of flats and maisonettes face each other across the pedestrian Rowley Way, whose gentle curve encloses the vista at either end. The larger terrace shields noise from the railway behind, each flat with an open space on the roof of that below. A third (smaller) terrace comprises houses with top-floor living rooms to give maximum light, set beyond a park landscaped by Janet Jack. As part of the scheme, Brown also designed a school and youth club for children with learning difficulties, which closed in 2012.

A home for the disabled, reception centre and shops were squeezed on to adjoining land so Brown's crescents were unsullied. Alexandra Road is beautifully crafted in white concrete, and it was listed to prevent insensitive repairs.

Frontage to Truman's Brewery

Brick Lane, Spitalfields

1973–6, Arup Associates

Listed grade II*, 24 March 1994

Joseph Truman brewed porter here from 1679, and his son Benjamin expanded the business in the 1740s. The director's house, remodelled in the 1770s, and head brewer's house of c.1834 survive, as do Georgian brewery buildings across Brick Lane. When the brewery demolished a terrace in Hanbury Street, local outrage made it clear that the redevelopment of its historic frontage to Brick Lane had to be better handled.

Arup Associates were commissioned in 1972 to provide offices, recreation facilities and warehousing. Their building linked the two houses and provided a common entrance with a stepped façade of mirror glass. This reflected the buildings opposite – seemingly completing a formal Georgian square – as well as the sky.

Mirror glass offered the ultimate in architectural minimalism. It was adopted in the United States from the early 1960s, arriving in Britain only a decade later with Norman Foster's work. Truman's was among its first uses in conservation.

Branch Hill Estate

Spedan Close, Hampstead

1974–8, Gordon Benson
and Alan Forsyth of
Camden Architect's Department

Listed grade II, 9 August 2010

This council estate was built in the grounds of an Edwardian mansion in Hampstead, where a restrictive covenant stipulated that development should be semi-detached and two storeys high. Benson and Forsyth had worked under Neave Brown and added a third dimension to his complex stepped section, pushing elements backwards as well as up. The flat roof of each house is the terrace of the next one up the hillside, reached by walkways or steel stairs from a courtyard below. The elevations are arguably more finessed than Brown's: the structural skeleton is board-marked and chamfered, and the infill is finished in smooth white concrete.

None of this came cheap, and the estate was attacked as financially irresponsible. Yet few could deny the sophistication of the architecture, the *Architects' Journal* considered it 'some of the highest-quality council accommodation in the country'. Yet the idealism that had built the welfare state was waning and Margaret Thatcher awaited election in 1979.

IBM centre

Green Park Way, Greenford

1977–80, Foster Associates

Listed grade II, 27 March 2013

Commissioned in 1975 following the success of his pilot offices at Cosham, Hampshire, Foster's office had designed a warehouse and distribution depot when IBM demanded that a computer support centre be built at Greenford within a year. The two elements are linked by a bridge over an access road but have been in separate ownership since 1997.

The buildings are set under a constant roofline, and were designed to be extended eastwards, as duly happened to the computer support centre, built first. This is a large-span steel structure clad with ribbed aluminium sheeting to the sides and fully glazed main façades. Off-the-peg cladding was used, but with specially detailed corners to enhance the building's profile, and a lime green frame. Foster first emerged as a builder of clean, cheap factory buildings, many for the computer industry. Greenford proved that he could build on a big scale for an international client without sacrificing the quality of his planning or detailing.

Floor 2

In an emergency
do not use escalators

LONDON:
CITY AND WESTMINSTER

Lloyd's Building, Lime
Street, City of London,
1981–6, Richard Rogers
Partnership

Chaucer, Coleridge, Shelley, Keats, Gilbert and Sullivan Houses, with accumulator tower

Churchill Gardens Estate, Pimlico

1947–54, Powell and Moya

Listed grade II, 22 December 1998

In 1943 London boroughs were ordered to produce housing plans for implementation at the end of the war. Westminster City Council identified an exceptionally large site, and in 1945 held an Empire-wide competition.

The winners were Philip Powell and Hidalgo Moya, 25 and 26 years old. They proposed tall blocks at right angles to the river along a winding estate road, with lower ranges (including houses) parallel to them. The initial four ten-storey blocks, named after poets, were inspired by the Bergpolder flats in Rotterdam (then recently visited) and Lubetkin's 'working-class flats' project of 1935. Glazed staircases and round lift tops punctuate the long façades, in a setting of neat paths and lawns. It was the first estate with a district heating system, fed by waste heat from Battersea Power Station, which was piped into a glazed accumulator tower.

Smaller flats followed at the western end of the site, beginning with Gilbert and Sullivan Houses, where glass dominates the façades. The estate was completed in 1962.

Hallfield Estate

Bishop's Bridge Road, Paddington

1949–56, Lindsay Drake and
Denys Lasdun (succeeding Tecton)

Listed grade II, 9 June 2011

The Hallfield Estate was conceived for 6,000 people by Paddington Council, which commissioned Tecton in 1946. The layout of long, ten-storey ranges, their living rooms facing south-west for sunshine, and with smaller, six-storey blocks set at right angles, has a lower density than the Churchill Gardens Estate (see p.494). Only part of the scheme was realized, in two phases modified by Drake and Lasdun after their partnership with Berthold Lubetkin terminated in 1948. They added communal buildings (The Forum, 1954–6) and Hallfield School (see p.503), and balconies to the lower blocks. The estate feels complete, large – there are 14 blocks – and a contrast to nearby stuccoed terraces, set below street level on three sides and retaining mature trees. Lubetkin's influence is evident in the sinuous road plan and patterned elevations that use tile, brick and concrete panels to create a chequerboard with the glazing. Screens project on the access elevations like giant puzzle-book mazes.

Parliament Square

City of Westminster

1950–1, George Grey Wornum

Landscape registered grade II,
26 November 1996

Parliament Square was formed when houses were cleared in the early nineteenth century, but was enlarged when in 1866–8 Sir Charles Barry created a setting for his Palace of Westminster.

It has always been blighted by traffic, and a scheme by the Ministry of Transport from 1935 was revived after the war and then accelerated for the Festival of Britain. Wornum was appointed in 1948 to develop the idea of a larger square with a new road to the west, amidst calls by Gordon Cullen for total pedestrianization. Wornum's layout was deliberately simple. He also controlled pedestrian access, with a path aligned on Westminster Abbey alongside retained plane trees on a raised terrace, for which he also designed lamp standards. Two catalpa trees on a subsidiary terrace to the north continue a row planted in New Palace Yard.

Set along the terraces are statues of statesmen, including Sir Winston Churchill (grade II), who glowers at the Houses of Parliament opposite.

Dutch Church

Austin Friars, City of London

1950–4, Arthur Bailey

Listed grade II, 25 September 1998

Edward VI granted a charter to Dutch Protestants as early as 1550, and they occupied the former monastery of Augustinian friars (founded in 1253) until its destruction in an air raid in 1940.

The new church occupied only half the area of the original, with the rest divided between open space and an office block. Bailey raised his chapel above a meeting hall, and created a columbarium for bodies disinterred during excavations. The careful stone detailing, revealing his training as an assistant of E. Vincent Harris, assumes a simple grandeur. This public building suits its status as the centre of a community as well as being a church. The crafted austerity is also appropriate to the Calvinist worship.

Glass was donated by the Church of Scotland (designed by William Wilson) and later the Worshipful Company of Carpenters (Hugh Easton). The west window, depicting the history of Dutch worship in Britain, is by Max Nauta. The organ was imported from the Netherlands.

219 Oxford Street

Westminster

1951–2, Ronald Ward and Partners

Listed grade II, 14 January 2002

It is unusual to find new offices and shops built before building licensing (a means of directing limited building materials to housing, schools and industry) was withdrawn in November 1954. This corner showroom, shop and offices commemorates the 1951 Festival of Britain.

The first drawings for the scheme date from 1950. However, the developer Jack Salmon then began to make changes to his business, Oxford Street Properties Ltd. The delay led the design to be revised, and to incorporate plaques of precast Carrara stone into the façade. They depict the Royal Festival Hall (see pp.546–7), the Festival of Britain logo devised by Abram Games and the demolished Dome of Discovery and Skylon. Their sculptor is unknown, but their quality is self-evident and they relate well to the banded metal windows of the corner composition.

Listing was secured when the building was proposed for demolition, and it was incorporated into a Zara store by John McAslan and Partners in 2004–5.

Time & Life Building

Bruton Street

1951–3, Michael Rosenauer
Interiors supervised by Hugh Casson

Listed grade II, 29 March 1988
Upgraded to II*, 26 April 2013

Licensing regulations (see p.498) could be circumvented by American investors using dollars. The plan reflects Rosenauer's experience in designing compact flats; so it could be glazed all round, he separated the building from its neighbour by a first-floor roof terrace, landscaped by Peter Shepheard. He then collaborated with Henry Moore, who designed a screen of four semi-abstract figures and installed *Draped Reclining Figure* on the terrace.

Casson and Misha Black reconvened their closest allies from the Festival of Britain to decorate the offices and dining rooms. They included R. Y. Goodden, Christopher and Robin Ironside, H. T. Cadbury-Brown, Leonard Manasseh and Oliver Cox, who recaptured the collaborative spirit of the Festival in dignified colours and materials appropriate to an office building.

Little of the interior survives except the entrance hall and Goodden's stair, but a judicial review in 1998 determined that the fixed works of art by Moore, Ben Nicholson and Geoffrey Clarke be returned. Maurice Lambert's *Symbol of Communication* hangs outside the main entrance.

1 Dean Trench Street

Westminster

1951–5, H. S. Goodhart-Rendel

Listed grade II, 29 March 1988

This house for Sir Michael Adeane replaces one built by Goodhart-Rendel in 1912 for his father, which was destroyed by bombing. This second design is more imaginative for its informality, after the pilastered and pedimented frontage of its predecessor, while remaining a belated example of the Edwardian town house. Its brick and strong white woodwork, with large projecting upper windows and dormers, is reminiscent of Beresford Pite's domestic architecture in its felicitous combination of Arts and Crafts with understated classical motifs. There are links, too, with the Chelsea houses of Norman Shaw and C. R. Ashbee. Although he is best remembered today for reviving our appreciation of Victorian architecture, there underlies in all Goodhart-Rendel's work of the 1950s a sympathy with the architecture of the era around 1910 when he began in practice.

Goodhart-Rendel built his own house and office at No. 60 Tufton Street in 1913, closing the vista of Dean Trench Street. This was also destroyed in the war, but was not rebuilt.

Westminster Kingsway College

Vincent Square, Pimlico

1951–3, 1955–7,
H. S. Goodhart-Rendel

Listed grade II*, 24 April 1998

The Westminster Technical Institute opened in 1893 and was extended in the 1930s, with the steelwork of a third phase abandoned in 1939. The latter enabled Goodhart-Rendel to secure a building licence in 1951, although it dictated much of his design and an assembly hall had to wait until 1955. Auguste Escoffier, chef at the Savoy, co-founded the first catering course here in 1910 and the private dining room is named after him. This and the entrance hall have classical motifs, developed from those of the earlier building but with black and red tiles and ebonized doors.

The exterior is even more striking. Goodhart-Rendel embellished his brickwork with a pierced parapet and red diaper patterns – the latter harmonizing with the building next door and indicating his abiding interest in the Arts and Crafts Movement. The entrance is in green slate with an incised panel by Joseph Ledger, while some windows have Gothick glazing details. The stair turret, begun in 1951, was extended with the completion of the scheme.

Notre Dame de France RC Church

Leicester Place, Soho

1953–5, Hector Corfiato

Listed grade II, 25 September 1998

In 1865 a French church opened to serve the community of hotel staff, chefs, musicians and milliners based around Leicester Square, in an iron structure built in the remains of Burford's Panorama, a circular diorama of 1793. This church was bombed in November 1940. Hector Corfiato created a space of extraordinary solidity and refinement, and one whose plan by chance anticipates the liturgical reforms of the following decade.

The decorating of the church was entrusted to René Varin, the French ambassador's cultural attaché. He commissioned the sculpture *Mater Misericordia* over the entrance from Georges Saupique and the Aubusson tapestry behind the altar. The Art Sacré movement in post-war France saw many leading artists and architects accepting church commissions in an integration of liturgical revival and avant-garde culture, and in 1960 the atheist poet Jean Cocteau painted a mural for the Lady chapel. His self-portrait is to the left of the altar.

Hallfield School

Inverness Terrace, Paddington

1953–5, Denys Lasdun
of Drake and Lasdun

Listed grade II, 29 March 1988
Upgraded to II*, 30 March 1993

Schools were always intended at Tecton's Spa Green Estate (see p.419) and Priory Green Estate, but only here was one realized by the original architects. It is more clearly Lasdun's than the adjoining housing in the Hallfield Estate (see p.495). He reacted against system building with a design that is keenly architectural, while providing a sense of intimacy for the smallest children.

Juniors and infants share a common entrance, which leads to assembly halls set one above the other and reminiscent of that by Gropius and Fry at Impington, Cambridge (1938). There is a mural by Gordon Cullen, also briefly of Tecton. The junior school comprises a two-storeyed spine, its cranked plan a miniature of that Lasdun later built at the University of East Anglia (see p.250). Lasdun likened the spine to a branch, and the infants' rooms to its leaves or petals. These are four pairs of classrooms clustered around a low corridor, whose round windows are set at the height of the smallest children. Additions by Caruso St John in 2001–5 have their own character.

Golden Lane Estate

off Goswell Road, City of London

1953–63, Chamberlin, Powell and Bon

Listed grade II (Crescent House grade II*), 4 December 1997

The City Corporation held a housing competition in 1951–2. Chamberlin, Powell and Bon submitted separate entries; when Geoffry Powell's won, the partnership was formed.

'There is no attempt at the informal in these courts,' they explained in 1957 of the difference between Golden Lane's introverted, grid-like plan and contemporary schemes. Deep basements left by bombed warehousing were exploited to make sunken gardens and tennis courts, and there is a sports centre, community centre, tenants' hall, shops and a pub. To achieve the maximum density, two-bedroom maisonettes were disposed around a tower of smaller flats, which at 16 storeys was briefly the tallest in Britain. It stands out for its aluminium and golden glass cladding, and for rooftop fins that mask water tanks and a garden. More small flats were added when the site was extended westwards to Goswell Road. Crescent House, hugging the curve of the road, introduced a tougher aesthetic of pick-marked concrete and dark timber, and anticipated the style of CPB's adjoining Barbican development then being designed (see pp.532–3).

45-46 Albemarle Street

Mayfair

1955–7, Ernö Goldfinger

Listed grade II, 23 April 1991

These paired shops and offices are pivotal in Goldfinger's career, anticipating his later works on a modest scale. It was among the first office schemes permitted following the abolition of building licences in 1954, and introduced him to Imry's, the developers with whom he also designed the later Alexander Fleming House (see p.576).

Albemarle Street combines modernism with an underlying Golden Section grid derived from Goldfinger's mentor, Auguste Perret. From him, too, comes the robustness of the frame. There is even a classical parapet – an expressive feature since removed from his later housing. The cladding is of Portland stone and muted Vitrolite panels.

There is a constructivist ideology in the way Goldfinger expressed every element in the façade. To maximize its letting potential while meeting council regulations, he cantilevered two bays forward, while clerestory glazing was set back to encourage more light into the building. Goldfinger also designed the interior of No. 46, though only the shopfront survives.

Bracken House

Friday Street, City of London

1955–9, Sir Albert Richardson
Listed grade II*, 13 August 1987

1988–92, Michael Hopkins
and Partners
Listed grade II*, 25 April 2013

Bracken House, reviled as conservative when built, was officially the first post-war building to be listed, saving it from demolition.

Despite Richardson's traditionalism in his later years, his London office buildings clearly express their steel structure behind their dignified classical dress. Bracken House was built for the *Financial Times*, its pinkish brick and Hollington sandstone a symbolic reference requested by its chairman, Lord Brendan Bracken, and topped by Richardson's distinctive curved copper cornice. The newspaper offices were in the north block, their entrance marked by an astrological clock whose central sun incorporates the features of Bracken's old boss, Sir Winston Churchill, while the skewed south block was rented out.

Richardson's central printing house was replaced with offices by Hopkins, which demonstrate how designation can encourage new design of comparable quality. His metal skeleton and tinted glass respect the proportions of Richardson's bookended composition within a 1990s aesthetic, with the proportions of both based on Guarino Guarini's Palazzo Carignano in Turin.

The Royal Military (Guards') Chapel

Wellington Barracks, Birdcage Walk

1955–6, H. S. Goodhart-Rendel
1962–3, Bruce George
of George Trew Dunn

Additions listed grade II*,
26 April 2012

The Guards' Chapel was built in 1838 for the Household Brigade (Her Majesty's Household Division) comprising the five regiments of Foot Guards and two Household Cavalry regiments. It was destroyed by a flying bomb in 1944 save for the apse added by G. E. Street in 1875–9, which remained miraculously unscathed. Goodhart-Rendel, a former Grenadier Guardsman, produced a war memorial cloister in 1955–6, but then died. George was commissioned to integrate this Soanian design, externally of brick, with Street's apse.

George achieved a surprising unity by concentrating natural top lighting and artificial light to highlight the nineteenth-century gold mosaic. Otherwise, dark Afromosia wood and white marble predominate, with aluminium panels by Geoffrey Clarke either side of the chancel arch. Slim angled windows of etched glass by Laurence Whistler and others light six narrow regimental chapels (the cavalry regiments share) and contrast with the surviving Victorian glass by Clayton and Bell set between an open narthex and a blind screen to the west – an effective variant of the Coventry Cathedral plan.

100 Pall Mall

Westminster

1958–62, Donald McMorran
with Duke and Simpson

Listed grade II, 24 November 1995

McMorran was the architect for the exterior of this large office building planned by Duke and Simpson for the developer Rudolph Palumbo. It features many of his favourite motifs. Here is his typical interplay of round arches, forming a distinguished entrance, contrasted with blank areas of Portland stone walling. The building, on the site of the bombed Carlton Club, had to fit alongside London's most prestigious row of nineteenth-century clubs, and shares the same air of gentlemanly confidence without extraneous detailing. Indeed, it shares something of the understatement of the Modern Movement, though the closest similarities are with the work of Italian Novecento architects such as Giovanni Muzio, active in Milan during the 1920s. The groin-vaulted entrance hall and stairwell continue this style.

St Vedast's Rectory

Foster Lane, City of London

1957–9, Stephen Dykes Bower

Listed grade II, 15 July 1998

This is an ingeniously planned building behind a classical frontage. St Vedast's Church had, since 1885, accommodated its incumbent in a series of City houses, until the burnt-out Fountain Tavern next door was acquired in 1952 and a new rectory erected on its site. Dykes Bower's first designs date from 1950, however, and formed a light-hearted addition to his restoration of the church, reconsecrated in 1962.

An arched doorway between the church and vicarage leads to a charming courtyard. Dykes Bower created a tiny, two-storeyed wooden south cloister, with an open loggia below a sashed gallery, linking the vicarage with the rear hall of 1691. He extended the loggia along the rear of the rectory, in the end wall of which is a relief head by Jacob Epstein. On the first floor, an iron balustrade and French windows suggest the style of c.1820. The interior is a complex sequence of spaces on four levels, where the living room features a mural by Hans Feibusch dated 1959.

Weeks Hall

Imperial College, Prince's Gardens

1957–9, Richard Sheppard,
Robson and Partners

Listed grade II, 30 March 1993

Imperial College became Britain's flagship of scientific and technical education in the 1950s, but government expenditure did not extend to halls of residence. It was left to the rector, Sir Patrick Linstead, to seek funding from industry for his vision of a community close to the college. In 1957, the engineering firm of Vickers gave £150,000 to build Weeks Hall in Prince's Gardens, named after their former chairman.

The tall, narrow building is quietly proportioned, with a strong vertical emphasis due to its tight site and setback glazed stair tower. Sheppard's team developed a congenial plan of eight floors of study bedrooms with shared kitchens and ground-floor common rooms, linked by a secondary spiral stair in a variant on the traditional collegiate plan that they repeated in their later college work. Here the room sizes are exceptionally large and the finishes exquisite.

More hostels built on the south side of Prince's Square by the same architects in 1960–8 were demolished with listed building consent in 2005, when Weeks Hall was refurbished.

Sanderson Hotel

50 Berners Street, Fitzrovia

1957–60, Reginald Uren
of Slater, Moberly and Uren

Listed grade II*, 23 January 1991

This prestige headquarters and showrooms were erected to celebrate the centenary of Arthur Sanderson and Son, art-decorators and furnishers. The architects were both specialist designers of department stores and surveyors to the Berners Estate, freeholders of the site.

Sanderson House eschewed effects. A curtain-walled building no higher than its neighbours, with no setbacks or decoration, it attracted attention by the subtle rhythm of its delicate mullions, more closely spaced in the centre of its frontage.

Sanderson moved out in 1992 and in 1999–2000, the building was remodelled as a hotel by Denton Corker Marshall with Philippe Starck. The façade has been restored, but ground-floor roadways were incorporated into a bar, leaving Philip Hicks's garden as a courtyard and retaining Jupp Dernbach-Mayen's polished boulder sculpture. The open showrooms have also been enclosed. What survives is the delicate staircase backed by a glass mural made up of fountain-like forms, designed by John Piper and made by Patrick Reyntiens. It is their largest secular work.

Embassy of the United States of America

Grosvenor Square

1957–60, Eero Saarinen,
with Yorke, Rosenberg and Mardall

Listed grade II, 21 October 2009

The United States embarked on an international building programme in the 1950s that reflected its new role in world politics. Modernism became a world-wide symbol of democracy (and of American companies) but the government had also to appease American traditionalists and address London building controls. It was the only embassy (properly a chancellery since the ambassador lives elsewhere) where a limited competition was held, won by Saarinen in 1956.

Saarinen set his building back, disrupting the square but later beneficial for security. His façades were a compromise of classical proportions and Portland stone (which never achieved the contrasts of soot blackening he anticipated), with an expressed structure and gold anodized aluminium. The concrete diagrid frame is externally visible where it supports the jettied upper storeys, but is most effective inside the tall ground-floor entrance and central lobby, former library and information areas. The quality of detailing stunned 1960s Britain. Theodore Roszak designed the eagle that gave stature to the cornice.

Rutherford School, now King Solomon Academy

Penfold Street, Marylebone

1958–60, Leonard Manasseh and Partners

Listed grade II*, 6 May 1998

Rutherford Secondary School was built for 780 boys on a tight site, replacing a board school that was subsequently demolished for the playground. The plan resembles that of London County Council comprehensives in placing the teaching rooms in one long curtain-walled block, along with the kitchens, boiler house and caretaker's flat. From the central entrance, a glazed link extends to a rear assembly hall with a pyramidal roof; the water tank on the main building is an upside-down pyramid.

Precasting allowed the school to be erected quickly; the mullions externally articulate the façades and are thicker internally to support the glazing. Coloured glass in the library catches the late sun, and the marbled entrance hall has a sculpture by Hubert Dalwood. Marble was among Manasseh's favourite materials; quarry tiles, glazed bricks and solid timber were chosen as similarly 'boy-proof' surfaces. Rutherford shows that a listed school can be sensitively restored and adapted as a modern academy, though the gymnasia have been replaced by new blocks.

26 St James's Place

Westminster

1959–60, Denys Lasdun and Partners

Listed grade II*, 22 December 1998

Lasdun was commissioned by the Malvin Investment Company, who had bought a derelict site overlooking Green Park and whose director wanted a glazed penthouse overlooking the park. Of the eight luxury flats, four enjoy a split-level 3:2 section, in which three storeys of smaller rooms to the north are set against two floors of high-ceiling living rooms facing the park. Lasdun had worked with Wells Coates at Palace Gate (1939), which had developed this section from that pioneered by Mosei Ginzburg's Narkomfin flats in 1920s Moscow.

The elevational treatment has the proportions of contrasting planes and horizontals found at Claredale Street (see p.443), but transformed into granite, mosaic and bronze. It is Lasdun's first truly mature work. Towards the park the split levels are expressed by vertical setbacks. The flats are striking, too, because they fit so happily into their setting, complementing John Vardy's Spencer House (1752–4) next door and showing Lasdun's concern for urban 'grain'.

Our Lady of the Rosary RC Church

Old Marylebone Road

1959–63, H. S. Goodhart-Rendel

Listed grade II, 25 September 1998

Goodhart-Rendel left designs in blue biro for this church, which was completed by his assistants Donald A. Reid and H. Lewis Curtis after his death. It replaced a smaller church next door.

The concealed site gave limited opportunity for the brick patternings that are a feature of Holy Trinity, Dockhead (see p.567). The interior, however, is Goodhart-Rendel's most uplifting space, remarkable for its loftiness and simplicity. With his preference for round arches, southern Romanesque sources played an important part in his work. The stark transverse pointed arches across the nave, pierced at the crown by triple round arches, are bold and uplifting, and were inspired by those at the Romanesque church of St Philibert Tournus in Burgundy. The need to construct these from reinforced concrete led to a coherent plastered finish throughout, in preference to the brick walls first suggested. The tiled sanctuary under narrow lancets is more imposing than that at Dockhead.

New Zealand House

Haymarket

1959–63, Robert Matthew,
Johnson-Marshall and Partners

Listed grade II, 24 November 1995

New Zealand House was long decried for being close to Trafalgar Square and for replacing the much admired Carlton Hotel. It is, however, London's finest 1960s tall office building.

New Zealand's support in the Suez Crisis of 1956 and Crown Estate immunity from most planning controls facilitated the tower, although the L-shaped tower originally proposed by Robert Matthew was reduced to 18 slim storeys in a simplification by Maurice Lee. The tower is a deceptively simple pattern of continuous horizontal bands of clear glazing set behind deep stone sills. It houses both diplomatic and commercial offices, and the penthouse Rainbow Room has spectacular views. The podium is more lavish and complex than its contemporaries. Passport counters and shops are on the ground and mezzanine floors, designed originally to also include a restaurant and expatriats' lounge. Above, the offices of the High Commission are lined in New Zealand marbles and hardwoods.

West footbridge, Zoological Gardens

Regent's Park

1960–1, Sir Hugh Casson, Neville Conder and Partners

Listed grade II, 25 May 1998

Franz Stengelhofen was appointed in 1947 to head the zoo's first architect's department and to prepare a development plan. Then Professor Lord Solly Zuckerman, Berthold Lubetkin's patron in the 1930s, returned to the Zoological Society and commissioned a more ambitious plan from Sir Hugh Casson. One element of Stengelhofen's work retained by Casson was the west footbridge, linking the Cotton Terraces either side of the canal and adjoining the Snowdon Aviary (see p.527). Because of the poor subsoil, a hinged form of construction was adopted, repeating that recently used at Clifton Bridge, Nottingham and on the Medway.

The bridge is 17.02m (56ft) long, with a suspended central span of 12.8m (42ft). The arched abutments are unusual in having extra steps tucked between them so that pedestrians can climb from a lower level directly on to the bridge. There are two light wells, enclosed by steel railings and teak handrails; a third has been replaced by benches on a raised plinth.

Millbank Tower

Westminster

1960–3, Douglas Marriott
of Ronald Ward and Partners

Listed grade II, 24 November 1995

The Vickers Tower, as originally named after its first head lessees and principal occupants, is a rare response to a Thameside location. Reflections from the river ripple across its grey-green curtain walling, as do changing cloud patterns. It shows the rapidity with which the British glass industry became sophisticated designers of curtain walling by the early 1960s.

Much of the cleverness of the building lies in its diabolo shape. It grew out of an arrangement for the lifts that was superseded, but since it gave a higher ratio of window to floor space and the architects liked it, they stuck with it. It resembles the Pirelli Tower in Milan, then newly completed, although the projecting stainless-steel mullions are derived from Gordon Bunshaft's Union Carbide Tower in New York. Ronald Ward and Partners are rarely credited for architectural sophistication, but here they refined the latest sources available. An ancillary eight-storey range has a complementary concave curve. Vickers's thirtieth-floor boardroom has been dismantled.

Royal College of Art

Kensington Gore

1960–3, H. T. Cadbury-Brown,
with Sir Hugh Casson and
Robert Goodden

Listed grade II, 11 July 2001

The Royal College of Art was founded to improve design in industry. Its prestige grew in the 1950s, when a permanent building was developed by its architectural staff. Goodden prepared the brief and Casson handled the committees, while the design was by Cadbury-Brown, then teaching in the sculpture department.

Cadbury-Brown wanted to balance Albert Hall Mansions east of the Royal Albert Hall with a corresponding block; because these were black with soot, he chose dark brick. The flexible workshops have industrial floor loadings, originally with the glass workshops at the top following their success in making the glass for Coventry Cathedral. Their different heights can be seen in the side elevations. The distinctive pairing of the top-floor windows followed the building grid of 5m (16ft 6in). To the west are offices, the library, and an elegant senior common room. To the east Cadbury-Brown and his wife Betty added a gallery (now remodelled internally), and it was a proposal to replace this with a taller block that prompted the listing.

1 Greystoke Place

City of London

1961, Yorke, Rosenberg and Mardall

Listed grade II, 24 November 1995

Yorke, Rosenberg and Mardall (YRM) expanded when in 1955 it secured the commission for Gatwick Airport. F. R. S. Yorke recruited three younger partners, David Allford, Randall Evans and Brian Henderson, who specialized in office buildings, for which this served as a flagship. The site was that of St Dunstan-in-the-West, whose graveyard forms a garden to the building.

The young YRM partners specialized in white tiles – a means of achieving a pure white finish without staining, and a module for modern or classical proportions. Rosenberg had used tiles in Prague in the 1930s, though a more probable source is the Maisons Jaoul; like Le Corbusier, YRM claimed never to cut a tile. With its irregular bays and setbacks, Greystoke Place was one of their most sculptural designs. There were originally five storeys of offices, the uppermost reserved for five of the six partners; Yorke asserted his supremacy by commissioning a penthouse flat.

Thai Airways

41 Albemarle Street, Westminster

1961–3, Peter Moro
Job architect, Michael Mellish

Listed grade II, 24 November 1995

Moro and Mellish designed these showrooms and offices for the leading furniture company Hille, bringing to the site the elegance and strong sense of geometry already seen at Moro's own house at 20 Blackheath Park (see p.562).

Moro's brief was to build the maximum permitted accommodation on the little site, including a basement car park. The result is a curtain-walled building of seven storeys to the front and three to the rear, on a cantilevered concrete frame with a glazed semi-circular staircase in between. The design's quality lies in its narrowly spaced black aluminium mullions, juxtaposed with silver-grey spandrel panels and a surprisingly rough-textured concrete frame where this is exposed at the rear. The original interiors, long gone, were by Robin Day, with whom Moro had collaborated on exhibition design before they worked together on the Royal Festival Hall.

Smithfield Poultry Market

West Smithfield

1961–3, T. P. Bennett and Son

Listed grade II, 24 July 2000

Smithfield was redeveloped in the 1860s as a market for carcases, with buildings by Horace Jones, architect and surveyor to the City of London. In 1958 fire destroyed the poultry market.

Sir Ove Arup and Partners engineered a new clear-span market hall with a shell concrete dome, which is flanked by covered driveways for deliveries and first-floor offices with their own small shell cylinder roofs. When built, Smithfield was the largest shell roof in Europe, at 68.58m (225ft) wide, and shell concrete construction remained popular for markets in the 1960s.

Externally the architects conceived a pattern of concrete and glass hexagons that is decorative while giving an opaque light to the unloading bays. Go inside, and the saucer dome – invisible from the street – is a real surprise, twinkling with lights. The whole interior is a coherent period piece, with tiling, Formica, blue fascias and contemporary signage, as is the basement bar.

Clareville House, formerly Stone's Chop House

Panton Street

1962–4, Albert Richardson and Eric Houfe

Listed grade II, 18 May 1995

Stone's Chop House opened in the 1770s, and until 1961 occupied two stuccoed houses with pub frontages. H. E. Popham wrote in 1937 that 'Stone's seems never to change, and, consistent with its traditions, preserves its eminent respectability . . . Long may Stone's remain as it is.'

But changed it was, under the management of Simpson's-in-the-Strand, although Richardson was an appropriate architect for a new building. In 1925 he had written *The English Inn Past and Present*, among the first books to glorify the English pub. He designed a five-storey office block with his signature setback attics, and a new Chop House in the middle of the Panton Street façade. Ground-floor columns and a Regency-style first floor hint at the old building. Both levels had restaurants, with a lounge overlooking the street on the first floor. Richardson's partner and son-in-law, Eric Houfe, conducted the site meetings and correspondence.

Stone's closed in 1981. The block was renovated by Lifshutz Davidson Sandilands in 2007.

The Economist Group

23–27 St James's Street
and 25–30 Bury Street

1962–4, Alison and Peter Smithson

Listed grade II*, 13 June 1988

The *Economist*'s chairman, Geoffrey Crowther, desired to consolidate scattered offices and to build himself a penthouse flat. Architects who had entered the Churchill College competition were approached, and the Smithsons were commissioned in 1960. The scheme comprised offices, with a bank and serviced bedsits for Boodle's club next door. Each was given a separate tower rising from a low podium that formed a pedestrian square, akin to their unbuilt schemes for Haupstadt, Berlin, and Churchill College. Narrow towers suited the clients' need for small flats and offices, while chamfered corners answered concerns about light levels in adjacent buildings while unifying the group – as does a bay added on the side of Boodle's club.

The Economist Group was one of the first schemes to develop large service and storage cores as an integral part of the design. It lies within a sequence of projects by the Smithsons that separated services from the main structure so that they could be readily updated, an idea that originated in their House of the Future from 1956. Windows and columns closely relate, while the Roach stone spandrels and mullions were designed to control staining and read clearly as cladding. The result is sophisticated and elegant, from a couple best known for heralding the brutalist aesthetic, and marks what they termed their 'shift' towards a tranquil, even 'ordinary' architecture intended for the client to personalize.

The scheme was listed when Skidmore, Owings & Merrill proposed to add two storeys to the 14-storey office tower. This was resisted but the interiors (largely by Alison) have since gone.

Corringham

13–16 Craven Hill Gardens,
Paddington

1962–4, Kenneth Frampton of
Douglas Stephen and Partners

Listed grade II, 21 January 1998

Douglas Stephen and Partners employed several architects who became better known as theorists and teachers. One was the critic Kenneth Frampton, who moved to the United States in 1966, leaving Corringham as his only significant building.

Corringham's 48 flats all have a dual aspect, as they are accessed from a central corridor placed only on alternate floors. Ancillary rooms and landings step over or under this low corridor – called a scissor section and developed by David Gregory Jones for the London County Council, where Margaret Dent (Mrs Douglas Stephen) was one of his colleagues. The elevations were inspired by the tough aesthetic of Lyons, Israel and Ellis, though the grouping of the entrance, lifts, heating and rubbish chutes into a distinct unit gives the block a powerful vertical emphasis, rather like Goldfinger's better-known towers. Otherwise Corringham is a slick, curtain-walled composition, to a regular grid. There are balconies on the rear elevation, overlooking a grassy square, and a projection on the upper five floors denotes larger, two-bedroom units.

Snowdon Aviary

Zoological Gardens, Regent's Park

1962–4, Lord Snowdon
and Cedric Price

Listed grade II*, 12 June 1998

A walk-through aviary was an important component of Sir Hugh Casson's revised plan of 1958, and was inspired by San Diego Zoo. As at the South Bank, he orchestrated a team of designers to produce buildings that were lively, experimental and varied. He introduced Snowdon and Price, while Price brought in Frank Newby as engineer.

The aviary belongs in the tradition of exhibition architecture. Newby had trained under Felix Samuely, engineer of the Skylon at the Festival of Britain, Britain's first sizeable tension structure. Snowdon's concept, refined by Newby, comprised two aluminium tetrahedra, between which are pairs of wider-gauged tubes anchored to the ground by heavy rocker bearings. This framework supports a web of steel cables in constant tension, covered by anodized aluminium netting. A tensile structure permitted a see-through effect in which the distinction between the inside and outside blurs, while the falling ground gives the aviary a spectacular site and an illusion of still greater structural complexity.

Elephant and Rhino Pavilion

Zoological Gardens, Regent's Park

1962–5, Casson, Conder and Partners

Listed grade II*, 12 June 1998

'This building', wrote the critic J. M. Richards, 'could be described in terms of an elephant's massive curves, its wrinkled hide and its curious silhouette.' It concludes a sequence of mid-century zoo buildings whose style reflects their occupants, from Tecton's penguin pool to the delicate Snowdon Aviary. Casson and Conder were indebted to Tecton's elephant house at Whipsnade, formed of 'turning circles' for each animal. Here the pens are clustered and projecting skylights over each one provide a theatrical lighting; chunky benches and brick walkways corral the surrounding humans. Outside, the huddle of copper towers suggests a group of animals gathered at a watering place. Casson produced sketches, calling it 'a saucy thing', but the principal design was Conder's.

The external finishes have to withstand the rough tenants, and the corrugated texture of exposed aggregate was devised to cause minimum injury to both parties. Conder had admired the finish on Twickenham Bridge, by Maxwell Ayrton from 1928–33.

St Paul's Cathedral School

New Change

1962–7, Architects' Co-Partnership

Listed grade II*, 3 January 2007

There were few more auspicious yet daunting sites in post-war London than this, nestled below the apse of St Paul's Cathedral on the site of Wren's bomb-damaged Church of St Augustine. The choir school, founded in the twelfth century, chose the modern design of the Architects' Co-Partnership as standing the test of time, after Seely and Paget's traditional scheme had been discredited by the Royal Fine Art Commission.

The new building had to incorporate St Augustine's surviving tower, where Paul Paget restored Hawksmoor's spire in 1966, and could rise no taller than its cornice. The Portland Roach stone and lead roofs acknowledge its seventeenth-century neighbours, and the long, slit windows reference Wren's pilasters. The bulk of the classrooms, halls, practice rooms and dormitories is reduced by being divided into four, maintaining views of St Paul's and providing collegiate quadrangles. Nikolaus Pevsner jokingly compared the roof to a 'funny hat' or 'edible fungus' but thought the scale and design of the building were 'evocatively right'.

Curzon Mayfair

Curzon Street, Mayfair

1963–6, H. G. Hammond
of Sir John Burnet, Tait and Partners

Listed grade II, 16 July 1997

The Curzon Mayfair replaced a 1930s art-house cinema of the same name by the same architects. The introduction of non-flammable film made it easier to build cinemas within larger commercial complexes, and the new building incorporated offices and flats, as well as a larger auditorium. The cinema is expressed as an unglazed block across the main street frontage that forms a strong contrast to the black-framed glazing above and below. The entrance foyer, to the side, includes a fibreglass screen that can be rolled across the box office when the building is closed.

The auditorium reacted against the stark simplicity of its predecessor. Its sculptured glass-fibre murals by William Mitchell disperse sound while giving a glowing, cave-like effect, and the illuminated coffered ceiling is by Victor Vasarely. Patterns of light are also played on to the 13.1m (43ft) screen – an example of the use of projection as an appropriate part of the architectural decoration. The rear part was sectioned off to make a small second screen in 2003.

City Police Station

Wood Street

1963–6, McMorran and Whitby

Listed grade II*, 24 April 1998

Wood Street Police Station culminated 25 years of building for London's police forces, with a design that looked back to inter-war classicism but also ahead to postmodernism. Even the functionalist *Architects' Journal* admitted that 'McMorran was a sincere and devoted architect who cared passionately about what he was doing. So, crazy though it is, this police station is in another class from the commercial trash nearby.' The closest analogies to what is McMorran's most imaginative work are with the Novecento Italiano and the Swedish architect Ivar Tengbom.

This is a building of two halves. The four-storey police station, with its heavily rusticated façade, accommodates the normal functions of a police station with a ceremonial hall for special constables on the piano nobile denoted by the larger windows. Behind, the pedimented 13-storey tower contains offices for traffic staff and residential bedsits, including hobbies rooms. Tower and station are linked by a basement containing recreational and conference facilities.

The Barbican

Barbican Centre, Guildhall School of Music and Drama, and City of London School for Girls

City of London

1963–82, Chamberlin, Powell and Bon

Listed grade II, 5 September 2001

Chamberlin, Powell and Bon (CPB), already designing the Golden Lane Estate (see p.504), were drawn to this extensive bomb-damaged site by the New Barbican Committee, which proposed flats as an alternative to more offices in the City. CPB combined flats and shops with the Guildhall School of Music and Drama, whose facilities were to serve as a modest arts centre out of school hours.

CPB's second proposals, in 1956, introduced the City's two secondary schools and the threatened Coal Exchange. As built, however, only the girls' school moved to Barbican, and only the Church of St Giles-without-Cripplegate and fragments of the medieval London Wall punctuate the ensemble of new buildings. The plan assumed virtually its present form in 1959. The towers assumed their triangular shape in 1961, when they were the tallest residential blocks in Europe. Work began in 1963 with a detached service block, Milton Court, sadly not listed and now demolished.

In 1964 the City decided that a larger concert hall and theatre would be more viable. The insertion of a 2,000-seat concert hall and 1,500-seat theatre into a scheme already under construction explains the congested plan. The Pit and the conference facilities are still later additions. But the library has dramatic views, and the theatre was planned around excellent sight lines, developed with the Royal Shakespeare Company. The fly tower and scene store are concealed by a conservatory that is wrapped around them.

The Barbican is one of the most ambitious new communities in Europe, executed without cutbacks over nearly 30 years. It combines CPB's fascination for social and land use planning with detailed design and sophisticated structure.

The Dell
(now Serpentine
Restaurant)

Hyde Park

1964, Patrick Gwynne

Listed grade II*, 11 January 1995

With this listing, Patrick Gwynne was belatedly recognized as among the most imaginative post-war designers, five years after his original Serpentine Restaurant in Hyde Park was demolished. It coincided with the National Trust's acquisition of his own house, The Homewood.

In 1963, private caterers were invited to build in the Royal Parks, and Gwynne won an invited competition for Charles Forte's two sites in Hyde Park. His first scheme for the smaller lakeside location resembled a two-storey wedding cake, but when car parking was refused the graceful, umbrella-like solution took shape. Its circular form takes advantage of the outlook: the cantilevered terrace over the lake balances the composition while leading the eye away from kitchens and lavatories hidden in the shrubbery.

The finishes are fine, especially the floor of Brescia Violetta marble, which runs unbroken from the café to the outside terraces. Tables, seats and counters were formed of precast terrazzo, and these survive externally. Gwynne's interior fittings were removed in 1979.

Lillington Gardens

Pimlico

1964–72, Darbourne and Darke

Phases I and II
Listed grade II*, 22 December 1998,

Phase III
Listed grade II, 20 December 2000

In 1961 the City of Westminster followed Churchill Gardens (see p.494) with a second major housing competition in Pimlico. The winner was John Darbourne, aged 26. The modest height and dark red brick were determined by G. E. Street's Church of St James the Less (1860–1). The housing forms a near, continuous wall around the site, creating secure play areas in the middle.

Lillington's originality was its complexity. Some ground-floor units are back to back, with private gardens, while upper flats have balconies and are entered from walkways planted with shrubs. Darbourne wanted tenants to associate themselves with a particular element rather than feel lost in an impersonal development. Phase III, begun in 1969 and including Pimlico Library, is differentiated by its tile-hung mansards. It has more family units, private gardens and far less public space. Pensioners' flats are set on the rooftops.

Lillington inspired many red brick estates in the 1970s. Yet its sources are firmly of c.1960, in Langham House Close (see p.572) and low-rise, high-density projects by Leslie Martin's studio.

Paddington Maintenance Depot

Harrow Road, Westminster

1966–8, Bicknell and Hamilton

Listed grade II*, 14 April 1994

Two buildings were erected for British Railway's fleet of parcel vans, in compensation for land taken for the M40. The budget was generous but the buildings were needed urgently, and the site between the Westway and Regent's Canal was extraordinarily confined. This is the last and finest of Bicknell and Hamilton's railway buildings, inspired by the modernism of the 1920s.

The low east block is concealed alongside the canal under the Harrow Road roundabout. It is a large, oval garage, whose cranked roof beams incorporate a high clerestory.

The west block pokes a distinctive snout over the Westway, like a tugboat with lift towers for funnels. Its service floors, designed for heavy loadings, are set down a steep ramp. The upper floors housed workshops, offices and mess rooms, linked by a curving stairwell detailed by Bicknell and sheathed in the same ceramic mosaic tiling as the exterior. There is a tactile muscularity in its curved corners and romanticism in its triangular plan. It was converted to offices in 2001.

125 Park Road

Regent's Park

1968–70, Farrell/Grimshaw
Partnership

Listed grade II, 28 December 2000

In 1966 Terry Farrell and Nicholas Grimshaw joined the Mercury Housing Society, an innovative co-ownership enterprise co-funded by the Housing Corporation and Cheltenham and Gloucester Building Society. It had a site with planning permission, and Farrell and Grimshaw's design for 40 small flats provided the maximum space allowed under financial yardsticks.

Though the building was jointly designed, Farrell's hand is clearly seen in the succinct plan, while the façade's continual strip windows and corrugated aluminium cladding suggest Grimshaw's more minimal approach. Each floor contained four flats set around a large central core housing services for the bathrooms, then a novel plan. Free-standing columns, continuous perimeter heating and regularly spaced electrical sockets encourage maximum flexibility; partitions can be altered, and some flats have been knocked together. There are fantastic views across Regent's Park and west London, and both Farrell and Grimshaw occupied penthouse flats in the block's early years.

Salters' Hall

Fore Street, City of London

1972–6, Sir Basil Spence,
Bonnington and Collins,
John S. Bonnington Partnership

Listed grade II, 18 November 2010

The livery halls are among the City's most fascinating buildings, despite wartime losses. Most were rebuilt traditionally after 1945, but not that of the Salters' Company founded in 1394, whose hall was destroyed in 1941. The first designs for its replacement in 1968 saw Spence suggesting Portland stone for a scheme led and completed by his partner Jack Bonnington.

Fine wrought-iron gates of 1887 screen the ground floor, which is open between square pilotis and with a glazed entrance to the side. The office levels are clad in aluminium curtain walling with smoke-coloured glass, but the building is defined by its reeded and striated 'corduroy' concrete, always partly painted. It befits the top-heavy massing, for the ceremonial rooms are on the fifth and sixth floors. These interiors, decorated by David Hicks, include the Court Room, lined in rosewood, and the double-height Livery Hall, with fluted ash panelling and an arched ceiling that are subliminally Gothick. Retractable screens mean they can be thrown together.

Wartski

14 Grafton Street, Mayfair

1974, John Bruckland

Listed grade II, 2 November 2012

Richard Seifert and Partners built a line of shops here in 1971–3. One was acquired by Wartski's, jewellers first established in North Wales but which opened a shop in Regent Street in 1911 and came to specialize in acquiring fine Russian works from the Soviet government in the 1920s.

The 1950s had seen the emergence of open shopfronts, with clear glass offering views into the shop behind. Boutiques and speciality shops challenged that approach from the mid-1960s, commissioning one-off façades using unusual, sometimes quirky, materials and motifs to create a distinctive image in which window displays were minimal. Wartski's rich design offers security, luxury and the semblance of a jewel box. A façade of patinated bronze boxes overhangs deep windows set between black polished granite pilasters, with black steps and stall risers of white marble. The projecting gold sign features the coat of arms of Elizabeth II. Bruckland was a specialist designer of exhibitions and interiors. Only the shopfront is listed.

Lloyd's Building

Lime Street, City of London

1981–6, Richard Rogers Partnership

Listed grade I, 19 December 2011

Lloyd's originated in 1688 in a coffee house, where seafarers and merchants met the first underwriters who insured their ships and cargoes. Its first purpose-built office was completed by Edwin Cooper in 1928, and its entrance arch survives. A second building, built by Terence Heysham in 1952–7, took as a board room Robert Adam's dining room from Bowood House in Wiltshire, then being demolished. When, in the late 1970s, an even larger building was required, the Richard Rogers Partnership won the commission.

Lloyd's is arguably Rogers's finest work. Their scheme provided a single vast trading space, the Room, with a built-in potential for expansion or contraction as the market required. A massive bank of escalators serves the four floors of this soaring atrium, with natural lighting from the arched roof and opaque side glazing inspired by Pierre Chareau's Maison de Verre in Paris. This unencumbered trading floor was realized by placing stainless-steel lift shafts, service towers and ventilation shafts outside the concrete frame, where they cut an extraordinary figure in the City landscape. The Adam Room was reconfigured to its original proportions and installed on the eleventh floor.

Lloyd's possesses an inspiring timelessness. Roger's design acknowledges such Victorian buildings as Leadenhall Market next door, yet its High-Tech design remains awe-inspiringly futuristic. The listing, which was warmly welcomed by both Lloyd's and Lord Rogers, recognizes the building's inherent flexibility, nods to its robustness and acknowledges its need to adjust as the markets change.

22 Parkside, Wimbledon,
1968–70, Richard and Su
Rogers with John Young

1–7, 25 and 39 Persant Road

Excalibur Estate, Bellingham

1945–6, Uni-Seco Ltd

Listed grade II, 16 March 2009

Under the Temporary Housing Act of 1944, 187 bungalows were built on land intended by the London County Council (LCC) as a park. The Act approved standardized bungalows by 11 companies, of which those by the Uni-Seco company were most numerous in London. A light timber frame clad in asbestos cement sheeting, the Uni-Seco is recognizable by its near-flat roof and corner windows, with the Mark 2 design also having a corner door. The Mark 3 has a central doorway and a much more logical plan, with two bedrooms and the living room on either side of a hallway. The kitchen and bathroom followed a standard ministry design.

The streets, narrower than was normally permitted and including pedestrian pathways, were named after Knights of the Round Table, continuing a policy in the LCC's adjoining Downham Estate. By 2004 this was England's largest surviving prefab estate. Lewisham Council propose to replace it with 371 new homes. English Heritage recommended that a group of 21 prefabs be listed, but only six recommendations were accepted by the government.

Passfields

Bromley Road, Bellingham

1949–50, Fry, Drew and Partners
Job architect, J. B. Shaw

Listed grade II, 22 December 1998

Maxwell Fry was a pioneer of modern housing design in the 1930s, but his expanded practice built little in England after the war.

Lewisham Council had acquired the small site before the war, so building could begin early. It was, however, constrained by the bustling Bromley Road, then still carrying trams and due to be widened. Fry set the nearest blocks at right angles, and placed a bigger block behind to shield a rear playground. The laundrette was one of the first designed for automatic washing machines.

The big block has two tiers of maisonettes, still rare in public housing and expressed by the engineers Ove Arup and Partners' use of a box frame construction, curved as at the Spa Green Estate (p.419) and here incorporating projecting balconies. Because it was begun after government cuts in 1947, funding was reduced, and having the upper floors as maisonettes meant that only one lift was needed. The estate won a Festival of Britain Merit Award for its mix of picturesque design and engineering innovation.

Royal Festival Hall

Belvedere Road, Lambeth

1949–51, London County Council: Robert Matthew, Leslie Martin and Peter Moro

Listed grade I, 29 March 1988

The Royal Festival Hall was the only permanent building erected on the South Bank for the Festival of Britain. Though it superficially resembled halls at Gothenberg (1933) and Malmö (1940), it was an extraordinarily rich and sophisticated achievement for its date and rapid building programme.

It was a replacement for the bombed Queen's Hall, and so was required to hold an enormous 3,000 seats. Matthew first suggested setting the auditorium above the foyer, though the detailed plan was Martin's. It was dubbed the 'egg in the box', since to prevent outside noise foyers surrounded the auditorium, which was expressed in a contrasting Derbyshire fossil stone. A restaurant ran across the river frontage, so access was from two entrances at the sides on different levels. The lower one, restored in the 1990s, remains the best way to experience the unfolding sequence of foyers.

The interiors defied the shortages of materials. Their detailing is tactile, from the cyma-curved auditorium boxes reminiscent of Lubetkin's balconies at Highpoint One, to thick staircase handrails and the 'net and ball' carpet motif. They were designed by Moro and his many enthusiastic ex-students, sidelining London County Council architects. The problem was the auditorium's dry acoustic, which was upgraded with Peter Parkin's novel assisted resonators in 1962–5 and by Kirkegaard Associates in 2005–7 in a renovation by Allies and Morrison.

The exterior was rebuilt in a savvier but blander modernism in 1963–5, when a large deck was installed over the complex ground levels between Waterloo Bridge and the river. An intended small hall was instead built alongside as the Queen Elizabeth Hall with the adjoining Hayward Gallery.

St George's Chapel

RAF Biggin Hill

1951, Wemyss Wylton Todd

Listed grade II, 1 December 2005

Set on top of the North Downs, Biggin Hill was the leading fighter aerodrome of the Battle of Britain. Of the airmen based there, 453 were killed. The desire to commemorate them, and the station, prompted a fundraising appeal backed by Sir Winston Churchill for 'a permanent shrine of remembrance' after a temporary chapel burned down in 1946. Air Chief Marshal Lord Dowding laid the foundation stone and it took five months to build.

Australian-born Wylton Todd served in the RAF and was a prisoner of war at Stammlager Luft III in Silesia, where he later designed the memorial to those shot in the Great Escape of 1944. At Biggin Hill, he produced a spare, Lombardic design in brick. The interior includes stained-glass windows by Hugh Easton, installed in 1955, depicting scenes of aerodrome life, along with casualty boards and other evocative items; glass by Goddard and Gibbs followed in the 1980s. The church's interest is historical; a Spitfire and a Hurricane stand sentinel outside.

Stockwell Bus Garage

Lansdowne Way, Stockwell

1951–4, Adie, Button and Partners

Listed grade II*, 29 March 1988

London's last trams were withdrawn in 1952, leaving a demand for garages to house the expanded bus fleet. There was steel for garages to replace those destroyed in the war, but for new depots, George Adie and Frederick Button resorted to shell concrete, aided by engineer A. E. Beer.

Peckham's bus garage, now demolished, repeated the construction popularized at the former bus depot in Bournemouth (see p.272). Stockwell is also spanned by ten concrete beams linked by thin barrel vaults and a ring beam, although its span of 59.1m (194ft) makes it a third wider than the Bournemouth garage, and it is also longer. The difference is the use of arched portal frames – giant ribs that rise from 4.87m (16ft) to 16.46m (54ft) at their centre. Between them, the arched cylindrical shells soar still higher, and the cathedral-like effect of their vaults is further enhanced by roof lights. To ensure adequate loadings, the frames' reinforcement bars were welded rather than lapped – perhaps the roof's greatest technical novelty. Some 200 buses can be garaged here.

Evolution House, formerly Australian House

Royal Botanic Gardens, Kew

1952, S. L. Rothwell, Ministry of Works

Listed grade II, 9 May 2011

While other materials were in short supply after 1945, aluminium was plentiful, but it was still rarely used for complete buildings. Britain led the way with the aircraft industries' promotion of prefabricated bungalows and schools, and with the 'Dome of Discovery' at the Festival of Britain. Aluminium alloys were welcomed for greenhouses as they were thought never to corrode, but this is the largest example anywhere of its date at 416sq. m (4,480sq. ft), developed with the engineer J. E. Temple.

The greenhouse was given by the Australian government following a visit by the director of Kew in 1949, and until 1994 housed plants from its deserts. The preformed galvanized frame of H10-WP aluminium is lightweight and resistant to corrosion, and has integrated ventilation, heating and cleaning systems. It rests on a plinth of reused bricks capped with a slate sill, the mortar flecked with coarse-grained grit. The Evolution House closed in 2013 to become an interpretation centre for the adjoining Temperance House.

St John's vicarage and caretaker's house

92 and 96 Vassall Road, Kennington

1952–4, H. S. Goodhart-Rendel

Listed grade II, 15 July 1998

These commissions, originally built as a convent and lodge for the Community of St Mary the Virgin, provided Harry Stuart Goodhart-Rendel with a rare opportunity to build in an updated version of the secular Gothic style. They were inspired by the adjacent Church of St John the Divine (of 1871–4 by G. E. Street), which he restored after incendiary damage. Street was one of Goodhart-Rendel's idols. John Betjeman believed that 'the house and cottage for the Wantage Sisters . . . are what Street would have designed in his best and most modest manner had he been asked to build such dwellings in south London'. The buildings are characterful without being pastiches.

A chapel in the gabled roof space of the former convent, now the vicarage, has become a delightful library, lit by the rose window that is a prominent feature to the side of the asymmetrical gabled façade. The caretaker's house forms a foil to this, resembling a lodge at its entrance, and with a hipped roof that serves to conceal its real size.

The Alton Estate

Ten Point Blocks, Alton East

1952-5, London County Council
Listed grade ll,
22 December 1998

Five slab blocks, Alton West

1955-8, London County Council
Listed grade II*,
22 December 1998

Old People's Bungalows, Danebury Avenue

1955-8, London County Council
Listed grade ll,
22 December 1998

Within the London boundary the only substantial housing sites were at Roehampton, a mix of large 1850s villas and eighteenth-century estates. It was partly to protect these sites from an unimaginative plan that the London County Council Architect's Department took command of the authority's housing design in 1950.

Alton East, originally 'Portsmouth Road', was developed by a socially minded team that included architects from the Hertfordshire schools programme. They replaced the villas with elegant towers or point blocks of 11 storeys, inspired by Swedish models, and keeping the Victorian planting they developed the lower slopes with houses and four-storey maisonettes, their red brick a contrast to the white brick and monochrome tile patterns of the points.

Alton West is stronger meat, developed by a younger generation who subsequently practised as Howell, Killick, Partridge and Amis. The valley site is laid out more formally, and the points, maisonettes, shops and a library are uniformly clad in storey-high concrete panels, first refined here. To the south, Mount Clare of 1776 and its surrounding trees were retained and fronted by old people's bungalows, their tall chimneys a cheerful anachronism in an otherwise modern vista. Still more striking are the five long, ten-storey slabs of maisonettes set across the valley on tall pilotis. After Harold Macmillan objected to the slabs being set in a line facing Richmond Park, they were set sideways into the hillside, to produce one of the great statements of modern architecture in London. Listing has recognized the importance of the most distinctive blocks, but the entire redevelopment and its landscaping deserves appreciation as an entity.

Church of St Luke

Diamond Street, Camberwell

1953–4, Arthur Martin, with Milner and Craze (executants)

Listed grade II, 13 April 2000

St Luke's replaced a church of 1876–7 bombed in the war. Its Byzantine design belongs as much to the 1930s as the 1950s, yet its broad transepts and central domed crossing make it admirably suited to modern liturgy. Although well massed, the simple brick exterior appears rather gaunt.

The interior, however, is surprisingly light and high, its central octagonal crossing and aisles defined by narrow columns on cushion capitals – a motif repeated in some of the fenestration and which gives an unexpected grace to the composition. Most notable of all are the cross-vistas produced by the combination of passage aisles with angled transepts. These are a simplified and more successful version of Martin's earlier church, St Luke's, Milber, Newton Abbot, built for his brother Keble Martin in the 1930s. Arthur Martin spent most of his working life as architect to the Duchy of Cornwall but he was from a strong High Church background and this, his last work, was a labour of love.

Elliott School (ARK Putney Academy)

Pullman Gardens, Putney

1953–6, London County Council
Group leader, George A. Trevett

Listed grade II, 30 March 1993

Elliott School is the finest of all the London County Council's (LCC) in-house comprehensive schools, but among the least recognized. Trevett's team of assistants is not fully known.

Elliott was built to serve the LCC's housing estate at Roehampton following a decision in 1947 to build comprehensives. The classrooms are in a four-storey teaching block, with a drama hall tucked into the lower part of the slope and an open-air theatre. To one side is a single-storey gymnasia and workshop block, and on the other a hall for 1,300 pupils, whose curves counter the bulk of the main block. Within the curtain-walled building, the variety of Elliott's decorative detail is remarkable, with tile and brick patterns, cyma balconies and wavy roofs. There are pilotis inspired by Le Corbusier, while the hall, cantilevered entrance canopy and end balconies have some affinities with Gropius and Tecton's work.

The school was reorganized in 2012 and the building was remodelled.

Parkleys

Ham

1954–6, 1958–9, Eric Lyons
for Bargood Estates, later
Span Developments Ltd

Listed grade II, 22 December 1998

Geoffrey Townsend gave up architecture in 1953 to operate as a developer, leaving his friend Eric Lyons to design the low-rise, high-density flats and terraces of houses they built together in south London's leafier suburbs. Span was one of the few private developers admired by the architectural press, and was very influential.

Their ideas reached maturity at Parkleys, flats designed for first-time buyers on endowment mortgages, which were pioneered by Townsend here. There are 169 flats in three sizes, arranged in two-storey, tile-hung terraces and courtyards, and three-storey blocks. The relatively high density is masked by the clever layout and dense planting that became a feature of Span estates. Parkleys was built over a nursery and used the old plant stock, with mushroom courtyard lamps designed by Lyons first used here. Townsend also introduced a management system that remains part of the Span ethos, whereby every leaseholder belongs to a company that elects a residents' committee to run the estate. This ensures that Parkleys has remained remarkably little altered.

Church of All Saints

Bridle Road, Spring Park, Croydon

1955–6, Curtis Green, Son and Lloyd

Listed grade II, 10 August 1998

All Saints was built with compensation money from St George's Church, Canterbury, bombed in 1942. St George's is commemorated by glass in the porch and is a reminder that Croydon was then within the Diocese of Canterbury.

All Saints has a west end baptistery, square nave and a long choir and sanctuary flanked by vestries and a Lady chapel. Its minimal Gothic style resembles that of Green's nearby Church of St George, Waddon, from 1932, with lancet windows and unmoulded transverse arches that define the main spaces; their form is repeated in the narrow aisle arcades. More unusual is the Lady chapel, whose length is interrupted by six stone columns.

It is easy to ignore the long succession of traditionally planned churches built in the 1950s. Curtis Green, his son and son-in-law were principally commercial architects, but their church work exemplifies an interest in good interior design. All Saints would have been elegant in the 1930s; for the 1950s, it is lavish, with its handmade bricks and big tiled roofs.

Lammas Green

Sydenham Hill Estate

1955–7, Donald McMorran

Listed grade II, 22 December 1998

McMorran chose a modern scheme when assessing the Golden Lane competition, yet his own work for the City Corporation remained traditional.

Here he designed 27 houses and 30 flats on the southern slopes of Sydenham Hill. The high land and views towards Kent add to the village-like character of Lammas Green. It replaced three houses owned by the Corporation, who insisted that their replacements should have no more than three storeys and that mature trees be kept. Rendered terraced houses, some stepped in pairs, surround three sides of a central green, with occasional dormers to heighten their picturesque qualities. The brown brick flats protect the houses from the main road. Their blocky massing of the tall stacks and shallow gables – clad in timber – are stylistically midway between Barn Field and Wood Field at Parkhill Road (see p.420) and his later North London estates. McMorran sought 'a community with its own life and identity', and also included a small community hall.

Fairlawn School

Honor Oak Road, Honor Oak

1955–7, Peter Moro
with Michael Mellish

Listed grade II, 17 December 2007

Such was the demand for primary schools that the London County Council passed some of its commissions (where time allowed) to private architects on an approved list. Moro, an architect noted, with his assistant Michael Mellish, for meticulous detailing, accordingly produced a neatly designed school for infants and juniors on a steep hillside with extensive views eastwards.

Like Lasdun's Hallfield School (see p.503), a line of linked pavilions on a staggered plan provides a mix of informal spaces for the infants. It is divided by the playground from a more grown-up design of two storeys for the juniors, curtain-walled on a concrete frame, and with sloping ceilings that maximize light. The main ornament is reserved for the steel-framed assembly hall, which also serves as a dining room, lined in timber and with an open-tread stair that leads directly to the upper cloakrooms and classrooms. An external mural by John Verney from 1958 was reinstated in 2008, but wood reliefs by Victor Pasmore disappeared years ago.

2, 4 and 6 Foxes' Dale

Blackheath Park

1957, Eric Lyons for
Span Developments Ltd

Listed grade II, 17 October 2011

Townsend and Lyons were introduced to Blackheath Park by the builder Leslie Bilsby, himself a developer there. Many of Span's most interesting schemes replaced bomb-damaged late Georgian houses or infilled backland sites here, encountering initial hostility from the planners but now recognized as contributing to the area's picturesque charm. Foxes' Dale is the only Span scheme of houses to be listed.

The houses have an unexpectedly deep ground floor plan, with the living room and study arranged around an internal courtyard behind the kitchen and dining area, giving a light and flexible open-plan living space. They are well appointed, with hardwood floors, fitted cupboards, and a sculptural spiral stair that saved space. No. 2 was chosen by *House and Garden* magazine as its 'House of Ideas' for 1957 and became the show home for an intended 19 houses to its T3 plan. At three storeys, the T3 was bigger than Lyons's other Blackheath houses, and at £5,975 so expensive that only this terrace of three was built.

St James's Church

Briarwood Road, Clapham Park

1957–8, N. F. Cachemaille-Day

Listed grade II, 25 September 1998

Cachemaille-Day's church replaced a proprietary chapel of 1829 by Lewis Vulliamy, which was bombed in 1940. The exterior is a simple brick box, but the interior is remarkable.

Nugent Francis Cachemaille-Day had worked for another church specialist, H. S. Goodhart-Rendel, in the 1920s when he studied contemporary German religious architecture. Having set up his own church practice in 1935, he began to explore the possibilities of concrete diagrid roofs to achieve broad spans and a sense of Gothic vaulted construction. An early example is the star-shaped Church of St Michael and All Angels, Wythenshawe, of 1937, but St James's is the most fully Gothic realization of the technique. Each rib crosses the church diagonally, intersecting with three other ribs en route. This geometrical pattern of squares gives the optical effect of a true tierceron vault. The ribs are given an extra dimension by having solid spandrels where they spring from the walls and the effect is dramatic. An extra set of columns denotes the chancel, in what was still a conventionally planned church.

20 Blackheath Park

Blackheath

1957–8, Peter Moro

Listed grade II, 29 March 1988
Upgraded to II*, 7 October 1999

Single-level dwellings were the vogue in the 1950s and 1960s, inspired by the Californian Case Study Houses, which exalted in open-planned, servant-free spaces surrounded by shady gardens. Marcel Breuer was the first to set such houses on a discreet plinth that housed such necessities as a garage and utility room underneath projecting living accommodation.

Moro developed this ideal notion for suburban living, slicing his house along its long, central spine so that the open living area and study overlooking the garden are a few steps lower than the dining area and kitchen, which thus permitted a clerestory to light the centre of the house. Like Breuer, Moro articulated the elevations by using different materials, here brick and render, but the internal timber finishes and overall calm simplicity are more reminiscent of Alvar Aalto.

Moro worked for Tecton, and designed the interiors of the Royal Festival Hall (see pp.546–7). His own house used only a limited palette of favourite colours with natural timber, dark steel and tiles.

The Finnish Church

Albion Street, Rotherhithe

1957–8, Cyril Mardall
of Yorke, Rosenberg and Mardall

Listed grade II, 29 March 1998

Cyril Sjöström was the son of a Finnish architect and an English opera singer, who adopted his mother's maiden name in 1944. He specialized in schools and housing, but he had been involved since the 1930s in planning a church for the Finnish Seamen's Mission, founded in 1882. The Surrey Docks were the point of entry for Scandinavian timber, and Norwegian and Swedish churches are nearby. The church aimed to serve a wider expatriate community from the first, however.

Mardall's design of 1954 was revised to become more flexible and yet compact, combining a church and meeting place within a single volume. A gallery café can be screened off or opened up as required, while a ground-floor reading room is separated from the church only by a free-standing stove and spiral staircase. It is simple, clearly Finnish and uncluttered by superficial details. It is England's only church with a sauna, designed by Mardall's architect wife, June Park.

Langham House Close

Ham Common

1957–8, James Stirling
and James Gowan

Listed grade II, 22 December 1998
Upgraded to II*, 18 May 2006

In 1955 Stirling was the first English architect to write about Le Corbusier's boldly expressed use of brick and concrete at the Maisons Jaoul (1953–5). Here was the honest use of materials for which Stirling and Gowan's generation had been searching.

The 30 private flats at Ham Common, for which Stirling was commissioned in 1955 by Luke Manusso, adopted the style of the Maisons Jaoul and details such as its concrete water spouts. With a budget of only £1,900 per flat, exposed concrete floor beams and brick walling were also cheap. The flats established the Maisons Jaoul as a model for British architecture as seen nowhere else. Stirling devised the taller block, Gowan the lower ranges, where the site was narrower. Stirling and Gowan also provided different interiors to the flats. Best are Gowan's large foyers to the two smaller blocks, with their concrete first-floor landings a bridge between glazed walls. While Stirling embraced other references, Gowan's later work remained true to brick modernism.

Royal National Theatre Studio

The Cut, Waterloo

1957–8, Lyons, Israel and Ellis
Assistants, John Miller and
Christopher Dean

Listed grade II, 20 March 2006

Waterloo's Old Vic Company was the forerunner of the National Theatre, but was hampered by having its workshops and costume department in Hampstead. It raised £90,000 from foreign tours to rebuild these facilities next door, and the raw, board-marked concrete and engineering brick were an appropriately workmanlike idiom. It demonstrates Lyons, Israel and Ellis's (LIE) move away from the clean slabs of their earlier schools towards a monumental style of broken silhouettes and radical shapes, taken further by former assistants Stirling and Gowan.

There is a highly glazed and panelled boardroom; otherwise the building housed ground-floor offices, first-floor wardrobe rooms and a scenic workshop that is top-lit with LIE's typically blocky skylights. A giant slot through the building, where a paint frame could be raised or lowered to aid the scene painters at work on the second floor, is expressed externally. In 1984 the building became a studio for theatre research.

St Mark's Church

Church Road, Biggin Hill

1957–9, Richard Gilbert Scott

Listed grade II, 16 November 2007

As Biggin Hill grew rapidly in the 1950s, Father Vivian Symons determined to replace its tin tabernacle, and with no money and materials he turned to the bomb-damaged Church of All Saints, Surrey Square, of 1893. Volunteers and members of Harrow School transported 125,000 bricks, 200 tons of stonework and all the roof timbers; the new building was christened 'the Moving Church'. A schoolboy neighbour introduced Sir Giles Scott to the project, which he passed to his son.

Richard Scott conceived a modern barn, but with Gothic tracery to the windows and a tapered tower. The old roof was set low on salvaged bricks and stone corbels. Father Symons etched 51 windows with scenes from the *Biblia Pauperum* using a dentist's drill. Scott designed the pews and organ case, while the reredos was inspired by his father's work at Liverpool Cathedral and incorporated a mural by Roland Pym featuring both the old church and the new. St Mark's is listed for its blend of old and new conceived at a time of austerity.

RC Most Holy Trinity Church

Dockhead, Bermondsey

1957–60, H. S. Goodhart-Rendel

Listed grade II, 25 September 1998
Upgraded to II*, 22 April 2015

In 1951, Goodhart-Rendel planned an ambitious replacement for this major Roman Catholic church, destroyed in the war, which was later simplified. The exterior is the culmination of his interest in patterned brickwork. The geometrical theme of hexagons and triangles, denoting the Trinity, is found throughout the building. It is most evident in the striking west front, whose twin hexagonal towers link to form a central arch, a device perhaps derived from Theodor Fischer's Garrison Church at Ulm of 1908. The design is also a rationalization of Goodhart-Rendel's uncompleted scheme for Prinknash Abbey, designed in 1938 following his conversion to Rome. The concentration of light from the south is borrowed from G. E. Street, while the round-arched windows are reminiscent of Beresford Pite.

The interior is light, vaulted in thin concrete, reinforced with Delta bronze for longevity. Relief panels behind the altar are by Atri Brown, as are the Stations of the Cross. The church and presbytery were completed after Goodhart-Rendel's death by his assistant, H. Lewis Curtis.

Rivoli Ballroom

350 Brockley Road, Crofton Park

1958–9

Listed grade II, 21 December 2007

From the street, this modest building is indistinguishable from the thousands of small suburban cinemas built before the First World War. Yet the Crofton Park Palace, opened in 1913, found a glamorous new use in 1959 – as a ballroom.

This was the era of American jive and swing bands, the lindy hop, jitterbug and rock 'n' roll, alongside the continued popularity of strict-tempo ballroom dancing. A local businessman and dancing devotee, Leonard Tomlin, bought the cinema in 1957 and inserted a luxuriant and exotic decorative scheme into its barrel-vaulted auditorium. Inspired by upmarket Art Deco ballrooms of the 1920s, the Rivoli has a Canadian maple-sprung dance floor, red velour walls, marquetry panelling, French chandeliers and Chinese lanterns. The ballroom is flanked by two narrow bars, one lined with booths and with a bar front of Arabesque interlaced patterns lit by saucer-shaped lamps. The aesthetic is kitsch and flamboyant. The building is still used as a dance hall.

Church of St Crispin with St Crispinian

Southwark Park Road, Bermondsey

1958–9, Thomas F. Ford

Listed grade II, 4 December 2000

Thomas Ford rebuilt many bombed churches for the Diocese of Southwark, including that of St Crispin, gutted in 1940. This interior has a rare homogeneity, its Greek cross plan under a central dome having a wide, shallow sanctuary with choir stalls to either side. It celebrates the Bermondsey leather industry in the coverings of the doors and pews, and in the dominating mural by Hans Feibusch commemorating St Crispin and St Crispinian, patron saints of shoes and leather. His protégé Phyllis Dear filled the dome with sky and clouds. Windows by M. C. Farrar Bell depicting leatherworking came from Christchurch, Jamaica Street, demolished in the 1960s.

Feibusch came to Britain after appearing in Hitler's exhibition of 'Degenerate Art' in 1938. The success of a mural for Collier's Wood Methodist Church led to a career in church decoration, much of it with Ford and most extensively in south London. St Crispin's was listed when it was threatened with demolition, and is now a nursery.

Christ Church

Blackfriars Road, Southwark

1958–9, R. Paxton Watson
and Barry Costin

Listed grade II, 26 October 2010

Christ Church is a modest neo-Georgian church, the third on this site and replacing that of 1738–41 destroyed in the war. It is listed for its stained-glass windows by Frederick W. Cole, installed in 1960. Celebrating the working lives of Southwark people, here may be observed printers, bakers, electricians, brewers, office workers and charwomen in historical and contemporary dress. Nearby historic places are depicted too, including St Paul's Cathedral, Bankside power station (now Tate Modern) and the River Thames, alongside a local housing estate and the weatherboarded houses of Southwark past. One window features a Routemaster bus and a London Transport bus stop for the nos. 4, 45 and 63; the 45 and 63 still serve the church. More windows were added in 1984–5.

The dignity of everyday life and work became a staple of church and community art in the post-war years. Christ Church, however, is a particularly enchanting example of this trend, unparalleled in its attention to detail.

1–26 Hallgate

Blackheath Park

1958–9, Eric Lyons
for Span Developments Ltd

Listed grade II, 22 December 1998

Hallgate was built as an entrance to a development of houses, The Hall, and has a sophistication not found in Eric Lyons earlier work at Parkleys (see p.536) and The Priory, Blackheath. The Hall is reached via a covered passage through the block.

Span secured a number of empty sites on the Cato Estate at Blackheath, for which Lyons produced little developments of flats and houses. It is the best place to see the evolution of their collaboration through the 1950s and 1960s. They have relatively high densities, up to 70 persons per acre, which was controversial in leafy Blackheath but make possible by intense planting.

Lyons's frustrations with planning inspectors are recorded at Hallgate. In a niche in the passageway wall is a sculpted figure, almost crushed under the concrete lintel he supports. By Keith Godwin, its title is *The Architect in Society*. 'If it is not a good likeness, it is roughly the way I feel at times,' Lyons explained in 1959.

Globe Academy

Harper Road, Elephant and Castle

1958–60, Chamberlin,
Powell and Bon

Listed grade II, 30 March 1993

Chamberlin, Powell and Bon sought to 'avoid specialization' in favour of 'fresh opportunities', seen in the buildings of their middle period such as Murray Edwards College (see p.235) and this school. Both buildings experimented with concrete forms, engineered by Flint and Neill.

The school was originally built as Two Saints School for 1,260 girls, with four-storey blocks set either side of three central gymnasia. Its most striking feature was its five-sided assembly hall, a stepped amphitheatre set over a broad walkway and topped by a hyperbolic paraboloid roof of five separate concrete shells with a central lantern. By supporting the shells at their low corners along the building's edge, the body of the hall (1,300.6m/ 14,000sq ft) could be free of columns. It is surrounded by five classrooms that were originally designed as house rooms to encourage smaller social groups within the large school.

The hall was retained and refurbished as the Pentagon Building in the school's rebuilding as an academy by Amanda Levete Architects, completed in 2010.

St Paul's Church

Lorrimore Square, Kennington

1958–60, John Wimbleton and H. G. Coulter of Woodroffe, Buchanan and Coulter

Listed grade II, 11 July 2001

St Paul's replaced a church of 1854 damaged in the war, and forms part of the Brandon Estate, the first major London County Council scheme to combine new housing with rehabilitated terraces. It includes extensive parish rooms, and screens can be opened into a hall at its west end.

Brick, concrete and copper are set over a high rubble stone plinth, symbolically reused from the old church, while the roof is a series of precast timber sections whose triangulation gives the new building its dramatic faceted appearance. The sections were delivered to the church ready assembled and sheathed in copper, and were hoisted into place.

The church's decoration is also lavish and very complete. The sequence of acoustic panels at the west end and the altar cloths are among the best surviving examples of the once prolific appliqué work of Gerald Holtom. The sanctuary figure of Christ is by Freda Skinner. This quirky, highly decorative 1950s style rapidly became old-fashioned with the Liturgical Movement, but is now being reappraised.

Mitcham Methodist Church

Cricket Green, Mitcham

1959, Edward Mills

Listed grade II, 5 March 2010

Mitcham is one of the finest nonconformist churches of the post-war years. Its designer, himself a Methodist, believed that church architecture had a moral dimension. In his primer of 1956, *The Modern Church*, Mills advocated the eloquence of using exposed materials, simplicity in composition and plan, and the value of community work.

These ideas are manifest at Mitcham. The church has a straightforward rectilinear plan enlivened by a dynamic folded concrete slab roof, engineered by Ove Arup and Partners. The roof's concertina extends beyond the nave wall to create a covered walkway linking the church to its community hall, conveying the importance of the church's social work. The nave has a fully glazed end bay, which throws light on to the riven York stone slabs of the wall behind the Lord's table. The church is little changed, retaining its original hardwood pews and choir stalls, organ and pulpit, also designed by Mills.

The Pavilion

Warren Road, Coombe,
Kingston-upon-Thames

1959–60, Oliver Hill

Listed grade II, 1 October 1999

The Pavilion is a late work by one of the most eclectic architects of the mid-century. Hill designed in both modern and traditional styles, with a versatility that makes some architectural historians question his pedigree. The Pavilion is a return to the neo-Georgian style he had used for London town houses in the interwar years, but reveals a greater richness and understanding of his sources.

Hill's interest in history can be seen in a book with John Cornforth, *English Country Houses: Caroline* (1966). The Pavilion demonstrates this knowledge of early neo-Palladianism, and a resemblance to a garden temple also reflects the growing awareness of such buildings in these years. The Pavilion has a three-bay front under a broad pediment, in which Hill placed the principal living room. This he flanked by small two-storey wings, each housing a staircase as well as the principal bedrooms. Seventeenth-century motifs are seen in the doorcases and stairs.

Metro Central Heights

formerly Alexander Fleming House, Newington Causeway, Elephant and Castle

1959–66, Ernö Goldfinger

Listed grade II, 8 July 2013

In 1958 Goldfinger and the developer Arnold Lee won a competition for speculative offices as part of the London County Council's rebuilding of the Elephant and Castle.

Three blocks were planned around a courtyard, with the fourth side added along with a pub and cinema in 1964–6. Goldfinger's Spartan concrete aesthetic was based on post-and-lintel construction to a 5.029m (16ft 6in) grid that followed the proportions of the Golden Section and was infilled with brick and grey Vitrolite. Set-back clerestory glazing to throw light into the interior is contrasted with projecting bays; only the last block had double glazing. Radiators were incorporated into the staircase balustrading. Yet Goldfinger lined the lift lobbies in marble and designed abstract glass panels with Kenneth Rowntree.

As offices (long the Ministry of Health), Alexander Fleming House was unpopular because it had the transparency of a goldfish bowl, rectified when in 2002 it was converted to flats. The concrete was painted and the Vitrolite clad with blue panels, but the structure itself survives.

Michael Faraday Memorial

Elephant and Castle

1960–1, Rodney Gordon, London County Council

Listed grade II, 21 June 1996

The Elephant and Castle area was redeveloped by the London County Council from the late 1950s. When a new electricity substation and transformer was required to convert AC to DC current for the Underground, its design was entrusted to Rodney Gordon, who subsequently joined Owen Luder and Partners.

Michael Faraday (1791–1867) was born nearby. He founded the science of electromagnetism, discovered electromotive power, and the first formula for stainless steel. The transformer station was therefore dedicated to him, and stainless steel was chosen after a glass inverted pyramid (revealing the glowing rectifiers) was rejected as likely to distract passing drivers.

Gordon realized that plain steel sheets would distort, so used dished panels whose refraction of light contrast with a Miesian black steel frame. It is one of their first uses in England, after Harrison and Abramowitz had used press-moulded panels on the Socony Mobil Building, New York, in 1956. Gordon claimed that his design was inspired by his Danish coffee table.

National Sports Centre

Crystal Palace

1960–4, Norman Engleback,
Bryn Jones and John Attenborough,
London County Council

Listed grade II*, 2 December 1997

In 1952, the London County Council took over the derelict Crystal Palace Park and appointed Sir Gerald Barry, fresh from the Festival of Britain, as consultant. He suggested a sports centre, and the hall designed in 1953–4 had similarities with a sketch by the Duke of Edinburgh, an early supporter. It was the first multipurpose hall designed in Britain, although not the first to be built, at a time when such facilities barely existed in Europe. Emphasis was given to swimming because there were few Olympic-sized pools in southern England.

The centre impresses by its planning and the homogeneity between the structural system and exterior design. Engleback's team placed the swimming and dry sports halls back to back, and a central A-frame between them supports the spectators' seating and cantilevered roof. The fan of bracing struts gives views over both halves of the building. Spurs continue as ribs across the roof and extend down the walls as glazing mullions, giving the building a drama only matched by that of the high diving board.

The Hall, Brunswick Park Primary School

Picton Street, Camberwell

1961–2, Stirling and Gowan

Listed grade II, 4 May 2011

The hall is a small but significant work, designed at the height of Stirling and Gowan's boisterous, short-lived partnership. It comprises three wedge-shaped sections and a boiler room, designed to be viewed in the round and with banks of windows on the taller elevations.

The headmistress wanted a gymnasium, but this was not included in the London County Council's brief, and the assembly and dining hall – for which Gowan made the preliminary design in 1958 as Stirling was teaching at Yale – remained low, with the central dip between the four sections indicating that the space could be subdivided. The embankment in which the building sits owed something to the vernacular architecture that both architects admired.

Gowan justified the square plan by the uncomfortably empty surroundings; a road between the hall and the 1920s school was to be closed when nearby prefabs were demolished, but never was. It also somewhat resembles the practice's four-square entry to the Churchill College competition, also surrounded by embankments.

3–35 South Row

Blackheath

1962–3, Eric Lyons for
Span Developments Ltd

Listed grade II, 21 June 1996

South Row is the most confidently modern of Lyons's work for Span. The rear terrace of houses is weatherboarded and as unassuming as Lyons's earlier works, but the block of flats at the front is massively executed in dark brown brick, designed by assistant Geoffrey Darke, with a partially exposed concrete frame that forms strong cornices and bands.

The difference also owes something to the prominent site, where local architects and London County Council had sought a pastiche of the bombed Georgian terrace Little Paragon. Lyons claimed an affinity between Span and the speculative builders of Georgian terraces that he used to justify his high densities and communal open spaces. South Row is, however, his least terrace-like design. That it is a square is revealed to outsiders through a broad, two-bay entrance cut through the ground floor of the flats and simply glazed.

Lilian Baylis School

Lollard Street, Lambeth

1962–4, Architects' Co-Partnership

Listed grade II, 20 December 2000

The Lilian Baylis School was the first of a clutch of comprehensive schools built by the London County Council in the 1960s to replace small nineteenth-century institutions.

In additions to an Islington school, Risinghill, the Architects' Co-Partnership had rejected the form of a single long slab popularized by London comprehensives such as Elliott School (see p.555) in favour of a series of low blocks around courtyards (demolished). The partner in charge, Kenneth Capon, felt that such a plan best suited a neighbourhood noted for its late Georgian squares. At Lilian Baylis, the pattern was repeated but the mainly two-storey blocks are more closely interconnected and the detailing more sophisticated. Most striking of all is the first-floor assembly hall, a square space surrounded by staging, panelled and with a diagrid roof. Listing was prompted by proposals to demolish the school and in 2013–14 it was converted to housing.

Meridian West

Diamond Terrace, Greenwich

1963–5, Julian Sofaer
1970s–1980s, E. Morton Wright

Listed grade II, 19 December 2007

Julian Sofaer is best known for schools and buildings for the Jewish community in London. Here, in what was his only private house, he aimed to achieve a harmony of proportion equivalent to music. He demonstrated a fresh, modern approach to traditional materials, with buff brick and timber including Western red cedar cladding, pine beams and a redwood ceiling. He also made a clear delineation between the formal public frontage and more informal, intimate family areas of this executive home.

The intriguing plan makes the most of its hillside setting, with the principal rooms on the first floor, reached via a stair to a bridge-like entrance lobby.

An extension to the south and entrance gates and garden walls were added by the architect-owner E. Morton Wright in a sympathetic style.

Pools on the Park

Old Deer Park, Richmond

1964–6, Leslie Gooday

Listed grade II, 16 January 1996

Leslie Gooday, who lived nearby for many years, specialized in exhibition design and private houses, and the baths at Richmond are exceptionally elegant. The complex is unusual in that in addition to two indoor pools for adults and learners, there is also an outdoor pool.

The breaking up of the entrance, changing and pool areas into distinctive masses scales down the impact of the building on the Old Deer Park. The roof is of copper with a deep eaves fascia over the pool, and is raised over the former diving area. It was designed to reduce the building's impact when oxidized green; renewed, it is again brown. Internally, the large and small pools occupy a single space, interrupted only by a cantilevered mezzanine gallery that cuts across the hall at a high level and continues externally as a sunbathing terrace with steps to the open-air pool. Additional sporting facilities have been contained in the existing envelope.

Phoenix School, formerly Eveline Lowe School

Marlborough Grove, Peckham

1966, David and Mary Medd with John Kay, Department of Education and Science

Listed grade II, 3 July 2006

Rural schools had been the Cinderellas of education until the Medds' brick school at Finmere designed two classrooms that could be used as a hall. Its success spotlighted the value of mixed age-range teaching and informed a new generation of inner-city schools, led by Eveline Lowe.

The plan provided for pupils aged between three and nine, grouped into three wings and with special provision for summer-born children. Those living in nearby tower blocks relished the rambling, single-storey arrangement. Covered verandahs provided outdoor activity areas, and interconnected spaces without corridors provided facilities for messy work, private study and group teaching; there were also quiet rooms, or kivas, a Pueblo Indian term. Such sub-divisions were subtly different to the open plans appearing elsewhere, which the Medds condemned.

Additions were made by John Pardey Architects to the front of the site in 2007–10, when the original building was refurbished.

1A Greenholm Road

Eltham

1966, 1973, Edward Cullinan
with Ian Pickering

Listed grade II, 12 October 2007

This house was designed for an MP, John Garrett, for whom Cullinan also made additions. The narrow infill plot enabled him to refine the long plan he had adopted at 62 Camden Mews (see p.460) on only a slightly larger scale, and explore the lighting of domestic spaces. A heavy construction of reused bricks on the ground floor provides privacy and enclosure for the ground floor's compact bedrooms, bathroom and garage. By contrast, the first floor is largely of timber, with glazed ends and a long clerestory that light an open-plan area with zones for living, dining and cooking arranged around a spiral staircase, which is encased in a sculptural brick stairwell. The greatest drama is in the roof's asymmetrical pitch, an external eye-catcher whose exposed roof trusses also dominate the interior. Cullinan also designed much of the surviving built-in furniture.

The linked garden room of 1973 is concealed beneath a grass ramp, like that at Maltings Chase (see p.255), replacing a timber ramp leading to the garden.

St Laurence's Church and Community Centre

Bromley Road, Catford

1967–8, Covell, Matthews and Partners

Listed grade II, 6 April 2012

When St Laurence's opened in 1968 it was known as the 'space-age' or 'Mod' church, its open metal spire likened to a satellite. Replacing a Victorian church demolished for the town hall's extension, for which £200,000 compensation was paid, the octagonal main space and hexagonal Lady chapel were among R. G. Covell's last and most liturgically advanced designs. The spire of the Lady chapel acts as a foil to the low, broad church, with its polygonal roof and corona in aluminium, stainless steel and gold.

The interior is rich in texture and most of its original fittings survive. It has a coffered fibreglass ceiling and abstract stained glass in dense blocks of colour by T. Carter Shapland, who also produced the glass altar cross. Curved pews, specially made, radiate in three banks.

The community hall was an integral part of the brief, and in 1969 the *Church Times* described it as 'a parish centre of a type unheard of this side of the Atlantic'.

2A Drax Avenue

Wimbledon

1967–9, Philip Dowson
of Arup Associates

Listed grade II, 7 February 2013

Philip Dowson was the one architect founder, in 1963, of Arup Associates. It was a parallel partnership to Sir Ove Arup and Partners, where his friend and client Jack Zunz was an engineer, a multidisciplinary practice where architects, engineers and surveyors worked together. It specialized in industrial, office and university buildings, but the partners designed houses for friends and colleagues.

What impresses is the consistency of Dowson's vision, the concrete block construction extending to garden walls that integrate indoor and outdoor volumes. Zunz had worked with Jørn Utzon in Sydney and wanted brick, but Dowson pressed hard and won. Spaces unfold from a narrow entrance alongside the semi-sunken garage, in a three-storey block that is subsidiary to a surprisingly large double-height living room placed at right angles. Clean lines are enhanced by frameless glazing. Built-in fittings and floorings of pine and beech soften the blockwork, well seen in the living room, which is entered up woodblock stairs and has a sunken central space.

10 Blackheath Park

Blackheath

1968–9, Patrick Gwynne

Listed grade II, 4 December 2000

The builder Leslie Bilsby commissioned three houses from Patrick Gwynne, all in Blackheath where he worked extensively for Span Developments, of which he was a director.

The slate walls and aluminium glazing were intended as a recessive contrast to the white Regency villas on either side. The splayed plan unifies the composition and provides angled views down the street, while stairs and ramps to front and back add to the space-age image.

The internal walls are lined in Gwynne's favourite black plastic covering, save for the central core, which is rendered. The layout, a central staircase around which the principal rooms form a chain, was regularly adopted by Gwynne in the 1960s. But here it had a particular logic, for Bilsby wanted rooms that could be thrown together for the drinks parties for which he was renowned. Gwynne provided a pentagonal room in each corner of the house, connected through pairs of red-lacquered sliding doors via intermediate spaces.

22 Parkside

Wimbledon

1968–70, Richard and Su Rogers
with John Young

Listed grade II*, 22 February 2013

Having built Creekvean for Su's parents in concrete block, the steel house for Rogers's parents was a progression from the Californian Case Study Houses and that at The Studio, Ulting (see pp.302 and 257). Anthony Hunt engineered an internal frame that reduced cold bridging and maintenance costs, and provided a clear space. The ends have uninterrupted glazing with sliding openings; the sides are sheathed in a skin of plastic-coated aluminium panels, exposed inside, with circular openings like the cat flap sealed by neoprene. Bracing was eliminated. Strong colours included the yellow frame, timber and blinds, and lime green sliding bedroom partitions. The kitchen is a free-standing steel unit with yellow cupboards.

A studio, originally intended for Rogers's mother's pottery, forms a buffer between the house and the street, and is itself protected by a landscaped mound. It was later adapted as a flat and as a design studio. The house was intended as a prototype, but remained a one-off.

Royal National Theatre

Upper Ground, Lambeth

1969–76, Sir Denys Lasdun and Partners

Listed grade II*, 23 June 1994

In 1942 the London County Council offered a site for a national theatre on the South Bank, and in 1963 Lasdun was commissioned to produce a theatre and opera house. When the latter was aborted in 1967, he was offered the present site.

The building takes its form from the two larger auditoria set at 45° to each other, denoted by a structural grid aligned on the Olivier that fixes the fly towers and main stairs and is seen in the foyers' coffering. Half-hexagon landings on the stairs provide unexpected views through the building. The Olivier Theatre with its corner apron stage and side slips is particularly inventive, and although the Lyttelton Theatre is a conventional end stage, the expression of the grid on an angle gives it the more interesting foyers. A third studio space, the galleried Cottesloe, now Dorfman Theatre, was designed by Iain Mackintosh.

The building was listed when an external walkway was threatened with demolition. In 2013–15, Haworth Tompkins revised subsequent interventions and extended backstage areas.

Queen's Road Estate

Richmond-upon-Thames

1978–83, Darbourne and Darke

Listed grade II, 6 July 2012

Queen's Road was developed from 1971 by London and Quadrant Housing for the Richmond Parish Lands Charity, to house lower- and middle-income families to a high standard and thereby encourage them to stay in an area that increasingly lacked affordable housing.

Applying the principles used in their award-winning housing at Lillington Gardens (see p.535), Darbourne and Darke's first and most imaginatively designed phase occupied a wooded site between existing Victorian streets and Richmond Park. The 91 units fit on to a plot of 1.18ha (3 acres) in an informal arrangement of blocky, close-knit terraces and closes, linked by covered passages. Two-, three- and four-storey flats, maisonettes and houses, some with a garage, are built of red-brown brick, with slate roofs. In 2011, anodized aluminium door and window units replaced the original brown-painted timber fittings. Road and pavement surfaces are integral to the design; street names are inscribed in flush ceramic panels. Only the first phase is listed.

MILITARY MONUMENTS OF THE COLD WAR
Listings and Schedulings

Those with a separate entry in the book shown in *italic*

TR1 hardened aircraft shelters, The 'Magic Mountain', Alconbury, Cambridgeshire
1983, 1989; listed II*, 10 September 2007

Atomic bombs store, RAF Barnham, Suffolk
1954-9; scheduled 29 May 2003,
listed II* and II, 24 June 2011

Gloucester Lodge heavy aircraft battery
New Blyth, Northumberland
1941, 1946-53; scheduled 30 January 2014

Royal Observer Corps
underground monitoring post
Zion Hill Farm, Brandsby, Crayke, York
1964; listed II, 10 April 2012

Bristol War Room
Flowers Hill, Brislington, Bristol
1953; listed II, 25 March 2013

War Room and Regional Seat of Government, Gilpin Road, Cambridge
1952-3, 1963; listed II, 18 July 2003

Blast Walls and related remains
former RAF Coltishall, Norfolk
c.1956; scheduled 7 March 2008

Central Government Headquarters Corsham, Wiltshire
1957-70; key parts scheduled 20 March 2013

RAF Daws Hill, High Wycombe
US headquarters bunker
1942, 1983; listed II*, 11 October 2013
Standby generator building
1980s; listed II, 11 October 2013

Regional Seat of Government
Dover Castle, Kent
1960s; scheduled guardianship
14 December 1999

Gates, Topsham Barracks
Topsham Rd, Exeter
1959; listed II, 18 June 1974

Transonic Tunnel, R133
Royal Aircraft Establishment, Farnborough
1939-42, 1951-6; listed I, 4 December 1996

Man Carrying Centrifuge Facility Building F49A, Farnborough
c.1952-5; listed II, 16 August 2007

Buildings for the UK's prototype atomic bomb, Fort Halstead, Kent
Buildings F16 and F17
1947; listed II*, 21 March 2012
Building Q14
c.1948-52; listed II, 25 February 2011

Atomic Weapons Research Establishment
Foulness, Essex
1947-53; scheduled 9 May 2013

Anti-Aircraft Operations Room Frodsham, Cheshire
c.1951; listed II, 18 March 2013

Submarine Escape Training Tank
HMS Dolphin, Fort Blockhouse,
Haslar Road, Gosport, Hampshire
1950-54; listed II, 26 June 2013

No. 2 Cavitation Tunnel (buildings 46 & 47), Haslar Rd, Gosport, Hants
1951-55; listed II, 22 July 2013

Civil Defence Sub-Division Control Centre
Gravesend, Kent
1954; listed II, 18 September 2013

Greenham Common, Berkshire
Former Control Tower
1951-3; listed II, 13 January 2012
Cruise Missile Complex
1980-3; scheduled 3 March 2003
Combat Support Building
1984-5; listed II, 2 September 2014
Former Wing Headquarters
c.1985; listed II*, 1 September 2014

Heavy Anti-Aircraft Gun Site
Halls Green Farm, Roydon, Essex
1948-50; scheduled 25 June 2001

Thor Missile Site, former RAF Harrington, Northamptonshire
1958-9; listed II, 17 June 2011

Royal Observer Corps post
Beacon Hill, Hinderwell, North Yorkshire
c.1960; scheduled 15 April 1980

War Room Bunker
Partingdale Lane, Mill Hill, Greater London
early 1950s; listed II, 2 December 2002

Anti-Aircraft Operations Room Shrubland Road, Mistley, Essex
1951; listed II, 22 May 2007

Cold War Radar Facilities
Neatishead, Norfolk
R30 Operations Room
1942-70s; listed II*, 22 February 2008
R3 Operations Block & R12 Equipment
Building
1952, 1967; listed II, 22 February 2008
Type 84 Radar Modulator Building
c.1963; scheduled 27 February 2008

Heavy Anti-Aircraft Battery
Norley, Cheshire
c.1950; scheduled 6 October 2003

Thor Missile Site
former RAF North Luffenham, Rutland
1958-9; listed II*, 17 June 2011

Control Tower, North Weald Airfield, Essex
1952; listed II, 19 April 2013

Regional Seat of Government
Chalfont Drive, Nottingham
1952-3, 1963; listed II, 18 July 2003

Royal Observer Corps Post
Beacon Hill, Pickering, North Yorkshire
c.1960; scheduled 7 July 2000

Former ROC Group Headquarters
Poltimore Park, Poltimore, Essex
1960-1; listed II, 8 April 2013

Site of Rotor radar site, Portland, Dorset
1950-1, scheduled 2 November 2004

War Room (The Citadel)
University of Reading, Berkshire
1953; listed II, 10 March 2009

Heavy Anti-Aircraft Gun Site
Sandpit Hill, Essex
1945-52; scheduled 9 March 2001

Royal Observer Corps
underground monitoring post
Castlehaw Tower, Sedburgh, Cumbria
1965; scheduled, date not recorded

Royal Observer Corps
underground monitoring post
South Creake, Norfolk
1950s; listed II, 13 August 2007

RAF Spadeadam Rocket Establishment
Gilsland, Brampton, Cumbria
1957-60; scheduled 10 October 2013
Blue Streak Rocket
1959; listed II, 10 October 2013

Royal Observer Corps
underground monitoring post
Keelby Road, Stallingborough,
North East Lincolnshire
1961; listed II, 23 May 2012

Swingate Chain Home Radar Station
Deal Road, Dover
Transmitter and receiver site
1936-62; listed II, 13 July 2012
Royal Observer Corps monitoring post
1962; listed II, 13 August 2012

Standby Generator
Threehammer Common,
Neatishead, Norfolk
1950-2; listed II, 22 February 2008

Anti-aircraft Site, Searson's Farm,
Trimley St Mary, Felixstowe
1946; scheduled 7 October 2014

RAF Upper Heyford, Oxfordshire
1950-2, 1970s; scheduled 30 November 2006
Nose dock hangars, control tower and
squadron headquarters
1950-2, 1970s; listed II, 7 April 2008

Royal Observer Corps
underground monitoring post
Southfield House, Skipsea, East Yorkshire
c.1959; scheduled 15 April 2004

Royal Ordnance Establishment now
Westcott Venture Park, Westcott,
Buckinghamshire
A–B and C–D propellant test stands
1947-9; listed II*, 23 May 2013
K2 test stand for solid propellant rocket
motors
1958-60; listed II*, 23 May 2013
P test stand for liquid propellants
1948-50, 55 and later; listed II, 23 May 2013
E test stand for liquid propellant engines
late 1950s; listed II, 23 May 2013
K1 test sand and related buildings, with
control tower
1967-8, 1959; listed II, 23 May 2013

Very Heavy Bomber Air Traffic Control
Tower, West Raynham, Norfolk
1945 and later; listed II, 13 June 2012

ROC monitoring posts
close to Westbury Beacon, Somerset
1953/1961; listed II, 21 August 2013

RAF Wittering, Peterborough
Nuclear fissile core stores, Buildings A09,
A10, A11, A14, A15, A27, Vw28, A29, and
A33
1952; listed II*, 11 July 2011
Gaydon Hangar
1952, listed II, 11 July 2011
Store and testing buildings
1952; listed II, 11 July 2011

Royal Observer Corps Group
Headquarters, York
1960–1; scheduled guardianship 21 June 2000

SCULPTURE AND MEMORIALS

**War memorial, St James the Great
Shakespeare Lane, Harvington,
Worcestershire**
1945; listed II, 23 May 2011

Memorial Figure
Dartington Hall, Totnes, Devon
Henry Moore, 1946; listed II*, 23 May 1993

**Concrete Figure of a Man
Lippitts Hill, Waltham Abbey, Essex**
Rudi Weber, 1946; listed II, 27 February 2003

**Home Guard War Memorial
Merryton Low, Fawfieldhead, Staffordshire**
1946; listed II, 19 March 2008

**Roosevelt Memorial
Grosvenor Square, Westminster**
William Reid Dick, 1946–48;
listed II, 14 January 1998

**Lychgate (war memorial)
St Mary's Church, Nunthorpe,
Middlesbrough**
Leslie Moore, 1947; listed II, 28 July 1988

**D Day Port Memorial
Weymouth, Dorset**
1947; listed II, 30 January 2009

**Southwood Memorial, St James's
Churchyard, Piccadilly, Westminster**
A. E. Richardson & Alfred F. Hardiman, 1947-8;
listed II, 15 April 1998

Three Standing Figures
Battersea Park, Wandsworth
Henry Moore, 1948; listed II, 30 March 1998
(shown right)

Polish Air Force Memorial
West End Road, Ruislip, Hillingdon
Mieczyslaw Lubelski, 1948;
listed II, 30 August 2002

Beattie and Jellicoe Memorial Fountains
Trafalgar Square, Westminster
E. L. Lutyens, Charles Wheeler & William
Macmillan, 1948; listed II*, 5 February 1970

War Memorial, Brantham Industrial Estate
Brantham, Suffolk
1948; listed II, 21 February 2011

Bus Shelter war memorial
The Green, Dunchurch, Warwickshire
Mr Castle, 1949; listed II, 7 November 2007

Lady Godiva, **Broadgate, Coventry**
William Reid Dick, 1949; listed II*, 15 April 1998

War memorial
Compton Bassett, North Wiltshire
1950; listed II, 12 November 2002

Civilian War Memorial to Parnall Aircraft
Co., St Mary's churchyard, Church Road,
Yate, South Gloucestershire
1950; listed II, 20 June 2013

War Memorial to Gramophone Co.
Cherry Lane Cemetery, Hayes, Middlesex
c.1950; listed II, 23 February 2010

Memorial Gates at Nevill Holt Hall School
Nevill Holt, Leicestershire
1950; listed II, 15 June 2002

Triton and Dryads Fountain
Regent's Park, Westminster
William Macmillan, 1950; listed II, 9 July 1998

World War II memorial at Manor Park
Cemetery, East Ham
Ralph Hobday, 1950; listed II, 17 August 2001

Lord Nelson Monument
Grand Parade, Southsea, Hampshire
F. Brook Hitch & H. J. Aldous, 1951;
listed II, 18 March 1999

Woman with a Fish
Delapre Gardens, Northampton
Frank Dobson, 1951; listed II, 15 April 1998

World War II war memorial, St John the
Baptist churchyard, Station Road, Harrow
1951; listed II, 27 September 2011

Youth
6 Bacon's Lane, Highgate, Camden
Daphne Hardy Henrion, 1951, 1959;
listed II, 10 August 2010
(shown above)

Citizens' war memorial
Chanterlands Avenue, Hull
1951; listed II, 21 January 1994

Lord Nelson Monument
Pembroke Gardens, Portsmouth
H. J. Aldous and F. Brook Hitch, 1951;
listed II, 18 March 1999

Contrapunctal Forms
Glebelands, Harlow, Essex
Barbara Hepworth, 1951-2; listed II, 15 April 1998
(shown right)

Turning Forms, **Marlborough School**
Watling Street, St Albans, Herts
Barbara Hepworth, 1951-2; listed II, 15 April 1998

Merchant Seamen's Memorial
Trinity Square, Tower Hamlets
Edward Maufe, 1952; listed II*, 15 April 1998

Merchant Navy Memorial
Georges Pier Head, Liverpool
S. H. Smith, C. F. Blythin & H. Tyson Smith, 1952;
listed II, 5 March 2010

Memorial to Civilian War Dead
Efford Cemetery, Plymouth
1952-53; listed II, 1 July 2013

Naval War Memorial
Bellevue Park, Lowestoft
F. H. Crossley & H. Tyson Smith, 1952-53;
listed II, 3 October 2000

Venus Fountain, Sloane Square
Kensington & Chelsea, London
Gilbert Ledward, 1953; listed II, 22 August 2006

Ghosts or *Descent from the Cross*
Campion House, Osterley, Hounslow
Andrew O'Connor, 1937, 1953;
listed II, 6 August 2003

War Memorial, Crayford Manor
Bexley, London
1954; listed II, 13 November 2012

Monolith Empyrean
Kenwood, Hampstead Lane, Hampstead
Barbara Hepworth, 1954; listed II, 15 April 1998

George VI, Carlton Gardens, Westminster
William McMillan, 1954; listed II, 9 January 1970

British Medical Association Memorial
Tavistock Square, Camden
James Woodford, 1954; listed II*, 15 April 1998

Sheep Shearer, **Momples Road**
Harlow, Essex
Ralph Brown, 1955; listed II, 15 April 1998

Statue of Field Marshall Jan Smuts
Parliament Square, Westminster
Jacob Epstein, 1956; listed II, 5 February 1970

Meat Porters, **Market Square**
Harlow, Essex
Ralph Brown, 1956-60; listed II, 15 April 1998

Falling Warrior, **Clare College, Cambridge**
Henry Moore, 1956-7; listed II, 15 April 1998

Bromhead Memorial
Richmond Cemetery, London
Cecil Thomas, 1957;
listed II, 11 September 2012

The Neighbours
Highbury Quadrant Estate, Islington
Siegfried Charoux, 1957-9;
listed II, 15 April 1998

Brookwood Memorial
Brookwood Cemetery, Woking, Surrey
Ralph Hobday, 1958; listed II, 23 July 2004

Blind Beggar and his Dog
Roman Road, Tower Hamlets
Elisabeth Frink, 1958; listed II*, 15 April 1998

Joyride
Town Square, Stevenage, Hertfordshire
Franta Belsky, 1958-9; listed II, 15 April 1998
(shown right)

Statue of Sir Walter Raleigh
Whitehall, Westminster
William Macmillan, 1959;
listed II, 5 February 1970

Sungazer, **Kingsdale School**
Alleyn Park, Southwark
William Turnbull, 1959; listed II, 15 April 1998

Striding Man, **William Penn School**
Red Post Hill, Southwark
Oliffe Richmond, 1959; listed II, 15 April 1998

Relief Mural, Bodington Hall
Otley Road, Leeds
Hubert Dalwood, 1959-62;
listed II, 30 October 2012

Statue of Captain John Smith
Bow Churchyard, Tower Hamlets
1960; listed II, 5 June 1972

Nine ceramic panels at the Fleet Building
70 Farringdon Street, City of London
Dorothy Annan, 1960;
listed II, 21 November 2011
Moved to Barbican Centre in 2013

The Watchers, **Alton Estate, Wandsworth**
Lynn Chadwick, 1960-3; listed II, 15 April 1998
Damaged. Remains in store in 2015

The Bull, Danebury Avenue, Wandsworth
Robert Clatworthy, 1961;
listed II*, 15 April 1998

Epidouros, **Malakoff, St Ives, Cornwall**
Barbara Hepworth, 1961; listed II, 15 April 1998

Fountain, Lambeth College
Brixton Hill, Lambeth
Kenneth Martin, 1961; listed II, 15 April 1998

Statue of Lord Trenchard
Victoria Embankment, Westminster
William Macmillan, 1961;
listed II, 5 February 1970

Two-Piece Reclining Figure No 3
Cooks Road, Southwark
Henry Moore, 1961-2; listed II, 15 April 1998

Pool and Sculpture
Town Square, Basildon, Essex
Maurice Lambert, 1962;
listed II, 22 December 1998

**Mural at Cromwell Secondary School
Blandford Road, Salford**
Alan Boyson, 1962; listed II, 19 August 2009
(shown below)

**Statue of Thomas Coram
Brunswick Square, Camden**
William Macmillan, 1963; listed II, 14 May 1974

Delight, **Finchale Road, Greenwich**
A. H. Gerrard, 1963-7; listed II, 15 April 1998

Hampstead Figure, **Avenue Road, Camden**
F. E. McWilliam, 1964; listed II, 6 August 1999

Corn King and Spring Queen
Wexham Springs, Bucks
William Mitchell, 1964; listed II, 15 April 1998

Kennedy Memorial, Runnymede, Surrey
Geoffrey Jellicoe, 1964-5;
listed II, 15 April 1998

**3 Totem Sculptures in Front Courtyard
Allerton Building, University of Salford,
Salford**
William Mitchell, 1966;
listed II, 26 January 2012
(shown right)

**Statue of Mahatma Gandhi
Tavistock Square, Camden**
Fredda Brilliant, 1968; listed II, 15 April 1974

Sculptural Wall, London Road, Manchester
Antony Hollaway, Harry M Fairhurst, 1968;
listed II, 10 June 2011

**Statue of Winston Churchill
The Green, Westerham, Kent**
Gift of the Yugoslav People, 1969;
listed II, 16 January 1975

Timepiece, **St Katharine's Dock,
Tower Hamlets**
Wendy Taylor, 1973; listed II, 26 April 2004

**Statue of Sir Winston Churchill
Parliament Square, Westminster**
Ivor Roberts-Jones, 1973;
listed II, 24 January 2008

INDEX

P

Pace, George Gaze 63, 69, 75, 88–90, 96, 102, 105, 145
Paddington Maintenance Depot, Westminster 536
Paget, Paul 203, 212, 529
Paine, Robert and Partners 374
Pall Mall (No 100), Westminster 508
Pall Mall Court, Manchester 71
Pank, Philip 480
Pardey, John 218, 334, 584
Park Hill, Sheffield 84–5
Park Lane (No 1), Sheffield 91
Park Road (No 125), Regent's Park 537
Parkes, David 244
Parkham Wood House, Brixham 291
Parkin, Peter 546
Parkleys, Ham 556, 571
Parkside (No 22), Wimbledon 589
Parliament Square, City of Westminster 496
Pasmore, Victor 29, 55
Passfields, Bellingham 545
Past Field, Henley-on-Thames 332
Paterson, Gavin and Son 20
Pattrick, Michael 384
The Pavilion, Kingston-upon-Thames 575
Peacock, Hodges and Robertson 202
Pearson, Charles B., Son and Partners 169
Pearson, H. W. (Bill) 112
The Pediment, Aynho 161
E. Pellicci café, Bethnal Green 418
Pennine Tower Restaurant, Forton 67
Pennyfathers Lane (No 5), Welwyn 198
Percey, Edmund C. 246, 247
Persant Road (Nos 1–7, 25 and 39), Bellingham 544
Phillimore, Claud 383
Phippen, Randall and Parkes 244
Phoenix 116
The Phoenix School, Bow 432
Phoenix School (formerly Eveline Lowe School), Peckham 584
Pickering, Ian 585
Piet, Zbigniew Jan 403
Pilkington Brothers' head offices, St Helens 55
Plesner, Ulrich 231
Point Royal, Easthampstead 336
Polish Air Force Memorial, Ruislip 595
Pollen, Francis 401
Pool and Sculpture, Basildon 597

Pools on the Park, Old Deer Park, Richmond 583
Poremba, Antoni 309
Potter, Robert 299
Potter and Hare 280, 287, 296, 297
Powell, Geoffry 448, 504
Powell, Philip 346, 494
Powell, Richard 259
Powell and Moya 249, 330, 346, 347, 352, 356, 377, 390, 494
Powers, Michael 243, 328, 339
Price, Cedric 527
Prichard, Lionel A. G. and Son 70
Provost's Lodgings, Oxford 327
Purcell Architects 347

Q

Queen Elizabeth II Court, Winchester 325
Queen's Park, Swindon 270
Queen's Road Estate, Richmond-upon-Thames 591
Queensgate Market, Huddersfield 109

R

Rackham, H. 290
Radar Training Station, Fleetwood 58
RAF Alconbury, Huntingdonshire 261
RAF Barnham, Thetford 201, 592
RAF Coltishall, Norfolk 592
RAF Daws Hill, High Wycombe 592
RAF Greenham Common, Berkshire 367
RAF Harrington, Daventry 165, 592
RAF Neatishead, Norfolk 238
RAF North Luffenham, Rutland 165, 593
RAF Spadeadam Rocket Establishment, Gilsland 593
RAF Upper Heyford, Heyford Park 321, 593
RAF Wittering, Peterborough 193, 593
Raleigh, Sir Walter (statue), Whitehall 597
Randall, Peter 244
RC Cathedral Church of SS Peter and Paul, Clifton 309
RC Chapel of the Most Holy Name, Shorncliffe 403
RC Church of Christ the King, Plymouth 293
RC Church of the Divine Motherhood & St Francis of Assisi, Midhurst 381

RC Church of the Good Shepherd, Woodthorpe 174
RC Church of the Holy Family, Pontefract 100
RC Church of Our Lady, Royal Leamington Spa 139
RC Church of St William of York, Stanmore 449
RC Church of SS Mary and Joseph, Poplar 428
RC Most Holy Trinity Church, Bermondsey 567
Reedley 46
Regent's Park Road (No 10), Primrose Hill 438
Regional Seat of Government, Cambridge 196
Regional Seat of Government, Dover Castle 592
Regional Seat of Government, Nottingham 158, 593
Reid, Donald A. 515
Reilly, Sir Charles 72
Relief Mural, Bodington Hall, Leeds 597
Renault Distribution Centre (Spectrum Building), Swindon 315
Renton Howard Wood Associates 111
Retail Market, Coventry 131
Reyniers, Peter 223
Reynolds and Scott 68
Rhinefield Bridge, Brockenhurst 319
Richardson, Sir Albert 208, 239, 506, 523
Richardson, Sir Albert, Houfe and Partners 458
Richardson Candles, Cambridge 208
Rigg Side (Anderton House), Goodleigh 310
River Cherwell footbridge, Oxford 318
Rivoli Ballroom, Crofton Park 568
Roberts, David 213, 243, 343
Roberts, Sir Gilbert 295
Roberts, Gwyn 109
Roberts, James A. 136
Robson, Geoffrey 329
Roche, Kevin 23
Rogers, Richard 256, 301, 540–1, 589
Rogers, Su 256, 301, 589
Roosevelt Memorial, Westminster 594
Rosehill Theatre, Moresby 20
Rosenauer, Michael 499
Rosenberg, Eugene 190
Rothwell, S. L. 550
Rotor radar site, Portland 593
The Rotunda, Birmingham 136
Rowe, Geoffrey 82

Royal Air Force 165
Royal Bank of Scotland, Plymouth 277
Royal Botanic Gardens, Kew 550
Royal College of Art, Kensington Gore 519
Royal College of Physicians, Regent's Park 452
Royal Festival Hall, Lambeth 498, 521, 546–7, 562
The Royal Military (Guards') Chapel, Wellington Barracks 507
Royal National Theatre, Lambeth 590
Royal National Theatre Studio, Waterloo 565
Royal Observer Corps Group Headquarters, Poltimore 593
Royal Observer Corps Group Headquarters (Cold War Bunker), York 93, 593
Royal Observer Corps monitoring post, Brandsby 592
Royal Observer Corps monitoring post, Hinderwell 592
Royal Observer Corps monitoring post, Pickering 593
Royal Observer Corps monitoring post, Sedburgh 593
Royal Observer Corps monitoring post, Skipsea 593
Royal Observer Corps monitoring post, South Creake 593
Royal Observer Corps monitoring post, Stallingborough 593
Royal Observer Corps monitoring post, Westbury Beacon 593
Royal Ordnance Establishment, Westcott 593
Runcorn-Widnes Bridge, Queensway 44
Rushbrooke, Bury St Edmunds 206
Rushmere Hall School, Ipswich 185
Rutherford School (King Solomon Academy), Marylebone 513
The Ryde, Hatfield 244
Ryder and Yates 26, 27

S

Saarinen, Eero 512
Sainsbury Centre for Visual Arts, University of East Anglia 264–5
St Aldate's Church, Gloucester 296
St Ambrose RC Church, Liverpool 53
St Anne's College, Oxford 338
St Anne's RC Church, Fawley 362

St Augustine's RC Church, Manchester 73

St Austell Library 289

St Catherine's College, Oxford 333

St Columba's Church, Kensington 429

St Crispin's School, Wokingham 322

St Cross Libraries, Oxford 337

St Dunstan's RC Church, Birmingham 152

St George Street (No 23), Canterbury 374

St George's Chapel, RAF Biggin Hill 548

St George's Church, Oakdale 287

St James's Church, Clapham Park 561

St James's Place (No 26), Westminster 514

St John's Church, Hatfield 217

St John's vicarage and caretaker's house, Kennington 551

St Joseph's RC Church, Newby 88

St Joseph's RC Church, Upton 39

St Joseph's RC Church, Wool 308

St Jude RC Church, Worsley Mesnes 70

St Laurence's Church and Community Centre, Catford 586

St Leonard's Church, Undercliff 376

St Luke's Church, Leagrave 203

St Margaret Clitherow RC Church, Threshfield 113

St Margaret of Scotland Catholic Church, Twickenham 481

St Mark's Church, Biggin Hilll 566

St Mark's Church, Broomhill 90

St Mark's Church, Chadderton 63

St Mary's Church, West Twyford 445

St Mary's Church, Willingdon 373

St Mary's Priory Church, Leyland 66

St Matthew's Church, Birmingham 142

St Michael and All Angels Church, London Fields 450

St Paul's Cathedral School, New Change 529

St Paul's Church, Bow Common 142, 446

St Paul's Church, Harlow 209

St Paul's Church, Kennington 573

St Paul's Church, Sheffield 86

St Peter's Church, Greenhill 101

St Raphael the Archangel RC Church, Millbrook 59

St Richard's RC Church, Chichester 380

St Saviour's Church, Fairweather Green 102

St Theresa's RC Church, Upholland 42

St Thomas More RC Church, Sheldon 150–1

St Vedast's Rectory, City of London 509

Salisbury Crematorium, Salisbury 290

Salters' Hall, City of London 538

Samuel, Edward 468

Samuely, Felix 170–1, 205

Sanderson, Ray 67

Sanderson Hotel, Fitzrovia 511

Sargent, Peter 101

Scargill Chapel, Kettlewell 89

Scherrer and Hicks 246, 247

School of Architecture, Cambridge 215

School of Oriental and African Studies, London 485

Schreiber House, Hampstead 464

Schwerdt, John and Partners 398

Scorer, Hugh Segar (Sam) 167, 168, 175

Scott, Adrian Gilbert 39, 376, 428

Scott, Brownrigg and Turner 396

Scott, Sir Giles Gilbert 39, 132, 150–1, 293, 302, 428, 441, 566

Scott, Richard Gilbert 150–1, 293, 566

Sculptural Wall, Manchester 598

sculpture 594–9

Seal, Mervyn 291

Seely, Hon. John 203, 212, 529

Seifert, Richard and Partners 234, 456, 539

Severels, Runcton 413

Severn Bridge 295

Seymour Harris (J) Partnership 109

Shaw, J. B. 545

The Shakespeare Centre, Stratford-upon-Avon 141

Sheep Shearer, Harlow 597

Sheffield City Architect's Department 84–5

Sheldon Bush lead shot tower, Bristol 306

Sheppard, Richard, Robson and Partners 229, 329, 473, 510

Sherren, Brian C. 277

Shippon, Meols Hall, Southport 57

Shopping Building (thecentre:mk), Milton Keynes 366

Shorten, Derrick 137

Silver Street (Nos 7–23) Stony Stratford 364

Sims, F. A. (Joe) 92

Skidmore, Owings & Merrill 179, 311, 459, 478, 524

Skinner, Bailey and Lubetkin 434

Skinner, Francis 419

Skip Shaft headframe, St Just 307

Slater, Moberly and Uren 511

Sloane Street (No 190, former Sekers), Knightsbridge 465

SMD Engineers 197

Smith, Ivor 84–5

Smith, Captain John (statue), Bow Churchyard 597

Smith, Michael 121

Smithdon High School, Hunstanton 194–5

Smithfield Poultry Market 522

Smithson, Alison and Peter 194–5, 204, 206, 294, 354, 524–5

Smuts, Field Marshall Jan (statue), Westminster 597

Snowdon, Lord 527

Snowdon Aviary, Regent's Park 517, 527, 528

Sofaer, Julian 582

Soissions, Louis de 202, 282

Solar Campus, Wallasey 56

Somerton Erleigh, Somerton 312

Sørensen, Eric 226

Sorrell House, Bosham Hoe 386

Souter, A. E. 277

South Downs House, Chichester 404

South Row (Nos 3–35), Blackheath 580

South Winds, Coventry 148

Southwood Memorial, St James's Churchyard, Piccadilly 594

Souza, Peter de 351

Spa Green Estate, Islington 419, 503, 545

Span Developments Ltd 219, 556, 560, 571, 580, 588

Spence, Sir Basil 132–3, 139, 236, 334, 387, 468

Spence, Sir Basil, Bonnington and Collins 358, 462, 538

Spence, Sir Basil and Partners 86–7, 387

Spence, John Urwin 358

Spence House and studio, Beaulieu River 334

The Spinney, Ipswich 225

Spring House (Cornford House), Cambridge 254

Standby Generator, Threehammer Common, Neatishead 593

Stanton Guildhouse, Stanton 300

Stark, Douglas Rogers 426

Stark, John and Partners 308

Stephen, Douglas and Partners 526

Stevenage Development Corporation 210

Stimpson and Walton 181

Stirling, H. J. W. 286

Stirling, James 170–1, 206, 215, 227, 252, 355, 410, 464, 564, 579

Stirling and Gowan 579

Stockwell Bus Garage, Stockwell 549

Stonecrop, Illmington 126

Stothert and Pitt 457

Stout and Litchfield 312, 341

Street, G. E. 299

Striding Man, William Penn School, Southwark 597

Stuart, Perry 184

The Studio, Ulting 256, 589

Studio at Chapel House, Horham 258

Submarine Escape Training Tank, HMS Dolphin, Gosport 592

Sulkin and Trevelyan Houses, Bethnal Green 439

Sunderlandwick Hall, Great Driffield 95

Sungazer, Kingsdale School, Southwark 597

Sunley House (formerly Barclays Bank), Maidstone 382

Sutton Place, Guildford 414

Swain, Henry 162

Swains Lane (No 81), Highgate 478

Swanscombe footbridge, Swanscombe Park 395

Swingate Chain Home Radar Station, Dover 593

Swiss Cottage Central Library, Camden 462

Synagogue and Amphitheatre, Carmel College 340

T

Tadeusz, Wladislaw 362

Tait, Gordon 43, 392

Tate & Lyle Sugar Silo, Liverpool 41

Taunton Deane Crematorium, Taunton 298

Tayler, Herbert 188

Tayler and Green 188–9, 199

Tayler and Green housing, Ditchingham 188

Team4 256, 301

Technical Block A, Heathrow 430

Teesdale, Windlesham 407

Teggin, Harry 71, 465

Templeton College, Kennington 352

Templewood School, Welwyn Garden City 186

Ten Point Blocks, Alton East 552–3

The first edition of this book grew out of the work of English Heritage's Post-War Steering Group. It commissioned reports from Christopher Dean, Bronwen Edwards, Roger Harper, Julian Holder, David Lawrence, Suzanne Marston, Mervyn Miller, Alan Powers, Andrew Saint, Andrew Smith, Bill Smyth and Paul Taylor. The book was the personal suggestion of Alan Howarth, Minister of State, and was generously funded by the DCMS and English Heritage.

This third edition was made possible by John Hudson, head of publications at Historic England, and Pavilion Books, where Polly Powell, Tina Persaud, Kristy Richardson and Fiona Corbridge have guided the book to publication. Paul Backhouse, Susie Barson, Roger Bowdler, John Cattell, Steve Cole, Emily Gee and Pete Herring at English Heritage have also given great support to the project, while Barnabas Calder, Alistair Fair and Alan Powers have provided stimulating discussion. The additional material on military buildings was only made possible with the help of Wayne Cocroft and Veronica Fiorato, who have checked all these entries. In particular it is a pleasure to record the assistance of Geraint Franklin (p.476) and advisers past and present in Designation Department who drafted some of the new entries. Their contributions are: Michael Bellamy (pp.126, 128, 148, 149, 152, 153, 154 and 155), Roger Bowdler (p.548), Tony Calladine (p.193), Sarah Charlesworth (pp.39, 50, 61, 62 and 75), Alison Clarke (pp.51, 82 and 113), Veronica Fiorato (pp.238, 323, 360, 362, 367, 370, 415, 582 and 585), Emily Gee (pp.36, 127, 366, 418, 422, 440, 450, 529, 540 and 584), Sarah Gibson (pp.165, 200, 201, 249 and 261), Esther Godfrey (pp.273, 277, 286 and 307), Jill Guthrie (pp.269 and 293), Julian Heath (p.380), David Hilton (pp.119 and 144), Amanda Hooper (pp.139, 141, 271, 274 and 282), Posy Metz (pp.382, 389, 394, 402 and 560), Hannah Parham (pp.457, 463, 486, 490, 495, 568, 570, 574 and 586), Trish Roberts (p.259), Caroline Skinner, Paul Stamper (pp.343, 365, 471 and 496), Jerome Tait (pp.284 and 302), Melissa Thompson (p.161), Myra Tolan Smith (p.192), Patience Trevor (pp.359, 364, 396, 442, 473, 477, 478, 487, 550 and 591), Rachel Williams (p.118) and Nicola Wray (p.67). It is the Designation Department, overseen by Dr Roger Bowdler, which advises Government on what should be listed and which is at the forefront of current policy.

Above all, James O. Davies and I would like to record our thanks to the buildings' owners and occupiers, too many to thank individually. Our enthusiasm for their buildings was shared by their warmth and generosity, and we hope that the book conveys something of the stimulation and rapport that resulted.

Elain Harwood and James O. Davies
January 2015

All photographs by James O. Davies / Historic England, except: James O. Davies (p.52); Mike Williams (p.95); Emily Gee (p.127); Derek Kendall / Historic England (pp.173 and 370); Steve Cole / Historic England (p. 192, 193, 201, 261 and 292); RIBA Library Photograph Collection (p.225); Alan Powers (p.231); Roger Thomas (p.238); Dennis Gilbert (p.312).

ACKNOWLEDGEMENTS